I0132158

REVOLUTIONS
AND REBELLIONS IN
AFGHANISTAN

REVOLUTIONS
AND REBELLIONS IN
AFGHANISTAN

ANTHROPOLOGICAL PERSPECTIVES

M. NAZIF SHAHRANI

ROBERT L. CANFIELD

INDIANA UNIVERSITY PRESS

This book is a publication of

Indiana University Press
Office of Scholarly Publishing
Herman B Wells Library 350
1320 East 10th Street
Bloomington, Indiana 47405 USA

iupress.org

© 2022 by Nazif Mohib Shahrani and Robert L. Canfield

All rights reserved
No part of this book may be reproduced or utilized in any form or
by any means, electronic or mechanical, including photocopying
and recording, or by any information storage and retrieval
system, without permission in writing from the publisher. The
Association of American University Presses' Resolution on
Permissions constitutes the only exception to this prohibition.

The paper used in this publication meets the minimum
requirements of the American National Standard
for Information Sciences—Permanence of Paper for
Printed Library Materials, ANSI Z39.48-1992.

Manufactured in the United States of America

Second printing 2022

Chapter 3, "The Evolution of Anti-Communist Resistance
in Eastern Nuristan" by Richard F. Strand, from the
original publication has been redacted in this edition.

Cataloging information is available from the Library of Congress.

ISBN 978-0-253-06677-0 (paperback)
ISBN 978-0-253-06678-7 (ebook)

For Samad, Abdurahim, Noorhadi, and the children of Afghanistan, with the hope that they may grow to live in a free, Islamic Afghanistan. And for all those who are fighting to make this dream a reality. Unfortunately, hopes which seem less and less likely after four decades now, in 2022. However, with those hopes the peoples of Afghanistan have kept their struggles for survival with dignity.

M.N.S.

For Kim, Howard, and Stephen, Afghanistan-born expatriates, beneficiaries of a rich childhood among a fabulous people.

R.L.C.

CONTENTS

Contents

Revolutions and Rebellions in Afghanistan: Anthropological Perspectives, published initially more than three decades ago, has been out of print for many years. The reprinting of this work—finally satisfying the requests of those who felt a need to have the volume in print—makes it possible for the current scholarly community to easily access data and analyses about how this prolonged conflict commenced. The descriptions and assessments of the ways in which the peoples of Afghanistan were responding to the shocks of the Afghan communist coup d'état of 1978 and the Soviet invasion of 1979—the threats they perceived and the ways they organized to respond then—provide reference points on how the country has changed through nearly four decades of war. The book also provides evidence of how many social conventions have remained the same. Familiar notions of obligation and authority have persisted throughout this period, even if various social alignments among groups may have shifted over time. That is, as the structures and expressions of social life in Afghanistan seem to have changed, the "inner necessities that animate it" have not.[1] The struggles of the peoples of Afghanistan for political survival, vividly articulated by the contributors to this work of more than three decades ago, are still animated and galvanized by their determined pursuit of, as yet unrealized, peace, justice, freedom, and dignity in this rapidly globalizing world.

The fact that much has changed in Afghanistan's social and political structures is amply documented in the new follow-up volume, *Modern Afghanistan: The Impact of 40 Years of War*.[2] In that work, a later generation of scholars offers further detailed, systematic accounts and analyses of the structures and alignments that have been operative in more recent times. They demonstrate that the "inner necessities" and moral idioms of earlier times are still vital—such as notions of authority and "kingship," manifest in a Kabul-centered, person-centered, extractive political economy; in their reliance on traditional kinship, tribal and ethnic loyalties, transformed by the identity politics of decades of war, rebellion, and post-Taliban failed attempts at reconstruction; in their uses and abuses of Islam, especially the concepts of *jihad* (armed and violent opposition) and *shura* (consultation), being deployed as grounds for mobilization and largely unrealized cooperation; and in the consequences of a political economy that is increasingly dependent on foreign subsidies.[3] These core elements of Afghanistan's contemporary political culture have been reinforced by the practices of the old, emergent, and aspiring power elites—the monarchists, Communists, secular nationalists, Pashtun/Afghan nationalists, Islamists of various stripes (global jihadists, Taliban, the Khorasan branch of Daesh [ISKP], etc.)—who continue to animate and at times seriously aggravate the chances for regaining national stability, peace, and security, increasingly desired by ordinary peoples of Afghanistan, both urban and rural, who are sick of war.

Contributors to *Revolutions and Rebellions in Afghanistan*, all of them anthropologists who had conducted field research in Afghanistan during the 1960s and 1970s, describe the responses and reactions of different segments of the peoples of Afghanistan to the Khalq/Parcham Communist party's revolutionary programs and the military intervention of their then patron, the former Soviet Union (Russia), from the perspectives of the local communities they had studied firsthand. These ethnographic accounts highlighted two important dimensions of the conflicts as they took shape: the moral and political struggle of the Afghanistanis (all the peoples of Afghanistan) to oppose an atheistic regime backed by the USSR, and the quest for a legitimate alternative state structure that could better realize social justice and a more inclusive politics that would accord with universal Muslim ideals as conceived by the then leaders of Afghanistan's Mujahidin.

The Mujahidin armed resistance of the 1980s resulted in the globalization of the Afghanistan jihad through the unprecedented support from Muslim majority nations of the world as well as the United States of America and several countries of Western Europe. The effort culminated in the defeat of the Soviet Red Army and its withdrawal in 1989, the unexpected collapse of the USSR itself and the end of the Cold War. In Afghanistan, it entailed the military triumph of the Mujahidin over the Afghan Communist regime (in 1992). However, the cherished goal of establishing a legitimate, inclusive Islamic government was never realized.

The military success of the 1980s was achieved through the efforts of the largely disenfranchised educated Muslim youth, both rural and urban. These elements steadily gained the support of the pious Muslim masses against the bankrupt traditional power elites and the atheistic Marxists who had sought to capture the extractive capabilities of the state to further their own interests with help from external patrons. The possibilities of a Mujahidin military success were anticipated by the contributors to *Revolutions and Rebellions in Afghanistan*. However, the likelihood of political failure after military victory was not expected. No one then could envisage the long, tortuous, and bloody ordeals the people of Afghanistan would suffer after the Mujahidin triumph of the early 1990s.

Afghanistan's four-decades-long war began as jihad—a grand Islamic ritual that symbolically colored not only the collective life of the nation but also the various agendas of the outsiders, Muslim and non-Muslim, who joined in the conflict. From the outset, the history of resistance against the Afghan Communists and their Soviet patrons, as rendered in this volume, was a collective struggle motivated by an alternative moral/political imagination. As Geertz has suggested: "The social history of the moral imagination is a single subject. . . . Single, but of course vast."[4] Sadly, for the Afghan participants and performers of jihad, the efforts of the many competing jihadi forces operative in this multiethnic and tribal society were for over four decades hampered by the perverse wishes of a new power elite that sought to establish an exclusive, extractive, centralizing political system similar to the kingship model they had known before the war. *Revolutions and Rebellions in Afghanistan* documented and analyzed the earliest conceptualizations and discourses about jihad as the ideological foundations of the moral/political struggle of the peoples of Afghanistan in the global stage of its time. As such, this book will provide a solid base for understanding the later manifestations of the concept of jihad by Taliban, Al Qaeda, and Daesh in the ongoing globalized conflict in Afghanistan.

The volume also ethnographically documents and analyzes how different segments of Afghan society understood their evolving roles in the existential drama of their Muslim nation. Afghan peasants and tribesmen viewed their role at the outset as Muslim patriots defending their faith and country. The traditional political and religious dignitaries conceived their role as leaders of the jihad. However, the rural and urban educated youth imagined their jihadi challenges more ideologically in opposing the Communist atheists who were promising revolutionary changes. Internal struggles gradually led to significant realignments of power relations between the old and the new structures, especially between the center and the peripheries.

Therefore, *Revolutions and Rebellions in Afghanistan* provides an important window for understanding and untangling the meanings associated with the grand Muslim ritual of jihad. It does so from the perspectives of the local citizenry as well as those looking from the outside at Afghanistan jihad as the social frame for unpacking the tortured history of the last four decades of modern Afghanistan. It also informs how Afghanistanis' selves of various types (ethnolinguistic, tribal, sectarian, local and regional within the "nation") have represented themselves to themselves and to others, identifying enemies and friends in the earliest phase of this long conflict, and the values and principles that have persisted and/or been reshaped according to the demands of the moment.

The penetrating analyses by anthropologists in this book will also make it possible to understand the later commoditization of jihad, especially to fight war by/for outside proxies, both near and afar. It will also help an understanding of the career paths of many jihadi freedom fighters who became "warlords" and then transformed themselves into partners of the United States and NATO forces. Their combined efforts at state-building and economic reconstruction, however, have failed over the past twenty years, turning the country over to the Taliban in August 2021, partners of Al Qaeda—perpetrators of the 9/11 tragedies in the United States and the reason for the onset of the so-called Global War on Terrorism.

Some of the key Mujahidin leaders at the time of the Soviet invasion, referenced in this book, have died violently; others have passed with old age. But many of them or at least their sons or proxies still are active in the country, either in the government or as participants in the activities of the Taliban and Daesh. A credibility gap and trust deficit have developed between the peoples of Afghanistan and the current power elites, even toward members of the international community who have empowered them.

In rural communities, social and political alignments still follow patterns extant at the time of the Soviet invasion—or are manifest in variants of earlier patterns of mobilization as described in *Revolutions and Rebellions in Afghanistan*. Also vastly changed is the political ecology of the region as well as the ways the major global powers have chosen to engage with the region. But, the social structures and political culture from which a future for Afghanistan must be constructed are in many respects the same, making the insights of anthropologists presented in this volume still relevant to understanding Afghanistan today.

We are grateful to the Institute of International Studies (IIS) at UC Berkeley for releasing their copyright for this book and to Jennika Baines and Bethany Mowry, acquisitions editors at Indiana University Press, and the Indiana University Press administration for their decision to publish this work again at this critical moment in Afghanistan's history. We also express our gratitude for the positive evaluation of the book by its past reviewers and readers. We are delighted that the book will be available to another generation of Afghanistan studies scholars and policy makers.

M. Nazif Shahrani *(Indiana University, Bloomington)*
Robert L. Canfield *(Washington University, St. Louis)*

1. Clifford Geertz, *Local Knowledge: Further Essays in Interpretive Anthropology* (New York: Basic Books, 1983), 55.

2. M. Nazif Shahrani, ed., *Modern Afghanistan: The Impact of 40 Years of War* (Bloomington: Indiana University Press, 2018).

3. See also M. Nazif Shahrani, "Afghanistan's Alternatives for Peace, Governance and Development: Transforming Subjects to Citizens & Rulers to Civil Servants," *Afghanistan Papers*, no. 2 (August 2009); and M. Nazif Shahrani, "Approaching Study of Political Culture in Afghanistan with Institutional Analysis and Development (IAD) and Social-Ecological Systems (SES) Frameworks," in *Sociocultural Systems: The Next Step in Army Cultural Capability*, eds. B. E. Strong, L. Babin, and L. Roan (Arlington, VA: US Army Research Institute for the Behavioral and Social Sciences, 2012), 169–192.

4. Gertz, Local Knowledge, 40.

PREFACE

This volume is the result of a day-long symposium of the 1980 meetings of the American Anthropological Association held in Washington, D.C. The objective of the symposium was to collect and compare the reports of scholarly authorities on the social condition of the various peoples of Afghanistan and their attitudes toward and understanding of the upheavals that had been taking place in their country. Policies that were being called "revolutionary" had been introduced by a group of Marxists who had taken over the government in 1978, and rebellions had sprung up all over the country. The media and foreign political observers were discussing these developments in terms of their national and international significance, but little was being said about what these developments meant to the peoples of Afghanistan themselves—how they interpreted the policies of the Marxist government and why they were responding so negatively. Unlike some of the political observers who have only recently taken an interest in Afghanistan and who were making pronouncements, the participants in the symposium have spent considerable amounts of time doing research in the country. Collectively they have studied many different peoples of Afghanistan from different ethnic, sectarian, and regional backgrounds: settled and nomadic, rural and urban, poor and middle class, educated and illiterate, traditional and progressive. Some of the scholars had done their research before the coup of 1978. Others had been in the country during the early period of the Marxist administration. Some have returned to the region to see people whom they had known—who were by then refugees in Pakistan—to learn what the civil war had done to them and what role, if any, they are playing in the conflict.

Eighteen scholars participated in the symposium. All but five of these have contributed to the present volume.*

*The symposium contributions of M. S. Noorzoy (University of Alberta) and Audrey C. Shalinsky (University of Wyoming) have appeared elsewhere; the comments of Gholam Ali Ayeen (University of Nebraska at Omaha) were not available in writing, and M. Jamil Hanifi (Northern Illinois University) and Schuyler Jones (Oxford University) chose not to contribute to the volume.

The book is organized into six parts. Part I consists of two introductory essays: the first (by M. Nazif Shahrani) relates the materials in this volume to the structure and current processes of change in Afghanistan society generally; the second (by Louis Dupree) chronicles the major events that led up to and followed the coup of 1978, which has had such a decisive impact on Afghanistan society. The next four parts of the book focus on specific regions of the country, each of them presenting problems characteristic to the region. Part II consists of essays on Nuristan (by Richard F. Strand and David J. Katz) and on the adjacent valley of Darra-i Nur (by R. Lincoln Keiser) in eastern Afghanistan. This has been an important region in the civil war: the first local uprising against the Marxist regime began in the Väygal (Waigal) Valley of Nuristan on 22 May 1978—hardly more than a month after the Marxist coup; Nuristani insurgence continues to this day. Part III is made up of three essays (by Shahrani, Thomas J. Barfield, and Hugh Beattie) covering the region of Qataghan and Badakhshan in northern and northeastern Afghanistan. Part IV has essays (by Robert L. Canfield and Richard Tapper) on social conditions in central and northwestern Afghanistan. The essays in Part V focus on the Pashtun—the Sheikhanzai in the western part of the country (by Bahram Tavakolian) and the Gilzai tribes of the southeast (by Jon W. Anderson). Part VI consists of articles (by Nancy Tapper and Nancy Hatch Dupree) on the effects of the government's policies on women, as well as some of the women's resistance activities.

It is unfortunate that detailed reports and analyses of all parts of the country are not available. We believe, however, that the essays presented here suggest social conditions and developments that have been extant generally throughout the country.

Robert L. Canfield

May 1984

ACKNOWLEDGMENTS

The editors received support and encouragement from many sources. They owe special appreciation to their colleagues, whose participation, patience, help, and cooperation made this work possible. Shahrani acknowledges with gratitude the support of Pitzer College—in particular Ronald Macaulay, Dean of Faculty, and Beverly Scales and Teresa Hidalgo, faculty assistants. Canfield gratefully acknowledges the support of the School of American Research in Santa Fe and Washington University in St. Louis. The enthusiastic support and interest of Carl G. Rosberg, Director of the Institute of International Studies, University of California, Berkeley, and the staff of the Institute, especially Paul M. Gilchrist, Principal Editor, have been greatly appreciated.

The editors and contributors have benefited from the critical comments of several anonymous readers. They have especially benefited from the discerning editorial counsel of Bojana Ristich, Senior Editor at the Institute of International Studies, who worked directly with each contributor, and through her care, dedication, and keen interest made the editors' task both more enjoyable and instructive.

Shahrani would like to express his special thanks to Mavis, who has been a constant source of help, inspiration, unwavering support, and encouragement. Canfield expresses his love and appreciation to Rita, who has both encouraged and forgiven his preoccupation with research and anthropology.

Of course any shortcomings in the work remain the responsibility of the editors.

NOTE ON TRANSLITERATION

In this work we transliterate local terms generally according to the system used in the *International Journal of Middle Eastern Studies*. However, to avoid an encumbered and esoteric appearance we omit diacritical marks in the text but provide them in the glossary.* The one exception to this rule is in the articles on Nuristan, in which a few special notations are made in accordance with standard linguistic transcriptions of South Asian languages. Because some vowel distinctions are retained in Afghanistan that have disappeared in Iranian Persian (the dialect most familiar to Western scholars), a transcription of the Dari (Afghan Persian) vowel system is provided in the chart below.

Vowel	As in Dari	Nearest English Sound
î	*shîr* (milk)	s<u>ee</u>k
i	*sir* (secret)	s<u>i</u>t
ê	*shêr* (lion)	<u>a</u>te
a	*sar* (head)	<u>a</u>t
û	*sûd* (interest)	b<u>oo</u>t
u	*sur* (in tune)	f<u>oo</u>t
ô	*shôr* (salty)	<u>o</u>re
â	*shâr*; formal: *shahr* (city)	c<u>au</u>ght

*The glossary is not inclusive of all words and names that appear in the text. Rather it contains only those which need the addition of diacritical marks for accurate transliteration.

NOTES ON CONTRIBUTORS

M. NAZIF SHAHRANI is Professor Emeritus of Anthropology at Indiana University.

ROBERT L. CANFIELD is Professor Emeritus of Sociocultural Anthropology at Washington University in St. Louis.

JON W. ANDERSON is Professor Emeritus of Anthropology at The Catholic University of America.

THOMAS J. BARFIELD is Professor of Anthropology at Boston University.

HUGH BEATTIE is Lecturer in Religious Studies at The Open University.

LOUIS DUPREE (1925–1989) was Senior Research Associate in Islamic and Arabic Development Studies at Duke University.

NANCY HATCH DUPREE (1927–2017) was Executive Coordinator of the Afghanistan Centre at Kabul University.

DAVID J. KATZ is Counselor of the Foreign Service of the United States of America, Retired.

R. LINCOLN KEISER is Professor Emeritus of Anthropology at Wesleyan University.

NANCY LINDISFARNE-TAPPER is Professor Emerita of Anthropology at the School of Oriental and African Studies, University of London.

RICHARD TAPPER is Professor Emeritus of Anthropology at the School of Oriental and African Studies, University of London.

BAHRAM TAVAKOLIAN is Professor Emeritus of Anthropology and Sociology at Denison University.

REVOLUTIONS
AND REBELLIONS IN
AFGHANISTAN

PART I

INTRODUCTION

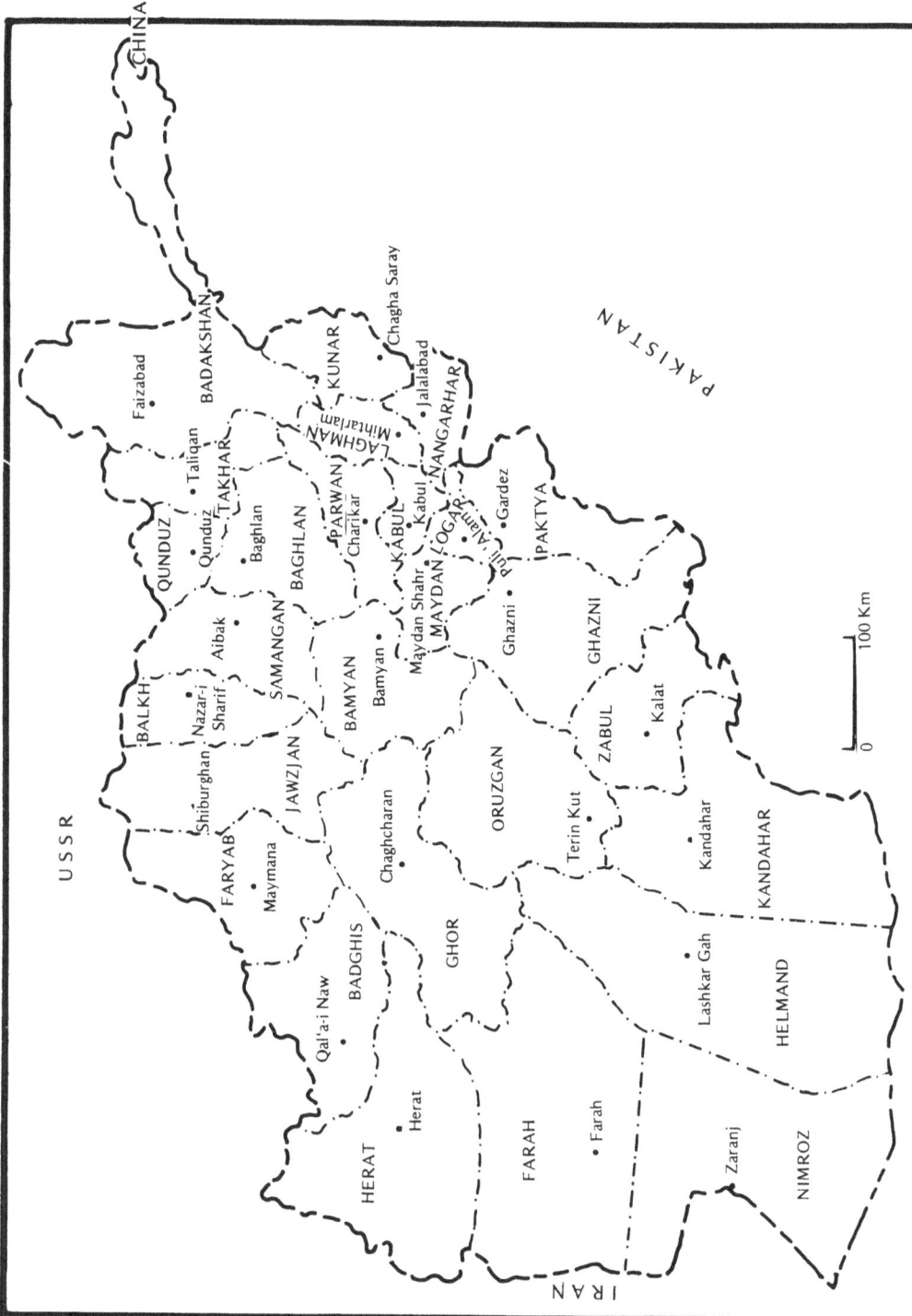

AFGHANISTAN: PROVINCES AND CAPITALS AFTER 1964

Chapter 1

INTRODUCTION: MARXIST "REVOLUTION" AND ISLAMIC RESISTANCE IN AFGHANISTAN

M. Nazif Shahrani

To students and observers of the current political and military crisis in Afghanistan, it is apparent that there is a multitude of conflicts and confrontations at various levels of society and with varying points of origin, motivations, and goals. How the contending groups are linked to the local-level social contexts and to the national-level historical processes in Afghanistan remains somewhat unclear. The contributions to this volume present the first in-depth examination of the social and historical contexts of the local-level popular armed resistance against the Soviet-inspired Marxist military takeover of the Kabul government on 27 April 1978 (the Saur Revolution) and the subsequent Soviet invasion and occupation of the country in December 1979.

The official Soviet and Afghan government view depicts the situation in Afghanistan as a classical "international socialist" battle against "world capitalist-imperialist forces." The view is made known in the West through a growing body of English-language Soviet publications on Afghanistan and by a number of Soviet and Communist

I would like to express my special gratitude to Robert L. Canfield for his unceasing support and many constructive comments and suggestions. This chapter has also benefited from the critical comments of a number of anonymous readers, as well as the helpful suggestions of a number of friends and colleagues: Tahir Ali, Jon Anderson, Don Brenneis, Allen Greenberger, David Katz, Kaveh Safa, Bahram Tavakolian, and Dana Ward. Most of the Soviet publications used in the chapter were made available to me by Austin L. Moede, M.D., a valued friend, and I owe him a special *tashakur*. Very special thanks are also due to Bojana Ristich, senior editor at the Institute of International Studies, Berkeley, for her many useful suggestions and her gentle insistence on consistency and clarity. Any shortcomings in presentation of facts and interpretation are mine alone.

sympathizers and supporters among leftist intellectuals and organizations.

Analyses of the crisis in Afghanistan by political observers, some scholars, and the media have focused primarily on the policies of the Afghan Communist government (a coalition of the Khalq and Parcham parties), a few Afghan resistance organizations outside the country, and, particularly, on the causes of the direct Soviet military intervention and its regional and international implications for East-West relations. What these analyses do not directly address is the context and the dynamics of the crisis inside Afghanistan. Commentators who have attempted to discuss the situation inside Afghanistan have frequently relied on a very narrow and reified knowledge of the country's history, culture, and politics. Their analyses are, for the most part, Kabul-centered and based on information which has been generally elicited from former Afghan government officials and members of the ruling strata who are now relocated in Western countries as "refugees."

The studies in this book differ from the existing literature on the Afghan crisis in at least two ways. First, with the exception of Louis Dupree's overview essay, none of the contributors addresses the political conflict exclusively at the national level or from the perspective of the former ruling elite. Instead each focuses on the perspectives of regional, local, tribal, ethnic, gender, and class groups which together represent the highly heterogeneous Afghan society. Second, the contributors do not presume any causal explanatory framework for the popular armed resistance. Rather they critically examine each ethnographic case in its own context in order to discern the reasons behind local responses to the conflict.

In this introductory chapter we shall attempt three things. First, to provide the reader with a broad historical and social framework so that individual contributions can be placed within the larger context of national socioeconomic and political developments. Second, to explore the place of Islam and the concept of *jihad* (holy war) in the political culture of Afghanistan. Third, to assess the direction of the current conflict by discussing how it evolved, how it has progressed, and what its prospects are. (We shall include a detailed study of the various resistance movements.) In the process, we hope to show not only how the chapters in this volume contribute to an understanding of the conflict, but also to examine significant issues concerning the conflict, about which there has been much speculation and misunderstanding. For instance, it has been contended that Afghanistan is primarily a tribal society and that the conflict is thus an example of tribal resistance against the consolidation of power by a central government. Some observers have also viewed the resistance movement as the reaction of "feudal lords" and tribal khans (chiefs) against the Marxist government's modernizing reforms, while others have seen it as a jihad waged by "Muslim fanatics" led by "reactionary clergy." Some have suggested that the resistance lacks an ideological basis and that its aim is a return to the status quo and the retention of feudalism, which would perpetuate the oppression, exploitation, backwardness, and ignorance of the Afghan people. We hope to provide a critical assessment of such contentions.

HISTORICAL AND SOCIAL FRAMEWORK

TRIBE, PERIPHERY, AND STATE IN AFGHANISTAN

From one perspective the conflict in Afghanistan is viewed as a confrontation between a "progressive" revolutionary government opposed by "traditionally independent mountain tribes who had in the past been paid subsidies by the central government, and among whom the bearing of arms was a natural feature of adult male life" (Halliday 1980a: 22). Faced with the loss of past privileges, the possibility of land redistribution, a control of smuggling across the borders and other forms of interference in their lives by the Kabul government, the tribes' natural response has been armed rebellion—the tactic they know best. Within this perspective there are a number of assumptions that are not borne out by ethnographic evidence—i.e., (1) Afghanistan is tribally organized throughout; (2) almost everyone in the countryside is armed; (3) most people are hostile to any form of central authority or outside interference; and (4) before the Khalq-Parcham Marxists took power the "tribes" enjoyed economic privileges directly through tax exemptions and government cash subsidies or indirectly through smuggling.

The assumption that Afghanistan is primarily a tribally organized society is a result of both overgeneralization and confusion between the system of agnatic descent for organizing social relations and tribe as a unit of military and political mobilization in the current conflict. Tribal ideology as a segmentary system organizing various levels of social groupings predominates only among the Pashtun and some nomadic segments of non-Pashtun groups such as Turkmen, Baluch, and Kirghiz, and the sedentary Nuristani (see Anderson, L. Dupree, R. Tapper, and Tavakolian in this volume).* The Pashtun, numerically the largest tribally organized group, are estimated at about 40-50 percent of the total population. They inhabit east, south, and southwestern parts of the country along the Pakistani borders, and there are colonies in parts of northern Afghanistan which were established during the last hundred years. Among the non-Pashtun sedentary populations such as Tajik, Farsiwan, Hazarah, and Uzbek, and "peasantized" Baluch and Turkmen, as well as numerous smaller minority populations, agnatic descent principles play a significant role in organizing socioeconomic ties, but these groups are not tribally organized

---

*An important factor influencing the notion that Afghanistan is a tribal society—and evident particularly in the earlier writings—has been the confusion (or ambiguity) between the more inclusive (national) referent of the term Afghan and its more exclusive (ethnolinguistic) referent, limited specifically to the Pashtun. The confusion may at least in part be due to the Kabul-centered orientation of earlier observers, who gained much of their information from government officials, who tended to convey the Pashtun nature of the Afghan society as a whole. Soviet researchers have, perhaps for political reasons, dealt with Afghanistan almost exclusively in terms of Pashtun society (e.g., see Editors of *Social Sciences Today* 1981). For Western researchers the tendency to equate the society of Afghanistan with that of the Pashtuns is further encouraged by the fact that there were many published accounts on the Pashtuns of the British-Indian North-West Frontier. These sources were and are extensively utilized; the Pashtun kinship principles of segmentary lineage and tribal structure and *Pashtunwali* (ideal Pashtun tribal codes of conduct) are presented in detail and are assumed to be applicable throughout the country. In contrast, until recently there has been a relative scarcity of detailed historical and ethnographic information about most non-Pashtun peoples. Therefore, even when writers acknowledged the presence of large numbers of such peoples, they were generally unable to discuss their social-organizational differences. Another significant reason for depicting Afghan society as Pashtun society has been the alleged role of the Pashtun tribes as king-makers, particularly since the civil war of 1929. Currently a relatively large Pashtun refugee population in Pakistan and the relatively easy access of Western journalists into Pashtun territories inside Afghanistan have further promoted the notion that the resistance in Afghanistan is primarily a Pashtun-dominated activity and therefore tribally organized (see Chaffetz 1979; N. Newell and R. Newell 1981; L. Dupree 1980b; Valenta 1980; Mukherjee 1981; and Harrison 1983).

in the same way as the Pashtun. In cases where tribal ideology exists, as among the Pashai and Nuristani, its role in the political processes is considerably different (see Keiser and Strand in this volume). More important, even among the Pashtun the role of tribe as a unit of military and political mobilization is often assumed rather than demonstrated through research.

The assumption that everyone in the countryside is armed is not accurate. Only small segments of rural Pashtun have been allowed to carry arms; with minor exceptions, in the towns and villages they never did. During this century a few rebellious Pashtun tribes have been suppressed, disarmed by the government, and forcibly relocated in the north (see Katz in this volume). Most of the non-Pashtun population, particularly in the northern, western, and central parts of the country, was disarmed by the government in the 1890s and again after the 1929 civil war. Except for hunting weapons, a strict policy of keeping the population unarmed has been enforced (see Shahrani in this volume).

The assumption that Afghanistan's rural population is hostile to any form of central authority or outside interference is true only of some nomadic segments of the population. (The most obvious instance of this kind of rural recalcitrance in this volume is presented by Tavakolian on the Sheikhanzai Pashtun in western Afghanistan.) Considerable autonomy may be common among nomadic Pashtun tribes due to their ecological and economic adaptation, but it is not so true of the vast majority of sedentary Pashtun. In fact, the relationship between Pashtun tribes and the Pashtun-dominated central government has varied historically. Local, tribal, and regional groups have sometimes supported and sometimes resisted the government (see Katz and Anderson in this volume; see also Anderson 1983a). Furthermore, it is important to note that from 1929 to 1975 all major rebellions against the government were instigated entirely by the Pashtun.

The relationship between the central government and the non-Pashtun ethnic groups has been complex. On the whole, their attitude toward the state has been ambivalent, characterized by neither active support nor active hostility. However, a degree of latent hostility toward both government authority and the Pashtun seems to be present among most of the minorities. The Nuristani, it has been suggested, tend to be particularly "anti-Afghan"—i.e., anti-Pashtun and anti-government, regardless of the latter's ideology or political aims (see Jones 1980). A combination of the culturally valued traits of aggressiveness and competitiveness among Nuristani men together with the Nuristanis' recent historical experiences of defeat and conversion to Islam by the Afghan state is said to account for their hostile attitudes. It has been asserted that the Nuristani would seize an opportunity of national confusion to take up arms against the state for cultural if not political reasons. On the other hand, both Katz and Strand (in this volume) argue that despite Nuristani misgivings about the Pashtun, the group long considered a strong relationship with the government in Kabul—over the heads of the local Pashtun—to its advantage. Katz and Strand conclude that the armed rebellion in Afghanistan, which began in Nuristan in 1978 and spread to the rest of the country, was not simply anti-state or anti-government as is often claimed; rather it was a Nuristani reaction to a particular *kind* of government, the Khalq-Parcham regime.

In northern, central, and western Afghanistan, the home territories of most of the non-Pashtun peoples, a strong central-government presence has existed for about one hundred years (see Barfield and Shahrani in this volume). People accepted government rule, and the kind of local autonomy enjoyed by some Pashtun tribes in the south was nonexistent. As in Nuristan, the establishment of central government rule was welcomed for at least one reason: it put an end to local and regional warfare. However, government rule in these regions was accompanied by an internal colonial policy of relocating large numbers of Pashtun nomads and peasants from the south and west. As a result, discrimination and injustice by the government against the local Turkic, Tajik, and Hazarah populations in education, social services, and political participation became rampant. These groups lost much of the rich land and water they had owned (see Korgun 1981: 135; N. Tapper 1973; Kakar 1979). In addition, there was flagrant economic oppression by some government-sponsored Pashtun khans (see Beattie, Shahrani, and R. Tapper in this volume). The groups had numerous justifiable grievances, yet between 1929 and 1975 no violent reaction against the government occurred.

Tax exemptions, government cash subsidies, and freedom to cross international frontiers were granted only to the Pashtun tribes who in 1929 had helped Nadir Shah depose the Tajik ruler, Habibullah (also known as Bacha-i Saqaw, "the water carrier's son"). Most Pashtun tribes—those in Kandahar, Ghazni, Logar, Kabul, and Nangarhar (among others)—were not exempted from conscription, and some previously exempted tribes began to be conscripted in the early 1960s. On the whole, a very limited number of persons and Pashtun tribes—those closest to the Pakistani borders—enjoyed direct and indirect economic, social, and political privileges as a result of Afghan government policies. There is no evidence that the Khalq-Parcham regime withdrew such privileges from these groups. On the contrary, after hostilities broke out, the Kabul government seems to have offered even more subsidies to the Pashtun tribal groups.* For the non-Pashtun, nontribal populations along the Soviet borders smuggling was never allowed, though for those living along the Iranian border the opportunities may have been slightly better, and there is no evidence that the Khalq-Parcham government has been any more successful in patrolling the borders than its predecessors.

With this discussion we do not intend to suggest that tribal formations in Afghanistan do not play an active part in the current conflict. Rather we wish to question, first, the generalized applicability of a tribal explanation in the current crisis, and second, to explore whether the motivating factor for the participation of the tribes is in fact the preservation of their alleged autonomy. As noted, even in areas where tribal ideology prevails, it does not imply a uniformly hostile attitude toward central authority. Furthermore, efforts to explain the crisis in terms of tribal resistance to authority tend to overlook two points. First, the Pashtun tribes along the Pakistani frontiers who traditionally enjoyed a degree of autonomy did not join the resistance until early spring 1979 (see Chaliand 1982: 48). Second, the major uprisings during 1978 and early 1979 began in areas where government traditionally had firm control and the people had benefited from its presence (e.g., Nuristan, Hazarajat, Baghlan, Kabul, and Herat). Thus it appears that the rebellions are aimed against a Communist government with strong ties to the Soviets and not simply against a modernizing and revolutionary state. Reactions toward the Khalq-Parcham regime and the Soviets are comprehensible

---

*Khalid (1980: 209) reports that in the summer of 1980 two million rubles were set aside by the Soviets and their clients in Kabul for direct cash payments to Pashtun tribes and their leaders in return for support of the government (also see Chaliand 1981: 31).

within the framework of the pervasive Islamic ideology in Afghanistan which we shall discuss below.

THE KHALQ-PARCHAM REGIME: REFORMS, REPRESSION, AND REBELLIONS

The Marxists have characterized Afghanistan before April 1978 as "a backward agrarian country, with a rigidly feudal way of life" (Grachev 1980: 23). A French Communist publication, *La Vie Ouvrière*, states that "With the exception of Kabul . . . the country has practically no electricity, no railroads, and very few highways. In a word, the Dark Ages" (quoted in Grachev 1980: 25). Another French publication, *France Nouvelle*, claims that "The make-up of Afghan society was simple. The land belonged to big feudal landowners who kept tenant farmers permanently in debt. . . . Besides, women can be sold" (quoted in Grachev 1980: 24). A researcher for the USSR Academy of Science, Ghulam Muradov, more accurately states the following:

> Hard labour, disease, hunger, poverty and illiteracy were the lot of the overwhelming majority of the Afghan people. They suffered from corruption rampant among government officials, arbitrariness and violence. . . . The peasants, workers, intellectuals, artisans and petty traders, deprived of elementary human rights, had at the same time no opportunity to conduct any legal organized struggle for their rights, as political parties were officially banned (1981: 179-80).

In an interview in *World Marxist Review* (April 1980), Babrak Karmal, the Soviet-installed leader of the Communist government in Kabul, claimed that

> The Saur Revolution was the inevitable and natural outcome of the whole of our country's earlier historical development, and of the steady growth of the antagonistic contradictions between a handful of exploiters and the working people of Afghanistan. Moreover, the Saur Revolution is part and parcel of the great revolutionary process . . . of the overthrow and abolition of the power of oppressors inaugurated by the October Revolution in Russia in 1917 (quoted in Grachev 1980: 33).

The declared aim of the Afghan Marxist revolution was

> to effect social, economic and cultural transformations . . . that would lead to the creation of a new and just democratic society in Afghanistan, where the exploitation of man by man, hunger, poverty, unemployment and illiteracy would be wiped out forever (Muradov 1981: 180).

The Khalq-Parcham almost immediately introduced a "far-reaching" program of reforms. However, it met with strong resistance and, ultimately, rebellion. In an assessment of the resistance, Leonid Brezhnev told a *Pravda* correspondent: "As has always been the case in history, the forces of the past banded together against the revolution" (quoted in Volkov et al. 1980: 9). Grachev claims that "The radical changes in Afghanistan evoked fierce counter-revolutionary resistance. The enemies of the popular government rose against the reforms in the country" (1980: 38). Another Marxist writer, Fred Halliday, claims that given the strength of traditional social structural principles in predominantly rural Afghanistan, "any attempt to reform such a system by appealing to the class interests of poor and landless peasants was bound to run into considerable difficulties" (1980a: 22; see also Silber 1980; Mukherjee 1981).* Similar sentiments are expressed, although not so explicitly, by other leftist writers, such as Charpentier (1979) and Dastarac and Levant (1980). Others have attributed the Khalq-Parcham government's problems more specifically to its lack of understanding of the social and economic realities of rural Afghanistan (e.g., see Paul 1980; Editors of *Pakistan Progressive* 1980; Roy 1981; and R. Newell 1979). Since the beginning of the "second" or "new stage" of the April revolution—i.e., after the Soviet invasion and occupation in December 1979—the Soviets and the Karmal regime place all the blame squarely on the shoulders of deposed President Hafizullah Amin, who was killed during the invasion. Muradov explains:

> Great harm to the Afghan revolution has been done by Hafizullah Amin who wormed his way to power by intrigues and deceit. [He] used impermissible methods in implementing such major

*For a theoretical discussion of the insignificant role of a poor and landless peasantry in various revolutionary movements, see Wolf 1969; Alavi 1965 and 1973; Kazemi and Abrahamian 1978.

transformations as the agrarian reform and the liquidation of adult illiteracy, which distorted their progressive essence. People's traditions and religious convictions were ignored, there were crude violations of revolutionary legality, arrests, and executions, without trial and/or investigations of innocent people (1981: 183; see also Grachev 1980: 42-49; Volkov et al. 1980: 83-97; Kasatkin 1980).

Because the Marxist regime, the Soviets, and many observers see the government's radical reform policies as the major cause of the resistance movement, it is prudent to examine the policies both in light of data presented in this volume and information that has become available recently, primarily from Communist publications.

On 9 May 1978, less than two weeks after the Khalq-Parcham party took power, it introduced most of its proposed reforms in a Radio Afghanistan broadcast. The thirty-point program, entitled "Basic Lines of Revolutionary Duties of the Government of the Democratic Republic of Afghanistan [DRA]," touched on a wide range of issues and promised numerous "democratic" changes—for example: land reform and abolition of "old feudal and pre-feudal relations" (Articles 1 and 2); a "democratic solution of national issues" (Art. 6); a "democratic solution of nomad issues" (Art. 13); support for the "national liberation movements in Asia, Africa and Latin America and struggle against old and new colonialism and imperialism" (Art. 27); and "respect [for] and abidance by the Universal Declaration of Human Rights and the Charter of the United Nations" (Art. 30).* The most widely discussed reforms of the DRA were introduced before the end of 1978 in Revolutionary Decrees Nos. 6, 7, and 8. They address (respectively) the "peasant problems" of land mortgage and indebtedness due to usurious practices; the democratic rights of women (limiting payments of brideprice and providing women freedom of choice in marriage); and land reform through confiscation and redistribution.

Decree No. 6: Land Mortgage and Indebtedness. Beattie (in this volume) points out that of the three most discussed decrees, only

*The full text of the document appeared in the *Kabul Times*; it is reproduced in Asia Society, Afghanistan Council, *Newsletter* 1979. For a summary of it, see Charpentier 1979.

No. 6 had any originality. (Marriage expenses and freedom of choice for women in marriage [No. 7] and land reform [No. 8] had been the subjects of repeated efforts at reform by previous governments dating back to the 1880s—and the efforts had shown little success [see also N. Tapper, N. Dupree, and L. Dupree in this volume].) The problems of land mortgage and indebtedness, while intensified in rural Afghanistan in recent decades due to an encroaching capitalist economy, have varied from province to province.* The reasons for the problems have included the generally low incomes of poor peasants, who could not meet government taxes or the costs of funerals, marriages, and other unexpected life-crisis situations. Many were thus forced to get loans at exhorbitant rates, often using their land as security. A Soviet economist, Vladimir Glukhoded, claims that

> Decree No. 6 . . . considerably eased the burden of usurious debts lying on the landless and land-hungry peasants, repealed the payment of interest on debts, as well as deferred mortgage payments, etc. According to estimates, the peasants were relieved from paying debts to the sum of about 30 thousand million afghanis (1981: 235; see also Grachev 1980: 26).†

---

*Louis Dupree (1973: 147, chart 11) provides the following average estimates (excluding Shiburghan province) of the distribution of agricultural land by form of tenure in the country in 1963: sharecropped—13.8 percent; mortgaged—5.5 percent; owner-operated—60.5 percent; and other (state-owned?)—20.2 percent. He also provides the following percentages for mortgaged lands within each province (wilayat) and three subprovinces (hukumat-i a'la): Nangarhar—43.6 percent; Farah—11.2 percent; Ghazni—11.2 percent; Parwan—9.1 percent; Kandahar—7.5 percent; Kabul—6.6 percent; Qataghan—5.8 percent; Oruzgan—5.8 percent; Girishk—5.7 percent; Paktya—3.7 percent; Mazar-i Sharif—1.5 percent; Ghor—1.2 percent; Badakhshan—0.8 percent; Herat—0.7 percent; Bamyan—0.6 percent; Maymana—0.6 percent (no data for Shiburghan). In 1964 the provincial boundaries were redrawn; some new provinces were added and some renamed.

†Based on the 1978-79 rate of exchange of U.S. $1.00 to about 30 afghanis (afs.), the Afghan peasants' debts amount to a staggering $1 billion according to Glukhoded's estimates. He does not give any indication for the basis of his estimates. However, it is important to note that in Afghanistan most rural, and even urban, mercantile loan arrangements are made informally between the contracting parties and are for the most part kept private. Sadhan Mukherjee of the Communist Party of India puts the overall peasant debt in Afghanistan at 722 million afs., spread among 4.3 million peasants (1981: 16). This figure seems negligible by comparison to Glukhoded's. On the basis of Mukherjee's estimates the average

While Decree No. 6 cancelled old debts, thus threatening the entire rural credit system, Beattie reports that the government did not provide new, reliable alternative sources of credit. Furthermore, conflicts developed when land titles were challenged by opportunists manipulating the provisions of the decree.

Decree No. 7: The Democratic Rights of Women. Decree No. 7 was intended to put an end to excessive wedding expenditures and the payment of large amounts of cash and goods in marriage, customs which not only supposedly undermined the dignity of women by treating them as a kind of family property, but also generally increased indebtedness and poverty. The decree limited the amount of payable *mahr* to 300 afs.,* set the minimum age for marriage at 16 for girls and 18 for boys, and stipulated free choice of marriage partners for girls. The decree anticipated a reduction in general indebtedness on the one hand, and a higher status for women on the other.

Nancy Tapper (in this volume) suggests that there is little difference between the marriage reforms of Decree No. 7 and those attempted by earlier regimes, from that of Amir 'Abdur Rahman (1880-1901) on. However, she believes that the reforms in Decree No. 7 attack symptoms rather than conditions of a social order. By focusing on the costs of marriage, the new government has either totally ignored or misunderstood that in Afghanistan marriage is the focus of most economic and political activity and the way by which individuals, families, and kinship and ethnic groups recognize and validate status.

Beattie (in this volume) reports that in the fall of 1978 people in Nahrin (northern Afghanistan) tried to observe the provisions of Decree No. 7 by holding less elaborate wedding celebrations. Some people who broke the new rules were said to have been prosecuted,

indebtedness per peasant amounts to only about 170 afs., or $5.70, compared to about 7,000 afs. ($230) using Glukhoded's estimates.

*Mahr in its strict Islamic sense is goods given to a bride by her husband at the time of marriage. It is for the bride alone, *not* her family; in theory she can take it with her in case of divorce or the death of her husband. Therefore, strictly speaking mahr is not "brideprice," although the Islamic prescription for mahr is used to legitimize the exchange of goods in the form of brideprice between families.

while some planned marriages were abruptly abandoned, resulting in rising tensions among individuals and general resentment toward the government (see also N. Dupree in this volume). Nancy Tapper believes that in the short run, rural women in Afghanistan will feel diminished in value, in their own eyes as well as those of their husbands and brothers, by being given away "free"; in the long run, she believes, marriage reforms such as proposed in Decree No. 7 are unlikely to succeed because they are formulated by a predominantly male Afghan elite and are generally based on Western models of production and gender roles. Nancy Dupree contends that the Khalq-Parcham regime has added only rhetoric and no substance to the reforms dealing with women's rights. She concludes that Decree No. 7 has sparked the resistance movement. However, it is important to note that the decree was promulgated in October 1978, well after the beginning of armed resistance in at least one region of the country, Nuristan (see Strand in this volume).

Decree No. 8: Land Reform. On the basis of UN and other international socioeconomic indicators, during the 1960s and 1970s Afghanistan was among the poorest and least developed countries in the world, with a per capita income of about $160 in 1975 (United Nations 1978: 14). (Soviet statistics put the figure at less than $100 before 1978 [Grachev 1980: 23].) The principal reason for such a low income is attributed to the fact that "About two thirds of the national income comes from agriculture. Some three-quarters of Afghanistan's exports are agricultural produce" (Glukhoded 1981: 228).

More than 85 percent of the country's estimated 15.5 million inhabitants are engaged in subsistence rural cultivation or nomadic pastoral activities. A little over one quarter of Afghanistan's land area of 65.2 million hectares (ha) is estimated to be potentially cultivable. Yet in the 1920s only one million ha was cultivated, in the 1960s, 3.5 million, and by the eve of the April 1978 revolution, about 7.8 million (see Gurevich 1981: 159; Glukhoded 1981: 229; Mukherjee 1981: 16). The principal cause of the rather remarkable increase in cultivated land during the last half century is thought to be the increasing sedentarization of nomads together with a population growth at an annual rate of slightly more than 2 percent (Afghanistan, Ministry of Planning 1972: 8; see also R. Tapper in this volume). Gurevich adds the following:

There is still much land that can be cultivated in Afghanistan . . . but it is not utilised mainly due to lack of water. The irrigation potential of small rivers and springs has in the main been exhausted. During [the last] several decades the best pastures were ploughed up for crops on arid lands [i.e., under the *lalmi* system, or rain cultivation] but harvests on this land were so unstable that there were no farms in the country that could operate solely on this basis (1981: 168).

Despite the increase in cultivated areas, the production rate of rural agriculture as a whole remained unchanged owing to extremely low levels of technology.* Moreover, Soviet writers and the Marxist government in Afghanistan claim that the archaic methods of production were accompanied by extremely backward agrarian relations, often characterized as "feudal," "semi-feudal" and "pre-feudal" (see, for example, Glukhoded 1981: 230-32). Although most researchers consider that small-scale peasant landownership predominates in Afghan villages, the Soviets and the Communist government claim that a substantial amount of rich cultivated land is owned by a small number of feudal and semi-feudal landlords. According to Glukhoded, 18-35 percent of all peasants are landless and "had to work the land belonging to big feudal lords on the basis of a shackling metayage, with the tenant paying a definite share of the harvest not only for the land he rented but also for the seeds, cattle and implements which the landlord leased to him" (1981: 231). Glukhoded further argues that "at the time of the April revolution, agricultural output had virtually reached the highest level of its natural progress under the prevailing social order" (1981: 233). He contends that the leaders of the DRA thus considered

the feudal exploitation of the landless and land-hungry peasants who comprised the bulk of the rural population [as] the main

---

*Gurevich (1981: 169) claims that per capita wheat production declined systematically from 181 kilograms in the early 1950s to about 141 kilograms in 1969-70. Official government statistics show a small increase in total annual production from 2 million tons in 1953 to 2.4 million tons in 1972. I believe the decrease in wheat production and the country's dependence on imported wheat during the 1960s and 1970s was due primarily to successive droughts and an increased cultivation of cash crops for export (such as cotton) in the best wheat-growing farmlands of northern Afghanistan.

16

reason for the abject poverty reigning in the Afghan village. They stressed that feudal and semi-feudal relations in the village pre-determined the general social backwardness of the country and retarded Afghanistan's economic progress. That is why the implementation of progressive transformations in agriculture has become task No. 1 of the revolutionary government (1981: 234-35).

Decree No. 8 was announced in December 1978. Attempts at land reform, like those concerning marriage, have been made as far back as the 1920s and as recently as the 1970s, during Muhammad Daoud's Republic of Afghanistan. As Beattie points out (in this volume), the major difference in the Khalq-Parcham land reform program was that it limited maximum land ownership by a family to the very low level of 30 *jiribs* (6 ha) of first-grade land or its equivalent. (Under Daoud's land reform the ceiling was 100 jiribs [20 ha] of first-grade land or its equivalent.) Another difference was that the Khalq-Parcham government did not stipulate any form of compensation for confiscated lands. (For a definition and classification of land in Decree No. 8, see Beattie in this volume.) Glukhoded states that "the main distinctive feature of the agrarian policy in the period . . . before the end of 1979 [i.e., the first stage of the revolution, before the Soviet invasion] was . . . alotting land to literally *all* landless and land-hungry peasants, including [an estimated 2.5 million] nomads" (1981: 236; emphasis in original).

In the absence of reliable statistics on landholdings in Afghanistan, it is very difficult to accurately assess the impact of the government's land reform policies. However, Glukhoded (1981: 230-31, 240-44) and Mukherjee (1981: 16-17) have recently compiled somewhat similar estimates, based on a variety of sources, including DRA government statistics and press reports. Both put the total fund of cultivable land at 7.8 million ha.* Of these only about 3.9 million ha were sown in 1978 (2.6 million irrigated and 1.3 million unirrigated according to Glukhoded; 3.5 million irrigated according to Mukherjee). Mukherjee adds that "1.4 million households [1.2 million

---

*By cultivable land I assume Glukhoded and Mukherjee mean land fit for ploughing or land which has been or is being used for cultivation, including croplands, orchards, and fallow lands. Of the total cultivable land, only 0.5 million ha of irrigated land is sown twice annually. (For similar statistics on land distribution, see Zekrya 1976: 12).

according to Glukhoded] owned land to the tune of 4.5 million hectares. The rest or 3.3 million hectares were in government hands" (1981: 16).*

Glukhoded's and Mukherjee's estimates are presented in Tables 1 and 2, which reveal the following: (1) More than 75 percent of Afghan families owned some land, and about 42 percent owned 1-6 ha of first-grade land (or its equivalent)—respectively the minimum and maximum land ownership targets or limits set by the DRA in Decree No. 8. About 25 percent of families (excluding nomads) are considered landless; approximately 29 percent own less than one ha of first-grade land (or its equivalent) and are considered "land-hungry peasants"; (2) A small percentage of families (4.3 percent according to Glukhoded and 9.0 percent according to Mukherjee) hold about 40 percent of all privately owned land. However, the average per family (about 15.5 ha according to Glukhoded and 18.3 ha according to Mukherjee) is not very high when compared to landholding standards in neighboring countries (e.g., Iran; see Kazemi and Abrahamian 1978). Mukherjee reports that among the "big feudal lords" only 39,000 families have surplus land (1981: 17). During the implementation of the agrarian reform program (January-July 1979), "about 330,000 hectares of land, recalculated on the first group basis, [were] confiscated from landlords (around 840,000 hectares in absolute figures)" (Glukhoded 1981: 243).[†] Glukhoded adds that if the surpluses of all big landowners were confiscated above the fixed maximum, "it would be possible to distribute not more than 430,000-500,000 hectares" (1981: 242).

The DRA government has been able to distribute only about 287,000 ha of first-grade land (or 765,000 ha in absolute figures) among 296,000 landless and "land-hungry" peasant families. Glukhoded admits that "To provide [the landless and "land-hungry" peasants] with plots no less than one hectare in size . . . 650,000 to

---

*Mukherjee's figures for the number of landowning families add up to 1.2 million and not 1.4 million as mentioned in his text (see Table 2 below). Figures based on data released in 1977 and cited in an interview by an Afghan Marxist put the number of people who owned land or herds at a little over one million (Editors of *Pakistan Progressive* 1980: 27).

[†]Mukherjee notes that only about 373,000 ha (presumably based on absolute landholding figures) were acquired from big landowning families (1981: 17).

Table 1

SIZE, OWNERSHIP, AND DISTRIBUTION OF LAND PRIVATELY HELD
BY FAMILY/HOUSEHOLD UNITS IN AFGHANISTAN

Size of Holding (Ha.)	Families Owning Land		Percent of Families Deserving Land[a]	Total Land Owned in Category (Ha.)	Percent of All Privately Held Land
	Number	Percent			
0	420,000-670,000[b]	0%	25.9	0	0%
0.1-1.0	470,000	39.0	29.0	520,000	26.0
1.0-2.0	450,000	37.5	27.7		
2.0-6.0	230,000	19.2	14.2	660,000	33.3
6.0 +	51,600	4.3	3.2	800,000	40.0

Source: Glukhoded 1981: 241-42.

[a]Calculations are based on 420,000 families.

[b]Figures do not include 2.0-2.5 million pastoral nomads who are considered "landless" and entitled to land.

NOTE: The figures are recalculated on the basis of first-grade land.

Table 2

SIZE, OWNERSHIP, AND DISTRIBUTION OF LAND PRIVATELY HELD
BY FAMILY/HOUSEHOLD UNITS IN AFGHANISTAN

Size of Holding (Ha.)	Families Owning Land		Total Land Owned in Category (Ha.)	Percent of All Privately Held Land
	Number	Percent		
0	N.A.	N.A.	N.A.	N.A.
0.1-2.0	805,000	67.0%	1,100,000	24.1%
2.1-4.0	161,000	13.4	738,000	16.0
4.1-6.0	125,000	10.4	702,000	15.6
6.0 +	109,000	9.0	2,000,000	44.4

Source: Mukherjee 1981: 16-18.

NOTE: The figures reflect estimates of absolute landholdings.

900,000 hectares of land are required, on the basis of the first group calculation" (1981: 242). He continues:

> On the whole, taking into account the possibility of utilising some additional resources (lands belonging to the state, concealed surpluses, etc.) the deficit of land in reaching the aim proclaimed by the reform was estimated at 230,000 to 350,000 hectares, recalculated on the first group basis. In actual fact, this deficit was considerably greater. First, we did not include the nomads in our calculations, who, under the law, are also entitled to receiving plots of land no less than one hectare in size. Secondly, the very classification of lands used for dividing them into equal plots, although it made it possible to compare lands varying in quality, was by no means always suitable for their mass distribution in small plots. It can hardly be considered feasible to create a peasant holding by granting a formerly landless peasant a 5 to 6-hectare plot of dry land of the sixth or seventh group, whose development is extremely difficult. This narrowed still more the possibilities of finding land resources to distribute them among peasants. Thus, in the existing conditions it proved practically impossible to grant plots of land one hectare in size, recalculated on the first group basis, to all landless and land-hungry peasants, including the nomads (1981: 242-43).

Critical of the government's land reform policies, Glukhoded says, "The implementation of this principle [equalized land distribution] is not justified by any theoretical considerations or practical experience" (1981: 240). He further states that "such a course of transformations in the [Afghan] village is by no means similar to the 'solution of the agrarian question even within the framework of democratic transformations'" (1981: 243). Yet he asserts that for the DRA government "the attainment of the basic aims of the reform was made dependent on the solution of the problem of alotting land to the peasants, which acquired an exaggerated, self-contained character" (1981: 235-36).

In addition to land confiscation and redistribution, the agrarian reform envisaged the creation of large-scale mechanized state farms (presumably in the 3.3 million ha owned by the state) and various types of cooperatives. Mukherjee reports that by the summer of 1981 some 1,210 agricultural cooperatives with 183,000 peasant members, 9 artisan cooperatives with 10,000 members, and 4 consumer cooperatives had been formed, successfully "making [peasants] more and more homogeneous as a class entity" (1981: 19). Glukhoded disagrees: "The organization of cooperatives could not yield positive results ... for it caused discontent among the peasants who were not duly prepared for being drawn into the cooperative movement" (1981: 241).

Problems of implementing the land reform continue at all levels of the government in Kabul. On 25 February 1982, while addressing a land reform meeting, Karmal bemoaned:

It must be mentioned with regret that a number of ministries and the related departments and the local party and state organs have not yet understood properly the boundaries of their responsibilities and still have not made use of the present possibilities for the realisation of measures taken towards the accomplishment of land and water reforms. For example, in a number of the provinces no adequate measures have been taken towards the realisation of the resolution dated 10th Jawza, 1360 [10 June 1981] of the Central Committee and the government concerning land reform (*Kabul New Times*, 2/25/82; also in Asia Society, Afghanistan Council, *Newsletter*, June 1982: 27).

From the above discussion it should be clear that the most critical factor in the agrarian problem in Afghanistan is and has been the shortage of cultivable land in general and irrigable land in particular; much less critical is the inequitable distribution of the available land. Therefore, the priority of the Khalq-Parcham government should have been land reclamation and programs for better and more efficient management of the available land and water. The government's main reason for the speedy introduction of its land reform program was, it seems, the anticipation that "the popularity of the government will increase as a result of ... land and anti-usury reforms and this will naturally strengthen the position of the Khalq government" (Charpentier 1979: 118; see also Silber 1980: 24). Perhaps this expectation in part explains the introduction of the program *after* the beginning of the armed opposition. However, the consequences of implementation have been quite contrary to the government's expectations—i.e., implementation has caused an intensification of the armed resistance.

Based on their field research in northern Afghanistan, Beattie and Shahrani (in this volume) indicate that most of the land in Nahrin district (Beattie) and Badakhshan province (Shahrani) is owned by small peasants, so that a confiscation and redistribution program may not have had much impact. In addition, in these areas, as elsewhere in the country, government officials have always been a principal source of oppression against villagers. In cases where local landlords have committed oppressive acts, they have done so with the full support of the government officials—as in the case of Nazarzai Pashtun khans in Saripul, discussed by R. Tapper in this volume. In fact most of the rich landowners in Afghanistan have been and are high-ranking government officials, the few clergy in the judiciary system, civilian administrators, and police and military officers. For the most part, they were the beneficiaries of the state lands—about 3.3 million ha of the total cultivable land available (42.3 percent). Indeed these officials were the exploiters of the landless and "land-hungry" peasants who had to lease lands from the state. Yet in the second stage of the April revolution, the government amended Decree No. 8 "in regards to the holdings of army men, tribals [chiefs?], religious bodies or individuals" (Mukherjee 1981: 19; see also Grachev 1980: 52).* The amendment seems to have once again benefited those in government service, particularly army officers and party members, as is attested in an interview with an Afghan Marxist:

> Part of the land was redistributed but the other things went to Party members. The houses seized from the comprador bourgeoisie, the large merchants, or previous bureaucrats did not become offices of the state but became private residences of the new bureaucrats. Cars seized from landowners and bankers were used by the sons and daughters of the new bureaucrats (Editors of *Pakistan Progressive* 1980: 41).

Thus despite the declared goals of the Kabul regime, both its policies and practices indicate that the Marxist revolution has been in the

---

*It is not clear what is meant by religious bodies in this instance. In Afghanistan, unlike in many other countries in the area, *waqf*, land held as a religious endowment by a religious institution, does not exist in any meaningful sense because such lands were appropriated by the Afghan monarchy during the reign of 'Abdur Rahman and again during the reign of Amir Amanullah (1919-29). An appropriation policy was enforced by subsequent governments (see Korgun 1981: 146; see also Shahrani in this volume).

first instance a transfer of power, wealth, and privileges from the old elite to the new.

In addition to agrarian reform, the Kabul government has pursued a number of less discussed policies, such as a literacy campaign (aimed mainly at females), price controls, anti-corruption measures, and the removal of *arbabs* (village headmen) at local administrative levels. As with Decrees Nos. 6-8, Beattie (in this volume) points out that these policies were not original but rather an intensification of existing trends. Despite the initial popularity of some of the measures, Beattie believes the overall reaction of the people was irritation and anger at the extent to which the government was interfering in their lives (see also L. Dupree in this volume).

It is clear that the policies of the Khalq-Parcham government produced many social and political tensions due to what Glukhoded has called "the errors and miscalculations made during the implementation of the agrarian reform and other social changes" (1981: 238).* Halliday offers an intriguing explanation for the armed resistance which followed: "Afghanistan is a country where political and social issues have tended to be settled by the gun and where the room for peacefully handling conflicts within the state, or between the state and subjects, is extremely limited" (1980a: 23). The consequence of this (natural?) propensity, according to Halliday, was that the tribesmen started shooting at Khalq-Parcham members on sight, and the regime retaliated with widespread brutality and repression against its opponents, thus causing an increase in the armed resistance (see also Paul 1980; Editors of *Pakistan Progressive* 1980; Medvedev 1980; and L. Dupree 1967 and in this volume). One difficulty with an explanation such as Halliday's—as we pointed out above—is that what is presented as a traditional way of resolving political issues between the state and its citizens may be true of only a segment of the Pashtun peoples—if then. It certainly does not apply to most non-Pashtun peoples of the country.

The Khalq-Parcham's reliance on force at the local level has played a major role in increasing the intensity of the armed resistance,

*Glukhoded adds that "a number of recent program documents of the People's Democratic Party and the revolutionary government of Afghanistan as well as . . . their leading figures [have] openly admitted the fact" (1981: 238).

23

spreading it, and causing it to continue. Barfield (in this volume) suggests that one of the major miscalculations of the Khalq-Parcham regime has been its failure to realize that the government bureaucracy it inherited was designed only to administer and not to introduce radical reform programs. When provincial officials were given the task of introducing an alien political ideology and implementing reform policies, the government began to collapse. In many instances, the special relations between previous governments and the local power elite were totally misunderstood and consequently ignored or abruptly broken off (see Strand and Katz in this volume). At the same time, the government began a program of political indoctrination among schoolchildren (see Keiser in this volume), interfered with religious practices (see Strand in this volume), and intensified its propaganda campaign in language that was incomprehensible to most of the population (see L. Dupree, Beattie, Shahrani, Keiser, and Katz in this volume). Even in cases where reforms were compatible with Islam, the Khalq-Parcham government failed to couch them in Islamic terms (see R. Tapper and N. Dupree in this volume). Equipped with a ready-made scapegoat in the deposed and executed Amin, Karmal offered the following explanation:

> Many of the mistakes and failings [of the Marxist government] were objectively inevitable, being the outcome of the country's backwardness, the absence of a strong working class and the fact that the Party is young, unseasoned, and does not have enough practical revolutionary experience. . . . We did not have sufficiently solid traditions of democratic centralism and collective leadership, and this led to some highly negative consequences. Important decisions were taken without the proper preparation, and elements of subjectivism and undue haste were in evidence. . . . Our People's traditions, religious beliefs, and way of life were ignored by the manner in which socioeconomic reforms were put into effect. Subjectivism and leftist extremes undermined such important projects as the agrarian reform (quoted in Glukhoded 1981: 238).

It should be apparent from our discussion that while there is a strong correlation between the Khalq-Parcham government's radical reform programs and the armed resistance, there seems to be no convincing evidence that the resistance is a response of ignorant and fiercely independent rural and tribal people to the *substantive and progressive nature* of the reforms. (Indeed on a theoretical level, the contention that the introduction of radical modernization and reform policies causes revolutions and rebellions is the subject of much debate among scholars; for example, see Huntington 1968; Aya 1979; Tilly 1973.) As a number of our contributors have suggested (Beattie, Barfield, L. Dupree, N. Dupree, and N. Tapper), very little in the reform policies is without precedence in the country. Furthermore, they have suggested that in the early months of Khalq-Parcham rule some of the proposed reforms were welcomed in some parts of the country. Two factors associated with the reforms appear to have contributed to the rise and expansion of the armed resistance. First, the reform policies were put forward by a political group closely identified with communism and the Soviet Union. Thus the legitimacy of its rule and its vision for the future were suspect. Second, the increasing reliance and eventual total dependence of the Khalq-Parcham regime upon the Soviet Union, the increasing use of force against suspected enemies, and the harsh manner in which the proposed reforms were implemented confirmed the people's fears regarding communism. The armed struggle in Afghanistan is universally expressed through the Islamic idiom of jihad, and it is to a discussion of Islam and jihad that we now turn.

THE PLACE OF ISLAM AND THE CONCEPT OF JIHAD

MISINTERPRETATIONS AND DEFINITIONS

The Soviets and the regime in Kabul have consistently maintained that the resistance movement in Afghanistan is led by "saboteur gangs," "mercenaries," and "counterrevolutionaries" who are simply the creations of the Western imperialist powers. They deny that the movement has an indigenous, independent Islamic political and ideological basis. Indeed members of the resistance are said by the Soviets and the Kabul regime to be neither Afghan nor Muslim, but merely "the willing helpers of imperialism."* The Soviets further

*The Soviets have published at least four books in English to support their claims that there are ties between the Afghan resistance with Western powers and the "reactionary regimes" in the region who are the clients of the imperialists:

charge that the Western imperialists are "hypocritical 'friends of Islam,' " who are using Islam to their own advantage, while "the Soviet Union is, and always has been, a friend of the peoples of the East and a friend of the peoples of the Muslim World" (Grachev 1980: 125).

While recent English-language Soviet publications addressing the current crisis in Afghanistan avoid directly attacking Islam as a backward and reactionary religion, a number of those analyzing the last four centuries in the history of Afghanistan have presented the negative role of Islam and religious authorities as a major consideration (see Editors of *Social Sciences Today* 1981, esp. articles by Aslanov, Arunova, Khalfin, and Korgun).* The role of Islam in the current crisis is addressed in the Western press by some sympathizers of the Saur Revolution. For example, Halliday claims that a "very potent counter-revolutionary factor is the simple fact that Afghanistan is a Muslim country, i.e. one in which there existed a popular ideology that could be mobilized by counter-revolutionary forces more effectively than is the case with any other religion in the world" (1980a: 23).

The Truth about Afghanistan: Documents, Facts and Eyewitness Reports (compiled by Volkov et al. 1980); *The Undeclared War: Imperialism vs. Afghanistan* (compiled by Grachev 1980); *Afghanistan: Onward March of the Revolution* (Ilyinsky 1982); and *Afghanistan Today: Impressions of a Journalist* (Petkov 1983). It should be pointed out that the members of the Islamic resistance movements in Muslim Central Asia against the Bolsheviks (1918-36), who were called *basmachi* (a Turkic term for robbers, plunderers) by the Russians, were subjected to similar charges—i.e., of being tools of British imperialism. It is also important to note that the Soviets are using the term basmachi to refer to the Afghan resisters, while their clients in Afghanistan have adopted the Persian term *ashrar* (insurgents with evil intentions). Many Western Marxist intellectuals and organizations also subscribe to the idea that the resistance in Afghanistan is the work of (among others) the United States, Pakistan, China, Egypt, and the Gulf states (e.g., see Stork 1980: 25-26; Paul 1980; Dastarac and Levant 1980; Khalid 1980; Charpentier 1979).

*The collection by the Editors of *Social Sciences Today*, which contains articles by some of the better-known Soviet experts on Afghanistan, claims in its foreword to "throw light on the basic stages of the struggle of Afghanistan's people for independence, against all attempts to impose the colonial yoke on them [!] " (p. 7). It is undoubtedly a representative sample of some six thousand works on Afghanistan that the Soviets claim to have published during the last sixty years.

Journalists and Western commentators generally present the Afghan conflict essentially as a religious war waged by traditional religious leaders and "fundamentalist" mullahs (learned men) and their faithful horde of tribal and rural followers against the invading Soviet forces and the urban-based atheist Khalq-Parcham government. Western writers use the same Islamic terms employed by Afghan resistance groups to identify the resistance effort and its participants—jihad and mujahidin (holy war and freedom fighters). Despite the use of Islamic terms, a great deal of confusion remains about the meaning, purpose, and structure of jihad in general and the armed struggle in Afghanistan in particular. As a recent publication of the mujahidin points out, some misunderstandings emanate from the image that has been presented of "holy warriors": "a bunch of blood-thirsty religious fanatics with swords in hand ready to behead anyone who does not profess Islam" (Editors of *Mirror of Jehad* 1982d: 3; see also Peters 1979: 4-6).* Canfield (in this volume) suggests that for most Westerners the image of a holy war fighter is of a fanatic who is willing to kill and die for a religious cause, and that such a person is assumed to be (among other things) narrow-minded, bigoted, and perhaps even cruel. The assumption persists not only among the general public, but is also propounded in the works of some observers (see Halliday 1980b: 71; Paul 1980: 14; N. Newell and R. Newell 1981: 147). Clearly such observers have disregarded a large body of mujahidin publications concerning the nature of jihad.[†] An examination of such publications, in addition to Soviet and Khalq-Parcham documents, is necessary for a thorough understanding of the current resistance.

---

*Ideological attacks on Islam have been a significant component of all European colonialist policies toward the Muslim world. Rudolph Peters states the following: "Western powers often justified their colonial expansion by the idea of a *mission civilisatrice*; it served their interests if Moslem society was depicted as backward and Islam as a religion of bloodthirsty, lecherous fanatics. Therefore, the unfavorable medieval image of Islam was revived" (1979: 110). The Soviet Union has depicted Islam in similar fashion in its own Muslim republics and in Afghanistan. (On the Soviet policy toward Islam in the Soviet Union, see Bennigsen and Lemercier-Quelquejay 1967, 1979; Bennigsen 1975, 1980-81; Kolarz 1966; Bociurkiw 1980-81; Bowers 1980-81. On Afghanistan, see Volkov et al. 1980; Grachev 1980).

[†]A detailed listing of mujahidin publications is provided in the addendum to the bibliography.

Jihad summarizes the ideological framework upon which the armed struggle in Afghanistan rests. The concept in Islamic political thought has many interrelated meanings. The term is derived from an Arabic verb (*jahada*) which means to strive or "[exert] oneself for some praiseworthy aim" (Peters 1979: 118; see also Peters 1977 and Sabiq N.D.: 1-8). In its religious sense, jihad means "to exert one's utmost endeavor in promoting the cause of Islam" (Editors of *Mirror of Jehad* 1982d: 3). Jihad may involve individual or collective effort and can take either a peaceful moral and spiritual form or direct or indirect participation in armed struggle. The most significant form of peaceful jihad at the individual level, which is called the greater jihad, is *jihad al-nafs*, or the struggle against oneself—i.e., "the struggle against one's bad inclinations and against seduction and enticement by nearby pleasures" (Peters 1979: 118; see also Editors of *Mirror of Jehad* 1982d: 8). Two more common forms of peaceful jihad are called the educational jihad. One, the *jihad al-tarbiyah*, entails the realization and spread of Islamic values and institutions within Muslim society. It is a "struggle for the good of society and against corruption and decadence. [This kind of jihad] is coextensive with the concept of *al-amr bi-l-ma'ruf wa-l-nahy 'an al-munkar* (commanding what is good and forbidding what is abominable)" (Peters 1979: 118). All Muslims are required to take part in this form of struggle and must "work with all their intellectual and material abilities for the realization of justice and equality between the people and for the spreading of security and human understanding, both among individuals and groups" (Muhammad Isma'il Ibrahim; quoted in Peters 1979: 118). The second is the *jihad al-da'wah*, an effort to "[spread] Islam amongst the unbelievers by peaceful means, such as argumentation and demonstration" (Peters 1979: 118). Both forms of educational jihad are sometimes also called the *jihad al-lisan* or *jihad al-qalam*, meaning "jihad of the tongue or jihad of the pen" (Peters 1979: 118-19).

The aim of armed jihad, which is most commonly translated as "holy war" in the West, "is not, as it was often supposed in the older European literature, the conversion by force of unbelievers" (Peters 1977: 3). Mahmud Shaltut, an Egyptian Islamic scholar, asserts the following after analyzing the Quranic verses on fighting: "The reason for which the Moslems have been ordered to fight is the aggression directed against them, expulsion from their dwellings, violation of

Allah's sacred institutions and attempts to persecute people for what they believe" (quoted in Peters 1977: 45; see also Peters 1979: 121-35). Shaltut further contends that "the Messenger [i.e., Prophet Muhammad] only fought those who fought him, and that his fighting had no other aim than repelling oppression, warding off rebellion and aggression and putting an end to persecution for the sake of religion" (quoted in Peters 1977: 75). He concludes that for Muslims "there are only three reasons for fighting . . . [:] to stop aggression, to protect the Mission of Islam, and to defend religious freedom. Only in these cases has Allah made fighting lawful and urged on to it" (Peters 1977: 55; see also p. 51).* As Peters points out, jihad in the sense of fighting "is further restricted by the phrase *fi sabil Allah*, in the way of Allah. This implies that jihad is not just plain ordinary war, but must be somehow connected with religion and the interest of believers" (1979: 120).† Taking note of Western colonial exploitation and oppression in the Muslim world, 'Abduh and Rida in *Tafsir al-Manar* explain:

> Fighting in the way of Allah is fighting in order to raise Allah's word, to safeguard His religion, to spread His mission and to defend His party. . . . Therefore, it comprises more than fighting for the sake of religion, because it includes defense of the religion and

*Two readers of an earlier draft of this manuscript noted that the definition of jihad expressed by Shaltut reflects a liberal apologist Islamic point of view and ignores the fact that theological definitions and historical practices in some instances have differed. That is, Muslim states have used jihad to expand their territorial domain as well as against their enemies within the Muslim world. The readers' points are well taken. However, my concern here is more sociologically than historically motivated, pertaining to the current resistance in Afghanistan rather than to the inconsistencies in historical uses by former Muslim rulers. The Afghan mujahidin who accept and emphasize the defensive aspect of jihad are likely to conduct their activities in accordance with their understanding of the concept.

†Jihad in the way of Allah is not restricted to the act of fighting: "Any activity that strengthens the military front and supports the jihad is also jihad in the way of Allah, like e.g. stepping up productivity, strengthening the internal front, financially contributing to war-efforts and looking after the fighters' families. The Prophet has said: *'Whoever supplies a warrior in the way of Allah with equipment, is also a warrior and whoever takes the place of a warrior in his family by means of [his] wealth, is also a warrior'*" (Muhammad Radja al-Mutadjalli; quoted in Peters 1979: 121; emphasis in original).

protection of its mission, but also defense of territory when an aggressor covetously plans to take possession of our countries and to enjoy the riches of our land (1948-53: vol. 2, p. 460; quoted in Peters 1979: 120).

For most Islamic intellectuals, peaceful jihad and the armed struggle are closely linked. Muhammad Abu Zahrah, a leading Islamic scholar, considers the peaceful jihad a prerequisite for fighting in the way of Allah:

Jihad begins with jihad against oneself by purifying one's soul from [bad] inclinations and passions and with its orientation toward Allah, [for one ought] not [to struggle] out of love for fame, or desire for pleasure or in hope of worldly matters. Whoever fights to show his courage and to acquire fame and money, cannot be regarded a *mudjahid*, for a *mudjahid* fights only to please Allah, to obtain what He has in store for him, to raise the truth and to make Allah's word the Highest (quoted in Peters 1979: 119-20; all additions in brackets are Peters').

ISLAM AND JIHAD IN THE POLITICAL CULTURE OF AFGHANISTAN

Islam and the ideals of jihad have remained constant and dynamic forces in the political processes of Afghanistan, particularly over the last two centuries. Canfield (in this volume) asserts that in a country where over 99 percent of the population is Muslim, religious and political concepts are merged in Islam (see also Anderson, Katz, Keiser, Shahrani, and Tavakolian). Historically political opposition to European colonialism in the Muslim world has provided the most important example of the inseparability of Islam from the political aspirations of Islamic societies. Peters points out the following:

[In societies] where ideology is entirely dominated by religion and where there is no separation between the realms of politics and that of religion, wars and revolts regardless of their actual causes, acquire a religious dimension in that their aims, their justifications and their appeals for support are expressed in religious terms. It is precisely the doctrine of jihad that provided this dimension in Islamic history (1979: 6).

In the history of Afghanistan (as in most other Muslim countries in the region), Islam and the concept of jihad have played very important but *varied* roles. Between 1747 (when the Afghan state was created) and 1880 the most important role of jihad was to mobilize the Afghan peoples against the direct military intervention of the British-India colonial power (1838-42 and 1878-80). As a result of successful jihads against foreign aggression and the realization of the role of Islam in the survival of the country, 'Abdur Rahman used the concept of jihad to consolidate the power of the central government over all tribal and local chiefs. In this effort he used government-administered *shari'a* (Islamic law) courts and the support of *'ulama* (Islamic scholars), thus providing the Afghan monarchy with a sacred blessing which it did not have until that time (see Ashraf Ghani 1983 and 1978). It is important to note that this sacred blessing and the government's claim to legitimate authority rested solely on the monarchy's claim to be the guardian of Islam and of Muslim territory.

In the face of constant Russian tsarist colonialist advances in the north and British intrigues in the south, at the turn of the twentieth century the ties between nationalism, centralized state power, and religion took strong root—so much so that by 1916 Mahmud Tarzi, one of Afghanistan's earliest and most ardent Islamic-minded intellectuals, restated the "organic analogy" among them in a series of articles in *Siraj al-Akhbar* (a leading newspaper) to explain the unity of the concepts of *din* (religion), *dawlat* (state), *watan* (country), and *millat* (nation) (see Farhadi 1977: 353-56). He referred to these four concepts as sacred terms and explained how their existence and survival were mutually determined:

If these three things—i.e. country, nation and state—did not exist, religion also becomes incomplete and useless. You may ask, why? I say, because history and daily events show us very clearly that those Muslim countries and nations who are brought under the sway of the rule of unbelievers and have lost their national and territorial independence to the oppressive colonialists have no freedom of religion. Just take a look around you: Do you think that those of our Muslim brothers who are living under the iron clasps of unbelievers and foreigners possess any freedom of religion, rights to a country, and national dignity, like we do? No! Never! Ever! (reprinted in Farhadi 1977: 345; see also Shorish 1984).

In 1919, shortly after his accession to the throne, Amir Amanullah Khan declared a jihad against Great Britain in order to gain Afghanistan's full independence. After a brief armed confrontation, Britain granted Afghanistan independence, and Amanullah became a national hero, gaining much popularity in other Muslim countries in the region as well. Following the jihad for independence, Amanullah advanced his claims to political authority on the basis of his defense of Islam and Muslim territory; however, he was at the same time determined to create a secular and modern nation-state, patterned after European colonial powers. Like many of his contemporaries in the Muslim world, Amanullah believed the colonialist charge that Islam was the cause of his country's backwardness, and he tried to imitate the West indiscriminately and rapidly. Unfortunately, as Burhanuddin Rabbani, the leader of Jamiat-i Islami Afghanistan (JIA— a leading resistance group), points out, "Instead of borrowing science and technology from the West [Amanullah] borrowed dressing fashion" (Editors of *Mirror of Jehad* 1982c: 10; see also Ghobar 1967: 812-13). Furthermore, the imitation of Western lifestyles and ideas was often accompanied by direct or indirect attacks on Islam (see Rodinson 1979).

Many of the reforms and modernization programs advocated during Amanullah's reign (1919-29) had the support of the nascent Afghan intelligentsia (*rushanfikran*). Moreover, Amanullah's efforts are still admired by many Afghans, both educated and illiterate, for they believe he was sincere in his aspirations to improve conditions for the people of Afghanistan.* However, despite Amanullah's reform-mindedness, his government suffered from mismanagement, corruption, nepotism, arbitrary rule, and oppressive practices. As a result, there were a number of rural armed uprisings and revolts. In a discussion of the "symbolics of power," Clifford Geertz states that not only does the central "political authority . . . [require] a cultural frame in which to define itself and advance its claims; . . . so does opposition to it" (1979: 168). Not surprisingly, the uprisings and revolts against Amanullah were justified as a jihad for an Islamic cause.

*Recently uncovered data raise the possibility that Amanullah may have had a strong Soviet connection and that his reform policies may have been directly influenced by Moscow (see Arnold 1981: 5-7; also see Khalili 1980: 91-101).

Opposition to Amanullah's rule did not begin as a jihad; rather it began as isolated tribal and peasant rebellions in response to specific cases of local government corruption and oppression, and it was generally led by rural khans (Poullada 1973: 94-98; see also Anderson in this volume). However, some of Amanullah's Western-inspired legal and social reform proposals apparently threatened the vested interests of traditional religious leaders, particularly *ruhani* (spiritual or Sufi leaders) in Kabul. In 1928, following the adoption of the last of Amanullah's recommended reforms by the National Grand Assembly (Loya Jirgah), the head of a powerful ruhani family, the Hazrat of Shor Bazar, "obtained the signatures of four hundred religious leaders to a petition opposing many of the proposed reforms and presented it to the King" (Poullada 1973: 169-70). Thus a major confrontation between the religious leaders and the king began. Soon, through effective propaganda by the ruhanis and some mullahs—especially "foreign mullahs" (*Mullaha-i Farangi*)*—the ongoing local rebellions were transformed into a cause against an "infidel king." The leadership of the rebellions was controlled and their actions sanctioned through *fitwas* (Islamic pronouncements) as an Islamic jihad.

The principal goal of the jihad against Amanullah was to remove him from the throne and thus to put an end to his reform policies. It was not in any way aimed against the unjust system of government which had given rise to the uprisings in the first place. In fact the jihad against Amanullah had no reformist or revolutionary ideology. As Poullada states, "At no time did political or ideological issues emerge as the subject of intelligent discussion or even propaganda because such issues did not exist" (1973: 208). As a result of the jihad, Amanullah was deposed, and the Musahiban dynasty (1929-78) was established by Nadir Khan.

Mullaha-i-Farangi refers to mullahs who, regardless of their origin, were allegedly working for the British. Some of them were said to be Muslims from the subcontinent who were sent into Afghanistan, while others may have been Afghans educated in India and recruited there. The expression is analagous to "Red Mullahs," who worked for the Bolsheviks. Prominent ruhani were variously referred to locally as *hazrat, naqib, sahibzadah, afandi,* etc.

THE LEGACY OF JIHAD AGAINST AMANULLAH

The successful use of jihad against the hasty reformer, King Amanullah, by an alliance of traditional religious leaders and rural khans had significant consequences for subsequent political developments in Afghanistan. For one thing, the Musahiban dynasty owed its rise to power to this alliance. Thus, initially unable to challenge the traditional forces, the new rulers adopted a policy of accommodation, cooption, and containment. For another, most of Amanullah's proposed reforms were abandoned. Islamic rhetoric was used to provide a cloak of legitimacy for the new regime. Many Pashtun tribal chiefs, official rural middlemen such as arbabs and *maliks* (village headmen), and important urban merchants were appointed as army officers and administrators, while prominent ruhanis and mullahs were appointed to the judiciary and state bureaucracy (see Ghobar 1967: 789-836; L. Dupree 1973: 441-45; Poullada 1973: 160-95; Gregorian 1967: 227-92). Many local magnates (*ashkhasi sarshinas* or *ashkhasi namdar*) were appointed or "elected" by the court to the two nominal houses of parliament, Majlis-i Shura (Consultative Assembly) and Majlis-i A'yan (Assembly of Elders or Lords).

By sharing power with the traditional religious and secular leaders, the Musahiban rulers were able to consolidate a measure of central authority in the country. However, they were fully aware of the tenuous loyalties of the traditional powerbrokers, and they were determined to create new bases of support among the younger generation to ensure the future of the monarchy. The most significant measures taken to achieve this long-term goal were the creation of a modern army and police force and the expansion of secular, Western-style education and a rationalized bureaucracy. However, the development of these modern institutions was measurably influenced by the Musahiban decision to accommodate the traditional ruling elite.

Recruits for the royal army and police were drawn primarily from among the sons of loyal Pashtun tribes and tribal chiefs, many of whom were already serving as army officers or bureaucrats in the government. A few were drawn from among the sons of non-Pashtun local notables under a form of court patronage known as *ghulam bacha* (literally, "slave boys" or "page boys," reminiscent of Ottoman practices). The ghulam bacha were "given" to the court by their families to be educated and trained as loyal servants. Between 1930

34

and the late 1950s recruitment procedures for the officer corps remained almost unchanged. Similarly the influence of the traditional elite, many of whom were already serving in the bureaucracy, was considerable in the government's attempt to expand secular and state-sponsored religious education. Between 1930 and the mid-1950s the government had limited resources for education, and the establishment of schools and recruitment of children to attend them was generally based on a system of court patronage. As a result, the development of education was not only very slow, but it was also uneven and for the most part favored urban areas, certain ethnolinguistic and tribal groups, and particularly families of the traditional elite who were considered loyal to the monarchy.

The Musahiban strategy of coopting traditional leadership proved effective—at least in the short run. Free of any serious challenge during the first decades of their rule, the Musahiban rulers began to govern with a firm hand. However, the new structure of power relations had important long-term local and national effects. On the local level, many of the traditional leaders who relied on community consensus, their own powers of persuasion, and exemplary authority were now effectively transformed into an official ruling elite with an independent source of coercive power and authority. Their association with government and often spatial isolation from their communities resulted in the gradual weakening of their ties and credibility as local leaders. In the face of official corruption and oppression, most communities turned to new local leaders, creating a parallel power structure to deal with community concerns (see Barfield, Canfield, Shahrani, and Tavakolian in this volume). Nationally the new official elite began to perpetuate itself through rampant nepotism and a patronage system, thus effectively reducing social and political mobility for those who were not already part of the ruling structure. As the bureaucracy matured, it became more ingrown.

The combined force of the old and new elite initially assured the Musahiban rule. The only political opposition during the first quarter of a century of rule came during the early 1950s. Wish Zalmayan (Awakened Youth), a small group of Kabul intellectuals founded in 1947, began in 1951 to call for a liberalization of politics and a constitutional monarchy. The government briefly experimented with the ideals of liberal politics, but it then silenced the opposition in 1952 (see L. Dupree 1973: 494-98). Nevertheless, the Awakened Youth movement was a clear forerunner of future developments in Afghan politics.

The factor which irrevocably influenced the policies and ultimately the political fortunes of the Musahiban dynasty—and perhaps the people of Afghanistan—was the influx of relatively large amounts of foreign aid beginning in 1956. Prime Minister Muhammad Daoud (1953-63), who engineered the flow of economic and military aid from both Eastern and Western bloc countries, regarded it as a principal means of strengthening the Musahiban rule and creating a well-integrated, strong, and modern nation-state. After the lesson of the Awakened Youth movement, the Daoud regime was intent upon utilizing some of the aid to educate larger numbers of Afghan youth and use them to achieve its goals. Yet the impact of foreign aid on Daoud's nation-building efforts was mixed and often paradoxical.

In 1956 the Soviet Union offered substantial amounts of military aid which provided the government with a new sense of security and a base of power capable of withstanding any traditional domestic challenge. As a result, the government made a major change in the recruitment policy of cadets for the officers corps, allowing the military academies to recruit candidates from all ethnolinguistic groups and social strata. In addition, the government began to recruit military conscripts from some Pashtun tribal areas that had until then been "exempt." Moreover, reforms for the emancipation of women were implemented, and opposition to them was dealt with quickly and ruthlessly.

By the mid 1950s the monarchy launched a program for "national integration." The principal vehicle was a series of five-year development plans. Through these plans the government intended to build a communication infrastructure, induce agricultural and industrial growth, expand education and social services, and make substantial improvements in social, economic, and political conditions. Foreign aid, primarily from the Soviet Union and the United States, financed 75 percent of the first three plans (1956-72).

To accomplish its goals the government needed the help of its well-entrenched but ill-equipped and generally corrupt bureaucrats. As a result, the outcomes of its economic development programs were very disappointing. The plans began with "the construction of a series of large infrastructural 'showy' and white-elephant-type projects [e.g., the Helmand and Nangarhar Valleys projects and Kandahar

International Airport]. Most of the projects were selected by non-economic criteria and did not pass the necessary feasibility tests" (Zekrya 1976: 212-13). There were virtually no increases in production, income, or employment. Only a very small segment of the population—primarily government officials, army officers, and the urban merchant class, who were also well represented in the bureaucracy—benefited economically. The majority of rural people and urban poor were not affected by the plans or were influenced negatively. As Zekrya points out,

[An important consequence of] fifteen years of planning efforts and . . . receiving one of the highest per capita amounts of external assistance in the developing world [was that Afghanistan] moved gradually from a level of food surplus to a level of self subsistence in food and finally to a state of growing food deficit (1976: 211).

While the government's economic development plans failed to realize the desired results, considerable improvements were made in the transportation infrastructure and in the expansion of secular education. Foreign aid had its most crucial impact upon education, producing important, unforeseen political consequences. With the flow of foreign aid, large numbers of schools were opened in the rural areas. (Education was perhaps the only tangible benefit of the development effort to reach some of these areas.) By the mid-1970s more than 800,000 Afghan youth were attending some 4,000 schools and over 600,000 had completed some formal education (see Chu et al. 1975: 76-83).

During the 1960s many educated youth were absorbed by an expanding government bureaucracy. In the late 1960s, however, the volume of foreign aid began to decline, and the bureaucracy had reached saturation. There were very few jobs in state-run industries and very little private development. It was increasingly difficult for high school and college graduates to find jobs and even harder to get into institutions of higher education. For the fortunate few who had already joined the lower ranks of the civil and military services, the prospects for job mobility within an already top-heavy bureaucracy largely manned by the old official elite seemed bleak.

The government favored an inculcation of secular and nationalistic values in the schools and did not make use of Islam to strengthen its authority or legitimacy. Although religious studies were kept in the curricula, they were often treated as inconsequential, particularly in the urban schools.* The government hoped that through increased secular education a kind of national civil politics would emerge, and that the newly educated youth would leave aside their primordial group loyalties and rally around the monarchy as the symbolic focus of a strong, new, civil Afghan nation-state. Not surprisingly, the schools did not produce the kind of "integrative revolution" within the polycultural Afghan society that the monarchy expected. Instead traditional loyalties and cleavages were for the most part modernized (see Geertz 1973: 255-310). The integrative revolution failed at least in part because the educational curriculum was not coordinated with the goals of national civil politics and in part because schools were allocated in favor of certain areas; both factors created tensions not only between Pashtun and non-Pashtun groups, but among Pashtun tribes as well.†

As a result of expanded education, large numbers of newly educated youth, particularly among the urban and rural poor, had become dependent on the government for their livelihood, but they felt no loyalty toward it. They witnessed social and economic changes in the urban centers but were not the beneficiaries. They also witnessed pervasive corruption among high government officials. Differential access to all forms of resources according to ethnolinguistic, regional, and class affiliations was becoming more pronounced through nepotism, favoritism, and the old patronage system. Economic conditions

---

*In an effort to curb the influences of traditional religious education, the government took direct control of formal religious schools and introduced non-religious subjects into the curriculum. Only graduates of these schools and the Faculty of Islamic Studies at Kabul University were eligible for government employment. Graduates of traditional *madrasah* (informal religious schools) could apply for such jobs only after certification by a government-run religious school.

†In the curriculum Pashto was imposed as the language of instruction for areas whose native language was other than Dari, even though students in those areas were bilingual in both Dari and their native tongue. In addition, the role of non-Pashtun in the history of the country was either not represented or misrepresented and distorted in the educational texts and other government publications. Differential allocation of schools and recruitment of students for higher education in government boarding schools in Kabul generally favored Muhammadzai over Ghilzai Pashtun and Pashtuns living in Nangarhar and Paktya over those in Kandahar and Ghazni. As a rule, fewer schools were allocated in non-Pashtun areas.

in the neglected rural agricultural areas were worsening due to improved communications and an increased penetration of world-market forces, which in turn increased rural out-migration. Consequently during the 1960s political discontent among the emergent intelligentsia rose. Paradoxically, at a time when the Musahiban rulers had achieved their long-sought goal of firmly controlling traditional political forces, the educated Afghans who had been trained by the regime to broaden its base of support were beginning to pose a strong political challenge.

A significant outcome of foreign aid and the government's development efforts was thus a new articulation of the power structure in the country. During much of the Musahiban rule there had been only two major political forces: foremost the royal household and the old and new ruling elite, and second the nonofficial, community-based traditional leaders who for the most part avoided contact with the authorities and were concerned with the welfare of their own communities above all else. Relations between the two were not confrontational; they involved keeping at a distance and maintaining a degree of mutual suspicion. A third element was added when the educated youth became alienated and began to call for radical social, economic, and political changes. Beginning in the mid-1960s they increasingly formed the primary political opposition in Kabul and other urban centers.

Despite their common complaints and grievances, however, the disenchanted intelligentsia did not represent a coherent political body with common goals. Differences among them came to the fore after the ratification of the liberal constitution of 1964, for which they were at least partly responsible. This constitution restricted the political role of members of the royal household (with the exception of the king), provided for more open parliamentary elections, and promised a free press and the formation of political parties. Taking advantage of the last promise, the educated youth began unofficially to organize themselves according to a broad spectrum of political ideologies. On 1 January 1965 the Khalq Communist Party was the first to make itself known.* Its emergence prompted the organization of an Islamic opposition group, called Jawanan-i Musulman (Muslim Youth)

---

*In 1965 the Khalq was the only Communist party in Afghanistan. In 1967 it split into two factions, Khalq and Parcham. The two factions formed a coalition in 1977, one year before their successful coup (see Arnold 1983).

but popularly known as Ikhwan al-Muslimin (Muslim Brethren) (see Shahrani in this volume). For different reasons the Khalq and Jawanan-i Musulman began to question the legitimacy of the monarchy and the government, and both advocated revolutionary change. At the same time, they actively opposed one another and often engaged in violent confrontations. Consistent with its policy of secularism, together with political pressures from the Soviet Union, the government let the Communists alone while severely suppressing Muslim Youth.

Muslim Youth became increasingly critical of Musahiban rule, not only for its failure to deliver on promises of economic development, social justice, and freedom and equality for citizens, or for the growing disparities of wealth and privilege between the elite and the masses of rural and urban poor, but more importantly for permitting foreign countries (particularly the Soviet Union) to exploit the country's natural and human resources to subvert Islam and the Muslim people through the Khalq. The organization thus aimed at the overthrow of the Musahiban dynasty as well as the official ruling class associated with it, strongly opposed all Communist movements in the country, and advocated the establishment of an Islamic government in Afghanistan. Shahid Habiburrahman, one of the leaders of the movement, described the system the group hoped to see established as follows:

> Islamic government has the duty to promote moral excellence, and the government itself should be an embodiment of superior morality. In the conduct of its duties, the government must be the model of moral and ethical excellence. In addition, it is the duty of the government to help spread the message of Allah and invite the people to the Way of God. It should also protect its citizens' rights, prevent any form of aggression and injustice against them, and eradicate cruelty, oppression and poverty in the nation. The government must also safeguard people's freedom and must make sure that the necessities of life for its citizens are made available. In the international arena, it must not only defend the oppressed peoples and oppose those who thrive on the blood [of the weak] and rob them of their human rights, but fight with all its strength all those powers who try to enslave and impose their will upon them. Otherwise, such a government does not fulfill its responsibilities and must be overthrown (1977: 35-36).

Under constant pressure from the government, Muslim Youth remained poorly organized and limited to educated, Islamic-minded youth. The Communists, free of such pressure and no doubt with external financial help, were better organized, and they succeeded in infiltrating the lower ranks of the army leadership. (Ironically this had been made possible by the government's decision in the mid-1950s to broaden its recruitment policies for military academies.) In 1973, with the help of the Parcham faction of the Communist Party, former Prime Minister Daoud, who had been out of power for ten years, staged a military coup, ousted his cousin and brother-in-law, King Muhammad Zahir, and established a republic (1973-78).

Long considered by Islamic-minded youth to be a friend of the Soviets and promoter of Communist elements and Soviet influence in the country, Daoud waged a brutal campaign against his opponents. He unleashed a particularly violent attack against Muslim Youth, jailing and killing many of its most promising leaders (most of them Kabul University faculty and students). In the summer of 1975 Muslim Youth groups staged armed attacks against the Daoud regime in several areas of the country, including the Panjsher Valley. Although initially successful, the attacks were soon repelled by superior government forces (Gall 1983: 80). Following their defeat, many members of the much weakened Islamic movement were forced underground or went into exile in Pakistan and elsewhere in the region.

Like the Muslim Youth movement, many of Daoud's other political rivals were eliminated under various pretexts. However, despite an apparent deterioration of relations between the Daoud regime and Khalq and Parcham, they were left unscathed during his rule. Although they had only a small membership—estimated at about 5,000—the two parties remained well organized and were once again able to infiltrate the lower echelons of the army leadership. Together they destroyed the Daoud regime and the Musahiban dynasty in the military coup of April 1978 (see Arnold 1983; Bradsher 1983; L. Dupree 1979a).

The assumption of power by the Khalq-Parcham touched off the current violent armed struggle—or jihad—and in turn led to the intervention of the Soviets. It is in light of the historical, socioeconomic, and political changes and continuities discussed above that we must analyze the current resistance in Afghanistan.

41

M. NAZIF SHAHRANI

THE ARMED RESISTANCE: EVOLUTION AND PROSPECTS

Within a few months of assuming power, the Khalq-Parcham party faced steadily growing armed opposition in many urban as well as rural areas. These uprisings, although initially uncoordinated and for the most part unrelated except for a common opposition to the Khalq-Parcham regime, were all expressed in terms of an Islamic jihad. (Even the government began to call its defense of "the gains of the revolution" a jihad against so-called imperialist lackeys.) Although the uprisings were waged by different groups and often for different reasons, the Western media and some scholars have characterized them as primarily a religious opposition led by tribal khans and traditional religious leaders simply to defend Islam. The differences between resistance groups have often been explained as those between "moderates" and "fundamentalists." The emphasis on the tribal, peripheral, traditional, and defensive aspects of the resistance has left unexamined the critical role of the educated segment of the Afghan population and the jihad it is waging. Fischer's comments on the Middle East are equally pertinent to Afghanistan:

> The pendulum . . . has become unhinged: Urbanization, education, and the world economy· have transformed the nature of politics. Old-style tribal revolts and local nativistic revolts still occur . . . but they are important primarily at the peripheries. . . . In the center, we have arrived in a complex world of a democratic mass politics where one needs to look below the "borrowed language and time-honored disguises" to the structural problem of mass society, a world where one needs to evaluate the demands phrased in traditional concepts of rights and duties in relation to these structural problems, and not just in abstract moral, cultural, or ideological terms (1982: 121).

In this section we shall analyze the changed nature of politics and look below the "borrowed language" of jihad and other "time-honored disguises," critically examine how people's motivations for jihad relate to the basic structural problems of Afghan society, and determine how the local rebellions meld with the revolutionary ideologies of the "complex world of mass politics" at the center.

At the time of the April coup, the Khalq-Parcham stepped into a virtual power vacuum because Daoud had already weakened or eliminated all organized opposition to his regime and no serious opposition remained. The Khalq-Parcham's ouster of the Daoud regime and destruction of the much despised Musahiban dynasty provided it with its principal claim to legitimacy.

For most illiterate rural populations the coup was just another *padshah gardushi* (literally, the succession of one monarch by another). Although such events involved some possible bloodshed among the contenders and were of concern to the center, they had little or no significance in the peripheries as long as rural routines were not disrupted. Therefore, the community-based traditional leaders were, as in the past, indifferent to the coup and its initial aftermath. However, bureaucrats in the provinces, rural and provincial teachers, and students and educated youth were much more in tune with their urban counterparts than with the rural masses, and their reactions varied depending on their political and ideological loyalties.

At the center the picture was far more complex. The much smaller, pro-Peking factions of the Afghan Communist party, Shu'la-i Jawid (Eternal Flame) and Sitami Milli, a Marxist anti-Pashtun group of youth from northern Afganistan, extended guarded but definite support to Khalq-Parcham (see Shahrani in this volume), as did Afghan Millat, a Pashtun nationalist/socialist group. In addition, the Khalq-Parcham had the sympathy, if not the support, of a segment of the generally politically inactive urban poor and a relatively large number of low- and middle-level government officials. (The sympathy was in large part due to the new regime's destruction of the corrupt Musahiban dynasty.) Many low-level officials who were entirely dependent on government salaries for their livelihood, particularly those from the urban poor, had little option but to accept the new order. Moreover, despite its harsh rhetoric against the old ruling elite, the Khalq-Parcham allowed most of them to leave the country unharmed (with the exception of Daoud and his immediate family and a few of his close associates). Some former ruling elite, among them Sayyid Ahmad Gailani, a prominent ruhani with strong ties to the monarchy, reportedly "attempted to cooperate with the Khalq government in its early weeks" (N. Newell and R. Newell 1981: 94).

Only members of Muslim Youth and other Islamic-minded intellectuals were truly alarmed by the rise to power of the Khalq-Parcham;

they opposed the government not only for ideological reasons, but also feared for their personal safety. Within weeks of the coup the regime began to move against pious individuals and suspected members of Muslim Youth. The group, whose members were drawn mostly from educated rural youth and recent migrants to urban areas, began to reorganize in small groups either in the urban areas or in the members' native rural homes. Some former leaders who were living in exile began to congregate in Peshawar, Pakistan, where they formed resistance organizations. Isolated and sporadic armed attacks against small government installations and well-known Communist officials began in Kabul and some provincial centers. In addition, a strong campaign was launched to inform the public about the anti-Islamic and pro-Soviet nature of the Khalq-Parcham regime. The government responded with increased repression and harsher retaliation against its suspected opponents (see L. Dupree in this volume).

Power struggles raged between the Khalq and Parcham factions in June-August 1978, and the Khalq faction, led by Nur M. Taraki and Amin, emerged victorious. However, the Khalqis were unwilling to share power with other Afghan Communist or secular nationalist groups, creating new tensions. The government's Marxist rhetoric, haphazard reforms, insensitivity toward and provocative actions against Islamic traditions, accompanied by an increased use of force against its suspected enemies, angered large segments of the population.

As local resistance grew, it was soon transformed into a national-level jihad. However, it is important to stress that neither the process of transformation nor the diversity of resistance organizations is strictly traditional. Each is indicative of both the altered nature of politics and of new structural relations between the center and the peripheries. Thus a detailed examination of the resistance organizations will enhance our understanding of the current situation in Afghanistan.

IDEOLOGY AND STRUCTURE OF THE RESISTANCE MOVEMENTS

Shortly after the beginning of large-scale armed opposition within Afghanistan in late 1978, attempts to organize formal resistance organizations outside the country, particularly in Pakistan, mushroomed. Most of the groups were organized by the educated youth. Not surprisingly, many were continuations, reorganizations, or new factions of groups in existence in Kabul during the 1960s and 1970s. A few new organizations, primarily from among the old aristocracy, were also formed, and some attempts were made at organizing people along ethnolinguistic lines.

On the basis of political ideology, most resistance organizations fall into one of two categories: (1) Groups which are inspired by Western ideologies of secular nationalism, socialism, Marxism, or Maoism; and (2) Groups organized according to the precepts of Islam. The best-known groups in the first category are Sazmani Azadibakhsh-i Mardum-i Afghanistan (SAMA—Organization for the Liberation of the Peoples of Afghanistan), a radical leftist group made up of the former members of the Communist Shu'la-i Jawid, and Afghan Millat (see Chaliand 1982: 58-59, and Khalid 1980). Membership in these groups is very small and drawn from among the urban intelligentsia. Their base of support is either extremely narrow or nonexistent. As a result, such groups have been the targets of attack by both the Kabul regime and the Islamic-based resistance groups. Some of them, such as Sitami Milli, have been completely wiped out (see Shahrani in this volume). The role of these groups has declined, and at present it appears to be negligible.

A large number of Islamic-oriented resistance organizations were formed, but only about seven of them have managed to gain recognition both inside Afghanistan and abroad and are now actively participating in the jihad. On the basis of leadership structure, political goals, external relations, and sources of support, these groups fall into two categories: the traditionalists and the Islamic revolutionaries. Basic differences between the two categories emanate from the basic structural differences of Afghan society.

There are three traditionalist organizations: (1) Jabha-i Milli Nijat (National Liberation Front), led by Sibghatullah Mujadidi; (2) Mahaz-i Milli Islami (Islamic National Front), led by Sayyid Ahmad Gailani; and (3) Harakat-i Inqilab-i Islami (Islamic Revolutionary Movement), led by Mawlawi Muhammad Nabi Muhammadi. Like Gailani, Mujadidi is a member of a well-known ruhani family who had strong ties with the Musahiban dynasty and the official ruling elite. Muhammadi, a traditional, madrasah-trained Islamic scholar, also had strong ties to the old regime; he has served as a deputy from Logar province in the Afghan parliament.

All three traditional organizations came into existence after the resistance had begun. Roy describes their leadership structure:

> [They] are organized according to a pattern of personal allegiances. They include leading figures from the former regime, tribal chiefs and traditionalist religious leaders trained in nongovernmental religious institutions. These parties are particularly well established in tribal Pathan [Pashtun] areas (in the south of the country) (1983: 12; see also N. Newell and R. Newell 1981: 93-94).

Their political goals are primarily the defense of Islam and the independence of Afghanistan. For them jihad in the present context means simply a war of liberation. Like their traditionalist predecessors during the jihad against Amanullah, they lack any reformist ideals for the country. Because much of their membership is from the old elite, they have been suspected of favoring the return of the monarchy. (These suspicions were confirmed when an alliance of the three traditionalist groups responded positively to a July 1983 appeal by former king Muhammad Zahir to the Afghan people to join under his leadership in the creation of a "National United Front" against the Soviet invaders [see Reshtia 1984].) The traditionalists have strong family and business ties in the West and are best known to Western journalists and researchers. They advocate direct military and financial help from the West and believe they cannot succeed without it. In the media they are often described as the Islamic "moderates" in the Afghan resistance.

The Islamic revolutionaries, who are ideologically and organizationally a continuation of the pre-1978 Muslim Youth, comprise four groups: (1) Jamiat-i Islami Afghanistan (JIA—Islamic Society of Afghanistan), led by Burhanuddin Rabbani; (2) Hizb-i Islami (Islamic Party), led by Gulbudin Hikmatyar; (3) Hizb-i Islami, led by Mawlawi M. Yunus Khalis;* and (4) Itihadi Islami Baray Azadyi Afghanistan (Islamic Alliance for the Liberation of Afghanistan), led by 'Abdur Rabbur Rasul Sayyaf. Rabbani and Sayyaf had studied at the Faculty

---

*The two Hizb-i Islami are the result of a factional split. The original group was led by Hikmatyar, and Khalis was his second in command. As a result of personal and tactical disagreements, Khalis left and formed his own party under the same name.

of Islamic Studies at Kabul University and at Al-Azhar University in Cairo; both were teachers at Kabul University. Hikmatyar was an engineering student at Kabul University. All three were actively involved in the leadership of Muslim Youth. Khalis, although educated in a madrasah, is a forward-looking Islamic intellectual and preacher. All of them are relatively young and come from modest rural backgrounds.

Initially the membership in and support for the Islamic revolutionary groups was not broad and was mostly made up of activist Islamic-minded rural and urban youth from middle- and lower-class backgrounds. Since the Soviet invasion the groups have drawn considerable additional support from community-based secular and religious leaders. The membership and support vary depending on the ethnolinguistic, regional, and ideological appeal of each group's national and local leaders.

For the Islamic revolutionary groups jihad in Afghanistan is not simply a war of liberation or a defense of Islam. It is also an armed struggle to establish an Islamic social and political order in the country (for details see Hizb-i Islami N.D.a: 7, 8; Hikmatyar 1980; JIA N.D.a: 7; and Editors of *Mirror of Jehad* 1982a: 10). The groups' forward-looking proposals for an alternative sociopolitical order have received little or no attention from journalists and scholars. Instead the groups are frequently dismissed as "fundamentalist."

The Islamic revolutionaries disagree with the traditionalist groups over the issue of the political future of Afghanistan. Unlike the traditionalists, the revolutionary groups consider a return to the status quo ante unthinkable, maintaining that the Musahiban regime was directly responsible for the tragedy that has ensued (see Rabbani 1976, N.D.a, and N.D.b; Rasul 1980; Hizb-i Islami N.D.b; and Habiburrahman 1977). Furthermore, they do not approve of the pro-Western policies of the traditionalists. They argue that the most obvious result of American and Soviet "peaceful competition" in Afghanistan over the past twenty-five years is the current crisis (see Kamrany 1969, Fry 1974, and Zekrya 1976). Their feelings are summed up as follows: "The Afghan mujahideen are now well aware that [Western capitalist] imperialism and Communism are like the two blades of a pair of scissors for the purpose of cutting the roots of our beloved religion, Islam" (Hizb-i Islami 1981; see also Hikmatyar 1983). They charge that the Western powers, particularly the United States, are not only not interested in a quick resolution of the conflict,

47

but also that their support of the traditionalist groups is undermining the struggle of the Muslim people of Afghanistan and will aid the Soviets and the Afghan Communists in achieving their aims.

There have been numerous attempts to bring all seven of the Islamic-based resistance groups into a single coalition. The most recent (summer 1981), a coalition called Itihadi Islami Mujahidini Afghanistan (Islamic Unity of Afghan Mujahidin), has been only partially successful. The leaders of the three traditionalist groups left the coalition shortly after its formation to establish the National United Front coalition. However, the deputy leaders of the three groups, all traditional Islamic scholars, elected to stay in the coalition with the four revolutionary groups.*

Despite strong political differences between the National United Front and Islamic Unity (both of which have headquarters in Pakistan), there is considerable cooperation among battlefield commanders—contrary to earlier media claims.[†] In addition, the role of large numbers of young educated Afghans (teachers, students, clerks, and low-level civil servants) from both rural and urban backgrounds is becoming increasingly apparent (see Shahrani and Strand in this volume). With time and experience they are taking leadership positions at all levels. Commander Ahmad Shah Mas'ud of the Panjsher Valley, Commander Amin Wardak of Wardak province, and Commander Zabihullah of Marmol, Mazar-i Sharif, are but a few well-known examples (see Gall 1983; Bain 1982: 92-99; and *Afghanistan Forum Newsletter* 1983: 21).

The most critical factor in the current jihad has been the relationship between the educated Islamic-minded youth and the rural and urban masses of Afghanistan. It is obvious that the peasant masses and local traditional leaders did not initially share the same vision of

*The deputy leaders who remained in the Islamic Unity coalition are Mawlawi Muhammad Mir (National Liberation Front); Mawlawi Mansoor (Islamic Revolutionary Movement); and Mo'azin (Islamic National Front). On the attempts at unification of the groups under a single leadership, see Editors of *Mirror of Jehad* 1982a, 1982b, 1982c; see also *Middle East Journal* 1982: 69, and *Afghanistan Forum Newsletter* 1983: 2.

[†]Indeed political disagreements among the resistance groups are sharpest among the groups living outside of Afghanistan—especially in Pakistan—and less prominent among the groups inside the country.

an Islamic future as the young revolutionaries. But Sayyaf contends that

> [this jihad] has had a deep effect on all the Muslims. It has brought us together. Today, the Afghans know one another. We have also found out in the process who is good and who is bad. Those who are sincere have gathered together in the way of Truth and have started to cooperate. They have started to live in an Islamic way, ... and they have started to taste the real meaning of jihad (1983: 11).

In their efforts to mobilize support, the mujahidin have focused on three elements: (1) the pervasive commitment to Islam among the masses; (2) a well-known and proven enemy, the Soviets and their Khalq-Parcham clients; and (3) the importance and popularity of local religious and secular leaders. There is little doubt that Islam provides a basis for unity between the national and local resistance movements. A number of contributors to this volume have noted the link between religion and politics (for example, see Tavakolian on the Sheikhanzai Pashtun nomads, Anderson on the Ghilzai Pashtun [Pakhtun], Katz on the Vaygal Valley Kalasha, Barfield on the Imam Sahib district in Qunduz province, and Richard Tapper on Saripul).

Most Afghans had suffered injustice and oppression at the hands of government officials, or knew of it, and accepted it as a normal (though not proper) part of government operations. However, the Marxist government introduced something *new* into the politics of Afghanistan—blatant atheism. The great majority of Afghans believed the usurpers were "infidels or else one's fellow-countrymen in the pay of infidels. No one in the lowest social strata, where nothing had shaken the faith in Islam, could fail to notice this" (Rodinson 1979: 5; in this volume see Keiser on the notion of the Communist regime as a *kafir* [infidel] government; see also Anderson and Barfield).

It was well known among both educated Afghans and some rural villagers that the Khalq-Parcham was Communist. Some observers have asserted that the Khalq-Parcham would nonetheless have gained credibility if it had presented its reforms using Islamic rhetoric. Indeed it has tried to do so since the Soviet invasion (see Muradov 1981: 192-95; Grachev 1980: 82-94; Volkov et al. 1980: 148-56; Mukherjee 1981; and Afghanistan National Fatherland Front 1981). However, thus far its attempts have produced no positive results, and it is unlikely that they will in the future. The regime cannot appropriate Islamic rhetoric simply by using it; the Soviet pretense of doing so over the past sixty years in Central Asia is well known in Afghanistan.

The Afghan people fear both communism and the Soviets. Their perception of communism as anti-Islamic has been significantly influenced by the presence of large refugee communities of Uzbek, Turkmen, Kirghiz, and Tajik (particularly in northern Afghanistan and Kabul)—groups who fled the Bolshevik suppression of Muslim peoples in Turkistan—i.e., Soviet Central Asia (see Shahrani in this volume).* Moreover, the Afghans perceive the Soviets as godless and immoral and "the Soviet way of life as antithetical to every value they hold dear" (R. Tapper in this volume, p. 246; see also N. Dupree on the attitude toward the young Afghan Communists). Some scholars allude to the "independent and national" character of the Khalq-Parcham regime (Harrison 1978; L. Dupree 1979a); however, most Afghans believe that the Khalq-Parcham is ideologically, politically, and morally dominated by the Soviets, and they view it in the same light—i.e., as an enemy of Islam and the Muslim peoples of Afghanistan.

The reliance of the mujahidin on traditional local leaders (particularly in rural Afghanistan) is justified both in historic terms and by the strong Islamic character of these leaders. As indicated above, local leaders have traditionally defended the interests of their communities against an indifferent central government. Local government officials, often outsiders contemptuous of the local population, could use or threaten to use force, coercion, and oppression, and they were invariably corrupt. Even village headmen, whether chosen by the villagers or appointed by the government, were, by virtue of their association with the administration, opportunistic, self-interested, and considered dishonorable (see Barfield, Katz, Shahrani, Strand and Tavakolian in this volume; Anderson reports that among the Ghilzai Pashtun, mullahs who were presumed to be in government service were doubly condemned, for both opportunism and doing the government's work). Moreover, locally powerful khans who rely on

---

*Previous Afghan governments have suppressed information on Soviet oppression of Central Asian Muslims from the educational curricula and the media, but the mujahidin are beginning to publicize it in their own publications, such as Rasul 1980; see also JIA N.D.b, N.D.c, N.D.d, Khalili 1980, and Shahrani 1981b.

the central government's power to enable them to exploit the local population are often targets of local opposition and revenge, especially in times of national political crisis, and they are never leaders of popular resistance movements (see Strand and Keiser in this volume).*

In contrast, local leadership in rural Afghanistan is based on voluntary, participatory, and often dyadic ties of mutual confidence and trust between leaders and followers. Local leaders often do not have official connections, and they emerge by gaining the support of individuals in their communities. They maintain their legitimacy by mediating among disputants within a community, safeguarding local interests against outside interference (including that of the local government), and defending such interests militarily when required (see Barfield, Strand, Keiser, Katz, and Anderson in this volume; see also Shahrani 1983).

Islamic values are a significant determinant of local leadership, for as Tavakolian contends in the case of the Sheikhanzai Pashtun nomads, "Sacred authority does not merely support political authority; it *is* political authority" (in this volume, p. 259). Local religious leaders can claim authority according to various criteria: learning (the criterion of mullahs and *mawlawis*—religious scholars and teachers); piety and spiritual achievements through *tariqa* (mystic orders or paths of religious devotion—the criteria of *walis, pirs,* and Sufis); significant ancestry (*hazrats, ishan, miyan, agha,* and *sayyid,*—among others); or combinations thereof. Each type of leader has a different following, depending on how he is perceived locally to protect community interests. Apart from officiating at various religious rituals, the principal task of religious leaders in peacetime is to mediate political conflicts within a community and with outsiders (see Anderson in this volume). Furthermore, through hospitality, charity, and generosity, they often help to equalize individual differences in wealth.

The authority of both secular and religious local leaders has remained extremely diffuse. While such diffuseness has ensured the

---

*Most official local leaders who had taken advantage of their official ties have been driven out of peripheral areas into Kabul, where, ironically, the Marxist regime protects them. In the same manner, most of the high government officials of the Musahiban dynasty have left the country and resettled in Europe or the United States.

survival of a traditional leadership structure parallel to the power structure of the local administration, it has also made it very difficult for political observers to take adequate account of it. Canfield (in this volume) argues that the local religious power structure in Afghanistan is not as ephemeral as it appears. Rather there exist organizational forms with particular features which he has referred to as "Islamic coalitions," and these can function as networks for collective public action. In an Islamic coalition many seemingly secular ties such as those of residence, affinity, common descent, and economic relationship coalesce, but all such ties have a strong Islamic aspect. In fact, Canfield states that "In the Islamic coalition political and social ideals are merged" (p. 288).

While the coalitions may not have played an important role in the national political arena in recent times, they have nevertheless been ready-made structural units. As such, they could be, and have been, used to mobilize Afghans against the Khalq-Parcham and Soviet forces (see Barfield, Canfield, Keiser, Shahrani, and Strand in this volume). An understanding of the dynamics of Islamic coalitions, particularly at the local and regional levels, can inform us about the structure and prospects of the current jihad in Afghanistan.

PROSPECTS OF THE RESISTANCE

It is significant that at the local levels of political and military action Islamic coalitions account for the relative successes of the mujahidin, but that on the regional and national levels they reflect the weaknesses of the Afghan resistance movements. Local networks are close-knit; they are based on intensely personal, participatory and community-oriented political processes and multiple social ties (as noted above). They give way to increasingly loose-knit networks based on impersonal, slightly hierarchical, and (eventually) abstract ideological principles, with little or no significant social density. Moreover, relations at the regional or national level become more explicitly voluntary (see Anderson in this volume). In the heterogeneous sociocultural and demographic mosaic of Afghanistan, the creation of a close-knit network of Islamic coalitions poses a major challenge to mujahidin leadership. In this volume some successes toward this end are reported at the regional level in Darra-i Nur

(Keiser), Nuristan (Strand), and Badakhshan (Shahrani),* and the creation of coalition groups among the resistance movements seems promising.

The Afghan resistance movements may have time on their side, but they face two significant impediments toward achieving strong and viable national coalitions (aside from their political and ideological differences discussed above). The first and perhaps less serious is that religious figures are generally considered special interest arbitrators rather than initiators of policies or programs. If the resistance is to succeed, these leaders will have to reshape their roles, projecting themselves as positive national leaders and overcoming their historical role as only mediators (see Anderson in this volume). (In the long run this impediment may pose greater problems for the older generation of ruhani or traditionalist coalition leaders than for some of the leaders of the Islamic Unity groups.)

The second is the deep-rooted problem of ethnicity. Ethnic tensions in general, and competition and conflict between Pashtuns and non-Pashtuns in particular, are a legacy of the divide-and-rule policy of the Musahiban dynasty (see, for example, R. Tapper, Katz, Strand, and Shahrani in this volume).† Furthermore, like many other issues in Afghanistan, ethnicity is not simply a political or secular one, but also Islamic. Ethnic problems are escalated to a moral level, and ethnic conflicts are often justified on Islamic grounds that can arouse strong emotions (see Tavakolian, Anderson, R. Tapper, Barfield, and Katz in this volume).

Because of the strong pro-Pashtun government bias in education and social services since the mid-1950s, interethnic conflicts can be particularly volatile among the young, educated segment of the population. As the leadership of the current struggle is for the most part

---

*Other regional coalitions include ones in Hazarajat (see Khalid 1980 and "B.M." 1982) and the Islamic Union of Northern Provinces of Afghanistan, formed in summer 1983.

†Interethnic suspicions between Pashtuns and non-Pashtuns seem to be a source of major concern in the present conflict in at least one area, Nuristan (see Katz in this volume). In Badakhshan, the Wakhi, Shughni, and Zibaki minorities have not supported the Tajik and Uzbek majority's struggle against the Khalq-Parcham largely because of a long history of ethnic discrimination and exploitation of the former by the latter (see Shahrani in this volume).

in their hands, the issue has gained a greater significance.* Mujahidin leaders who emphasize the Islamic concept of *umma*, a community and brotherhood of all Muslims, largely consider ethnicity a non-issue. In contrast, the Khalq-Parcham and the Soviets have tried to take advantage of it by introducing a "nationalities policy" that clearly mimics the nationality policy of the Soviet Union in almost every detail (see Naby 1980). The result has been an emphasis on ethnic differences and a renewed competition for government favors.

In addition to these two internal impediments, the resistance movements are subject to Soviet propaganda aimed at undermining the credibility of the mujahidin. Two accusations require particular comment. First, the mujahidin leadership has been accused of connections with the U.S. Central Intelligence Agency (CIA) and therefore of representing Western imperialist interests.[†] Members of the Islamic Unity coalition have rejected Soviet attempts to represent the resistance as another East-West confrontation (see JIA N.D.e), and (as noted) they have condemned the pro-Western policies of the traditionalists.

The second charge is that reactionary Islamic fundamentalists are against social and economic reforms, education, progress, and modernization, and that they seek a return to seventh-century Islam and feudalism, oppression, and backwardness. This charge is made not only by the Soviets, but by some Western writers as well. For the most part, it is based on poorly understood and often misconceived historical facts. Geertz suggests that "The relevance of historical facts for sociological analysis . . . rests on the perception that though both the structure and the expressions of social life change, the inner

---

*One of the principal factors influencing the ethnic attitudes of the young educated Afghans (particularly Pashtun vs. non-Pashtun) has been the so-called "Pashtunistan Issue." The issue, concerning territorial claims by Pashtun peoples living in Pakistan, was raised by the Musahiban dynasty, particularly Daoud in the 1950s. The Afghan government's Pashtunistan policy was supported by the Soviets, who used it as a principal means of access into the country's affairs (see L. Dupree 1973: 493, 541).

[†]To support this accusation the Soviets have named as rebel leaders and CIA agents two virtually unknown individuals of Afghan descent living in the United States. They have also named as a CIA agent at least one other individual living in the United States who is allegedly connected with the traditionalist groups (see Volkov et al. 1980: 39-54). No specific charges have been made against any of the mujahidin leaders recognized as such by the Afghans themselves.

54

necessities that animate it do not" (1977: 167). Such "unchanging inner necessities" and the way Islam has addressed them are underscored by Rabbani:

First I should explain a common misunderstanding. When we say we want a government on the model of the early Islamic pattern, many people think we want to move history backward and have . . . living condition[s] exactly the same as 14 centuries ago. They think a government based on that model cannot be compatible with the conditions of the electronic age. But the issue is not as simple as they think. . . . We believe those principles [from the time of the Prophet Muhammad] are applicable in national and international affairs today as much as they were at that time. . . . Justice is an Islamic principle. . . . The implementation of justice is as much applicable today as it was at that time. Islam enjoins seeking knowledge as a duty of every Muslim—man and woman. Today the form of seeking knowledge might be different. . . . But seeking knowledge is as practical today as it was 14 centuries ago—and even much more [so]. . . . Shoora (council) is an Islamic principle. It is the order of the Holy Quran to Muslims to decide their affairs on the basis of consultation. This is almost the same thing you have as parliament today. . . . We do not see any difficulties in applying Islam in our society: the Islam which is not an impediment in the way of knowledge, science, technology, peace and justice and the Islam which is an obstacle and enemy to oppression, corruption, ignorance, exploitation and imperialism (Editors of *Mirror of Jehad* 1982c: 9-10).

The Islamic Unity coalition has programs for economic, social, educational, and technological reform and modernization—for example, land reclamation and redistribution according to need; expansion of mechanized farming; confiscation of the wealth and property of those who have accumulated them through embezzlement, corruption, and other illegal means; income and net worth reporting by all government employees; and profit-sharing in large enterprises (see Hizb-i Islami N.D.a; JIA N.D.a; Editors of *Mirror of Jehad* 1982a: 8-13). The coalition has already laid down a network of schools (grades 1-12) among the refugee communities in Pakistan, as well as in some rural areas inside Afghanistan under mujahidin control. Curricula development and publication of textbooks reflecting Islamic revolutionary ideals are well on the way (Shorish 1983).

In sum, the present armed conflict is on two levels. On the first and more obvious, it is a jihad in defense of Islam and Afghanistan against the direct Soviet military intervention. At this level for most Afghans it is as much a moral and Islamic struggle as a political struggle against a superpower. On the second level, the conflict concerns the problem of legitimate state authority and reflects the structural problems within Afghan society which emerged initially as a conflict between the disenfranchised educated youth and a morally bankrupt traditional aristocracy when a secularized Marxist intelligentsia seized power.

In this tripartite struggle among Marxists, traditionalists, and Islamic revolutionary youth, the principal objective of all parties has been to gain the support of the Afghan masses. Unable to mobilize support, the Marxists have "invited" the Red Army to keep them in power. The traditionalists enjoy the loyalty of some Pashtun tribes, religious leaders, and officials of the former regime. Their base of support, broader a few years ago, appears to be steadily declining. In contrast, the Islamic revolutionary groups have gained substantial local support throughout the country and strengthened their national posture through the coalition of Islamic Unity. The principal victims of this struggle have been the Afghan rural population. At the same time, however, the largely self-sufficient subsistence farmers have made the struggle possible.

There are increasing signs that Afghanistan is witnessing a true Islamic revolution in which the mujahidin are increasingly beating the Soviets at their own game

> [using] the very methods that Moscow has been instigating among liberation groups in Latin American, African, and other third-world countries. But unlike Moscow's often direct military support for its bevy of liberation movements, the Afghans do not receive the same benefits from the West (Girardet 1982, 26 July).

The lack of organizational linkage between the mujahidin groups and outside powers, particularly the superpowers, makes the Afghan struggle distinct in the recent history of liberation movements. At the same time, the absence of a single charismatic leader within the mujahidin ranks may decrease the risks of a totalitarian regime if the mujahidin are victorious.* The departure of the mujahidin from the familiar leadership pattern of other liberation movements is considered by many Western researchers to be a sign of weakness and evidence of the chaos they believe traditionally reigned in Afghanistan (see for example Azoy 1982, N. Newell and R. Newell 1981, and Chaliand 1982). However, the diffused power structure of the mujahidin, based on village- and community-level political and military leadership, has proven resilient and effective against a militarily superior enemy.

In this jihad Girardet has noted that "Russia's most formidable foe is not a military one, but Islam. . . . Difficult for the Western (and Russian) mind to understand, faith is the greatest strength of the Afghan, whose whole approach to life is closely bound to his constant struggle for survival" (1982, 26 July). To understand the depth of determination of the Afghans, the Soviets could take note of the observation by Khalfin on the British dilemma during the Second Anglo-Afghan War (1878-80). Following an attack on the British Mission in Kabul, a British army unit was sent there on a punitive mission. After capturing Kabul, the British

> burnt down neighboring villages and brutally dealt with those sus-
> pected of the attack on the mission. . . . However, the policy of
> terror proved ineffective, the country was in the grip of a guerilla
> movement, the British troops were blocked in large cities. Their
> henchmen were killed as soon as they ceased to be heavily guarded.
> In Kabul the interventionists felt safe only behind the walls of the
> Sherpur fortress (Khalfin 1981: 108).

The crisis in Afghanistan is by no means over. One hopes that the importance of the "revolution" and rebellions will become more evident to the West. Both direct and indirect Western involvement is likely to escalate because the geopolitical implications of the Soviet presence in Afghanistan are seen as ominous (Canfield 1981). The situation cannot be resolved without the active participation of the people of Afghanistan, and a solution will require a knowledge and understanding of local realities. It is hoped that the first-hand reports in this volume will offer such information.

*The absence of a strong mujahidin leadership could also mean that they may not be able to form a government at all. However, if the existing coalitions survive, they should be able to form a government run by a collective leadership.

Chapter 2

THE MARXIST REGIMES AND THE SOVIET PRESENCE IN AFGHANISTAN: AN AGES-OLD CULTURE RESPONDS TO LATE TWENTIETH-CENTURY AGGRESSION

Louis Dupree

Seven "Rs" can be used to characterize the political processes in Afghanistan since April 1978: revolution,* repression, rhetoric, reforms, revolts, refugees, and Russians.[†] Before we discuss these in detail, let us turn briefly to history.

In July 1973 the monarchy which had dominated Afghan politics at the center for almost 150 years was overthrown by Muhammad Daoud Khan, first cousin and brother-in-law to King Muhammad Zahir, who had reigned since 1933 (L. Dupree 1980a: 477-658, 753-60).** Daoud had been prime minister from 1953 to 1963 (pp. 499-558), when Zahir Shah replaced him with Dr. Muhammad Yusuf (a commoner—unlike Daoud), and a ten-year experiment in constitutional monarchy began (pp. 559-666).[††] The experiment failed partly because the king listened to the advice of the more conservative members of his family and staff and failed to take the steps necessary to implement the constitution introduced in 1964—basically steps to broaden the base of political participation. The failure of seven Western-educated (U.S. and Western Europe) prime ministers (including Yusuf) and cabinets to implement Western-oriented programs also contributed to deterioration on the political scene.

---

*Actually "revolution" is too strong. What occurred on 27 April 1978 was a *coup d'état*, but those who perpetrated the coup called it an *inqilab*—"revolution" in Persian—and it has become generally known as the Saur Revolution.

[†]Now an eighth "R" can be added to the list—Reagan.

**The monarchy had been of the Muhammadzai lineage of the Durrani Pashtun tribe (L. Dupree 1980a: 333, 366-67).

[††]Details can be found in L. Dupree 1978a, 1978b, 1979b, and 1980g.

During his ten years out of power, Daoud held running seminars with some of the young military officers he had sent to the USSR for advanced training. Many had been converted to socialism, but so had a number of nonmilitary students educated in Western Europe and the United States.* With the support of many members of Parcham (The Banner), a major leftist party with strong support among the intelligentsia and the bureaucracy, Daoud seized power in an almost bloodless coup on 17 July 1973, while the king lolled in the mud baths of Ischia, Italy.

THE REPUBLIC OF AFGHANISTAN (1973-78)

Daoud became president, prime minister, and founder of the Republic of Afghanistan on 17 July 1973. Prior to his overthrow and death in a second leftist coup, Daoud charted a reasonable path for Afghanistan but made several fundamental mistakes along the way. He alienated his leftist supporters by sending many in the Parcham party (including the police) to staff district and subdistrict positions and spread the message of the new republic. The city-wise, detribalized Parcham activists ran headlong into the rural power elites. Within months some of these reformers became frustrated and realized that change would be slow and consistent with existing cultural patterns. Some turned cynically to corruption based on well-established precedents. Others returned to Kabul and resigned—or were dismissed for leaving their posts without permission.

In February 1977 a new constitution was passed with several significant changes made by the Loya Jirgah (Great National Assembly—partly elected, partly appointed.)† In March the Republic of Afghanistan, after four and one half years of an on-again, off-again, mostly paperbound reform program, waited for Daoud to appoint a new cabinet.** Daoud and his brother and close adviser, Muhammad

*A joke making the rounds in Kabul in the 1960s and 1970s went as follows: "Russians turn out anti-Communists; Americans train Communists."

†Of the 131 articles in the constitution, 34 were amended and 6 new articles added, mainly defining and enhancing the role of the judiciary and transferring police investigative powers to the attorney general's office.

**The program included land reforms (July 1975), a civil service reforms act (June 1977), and—for the first time since King Amanullah (1919-29)—a codified

Naim Khan, indicated several times that the new cabinet would embrace all political spectra, from moderate religious leaders to moderate leftist leaders (personal communications).

In March 1977, however, Daoud reverted to the behavior of an old-style tribal khan. He appointed or reappointed friends, sons of friends, sycophants, and even collateral members of the deposed royal family to his new cabinet and other high ministry positions. Even Muhammad Naim broke with Daoud over the president's continued favoritism of the rightists in the cabinet. (In April 1981 I interviewed one of Daoud's personal physicians, who indicated that the president had been suffering from rampant senility for the last year of his life.) Furthermore, Daoud began to draw away from his close relationship with the USSR and entered into a network of military and economic agreements with the Muslim world, particularly neighboring Pakistan and Iran.

Confronted with Daoud's increasing dependence on an "inner cabinet" of conservatives, the two major leftist groups, Parcham and Khalq (The Masses), reunited in July 1977 after a ten-year separation. Post-World War II leftist movements in Afghanistan have been miniscule, fragmented, and on the whole home-grown. Their leaders have been well-known, many having participated in the 1965 and 1969 elections held under the 1964 constitution.

The Khalq—officially the Jamhuriyat-i Demokratik-i Khalqi Afghanistan (People's Democratic Party of Afghanistan—PDPA) was the first major leftist party to emerge, founded on 1 January 1965. The Parcham branch of the PDPA was formed in June 1967, primarily as a result of personal struggles for power within the Khalq: Nur Muhammad Taraki (Secretary-General) and Hafizullah Amin (Khalq) vs. Babrak Karmal (Parcham). In addition, the Khalq faction preached the primacy of the class struggle, but the Parcham leadership wanted to form an anti-government united front to oppose the monarchy (L. Dupree 1979c).*

penal code and civil code, based on secular law but not violating general Islamic principles.

*Political parties were technically illegal in Afghanistan from 1973 until 1978, although several functioned unofficially—but openly. No *underground* Communist party dominated by the USSR existed (see L. Dupree 1971: ap. A, pp. 31-32).

Parcham's association with an increasingly unpopular government (and the "defanging" of Parcham when Daoud sent the bulk of its cadre to the countryside immediately after the 1973 coup) undermined Parcham's appeal. Khalq, meanwhile, had not been idle. The official Khalq history claims the faction began to recruit cadre among the military after the 1973 Daoud coup, but from my conversations and observations over the years it would appear that recruitment was initiated in the late 1960s. Parcham had been considered by many as the most pro-Soviet of the leftist parties; military officers (even those trained in the USSR) tended to be more nationalist than socialist, more pro-Afghan than pro-Soviet, so they usually gravitated to Khalq.

Khalq stepped up its recruitment of military cadre after Daoud announced his March 1977 cabinet. Taraki had made several attempts to meet Daoud but had been blocked by Daoud's "inner cabinet" mafia. By summer 1977, support for the republic had largely dissipated, and the possibility that Taraki might succeed Daoud, legally or illegally, was widely discussed at Kabul University and throughout the Afghan intellectual community. Babrak Karmal, Parcham's leader since its split with Khalq in 1967, alienated from Daoud and sensing that the republic was doomed, negotiated the reunion with Khalq, forming a united front of opposition.

Daoud finally seemed to recognize the seriousness of the opposition by early April 1978, and family members were able to effect a reconciliation between Daoud and Naim. On 17 April, the president told his family that he planned to announce new administrative reforms, broaden the base of power in the Central Committee, establish a new cabinet of technocrats which would include moderate leftists, and hold elections in a year or so. Ten days later Daoud's concepts of reform had become academic.

REVOLUTION

The April 1978 coup was accidental in that a series of unplanned events precipitated and ordained its eventual outcome.* The first accident occurred on 17 April (the day Daoud decided to make

*For an hour-by-hour account of the coup, see L. Dupree 1979d.

major changes in his government), when Mir Akbar Khaybar, a well-known Parcham ideologue (and former high-ranking police officer), was murdered by persons unknown.* Massive demonstrations at the burial site for Khaybar on 19 April surprised most Afghan and foreign observers. An estimated 10-15,000 mourners took to the streets, marching past the U.S. Embassy and shouting the usual anti-American slogans.

Alarmed, the government immediately arrested the leftist leadership, with the notable exception of Amin, who had time to contact certain party members within the armed forces and police before he was arrested. A makeshift coup was planned and launched. The coup succeeded in less than twenty-four hours, and Daoud and about thirty members of his family (including Naim) were killed.

Taraki became President of the Revolutionary Council and Prime Minister of the Democratic Republic of Afghanistan (DRA). The two main competitors for power, Amin and Babrak Karmal, became deputy prime ministers, but this arrangement did not last long. In all their public announcements the leaders of the DRA insisted they were not Communists.[†] The ultimate demise of Taraki and Amin as a result of Soviet machinations gives their contentions some credibility.

In the first DRA cabinet (twenty-one persons) only four members (three military and one civilian) had received training in the USSR, and they considered themselves nationalists, not pro-Soviet. Almost all the cabinet members spoke English; only the four educated in the USSR spoke Russian (Halliday 1978; L. Dupree 1979b). The DRA's policies, the cabinet announced, would be based on Afghan nationalism, respect for Islam, social and economic justice, and implementation of foreign agreements signed by previous Afghan governments.

---

*A blanket of silence descended over the incident after the coup. Was Khaybar killed by the Daoud government (believed by many at the time) or by rival (Khalq?) leftists (as I believe)? The question remains.

[†]For purposes of this chapter I define Communists as those who come directly under Moscow's control. The term communist (lower case) refers to nonaligned Marxists, mainly Third World nationalists who are often misunderstood and misinterpreted by outsiders. The controversial points mentioned in this section are discussed in detail in L. Dupree forthcoming.

REPRESSION

Few could object to the noble goals of the DRA, but as often happens after a bloody coup, the regime's initial interests revolved about legitimacy and security at the expense of human rights and a disrupted economy (L. Dupree 1980d). To achieve a shaky legitimacy, the leadership of the PDPA claimed to be the inheritors of the mantle of King Amanullah, whose attempts at modernization had failed (Poullada 1973; Stewart 1973). According to the DRA rhetoric, almost half a century of Afghan history had ceased to exist except as an example of a nation living in "fear, deprivation [and] destitution," when "abuse of state power [had] reached a climax. Corruption, tyranny, and plunder had been the way of life in the fake republic of Daoud."*

The DRA did not invent repression and torture in Afghanistan; however, although previous regimes could not claim high ratings in human rights, the DRA went far beyond the allowable bounds of cultural deviance by Afghan standards. Most of the DRA leadership had spent varying periods of time in jail, and most had managed to survive. Many had held high positions in pre-DRA governments. Few, however, survived the after-effects of their own "revolution."

The PDPA leadership made several critical initial errors. Chief among these was that instead of calling on all Western-trained technocrats, bureaucrats, and intellectuals to assist in the building of a new Afghan society, it considered those who would not enthusiastically support the DRA's programs as enemies. A number of newly independent Third World nations have committed and continue to commit this fatal error. Opposition to a regime or its proposed programs is not *necessarily* preparation to overthrow it—but suppression of an opposition can force the opposition to revolt.

Successive phases of repression occurred before the Soviet intervention of December 1979. Each step by the DRA seemed almost designed to alienate every major segment of Afghan society. The jails quickly filled to overflowing with important surviving members of the former royal family and collateral relatives, as well as large numbers of qualified technocrats whose only crime had been to hold responsible positions in previous regimes. The PDPA replaced these valuable

*_Kabul Times_, 5/4/78; this was the first issue after the coup.

human assets with party members, qualified or not. The new cabinet ministers and deputy ministers were generally competent, but there was a great shortage of experienced, action-oriented, middle- to upper-level administrators—and the shortage accelerated as the months passed and repression escalated.

Reshufflings at the top followed what had become a Third World pattern. When coalitions of the left (or right) topple a Third World regime, they fission almost immediately. The Khalq-Parcham graft was no exception. The Muhammadzai eliminated, the dominant Khalq leadership removed Parcham's ambitious leader Babrak and his followers from positions of power in a traditional Afghan manner. The Revolutionary Council exiled Babrak and his lieutenants to ambassadorships, a pattern utilized by Daoud and previous Afghan leaders to immobilize opposition.* Taraki and Amin then moved against a more formidable group: the nationalist Muslim factions in and out of the cabinet.

In late August 1978 the regime arrested numbers of high-ranking military officers and civilians for plotting to overthrow the regime. The confessions of those arrested—extracted by means usually employed in Afghanistan regardless of the regime in power (physical and mental torture, threats to family members)—were broadcast over Radio Afghanistan, and the government-controlled press published facsimiles of the confessions in the handwriting of the accused (a tactic also employed in the past). The confessions implicated Babrak as instigator and ringleader of the overthrow plot, but most of those involved appeared to have been more nationalist and Muslim than Parcham in orientation and to have favored a genuinely nonaligned Afghanistan. The confessions obtained and Parcham implicated, the DRA ordered Babrak and other Parcham ambassadors home. Under the circumstances they refused and disappeared into Eastern Europe and/or the Soviet Union to serve as Soviet political soilbanks.

---

*In July 1978 Babrak was posted to Prague, Nur Muhammad Nur (Minister of the Interior) to Washington, 'Abdul Wakil (Central Committee) to London, and Mahmud Baryalay (Babrak's brother) to Islamabad. Dr. Anahita (Minister of Social Affairs and Tourism) went to Belgrade. She was the only woman in Taraki's first cabinet (but not the first woman to serve in Afghan cabinets). With Dr. Anahita's departure, her important ministry was abolished. Tourism reverted to the Afghan Air Authority.

RHETORIC AND REFORMS

As the Khalq regime preempted the leftists and nationalists, it decreed a series of administrative procedures and far-reaching reforms. As presented, the reforms ran counter to major Afghan cultural, social, and economic institutions. (Ample evidence of this is provided in other chapters of this volume.) Too much was attempted too fast, without adequate preparation, qualified personnel, or a broad base of popular support. Some reforms contradicted each other or even had internal inconsistencies (L. Dupree 1980c).*

Most objectionable, the reforms and other pronouncements were couched in Marxist dialectic translated directly into Persian and Pashto, and they sounded somewhat stilted to Afghans, most of whom heard them over Radio Afghanistan.[†] Furthermore, much of the rhetoric out of Soviet Central Asia was now to be heard over Radio Afghanistan. It caused the nonliterate rural population and many in the literate urban elite to consider the new DRA Communist, and therefore Soviet-dominated.

It is interesting to note that the reform programs of the DRA were remarkably similar to those announced by Daoud's republic. But Daoud had presented his reforms to the Afghan people in classical Dari (Afghan Persian) and Pashto and had not used Marxist dialectic.**

---

*For details on the so-called "women's reforms," see the contribution in this volume by Nancy Hatch Dupree.

[†]The transistor radio has created a revolution in communication in the Third World in the past decade or so. No Afghan village or herdsmen's camp exists without at least one of these radios, which can usually pick up Radio Beijing, the Voice of America, the British Broadcasting Corporation (BBC), Radio Moscow, and several stations broadcasting out of Soviet Central Asia in languages which Afghans understand.

**Marxist dialectic sounds stilted not only in Persian and Pashto, but also in most English translations of Russian. Friends of mine who read Russian assure me that the dialectic (perverted by many Leninist and Stalinist doctrines) also sounds stilted in Russian. The only language in which it sounds at home is German, in which Marx wrote most of his works.

REVOLTS

Except for sporadic attacks from Pakistan by the Hizb-i Islami (Islamic Party), a dissident Muslim fundamentalist group led by Engineer Gulbudin Hikmatyar, most of the opposition was quiet in Afghanistan from the April coup until late August-early September 1978. But periodic explosions (usually harmless) rocked Kabul, and the opposition began to clandestinely publish and distribute a plethora of anti-government publications (called *Shab-Namah*—Evening News). These incidents reminded the DRA that opposition to the regime in reality did exist.

Several factors account for the relative lack of early reaction against the DRA. For one thing, the coup had come as a surprise; for another, most people in the urban centers were willing to give the regime a chance to succeed under its initially articulated guidelines. Furthermore, spring and summer are months of major economic activity (farming and herding) in the countryside. Students of warfare often overlook (or underestimate) the relationship between leisure time and fighting in the annual cycle of preindustrial peoples. Even after preindustrial societies had had contact with—and often been dominated by—technologically superior imperialists, warfare continued to play a major *seasonal* role in some of them, through annual feuds or through institutionalized avoidance, which is really another variety of conflict.*

In rural Afghanistan from early spring through early fall, the intensity of the agricultural and herding cycle forces people to work cooperatively, which usually acts as a check on tensions that may arise. Normally, local feuds end in time for the spring planting. Women from fighting factions literally "place the stone on the mountain"—i.e., stones are piled at a traditional spot—a signal for the feuds to end and the farming to begin. (It is the equivalent of the American

---

*For a discussion of how seasonal warfare affected imperialist tactics, see L. Dupree 1977a. I cannot resist quoting Terence Hanburg White, *The Once and Future King* (New York: Putnam, 1958): "Look at the Norman myths about legendary figures like the Angevin kings. From William the Conqueror to Henry the Third, they indulged in warfare seasonally. The season came round, and off they went in splendid armour which reduced the risk of injury to a foxhunter's minimum. Look at the decisive battle of Brenneville in which a field of 900 knights took part, and only three were killed" (p. 235).

Indian "burying the hatchet.") A period of relative leisure drifts in with fall and lasts until the spring planting or migration with the herds. During the slack months agricultural tools, mud huts, tents, and other nomadic gear require only a relatively short time to repair, and few other diversions exist. Long periods of inactivity and intimate contact can bring latent aggression to the surface.

Despite the formalized system of reciprocal rights and obligations in rural Afghanistan, tensions build up between individuals, families, and lineages. In-group tensions usually relate to the inheritance of property, mate preference, and honor (L. Dupree and L. Albert 1974: ch. 1; Ahmed 1980). Islamic law and local customs carefully delineate inheritance patterns, but wily brothers and uncles sometimes trick less wily brothers and nephews. Disagreements can cause families to break up and form new kin units. (It is this process that often produces the self-perpetuating blood feud.)

Competition for mates can also precipitate crises within groups. The preferred mate for a male is his father's brother's daughter, or as close to that kin status as possible. Thus male cousins are potential or real rivals for daughters of paternal uncles. The ideal mate often cannot be attained, however, and marriages with mother's brother's daughter and even mother's or father's sister's daughter are not uncommon (Centlivres 1972; Knabe 1977b). Competition for mates is further intensified because the adult male to female ratio is about 116 : 100 (USAID 1975). Families traditionally arrange marriages without close consultation with the principles, who ideally accept without complaint. Absence of open protest, however, does not necessarily imply the absence of subsurface negative tensions in either or both potential mates.

The core of the institutions of inheritance and marriage (basically the role and status of women [N. Dupree 1979; A. Amin 1973]) involves concepts of honor; in the ultimate sense, the men who fight out-group feuds fight for honor. Feuds may last for several generations, and current participants may have only hazy notions regarding the origin of a conflict. At times feuds may lie dormant for several years and then unpredictably explode with violence. The tribesmen of Afghanistan can be described as having a short fuse and a long feud.

But the feuds have positive functions. They help channel in-group feuding over property rights and mate-preference toward violence against neighboring groups—i.e., they serve to externalize internal aggressions. One function of the feud is to perpetuate one's own group, not to destroy other groups. Therefore, blood must always be about equally spilled, and property equally destroyed or taken. If one side gains materially at another's expense, the seasonal feud might extend into the farming or herding cycle—contrary to the interests of both sides (L. Dupree 1980b).

If a central government goes beyond the bounds of cultural deviance, Afghan ethnolinguistic groups may destroy local government offices and may even kill some civil officials and military personnel. But such attacks are merely a traditional way to express an opinion, to disagree with and challenge certain government policies or oppression by government officials. They are not necessarily launched to overthrow the regime in power.*

In late August 1978 the regional revolts began right on schedule— i.e., at the beginning of the slack season. Nuristan was the first to launch a traditional attack, quickly followed by the rest of the Kunar Valley and the provinces of Paktya, Badakhshan, Kapisa/Parwan, Oruzgan, Badghis, Balkh, Ghazni, Farah, and Herat. The DRA should have responded in the traditional way. It should have sent just enough armed force into the field to stop the tribal movements and then called a Loya Jirgah of the regional power elites, religious leaders, high government officials, and prominent intellectuals to talk out problems.

A new factor had been added in late summer 1978, however: the DRA had a Soviet-equipped and trained military, and it overreacted— as have many Third World central governments when faced with opposition from the countryside. Villages were bombed and napalmed and much blood shed. Government reprisals continued throughout the fall and winter of 1978-79, and revolts spread to every province in Afghanistan. As the spring approached, tribesmen did not return to their normal agricultural cycle—a culturally oriented signal to the government in Kabul. They continued to fight throughout the spring and summer of 1979. *Now* they were fighting to *overthrow*. By late summer Afghan military (draftee) units began to desert in large

---

*Two examples of attacks which were not necessarily intended to overthrow regimes but to challenge central government policies are the 1929 civil war in Afghanistan (Poullada 1973; Stewart 1973) and the post-World War II march of the Iranian tribes on Tehran (Avery 1967).

numbers. The fighting had ceased to be a winter interlude, and the troops did not want to fight against fellow Afghans.

The DRA government responded to tribal threats by requesting (and receiving) more Soviet military advisers and more sophisticated equipment. The Soviets did not want to be accused of deserting a new "socialist friend" in distress. By late 1979 most observers agreed the DRA was in serious trouble, and it was doubted that the regime could survive unless the Soviets directly intervened.*

Sayyid Ahmad Gailani, leader of one of the numerous Afghan groups operating out of Peshawar, went to London in the fall of 1979 and broadcasted a message over the BBC Overseas Service to the world. His effort had the backing of all but the most fundamentalist Muslim groups. His message was simple and straightforward: Our war is not with the Soviet Union nor with the Soviet people; our war is with the DRA regime in Kabul, and when the regime falls, we shall do nothing to disturb the "special relationship" that Afghanistan has had with the USSR since the late 1950s.

The "special relationship" had never been put into writing or even articulated. But in essence it meant that the Afghans never publicly went against the Soviets in international forums (such as the United Nations)—although they have privately disagreed with certain policies from time to time. In return, the Afghans accepted aid and trade from nations wishing to engage in these two interlocking institutions and sent students to countries around the world.

REFUGEES AND RUSSIANS

Fundamentally the Soviets had two choices regarding Afghanistan: to invade or not to invade. They chose to invade. I did not think

---

*While foreign intervention is not the focus here, it is worth noting that the Soviets claimed that several nations (the United States, People's Republic of China, United Kingdom, Pakistan, Iran, Egypt, and Israel) were actively intervening in Afghanistan, training and supplying arms to anti-government groups. Whatever aid existed, it had not been very effective—yet—according to guerrilla leaders with whom I spoke at the time. Here I am attempting to show that Afghan *culture* responded to a perceived threat from both the activities of the DRA and the Soviet intervention. I have discussed the intervention issue in L. Dupree forthcoming.

they would take such a hazardous step (L. Dupree: 1979a, 1979b)—mainly because if the Soviets invaded Afghanistan it would be the first Soviet aggression since World War II on an independent and nonaligned territory—an important and potentially dangerous precedent.* Czechoslovakia and Hungary were not in the same category as Afghanistan. They were considered by NATO and the rest of the world as part of the Soviet bloc and members of the Warsaw Pact, but Afghanistan was not.

Probably the Soviets planned a Dominican Republic-type operation: eliminate the government in power, replace it with a puppet government, and leave within ninety days, having effectively extended their control to the borders of Pakistan.† Many of the invading troops (some estimates reach as high as 40 percent) were reservists called to active duty to fulfill their military requirements. In addition, the Soviets sent in a large number of troops (mainly reservists) from the Muslim republics of Soviet Central Asia, reasoning that the Muslim troops, sharing common cultures and languages with the Afghans, would fraternize successfully with them—particularly the Tajiks and Uzbeks. The assessment proved correct. The Central Asians mingled with the local Afghan population in the cities and were rather disturbed to find that no foreign troops (other than from the USSR) were inside Afghanistan.

The Soviets have never been completely successful in the "Russofication" of their Central Asian republics and have always feared that influences from the south (Turkey, Iran, Afghanistan) would infiltrate across the border. The Soviet Central Asians feel an affinity with peoples to the south which is more cultural than exclusively religious. Soviet statistics alone indicate that by 2000 A.D. the total population of the USSR will be 53 percent non-Russian. Moreover, about one third of all Soviet citizens will be Muslim (d'Encausse 1978). These data obviously worry the Soviets, and the Islamic resurgence on their southern borders takes on increasingly political—instead of religious—aspects (L. Dupree 1980h).

---

*For discussions of the Soviet intervention in Afghanistan, see the following (among others): L. Dupree 1980g; Griffiths 1981; N. Newell and R. Newell 1981; Khalilzad 1980.

†A joke in Moscow among intellectuals in 1981:
Question: "Why are we still in Afghanistan?"
Answer: "We're still looking for the people who invited us in."

A small number of Central Asian Muslim troops deserted to fight with the Afghan *mujahidin* (freedom fighters). The Soviets reacted by shipping most of the Muslim troops back to Central Asia by the end of February 1980. As a final gesture of cultural affinity with the Afghans, many Muslim troops combed the bazaars of Kabul and elsewhere for Qurans to take home.

When they invaded Afghanistan on Christmas Eve 1979 (85,000 troops ultimately entered Afghanistan), the Soviets had either for-gotten—or ignored—the history and culture of Afghanistan. Twice in the nineteenth century Afghan tribes and ethnic groups had united regionally to drive invading British armies from their country. This statement runs counter to traditional British historical accounts, but studies of the First (1838-42) and Second (1878-80) Anglo-Afghan Wars have brought me to this conclusion.* Politically, and in the broadest sense militarily, the British did not win—even if they did not unilaterally lose—those two wars.

Relatively speaking, few Afghans were involved in the fighting before the Soviet invasion. The invasion triggered off another Afghan cultural response. Many Afghan tribes who were traditional enemies "placed the stone on the mountain" for the duration.

Afghan kin units (in almost all areas) are based on vertically structured segmentary lineages which territorially neighbor other line-ages which compete with them locally in the off-agricultural season (as discussed above). However, when an outside *horizontal* force threatens the vertical lineage, the tribes unite locally to resist and, if possible, throw out the invaders. Traditional enemies—such as the Mangal and Jadran Pashtun from Paktya—have united to fight against the Soviets, just as they did one hundred years ago to fight the British. Even disparate ethnolinguistic groups within regions have united at least militarily (and ultimately will unite politically) to resist the invaders and the puppet regime.

Soviet tactics have helped accelerate the extension of regional power. Afghanistan, like Vietnam—although with completely dif-ferent terrain—is superb country for guerrillas. The invading Soviet divisions came into Afghanistan with the same equipment—e.g.,

---

*I am writing a book on *The First Anglo-Afghan War (1838-1842): Myth as History and History as Myth* (tentative title). For a preliminary statement, see L. Dupree 1976b.

tanks—and organization they would use in the plains of Eastern Europe. Tactics quickly began to break down because Afghanistan is definitely not tank country. In addition, infantry search-and-destroy tactics and simple bombing and napalming have not worked, and the Soviets have had to rely more and more on their most effective weapons system: the highly vaunted Mi-24 (Hind) armored gunship, for which the mujahidin have no defense—yet. (They obviously need surface-to-air shoulder-fired missiles.)

The Mi-24s roam up and down valleys with impunity, implementing two main Soviet tactical elements: rubbleization of the countryside and migratory genocide. Mud-brick or stone-hut villages can be reduced to rubble in a matter of minutes; the object of such destruction is apparently to drive the Afghans out of their country into unstable Pakistan and Iran. The logic is inescapable: a dead Afghan is of no use whatsoever to the Soviets, but a live Afghan in Pakistan or Iran (among similar ethnolinguistic and tribal groups) may accentuate the instability of two countries still trying to find their own identity in the modern world (Harrison 1981). Fewer than 500,000 refugees were in Pakistan and Iran at the time of the Soviet invasion. Since the Soviet intervention the number has jumped to approximately three million—the world's largest refugee problem; Iran has about two million (UN High Commission for Refugees [Geneva] 1981; personal communication).

The tactics of rubbleization and migratory genocide have backfired on the Soviets, however—at least temporarily. The fact that entire valleys have been denuded of people has encouraged new patterns of transethnic unity. Guerrilla leaders, their villages destroyed, have taken their families to Pakistan and returned to their own areas. Because they no longer have to worry about the safety of their families and the sanctity of their villages, groups can coalesce into larger units and range more widely over expanded zones of responsibility.

It is important that the processes of extension of local power beyond its traditional boundaries be permitted to evolve naturally without outside interference. The mujahidin do not want—nor do they need—foreign troops, mercenaries or otherwise. By their own account, what they need are guns, medicine, and food.

The current situation in Afghanistan most resembles the evolution of the Yugoslav partisan movement during World War II. Initially individual Yugoslav ethnolinguistic groups resisted the Germans and

Italians independently. As the war progressed, larger units evolved around basic ideologies: the royalists under Draža Mihajlović and the leftists under Tito. The groups came together in military and political groupings but never lost their basic ethnolinguistic identity. Out of these patterns emerged Tito's federation of autonomous regions and socialist republics.

It is to be hoped that the unifying process will continue in Afghanistan. Local units should combine into multiethnic regional units, then link up, at a final phase, into a national liberation movement.

Whether the Russians leave Afghanistan or not, nothing will ever be the same. Afghan historical and cultural patterns, much altered but still recognizable as Afghan, will probably emerge victorious—unless superpower confrontations explode into World War III.*

*A number of books on Afghanistan have been published since this manuscript was submitted for publication, among them the following: *Afghanistan: The Target of Imperialism* 1983; T. Amin 1982; Arnold 1981 and 1983; Bhargava 1983; Bradsher 1983; Chaliand 1982; Hammond 1984; Hyman 1982; Male 1982; Manzar 1980; Misra 1981; Monks 1981; Nayar 1981; Ratnam 1981; Rubinstein 1982; Victor 1983; Vogel 1980; Volkov et al. 1980; and Wiegandt 1980.

PART II

NURISTAN

AND

EASTERN AFGHANISTAN

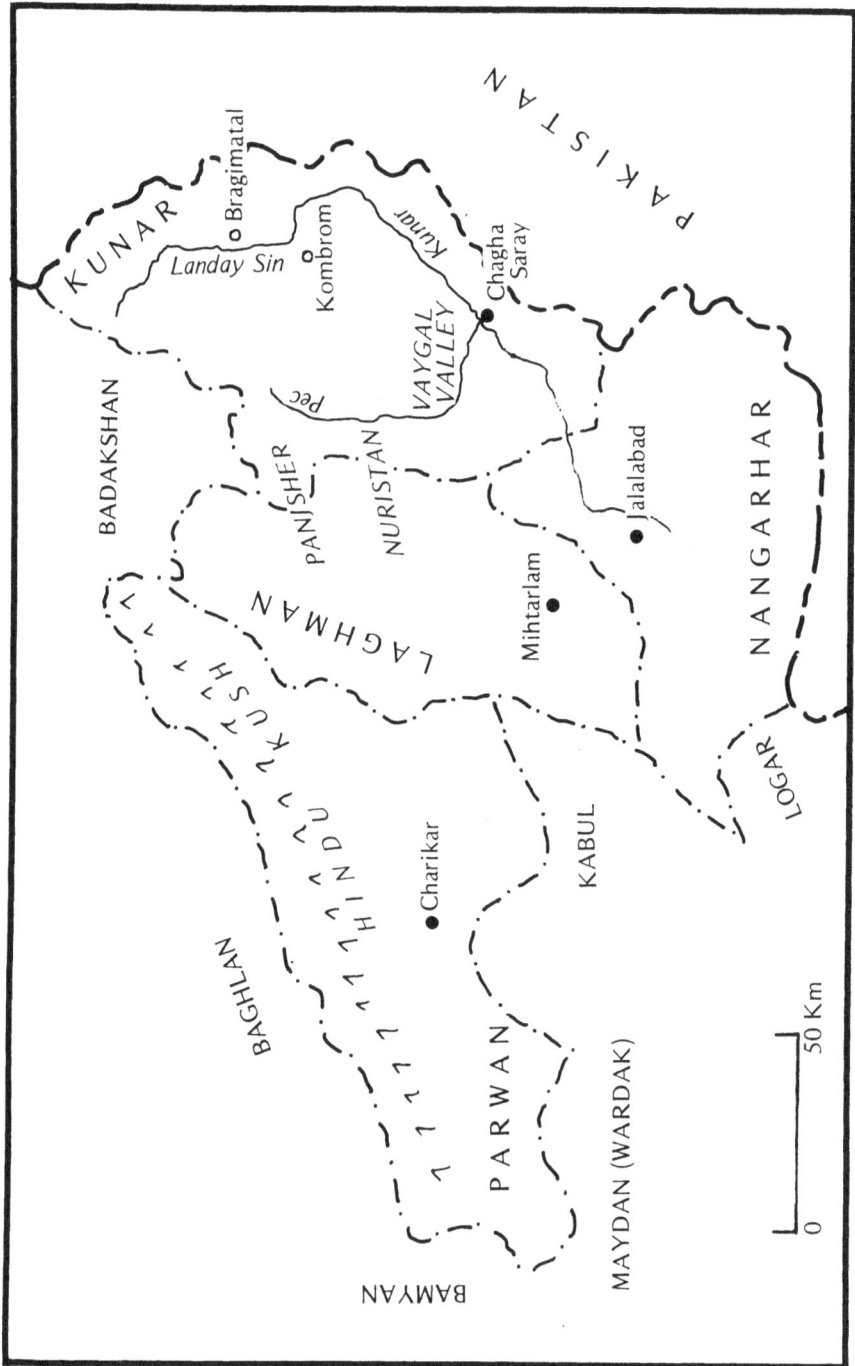

NURISTAN AND EASTERN AFGHANISTAN

Chapter 3, "The Evolution of Anti-Communist Resistance in Eastern Nuristan" by Richard F. Strand, from the original publication has been redacted in this edition.

Chapter 4

RESPONSES TO CENTRAL AUTHORITY IN NURISTAN:
THE CASE OF THE VÄYGAL VALLEY KALASHA*

David J. Katz

The acceptance of Afghan sovereignty and incorporation into the Afghan state have had dramatically different consequences for different Nuristani communities. Strong ties developed between the Kalasha people in the Väygal Valley of south-central Nuristan and their Afghan rulers. These bonds, which grew stronger during the decades following their conquest in the 1890s by Amir 'Abdur Rahman, were characterized by loyalty, respect, and mutual benefit. Relations between the Kalasha and the Afghan government weathered eight decades free of the frustrations and tensions that had alienated many other rural Afghans from their central government. However, the 1978 Saur Revolution brought changes that drove the Kalasha (along with other Nuristanis and neighboring non-Nuristanis) to renounce the government and their ties to it.

In this chapter we shall examine the pre-1978 Kalasha-government relationship and the factors contributing to an unprecedented insurrection by these inhabitants of the Väygal Valley in that year.

*"Väygal" is a more accurate transliteration for the Kalasha pronunciation of this word, although "Waigal" is the more widely used spelling.

Grateful acknowledgment of support for this research is hereby given to the National Institute of Mental Health, Research Training Grant USPHS/MH 10576. In addition, I wish to thank Mr. Muhammad Alam Melabar, Faculty of Letters, Kabul University; the Office of Cultural Relations, Ministry of Foreign Affairs, Government of Afghanistan; the Office of Cultural Relations, Kabul University; Mr. Ghulam Nabi; and Dr. Jon Sommers, Executive Director, Afghan-American Educational Commission. Without their generous assistance, patience, and understanding, the research would have been impossible.

The presentation is based primarily on material collected during ethnographic fieldwork in Afghanistan between August 1975 and July 1977.* Media reports, correspondence, and interviews with individuals familiar with the current conditions in Nuristan are sources for the discussion of the situation since 1978. However, conclusions concerning post-1978 events must remain tentative until they can be verified through additional field study.

SITUATING NURISTAN AND THE KALASHA

Nuristan is a five-thousand-square-mile region strategically situated in northeastern Afghanistan. For millennia, caravans, religious pilgrims, explorers, and armies traversed routes through and around Nuristan, linking the plains of the South Asian subcontinent to the fertile valleys of central Afghanistan and the Oxus River (Amu Darya) basin in Central Asia. Nuristan's precise population is unknown, but estimates range from sixty to one hundred thousand. About eighty-five hundred Nuristanis inhabit the Vaygal Valley, living mainly in nine corporate communities called deš. Most members of each deš reside full-time in a compact, year-round village located at about seven thousand feet, an elevation midway between their highest and lowest zones of economic utilization, while the remaining members have moved to recently founded hamlets in outlying areas. Each deš is politically autonomous and exercises exclusive control over resources in its territory. Villages lie hours distant from one another; travel between them is only by means of rugged footpaths.

No corporate organization, economic or political, exists at levels more inclusive than the individual deš. Kalasha is an ethnic identity that Vaygal Valley residents share with inhabitants of five other major valleys spanning much of southern Nuristan. Attributes unique to Vaygal Valley Kalasha are mainly based on their relative proximity, frequent interactions with one another, and common recent history. Coresidence in the Vaygal Valley and the resultant attributes allow consideration of the nine deš as a unit as long as it is understood that these communities together do not constitute a bounded and discrete ethnic or political entity.

---

*A total of sixteen months was spent in the Vaygal Valley.

Primarily Kalasha practice a type of mixed mountain agriculture involving cereal cultivation on intensively farmed, irrigated terraces and small animal pastoralism. Pastures used by virtually all village herds lie entirely within the contiguous deš-controlled territory. Secondary subsistence activities include fruit and nut cultivation, bee-keeping, and some vegetable cultivation. A sexual division of labor is maintained for the basic production modes: women have responsibility for cereal cultivation, while animal husbandry and dairy production remain the exclusive province of men. In recent decades this division has changed somewhat as large areas of low-elevation winter range have been turned into fields. Although women still do most of the work on these highly productive fields, men assist with plowing and harvesting.

Ancestors of the Väygal Valley Kalasha have lived in the Nuristan mountain valleys for centuries. Before their conversion to Islam, Kalasha and other non-Muslims in the region practiced polytheistic religions. Muslims called them *Kafirs* (Arabic for infidel) and their land Kafiristan. Following their conversion, the Kafirs became known as Nuristanis, and their country Nuristan (Arabic for "Land of Light"—an allusion to their recent Islamic enlightenment).

Kafiristan and the nearby lowlands were the last independent areas within the political boundaries of modern Afghanistan. Historical accounts describe bitter hostilities between different groups in what is now Nuristan and the adjoining Kunar River basin lowlands before the region's incorporation into the Afghan state (Robertson 1896). Specific reasons for these conflicts, particularly those between Väygal Valley villagers and their neighbors, are not known. Religious differences, often cited as the primary cause of animosity—especially before Kafirs converted—fail to account for all hostilities since Kalasha fought fellow Kafirs as well as Muslim Pakhtuns.* Nor were relations between Kafirs and Muslims consistently hostile. Trade between religiously different villages was frequent, and on occasion religious differences were set aside to form alliances for fighting

---

*"Pakhtun" is used here only for persons who identify themselves as ethnic Pakhtuns. The term "Afghan" will be used to identify citizens of Afghanistan regardless of ethnic affiliation. However, Kalasha and many other Afghans often use these terms interchangeably when referring to ethnic Pakhtuns. "Pakhtun" represents the dialectical usage among the eastern tribes, although "Pashtun" is the more widely used spelling.

common enemies. Territorial conflicts, slave raids, kidnappings for ransom, plunder and vengeance for previous hostile acts – all provoked confrontations between groups in this area.

Whatever the specific causes of these hostilities, one consequence for the Kalasha was a preoccupation with security. Kalasha villages were surrounded by more numerous, stronger, and better armed groups who were bent on destroying them and usurping their lands. The survival of Kalasha villages depended on careful, unrelenting attention to defensive arrangements. Even provocative raids by Kalasha warriors deep into enemy territory contributed to their security since these forced their enemies into taking defensive precautions, thereby diverting manpower from aggression against Kalasha.

Väygal Valley villages are difficult to attack. Most are surrounded by trackless rugged mountains which serve as buffers between the village center with its adjacent fields and neighboring populations. Vast tracts of rich arable land in the warmer lower elevations which were under Kalasha control but too close to enemy territory could not be farmed out of fear for workers' safety and because of the impossibility of protecting standing crops and irrigation systems against vandalism. Thus despite the economic potential of Kalasha lands, famines and food shortages were not uncommon during the Kafir era.

Before 1978 the most worrisome challenges to Väygal Valley Kalasha came from neighboring non-Nuristani populations. These people, mainly Safi Pakhtun subsistence farmers, have suffered for decades from severe overpopulation, unemployment, and lack of opportunities in their lowland territory, and they have continually pressed for access to the resource-rich highlands. In the middle Peč River Valley (to the south of Nuristan) the only direction for Safi expansion is into territory controlled by mountain-dwelling non-Safi peoples including the Kalasha.

From the time the Väygal Valley Kalasha accepted Afghan sovereignty until 1978, neither central government coercion nor its threat was needed for their integration into Afghanistan. Kalasha saw their strong ties to the government as in their own best interests. The government preserved peace in the region, thereby reducing the people's time-consuming and expensive preoccupation with defense and security. It also provided numerous opportunities and benefits for individuals and communities, including jobs, medical treatment, and education. The Saur Revolution and actions of the Marxist government destroyed this mutually beneficial arrangement. No longer did Kalasha perceive ties to the government as serving their interests. The threat from the Marxist government, implied by its new policies, superseded any threats local competitors had posed.

CONQUEST AND CONVERSION IN THE VÄYGAL VALLEY

The Afghan government's conquest and conversion of the Kafirs differed throughout Kafiristan. Nuristani attitudes toward and relations with the government have in large measure been affected by their experiences at that time. Given the rugged terrain and the logistical nightmares of military campaigns into roadless Kafiristan, 'Abdur Rahman sought to achieve his objectives without undertaking military operations whenever possible. The Afghan commanders initially attempted to negotiate settlements with local leaders; only when this failed did the Afghan army march on intransigent villages. Residents of Kafiristan's far eastern and western valleys resisted the amir's forces. Their refusal to accept Afghan sovereignty led to harsh treatment when they were finally subdued. The Afghan commander of the area including the Väygal Valley Kalasha summoned their leaders to his headquarters at Chagha Saray. There they negotiated a peaceful surrender after the Kalasha representatives acceded to the Afghan commander's demand that they renounce their faith and convert to Islam.

Kalasha initially reacted to their conquest and conversion with ambivalence. They had traded their independence and autonomy for a government presence in the region that halted local warfare, slave raids, and kidnappings. Kalasha informants, some of whom were alive at the time of conquest, recalled how their people welcomed a new freedom from fear. Shahrani (1979b) notes a similar acceptance of the Kabul government's presence by residents in Afghan Turkistan at about the same time. As in the Väygal Valley, the population responded passively because "the prevailing Kabul authority put an end to the chronic warfare in the area that had sapped the human resources of the inhabitants" (p. 180). The pacification of the region allowed some Väygal Valley Kalasha villages to begin developing fields and irrigation systems in parts of their lowland territory which had previously been used only as winter range for herds guarded by well-armed and brave herders.

Conversion to Islam brought no immediate radical restructuring of Kalasha society. Mullahs sent by the government to the villages stopped the most patent non-Islamic customs and instructed residents in Islamic fundamentals and practices, and the instruction was gradualistic in its orientation to social and cultural change. Local political organization and leadership were left largely intact, although these slowly changed on their own, largely due to altered sociopolitical conditions arising from the cessation of hostilities.

As new converts, the former Kafirs enjoyed a privileged status. Their treatment by the amir contrasted sharply to his harsh and cruel treatment of recently subjugated Muslim populations: "In contrast with his policy towards other rebellious groups, the Amir's treatment of the Kafirs was almost paternal. He made particular efforts to educate them in Islamic and Afghan ways" (Kakar 1971:202). 'Abdur Rahman sought to avoid sowing the seeds of future insurrections among the Kafirs. He did not relish the prospect of strategically situated Nuristan becoming a stronghold for disgruntled religious zealots at a time when he was trying to subdue the powerful Afghan religious establishment. Government mullahs in Nuristan taught doctrines equating Islam and the state, stressing that service and dedication to Islam, the Afghan state, and the amir were one and the same (Ashraf Ghani 1978).

Except for mullahs in every village, the only significant government presence was a single outpost (*hukumat*) at Akala, a centrally located hamlet in the Kalasha portion of the Väygal Valley. A district administrator (*hakim*) and a small detachment of soldiers were charged with governing the region, preserving peace, and guaranteeing the mullahs' security. The amir regarded the Kafirs as a people uninvolved in the constant political maneuvering and intrigues endemic among Pakhtun groups. In addition, Kafirs lacked the numbers and political experience to pose an independent threat to his rule. "The Amir ... wished to make the Kafirs, who had no previous loyalty, attached to his dynasty—a policy which has been consistently pursued by his successors even to the present day" (Kakar 1971:208).

Kalasha integration into Afghanistan proceeded smoothly and uneventfully. No Kalasha were exiled to remote locations in the country, nor was there any significant resettlement of non-Nuristanis on Kalasha land. However, the government demanded that a number of young women and men from each village be sent to Kabul. The girls went to the amir's harem or to members of his court as wives or consorts. The boys initially served as pages or servants in the court. Many were later trained as mullahs or given military commissions or civil appointments. In effect, these youths were hostages who assured the continued obedience of their kin and fellow villagers to the amir. But at the same time their presence facilitated the integration of the Nuristanis into the Afghan state. Ties of blood and marriage between Kalasha and members of the court and government forged important bonds between them and members of the Afghan elite.

In the decades following their conquest Väygal Valley Kalasha were left to themselves as long as they created no disturbances, did not openly challenge the government, supplied the required number of conscripts, paid their annual taxes, and helped provision the soldiers garrisoned at the hukumat at Akala. Eventually the outpost was moved to the more accessible Peč River lowlands. The government apparently saw no need to maintain an active presence in the Väygal Valley.

Stability in the region was shattered by a major uprising in 1946 among the Safi Pakhtuns residing in the Peč and Kunar lowlands. This insurrection tested the allegiance of Väygal Valley residents to the government. By refusing to support the Safis and openly backing the government, they reaffirmed and strengthened their ties to it. Fifteen years later, during heightened tensions between Afghanistan and Pakistan, valley residents again actively supported the government by staging clandestine raids into Pakistani territory.

The Kalasha-government relationship culminated during the era of the Republic of Afghanistan (1973-78) under Muhammad Daoud. Military officers from the valley were promoted to important commands; the number of valley students receiving higher education and advanced degrees grew; government programs in the area increased markedly; existing roads were upgraded and new ones were planned. Authorities responded favorably to many locally initiated requests for government-subsidized projects directly benefiting the Kalasha.

The treatment of Nuristanis by 'Abdur Rahman and his successors reflects the attitudes of the cosmopolitan Kabul elite toward them. Nuristanis exemplified the ideals of bravery, love of freedom, simplicity, and ability to survive in a harsh and hostile environment. The physical features of many Nuristanis, which are more typical of northern Europeans than of other Afghan peoples—especially their fair complexions and blue eyes—also endeared them to the elite, making them highly desired as servants, concubines, and wives.

Relations between Safi Pakhtuns and the government have been less satisfactory. Their 1946 rebellion climaxed a stormy history of conflicts and tensions. Unlike the Kalasha, Safis had initially refused offers to peacefully accept the amir's sovereignty. After they were defeated militarily (by Afghan forces guided by Kalasha warriors around Safi defenses), Shinwari and Muhmand Pakhtuns from areas adjoining the Durand Line (Afghanistan's boundary with British India) were resettled in the middle Peč basin. This additional population aggravated the already serious shortage of arable land in the Peč lowlands, forcing the Safis to intensify their farming practices, develop every bit of land suitable for cultivation, build elaborate and costly irrigation systems, and pursue what for them were new economic activities—including herding, thereby putting them into direct economic competition with their Kalasha neighbors. To make matters worse, Safis laid claim to arable land lying on what Kalasha contended was their side of a disputed boundary separating the territories controlled by the two populations.

The government suppressed the Safi rebellion in 1947, and many Safi leaders were jailed or exiled. Since this defeat the lowlands have continued to seethe with resentment toward the government. During the Republican era, Islamic activists capitalized on the antigovernment sentiments of many Safis and worked to transform their political and economic grievances into emotionally charged religious issues. In 1975 a group of lowland residents—including local religious leaders—murdered the police commandant at Manugi.

Although Safi enmity has been directed chiefly at the government, they also bitterly resented their former enemies in the Väygal Valley who sided with the government and refused to support their struggles. Many Safis believe that Kalasha have consistently received preferential treatment from the central authorities. Indeed, as noted, significant differences characterize the historical relations between the government and these two neighboring populations. The history of these relations is opposite to what would be expected from a widely held assumption among Afghanistan's non-Pakhtuns that the Pakhtun-dominated government systematically promotes Pakhtun interests at the expense of non-Pakhtuns throughout the country

(Anderson 1978b:4). Factors accounting for the differences in the relations between rural Afghan populations and the government can be found through an examination of the conception of government by these populations.

CONCEPTS OF GOVERNMENT STRUCTURE AMONG KALASHA

Väygal Valley Kalasha distinguish three governmental levels: a local level, an intermediate level, and a top level of central government in Kabul. In Afghanistan government administration and policy-making are highly centralized. Administrative units—the provinces, subprovinces, and districts—supposedly act on instructions from the center rather than on their own initiative.

Local government for the Väygal Valley is at Manugi in the Peč lowlands, near the confluence of the Väygal and Peč rivers. Officials at the *wuluswali* (district headquarters) constitute the administrative connection between officially recognized villages and the government. Although representatives from many ministries and departments are stationed there, the most important officials are the *wuluswal* (civil administrator), the *commandant* (police commander), and the *qazi* (religious judge). These officials are nearly always ethnic Pakhtuns from distant parts of Afghanistan. Many of them do not hide the disdain they feel for non-Pakhtun Afghans.

Officials usually remain at the wuluswali for tours seldom lasting longer than a few years. This policy is intended in principle to reduce opportunities for official partisanship in disputes and the overinvolvement of officials in local politics. Such opportunities are tempting because all government officials at the district level are poorly paid. Few can resist supplementing their meager salaries by extralegal means.

Administrators at the Manugi wuluswali are quite isolated from the central government; thus they actually wield extensive discretionary power. District affairs are usually conducted with expediency and informality rather than adherence to established codified procedures. Such informality generally benefits all parties since it is very expensive, time-consuming, and frustrating to follow official practices and regulations.

The top officials stationed at Manugi remain at or near their headquarters. Most never visit the mountain villages in their jurisdiction since the nearest ones lie hours distant and are accessible only by steep and rocky footpaths. Instead officials prefer working through and with community headmen, who are summoned to the wuluswali. As a result, these top officials have little direct knowledge of the Kalasha, their territory, or their particular circumstances. Second-echelon local government employees — many of whom reside permanently in the lowlands — must advise and inform the administrators about the details of their jurisdiction.

For Kalasha the second level of government consists of all administrative echelons between the wuluswali and the central authorities. During the 1970s these comprised the subprovince (*loy wuluswali*), with offices at Chagha Saray, and the province (*wilayat*), with headquarters at Jalalabad.* Contact with officials at this intermediate level usually follows unsuccessful dealings with local officials. However, little is ever decisively settled by officials at this level. Matters serious enough to reach them are usually serious enough that the officials do not have the legal prerogatives to resolve them. Kalasha regard this level as useless, only adding to the expense, frustration, and time needed to resolve matters that cannot be settled at the wuluswali.

The highest level, the central government, is identified with the head of state and the numerous departments, offices, and ministries located in Kabul. At this level the officials are authorized and expected to act decisively. Surrounding these officials, however, are countless bureaucrats, each with a specific role which in principle cannot be ignored in the conduct of official business. Problems at this level of government seldom fall within the jurisdiction of one office or ministry. Petitioners usually shuttle between offices for days or weeks collecting signatures and authorizations before they can submit their problems for final consideration. The expenses incurred by

*By 1977 the province of Nangarhar, which included Nuristan, was split into two provinces. Central and eastern Nuristan became part of the new province of Kunarhar, with its administrative center at Chagha Saray (Asadabad) — a situation existing before a change had consolidated the two provinces years earlier. The elevation of Kunarhar from a subprovince to a province suggests that the government wanted to accord greater attention to the specific conditions and problems in the upper Kunar region.

petitioners are tremendous. In addition to fees and bribes, there are costs for lodging, meals, and transportation.

Decisions made by the central government are not implemented until they have worked their way down to authorities at the local level. By the time this occurs, personnel changes, new regulations, or other circumstances can lead to the reconsideration of a particular issue, and an Afghan who has petitioned the government about this issue may have to begin the entire request process anew. Hotly contested disputes often continue bouncing between different courts and jurisdictions for years, even decades, without a final settlement. When a litigant sees that he is on the verge of losing his case, he can use many tactics to block or delay a judgment, while local government officials are reluctant to dispose of cases since a final resolution will eliminate opportunities for them to exact considerations from the litigants.

To Väygal Valley Kalasha the wuluswali and the central government are the most important levels. The intermediate level is seen as little more than an administrative channel that must be traversed in the process of getting from one important level to the other. Perceptions and evaluations of the government are conditioned by the experiences Kalasha have on the two important levels. Two aspects of relations with the government are critical for shaping their attitudes: (1) the degree of government involvement in their affairs, and (2) the effective access they have to the government for receiving consideration, benefit, and redress.

GOVERNMENT INVOLVEMENT IN LOCAL AFFAIRS

Circumstances that facilitate unwanted government involvement in a rural community are expected to heighten the resentment of residents toward the responsible officials, institutions, and the government in general. In Nuristan and elsewhere in rural Afghanistan two factors determine a community's susceptibility to government meddling: its accessibility to officials because of its proximity to government outposts, and the government's perceived need for involvement in the community.

During the Republican era, except for a few schoolteachers, there was no permanent government presence in any Väygal Valley village. The lack of roads and trails suitable for horses made these villages unappealing targets for government interference. In partial result (as we noted above), local government officials were largely ignorant of affairs in these communities, and residents went to great lengths to make certain that officials knew as little as possible about their villages. As long as nothing occurred in the villages which threatened regional security or required government attention, these officials took few steps to learn what was going on there. Until 1978 the valley was generally peaceful and law-abiding. Therefore, overall government interest in Väygal Valley communities was slight. When the government intervened, it was usually in response to requests by a community's leaders. Since these initiatives originated locally, residents did not regard them as undue interference. Thus residents for the most part controlled the extent and pace of their integration into the Afghan state, and the government avoided confrontations with the populace.

The central government imposed few demands on the Kalasha; they chiefly involved taxes and military conscription. Taxes—a miniscule sum paid annually by every household—were more symbolic than a significant portion of a household's earnings. No taxes were levied on land, herds, grain, or other resources or produce. Taxes were collected indirectly. After lineage headmen received taxes from each household in their lineage, they turned them over to a government-recognized deš headman, who in turn delivered them to the revenue collector at Manugi. Military conscription was handled in an indirect manner as well. Each community sent a designated number of conscripts, but conscript selection was left up to the community. (In most other parts of Afghanistan conscription was universal for males twenty-one years of age and older.) These low demands fostered low expectations on the part of the Kalasha. They did not hold the government accountable for the way their taxes were spent, nor did they expect the taxes to be returned to their communities in concrete goods or services.

Unlike the central government, which left the Väygal Valley Kalasha to themselves, the local government was a genuine source of concern to the residents. Interference and meddling—usually unofficial—occurred as local administrators used their offices for personal gain. In return for condoning expedient and unofficial settlements, these officials expected payments. For that reason, few purely intra-community or intra-valley disputes ever reached their attention. Väygal Valley residents fully appreciated the added expenses involved in taking disputes to the government. They also recognized that a need remained to achieve locally acceptable solutions regardless of government-mediated settlements. Therefore, the government usually became involved only in disputes where one party felt unable to obtain a satisfactory resolution in his own community. Typical cases involving Kalasha that reached the government arose from transactions between them and Safi merchants and moneylenders. Since Kalasha economic production is still predominantly subsistence-oriented, little cash circulates in the village economy. When cash is needed, valley residents must often borrow from lowland shopkeepers or traders. With few means among rural populations for resolving interethnic problems, disputes over Kalasha debts often ended up before the government.

For the typical Kalasha virtually any contact with the local government proves expensive. In addition to a litigant's direct expenses—official and unofficial—he must bear the costs of meals and lodging while he remains at the government outpost; moreover, during the time he is away his productivity is lost to his village. There is also the risk of an even greater loss if a judgment results in a jail sentence or fine. Moreover, most Väygal Valley residents are ill-prepared to deal with local officials. Few Kalasha are literate and many cannot converse in Pakhto, the language used for government business throughout eastern Afghanistan. Frightened by an unfamiliar situation and powerful officials, these uneducated herders and farmers are unable to effectively present their cases. If litigation appears inevitable, Kalasha frequently agree to a settlement regardless of their case's merits simply because the expenses and risks involved in winning a favorable judgment usually exceed any possible gains.

Despite many Pakhtun officials' ethnic bias against Kalasha and occasional collusion between these officials and Safi litigants in disputes involving Nuristanis, lowland residents were not immune to official meddling. The proximity of the Pakhtun villages to the wuluswali brought far greater interference in their affairs than in those of the more remote Kalasha villages. This meddling has been one factor accounting for the strong anti-government sentiments throughout the lowland population. (Government interference in the Peč lowlands is similar to the situation of the Landay Sin region of eastern Nuristan, where there are two government outposts, one near Kómbŕom [Kamdesh] and another at Bŕagimatal.

Although local interference is not regarded as official policy, it nevertheless reflects poorly on the administrative competence of the central authorities. Kalasha have no expectation that Pakhtun officials stationed at the wuluswali will have any positive sentiments toward them, nor are they surprised that these officials use their positions for personal gain. It is the few officials who have performed honestly— "as Muslims"—who are notable and are affectionately remembered by Kalasha leaders who regularly deal with the local government.

ACCESS TO THE GOVERNMENT

As access to Kalasha and Safi villages by the government varies, so too does accessibility to the government by these two populations—albeit in reverse proportions. In order for an Afghan to successfully petition his government, he must have *effective* access to it. "Effective" is the critical factor since all communities and individuals in principle have access to their government through local administrators. However, access at the local level is rarely effective because most important decisions are made at the top level. With demand for government-controlled benefits, opportunities, and resources far greater than the supply, successful petitioners must be able to separate their requests from innumerable equally valid ones and shepherd them through local and intermediate bureaucracies to the top. Not only is the most effective access to the Afghan government at its center, but in gaining this access, a petitioner aims to penetrate the bureaucracy at a point as close to the highest levels as possible, thereby circumventing officials and departments which in effect do little more than delay and complicate matters.

Kalasha effective access to the highest levels is mainly through informal contacts, of which they rely on three types. First, they rely on the urban-dwelling elite of Nuristani ancestry, including descendants of Nuristani women who were taken to Kabul shortly after Kafiristan's conquest, as well as the sons and grandsons of Nuristanis who served in government and settled in Kabul. By virtue of their long experience in Kabul and in government, these individuals often have a network of coworkers, friends, and relatives stretching to top decision-makers. Kalasha military officers and civilian government employees constitute a second avenue to the top levels. These individuals, most of whom attended Kabul boarding schools and later enrolled in the university or military academy, have former class-mates, colleagues, and friends serving in many branches of government. A third link has been directly to members of the royal family or the head of state. King Zahir and President Daoud made visits to the Väygal Valley. Both granted delegations from the valley audiences on many occasions, and both responded positively to Kalasha petitions brought to their personal attention.

Communities and individuals having effective access to their government are more likely to hold positive attitudes toward government than those without such access. In this respect Kalasha have been far better situated than Safi Pakhtuns, whose history of troubled relations with the government and lack of informal contacts put them at a disadvantage in dealing with the central authorities. At the local government level, compared to their Safi neighbors, Kalasha were the outsiders, but at the top government level they have been the ones with effective access. Kalasha effective access to top officials offset the disadvantages they often experienced in dealing with local officials. In 1976, for example, one exceptionally greedy wuluswal at Manugi was abruptly dismissed after a Kalasha civil servant complained to a high Interior Ministry official. This civil servant was a former classmate of the wuluswal and also a friend and confidant of the wuluswal's superior. (Unaware that it was the civil servant's complaint that prompted the dismissal, the dejected wuluswal unsuccessfully begged the civil servant to intercede on his behalf with his superior.)

During the 1970s Väygal Valley Kalasha used their effective access for building and enlarging public schools in several villages, sponsoring inoculation programs for livestock, and winning approval for the construction of a road into their valley. Individuals used this access to enroll their children in the finest schools, obtain government employment, get quality medical treatment and hospitalization, and receive serious consideration for their petitions.

Kalasha appreciated their network of informal contacts because it meant they did not have to resort to cruder tactics for gaining the government's attention. Their confidence in their influence on the government was such that they even sought a permanent government presence in the Väygal Valley: they petitioned for the construction of an *alaqadari* (subdistrict outpost) and a road leading up the valley to it. Kalasha apparently expected that their connections to the central government would allow them to control local officials while at the same time ending what they perceived to be Pakhtun advantages with the local government as long as it was located in Safi territory.

KALASHA ATTITUDES TOWARD THE GOVERNMENT IN THE 1970s

As noted, before the Saur Revolution most Väygal Valley Kalasha were strong government partisans. The government had after all brought them Islamic enlightenment, the potential for their salvation, and a divinely sanctioned moral and social order. Kalasha saw the state and Islam as indivisible: their government service was service to Islam, and defending their country was a defense of their faith. Moreover, the government had brought peace to the region, decisively ending the threats and fears which had previously occupied their lives.

Governmental paternalism reinforced Kalasha loyalties. Even the government's demands after the conquest that youths from every village be sent to Kabul are in retrospect interpreted by Kalasha as having had long-term benefits. The government actively encouraged the education and training of Nuristani youths and their employment by the government. In addition, Kalasha had strong personal ties to and affection for the former king and President Daoud, whose visits to the valley demonstrated their interest in the Kalasha.

Along with these positive sentiments, Kalasha held negative attitudes and evaluations largely as a result of their experience with local-level officials. However, although most local officials were viewed with disdain, they could be neutralized either by avoidance or by Kalasha effective access to the central authorities.

Not only did Väygal Valley Kalasha differently evaluate the local and top levels of government, but they also differentiated between the government's interests and those of ethnic Pakhtuns. Kalasha did not consider the government as merely the political means for projecting and expanding Pakhtun domination and control over non-Pakhtun areas and peoples. Indeed they found their own interests coincided with government interests to a far greater extent than those of the local Safi Pakhtuns.

The generally positive Kalasha opinion of the government prevailed during the Republican era among both rural-dwelling Kalasha and those living and working in Kabul and elsewhere outside their valley home. However, a growing minority was becoming far more negative in its attitudes toward the Afghan government. For the most part, the criticisms of this minority paralleled Islamic fundamentalists' complaints with the government. Sympathy for fundamentalist criticisms was more prevalent among the lowland Pakhtuns than among the Kalasha because the fundamentalists offered an ideological justification for long-standing Safi grievances against the government. Kalasha supporters of this fundamentalism included former slaves who were still denied full participation in community political and economic life and zealous individuals, called *sheikhs*, who eagerly sought to eradicate all practices and customs carrying the slightest tinge of a non-Islamic heritage. These local fundamentalist activists received support, moral and otherwise, from Pakistan, where many mullahs from eastern Afghanistan are trained. Political differences between Afghanistan and Pakistan—mainly centering on Afghanistan's contention that the predominately Pashtun regions of Pakistan should be a sovereign state called Pashtunistan—have at times led each country to encourage subversion of the other through propaganda and covert backing of anti-government elements.

In the Väygal Valley opposition to the government during the mid-1970s remained relatively innocuous and unsophisticated. Instead of actively working against the government, Kalasha fundamentalists concentrated on broadening their power base among their fellow villagers. Most Kalasha fundamentalists were unfamiliar with national politics, and few had any personal grounds for complaints against the government. To a large extent, they merely parroted the more politically astute Pakhtun fundamentalist complaints about the non-Islamic character of the Daoud regime.

POST-SAUR REVOLUTION PERCEPTIONS AMONG KALASHA

The Saur Revolution of 1978 radically altered Kalasha perceptions and evaluations of the government. Where unwanted government involvement in their lives had previously been restricted to greedy local officials, Afghanistan's new leaders promised major social and economic reforms that could be implemented only by government intervention in aspects of life outside its traditional purview. Although earlier regimes had promised similar reforms, the Marxist government actively sought to implement them. Furthermore, the speed at which reform decrees were issued and programs initiated suggested that the regime intended to become profoundly involved in rural communities largely on its own terms. It quickly became apparent, however, that even with foreign backing, the new regime could not impose its reforms on the country in the face of widespread popular resistance.

The populations most susceptible to the government-mandated changes were ones that had always been most vulnerable to meddling by local officials. Väygal Valley Kalasha in their isolated villages had little to fear immediately from the new policies. However, the massive purges following the coup d'état in April virtually eliminated Kalasha links to the top government level. Officials from the Daoud regime, including many high-ranking civil servants and military officers, were replaced. Nuristanis who had held influential positions were suspect due to their long-standing loyalty to the Afghan royal family and President Daoud. Many urban Nuristanis who were not arrested fled to the relative security of their mountain villages.

The new regime's Marxist rhetoric undermined the traditional ideological justification for the Afghan government by distancing it and its leaders from Islam. Government pronouncements were antagonistic and confrontational at a time when the government had not yet consolidated significant popular political support. Linking its rural reforms to a non-Islamic ideology and social theory played directly into the hands of Islamic fundamentalists, who could accuse it of failing to conform to Islam. Moreover, the Marxist government's accountability was to its foreign patron, the Soviet Union, the source of its strength and guarantor of its survival, rather than to the Afghan people. This situation, unprecedented in modern Afghan history, meant that the central authorities, unfettered by traditional constraints on their power, could attempt to impose their will as never before on rural Afghans.

The Marxist government sought to win some support by promising to recognize and accommodate ethnic minorities officially ignored by previous governments (Naby 1980). Väygal Valley Kalasha probably regarded these promises with skepticism given the good relationship that had existed between them and the deposed leaders, the treatment their people had already suffered at the hands of the new regime, and their doubts about the Marxists' concordance with

Islam. These suspicions were compounded by a recognition that the Communist party's dominant faction — the Khalq — consisted mainly of Pakhtuns from rural areas. Kalasha had no reason to expect that these leaders would either tolerate or accommodate the legitimate interests of non-Pakhtun ethnic populations.

The Marxists inherited an administrative organization which had no experience implementing large-scale unpopular reforms in rural regions. Purges and personnel changes following the coup further weakened the rural administrative machinery. The Marxists' only realistic hope for successful implementation of their reforms was that rural dwellers would voluntarily accept them. But the government's inflammatory rhetoric and its arrogant distancing from Islam and the trappings of Islamic legitimacy, together with its headstrong approach to reform, doomed its efforts regardless of the good intentions behind them.

Responses to the government efforts that precipitated insurrection in the Väygal Valley and the middle Pec̆ lowlands followed familiar lines. Although precise details are unavailable, the general outlines of the uprising, one of the first against the Marxist government, demonstrate once again differences between Safi and Kalasha relations with the government.

Late in the summer of 1978 the military detachment stationed at the Manugi wuluswali arrested and held a number of Safi religious activists from the Pec̆ lowlands. Irate Safis attacked and murdered the local commandant and several soldiers and made off with their weapons. The government retaliated by burning the village of Nang-alam, destroying it and nearly all the grain stored from a recently completed harvest. Lowland dwellers fled to the security of the nearby highlands; many sought refuge with their friends and trading partners in Väygal Valley villages. The government, apparently aware — although belatedly — of the volatile situation and the possibility that hostilities could spread, sent a delegation to negotiate a settlement and report back on the people's grievances. Included in this delegation were most of the few remaining Kalasha government employees who were not in jail.

Although Kalasha communities sheltered and fed the fleeing Safis, they refused to side with them in their dispute with the government. Many Kalasha leaders reportedly regarded the conflict as only the latest episode in the long-standing tensions between Safis and the government; they saw little to be gained and much to lose by becoming embroiled in a dispute which did not directly involve their interests. Despite the cautious attitude of many Kalasha leaders, Safis found support among fundamentalist Kalasha in the four northern villages of the Väygal Valley that have no common borders with the Safis and therefore have had fewer disputes with them. Some of these Kalasha fundamentalists joined Safis in staging raids on the military forces occupying the lowlands.

The negotiation team sent by the government was unsuccessful. Other uprisings were occurring, and the possibilities for a settlement to the dispute with the Safis decreased as government control eroded throughout the region. At least some Kalasha members of the negotiating team chose to remain in their villages. By sending negotiators to the Väygal Valley, the government had shown its concern with preventing the insurrection from spreading from the lowlands into Nuristan. Perhaps it recognized—as had previous Afghan governments—how dangerous it would be to have strategically situated Nuristan in open rebellion. As subsequent events have clearly demonstrated, the costs and problems of conducting military operations to regain control of Nuristan are too great for the government. In the Peč Valley government forces have been able to retake and hold the lowlands, including Manugi and Nangalam. However, they have not been able to do more than attack Väygal Valley villages from the air. The Väygal Valley, like virtually all other parts of Nuristan, remains entirely outside of government control.

POST-SAUR REVOLUTION POLITICS IN THE VÄYGAL VALLEY

Despite their stake in peace and stability, the response of Väygal Valley Kalasha to the Marxist regime has cast them into an anarchic situation. How are the interests that led Kalasha to establish and nurture strong links to the government for over eighty years expressed in this new situation? Current information available on Nuristan, and the Väygal Valley in particular, corroborates much that was apparent during my field research in the mid-1970s. Although national political conditions have changed, nothing suggests a shift in people's attitudes about the kind of social and political organization they want for their communities and the type of relations they want with outsiders and with the Afghan government. As in the past, two political orientations prevail: many Väygal Valley Kalasha, called here conservatives, seek a system similar to the one that existed before 1978; others insist on building a new society based on an Islamic fundamentalist program.

Long after the national and international dimensions of the current state of hostilities fade, the local problems that have always been central to Kalasha will remain. Nothing short of the depopulation of the lowlands by emigration or mass extermination will reduce the potential for conflict and competition between Kalasha and their Safi neighbors. The main cause of tension between these populations—the juxtaposition of the overpopulated, resource-scarce Pakhtun lands with the underpopulated, resource-abundant Nuristani lands—will remain. For this persistent problem local proponents of the two orientations advance different solutions and find serious grounds for disagreement.

Kalasha conservatives express skepticism about the benefits promised from any radical political reorganization, whether tied to Islam or some other doctrine. They seek relations with the central authorities which, as before 1978, would afford them security, local control of local affairs, and opportunities to derive benefits from the government. While they do not categorically oppose government involvement in their communities, they view it with suspicion and wish to exercise control over the government's role in their affairs. In addition, the conservatives seek a strong (albeit limited) government presence in the region that would guarantee their external security and maintain peace among local populations. Essential components of this presence would be institutions and procedures for settling disputes that cannot be handled by nongovernmental means.

The fundamentalists call for the radical restructuring of the Afghan economy, polity, and society based on an explicit Islamic mandate. For local problems they propose new solutions: Ethnic distinctions between Pakhtuns and Nuristanis will be deemphasized since these are supposedly un-Islamic and only create invidious divisions among Muslims. In their place will be a new, larger-scale order characterized by authentic brotherhood based on the equality of all Muslims within the community of the faithful. Proponents of this fundamentalist approach consider the pre-1978 political order as irrevocably flawed. Unlike the conservatives, who seek an unassertive central government, fundamentalists define government's proper role as intrusive, activist, and dogmatic. However, government will be guided by its Islamic mandate to do whatever necessary to establish the Islamic order throughout the country.

Local support for the two programs is now more equally divided than before 1978. Fundamentalists were formerly a small minority in most Kalasha communities. Even in villages where they had achieved some influence, they avoided antagonizing the government. Conservatives, who supported the government during the Republican era, were in turn backed by the government, which bolstered their influence by favorably responding to their initiatives. Reports as recent as March 1984 suggest that the conservatives have retained overt political control through most of Nuristan and in nearly every Väygal Valley community.

Unlike the conservatives, fundamentalists have extensive experience with oppositional politics. As in the past, Kalasha fundamentalists benefit from association with fellow fundamentalists throughout the region. In addition, fundamentalists in eastern Afghanistan draw support from fundamentalists in other countries—especially Pakistan, where the powerful fundamentalist Jamiat-i Islami organization maintains a vast network of religious schools, influential political connections, theologians, financial backers, and propaganda outlets.

Conservatives now face several disadvantages compared to the fundamentalists. First, they are vulnerable to charges that they seek to reinstate a political order riddled with corruption, injustice, and exploitation. Second, they are criticized for wanting to reestablish an order where the same type of secular, non-Islamic movements that toppled the regime in 1978 could again emerge. Third, although they want the new order to be Islamic, they lack a coherent and clearly articulated Islamic ideological program comparable to that of the fundamentalists. Finally, many conservatives are perceived as motivated by fear of losing their power and dominant position in society (both as individuals and as a group); their removal from power is implicit in the fundamentalist agenda.

Despite their disadvantages, conservative leaders regard the fundamentalist program as susceptible to corruption or exploitation. Locally they fear that the lowland Pakhtuns will use a revolutionary Islamic program as a smokescreen for yet another—and perhaps the decisive—attempt at expansion. They fear that the fundamentalist agenda will trigger irreversible changes which will seal once and for all the fate of Kalasha. Once Kalasha resources become accessible to Muslims from outside the community, conservatives fear that Kalasha will be shoved into subservient status in their own land—Pakhtun professions of commitment to Islamic principles and Muslim brotherhood notwithstanding. They cite numerous historical instances throughout the Kunar basin, where Pakhtuns initially insinuated themselves into a village or region, voicing the best of intentions, and then through deceit and guile wrested control and property from the original residents.

Prominent Väygal Valley opponents of the fundamentalists include many rural political leaders, especially those in the villages bordering on Pakhtun territory. These leaders have direct experience with Pakhtun predatory expansionism and are acutely sensitive to the threat it poses. Other important opponents of the fundamentalists include many former members of the urban educated elite. Their experience with national politics makes them aware of the need to preserve a strong ethnic identity distinct from Pakhtuns in order to protect their interests on the national level.

Conservatives and fundamentalists are equally opposed to the Marxist regime. Evidence on the different types of opposition to the Soviet-backed government reflects a basic continuity of concerns from the Kafir era. Conservatives and fundamentalists remain vitally concerned with local issues, and each group believes its program holds the greatest promise for reestablishing security and peace with neighboring peoples. National and international considerations, while not irrelevant, are most salient as they affect local issues.

Analyses of the insurrections throughout Afghanistan against the Marxist government have stressed their religious rationale, character, and aspirations. The long-standing concerns of Väygal Valley Kalasha assume an importance equal if not actually greater than the strictly religious considerations. This is not to downplay Islam's importance since it remains the only ideology familiar to the population that holds the hope for personal salvation and a life in a just society in this world. However, the critical abiding interests of Väygal Valley Kalasha are with preserving security, peace, and control over their resources and lives. Through their rebellion, whatever the particular ideological rationale, Väygal Valley Kalasha show that they do not believe the current government can satisfy these interests.

CONCLUSIONS

Coercion and its threat have not been the critical factors sustaining the allegiance of Väygal Valley Kalasha to the Afghan government. Nor did propaganda, subsidies, or bribes figure importantly in maintaining the allegiance. Strong ties proved mutually beneficial and fostered Kalasha's acceptance of the government. The post-Saur Revolution Marxist government destroyed the bases for this historically nurtured relationship. The current insurrection cannot be interpreted as either a Kalasha rejection of a strong government presence in their region or an unwillingness to be incorporated into a larger state.

When leaders from the valley communities peacefully accepted Afghan sovereignty over eighty years ago, they recognized that their most serious threats came from other groups in the region. A phrase I repeatedly heard succinctly expresses Kalasha perceptions of the threat posed by local Pakhtuns: "We are few; they are many." Outnumbered by the lowland dwellers and rich in lands and resources, the Kalasha feel the prospects are slim for continued well-being and independence in a political environment where each community must fend for itself. Kalasha have little interest in promoting anarchy since they are the ones with the most to lose.

Few Kalasha have an extensive knowledge of their history. However, most know that their lands were previously inhabited by groups who were driven out, killed, or vanished as distinct peoples. Kalasha understand that they are immigrants to their land. They know they wrested their territory from man and nature and have had to continuously fight to preserve control over it. Eighty years ago, when Kalasha found themselves surrounded by enemies they could not defeat, they decided it was in their best interests to accept the Afghan government and support its presence in the region. In effect, they assured themselves the greatest degree of freedom by partially surrendering their autonomy to the state.

While their previous relations with the government were mutually beneficial, they were not ideal. If the government did little harm to Kalasha, it largely did little at all. Compared to their Kafir past and their current situation, however, their relations with the government from their conquest until 1978 were neither coercive nor repressive. Generations of Kalasha lived essentially free from fears for their security, and the central authorities treated Kalasha with some sensitivity and responsiveness.

In its details the case of Väygal Valley Kalasha differs from cases elsewhere in Nuristan and in other rural Afghan communities. Kalasha bore little bitterness about their conquest and conversion. Subsequent events solidified and reaffirmed their ties to the government. Their geographic situation effectively insulated them from the most oppressive aspects of contact with local authorities. In addition, Kalasha were fortunate to have many strong ties to high-ranking officials. The most serious concern for Kalasha, that of security, brought a convergence between their interests and those of the government. All these factors fostered a relationship with the Afghan government which was more desirable for the Kalasha than it would have been for many other rural populations.

Despite its distinctiveness, certain conclusions can be drawn from the Kalasha case which apply to groups elsewhere in Afghanistan. First, rural residents distinguish between the comportment of local administrators and the legitimacy of the central authorities, and evaluations of both levels contribute to overall assessments of the government. Second, non-Pakhtun Afghans do not all consider the interests of the Afghan government identical to the interests of the ethnic Pakhtun segment of the population. The disdain of Kalasha for their Safi neighbors and local Pakhtun officials was not generalized to the Pakhtun-dominated government. Third, relations between rural communities and the government are shaped to some extent by the character of local intergroup relations and competition.

Väygal Valley Kalasha did not and do not value more the complete autonomy of their pre-conquest past than the peace and security gained by their submission to the government. Their rejection of the Marxists and their willful return to an anarchic situation show how deeply they abhor and distrust the present government.

Chapter 5

THE REBELLION IN DARRA-I NUR

R. Lincoln Keiser

THE REBELLION: QUESTIONS AND PARADOXES

On 27 April 1978, Afghan Communist revolutionaries led by
Nur Muhammad Taraki and Hafizullah Amin overthrew the government of Muhammad Daoud, thus ending the rule of the Muhammadzai, the Pashtun royal lineage that had dominated Afghan politics for
one hundred and fifty years. The officials of the new Communist
government were almost exclusively members of the educated elite
and had neither sympathy for nor understanding of the tribal and
peasant rural population that comprised the majority of Afghanistan's
people. Lacking legitimacy in the eyes of most Afghans and handicapped by narrow, doctrinaire views, officials of the Communist
regime quickly succeeded in alienating large sections of the population. Beginning at first with isolated uprisings, armed rebellion finally
spread throughout the country. By early winter 1979 it was apparent
that the Afghan military was incapable of containing the rebellion
despite massive Soviet aid. Thus in December of that year units from
the Soviet army and air force crossed the Afghan border and occupied
strategic roads, cities, and bases in the country. Ferocious and bloody
fighting between Afghan guerrillas and the Soviet invaders ensued—
fighting which continues to the present. In this struggle an often
ragtag, poorly armed assortment of peasants, tribesmen, and urban
dwellers divided by ideological and ethnic differences has so far
proven a match for the Soviet Union. This not only continues to
surprise Western military "experts," but poses perplexing questions
relating to the nature of popular rebellions as well. In this chapter
we shall attempt to provide some understanding of the rebellion in

Afghanistan through an analysis of events in one small rural area, the Darra-i Nur Valley of Nangarhar province.

Darra-i Nur, a side valley within the Kunar River valley system, is located about twenty-five miles from the city of Jalalabad. It begins in the Kund mountains and extends for about fifteen miles before opening into the main Kunar Valley near the town of Shewa. Darra-i Nur itself is a valley system in miniature: small tributary valleys branch off at various locations along its length. At the village of Panj Ulla, roughly eight miles from its mouth, the main valley forks. One arm extends to the northwest toward Laghman, while the other extends to the northeast and broadens to form a large bowl, a formation not uncommon to mountain valleys in Central Asia.

About 10,000 people inhabit Darra-i Nur, scattered in settlements ranging from compact villages to dispersed homesteads. They speak various dialects of what linguists call Pashai, a language belonging to the Dardic branch of Indo-Aryan. Some of these dialects have distinct local names, and some are mutually unintelligible. However, no one in the valley uses "Pashai" in reference to his/her language, and it is never used as an ethnic appelation.*

Fighting between the inhabitants of Darra-i Nur and troops of the Communist government broke out in the winter of 1979. The first organized opposition began in Kashmund Qala, a highland village located in a tributary of the main valley. Mir Beg, an influential leader from that village, led the initial fighting, which began when the men of Kashmund Qala surprised a contingent of the Afghan army stationed at Panj Ulla. After early rebel success, the resistance of the government troops stiffened; the battle lasted five days. During the first part of the fighting the rebels captured modern weapons, making it impossible for the government forces to hold out against them. As a result, the government troops evacuated Panj Ulla and fled a few miles south to a primary school, leaving a large store of modern weapons and ammunition behind.

Due at least partially to widespread political discontent in the valley, Mir Beg had succeeded in gaining the cooperation of the politically important groups and factions in Darra-i Nur, as well as the Pashto-speaking Safis of the lower Kunar—a particularly noteworthy achievement given the intense rivalries and deep-seated animosities

*For a detailed analysis of Pashai ethnicity, see Ovesen (1982).

that had previously divided the various groups in the area. In these rivalries tribes, village clusters, and factions were the meaningful entities; Darra-i Nur itself was never perceived as a significant corporate political unit. By building a political alliance that spanned tribal and factional differences and creating a military organization that crosscut earlier political divisions, Mir Beg successfully altered the political structure in a fundamental manner.

Led by Mir Beg and armed with newly captured weapons, forces from this new alliance attacked and destroyed the government troops barricaded in the primary school; the entire valley was now in rebel hands. Unfortunately for the rebels, however, in spring 1980 a new government force armed with tanks and augmented by Soviet advisors attacked the valley from the government-held base at Shewa. The lower Darra-i Nur is wide and transversed by a relatively good road, so the tanks could operate effectively in that part of the valley. The tanks provided the government troops with an advantage that the rebel forces could not overcome, and they were forced to retreat to the more rugged terrain in the surrounding mountains. The government troops were unable to advance beyond the end of the road, effectively reducing the fighting to isolated encounters. This respite gave the rebels an opportunity to reorganize their forces and refine their techniques for destroying tanks with homemade mines, gasoline-soaked blankets, and fire bombs. When they finally counterattacked, the rebels defeated the government troops, who evacuated the valley and retreated to their base at Shewa. As of 1980 the Soviet-supported government troops had not been able to retake Darra-i Nur.

The events related above suggest a number of questions: (1) Why did the people of Darra-i Nur take up arms against a vastly superior military force armed with sophisticated modern weapons? (2) Why did the valley's inhabitants forge an alliance not only with one another, but with the Kunar valley Safis as well? and (3) Why was a highland leader able to organize the alliance and change politics in the valley in such fundamental ways? These are perplexing questions for a number of reasons. First, animosity has existed between the people of Darra-i Nur and the Pashtun-dominated central government in Kabul since the valley was first incorporated into the modern Afghan state in the late nineteenth century. Yet incidents of rebellion had been few, and they had usually occurred when the government's military strength in the valley was crippled due to political upheavals and weak leadership in Kabul. Given this history, one would not have expected the people of Darra-i Nur to rebel against the Taraki/Amin regime. For one thing, it would not have been surprising if they had viewed this regime as they viewed the previous Muhammadzai governments—as a slightly different, but similar manifestation of Pashtun domination. (Amin, the most powerful leader in the new regime, was an ethnic Pashtun infamous for his Pashtun chauvinism.) For another, the military strength of the Communist regime at first appeared substantial. The Afghan military was supplied by the Soviet Union with modern small arms, tanks, fighter bombers, and helicopter gunships. The army was advised by military personnel from Eastern Europe well trained in techniques of modern warfare. Moreover, the government apparatus was organized, and political leadership was entrenched. In short, in certain respects the situation following the Communist coup was similar to situations during the Muhammadzai period when Darra-i Nur had remained relatively peaceful.

Second, on the occasions when open opposition to the central government had occurred, competing political groups and factions in the valley had usually taken advantage of the central government's military weakness to resume warfare among themselves rather than to attack government troops in the area. During these times cooperation among rival political groups in the valley was rare, and alliances were unusual between the peoples of Darra-i Nur and the Kunar Valley Safis, who for centuries had been considered hated enemies.

Third, prior to the rebellion the leaders in Darra-i Nur who were most influential outside their own local area were generally large landowners, or *khans*, whose holdings were in the agriculturally rich lower valley. An obvious example was Malak Baba, whose wealth and fame were known throughout the region. Malak Baba had numerous political connections outside the valley and was so well known that he was jailed for a time by the Communist government immediately following the April revolution.* One would expect that if anyone were to successfully create a viable alliance in Darra-i Nur, it would be a lowland khan such as Malak Baba, whose widespread respect and influence could be used to forge political allegiances. Yet the leader

---

*It is interesting that Malak Baba shared a jail cell with Muhammad Anwar, who became the rebel commander of an upper Kunar Valley alliance. (For details, see the chapter by Richard Strand above.)

who emerged, Mir Beg, was from a highland village and had not previously been particularly influential outside the valley.

To gain an understanding of the rebellion in Darra-i Nur and at least partially answer the questions posed above, it will be necessary to isolate and analyze a number of interconnected elements. Thus I shall attempt to explain the nature of local government in Afghanistan, discuss changes that occurred in the relationship between the inhabitants of the valley and the central government both during the time of Daoud and following the April revolution, look at political ideology as expressed in symbols to see how such symbols motivate people to political action, and analyze the environmental and social structural features necessary for understanding traditional political leadership in the valley.

LOCAL GOVERNMENT BEFORE AND AFTER THE APRIL (SAUR) REVOLUTION

In 1968, while I was involved in field research in Darra-i Nur, the valley was a subdivision of the Shewa district. It was under the joint administrative control of a subdistrict commissioner, or *alaqadar*, and a police commandant. In addition, the Afghan court system was represented by a full-time clerk. The valley itself was too small to have a *qazi*, or Muslim judge, in residence, but it was visited from time to time by a qazi stationed at the district headquarters in Shewa. There was a local jail at Panj Ulla, the government headquarters in the valley. The alaqadar was assisted by a clerk, scribe, jailkeeper, tax collector, and various personal servants, all of whom were responsible for many of the day-to-day administrative tasks. The police commandant had a small detachment of paramilitary police to enforce government policy.

Although these officials received nominal salaries from the government, these were insufficient to meet even basic needs. Most of their income came from bribes extracted from the valley's inhabitants. Since the alaqadar and commandant were not closely supervised by their superiors and since bribery was built into the system, it might appear that government free from corruption was impossible. However, bribery was not officially recognized and was not given overt legitimacy. If an alaqadar or police commandant were too blatant in

his demands, concerted action by local political leaders could be organized against him and charges of corruption made to his superiors.
Such charges were effective because much of the male population
in Darra-i Nur was armed, and the control of the government was
thought to be tenuous by government officials themselves. Although
armed uprisings were few, the government perceived the possibility
of such opposition as very real. Therefore if an alaqadar or commandant made himself so despised that an uprising were threatened, he
was quickly replaced. Because officials knew that abusive demands
could lead to their replacement, most kept their demands at a level
acceptable to the local people.

Since local officials were dependent on bribes for a large part of
their livelihood, they were to a degree dependent on the good graces
of the local population. As a result, a balance was struck between
government representatives and the people of Darra-i Nur. In many
respects villages were left to run their own affairs, but taxes were
collected, men were conscripted, and the legitimate right of the government to handle certain kinds of civil and criminal cases was recognized. Successful alaqadars had at least some respect for local customs
and considerable understanding of the structure and organization of
local politics.*

The recognition of the government's legitimate right to rule is
especially important. As political anthropologists have known for
some time, no political system can function effectively without an
acceptance of its legitimacy by its members. In Darra-i Nur (and
Afghanistan as a whole) the judicial arm of the government was intertwined with Muslim ideology; thus in the context of civil and criminal
justice the government symbolized Islam. This was an important—if
not the most important—factor in local acknowledgment of the central government's legitimacy. As we shall see, it is particularly relevant
for understanding the Darra-i Nur rebellion.

Changes in the local political system began to occur prior to
the Saur Revolution. When Daoud first came to power, he included
members of leftist parties in his government. Later he reversed this
policy and attempted to purge Communists from the government.

---

*Acceptable balances between government officials and local residents seem
to have been fairly common in Afghanistan; for example, see Uberoi (1968) for
a discussion of how bribery operated in the Andarab district of northern Afghanistan.

Many were sent to the provinces as government officials and school-teachers. Most of these were members of the urban elite who had little experience interacting with rural people. They were harshly doctrinaire, despised local customs, and had no understanding of local politics (Strand 1980). It is not surprising that they rapidly aroused the distrust and dislike of the rural population.

After the revolution, changes accelerated. The new officials charged with rural administration were at first flushed with revolutionary zeal, and (at least on the surface) adamantly opposed to the old system of bribery, claiming that it was a manifestation of the decadence of the previous Muhammadzai regimes.* To the inhabitants of Darra-i Nur this meant that government officials would no longer be dependent on bribes and thus would have no reason to respect local customs or accommodate indigenous political leaders. The local population felt threatened with the loss of a particularly effective means of controlling government policy in its area. The fabric of the previous political system in which indigenous political structures were integrated with the state bureaucracy threatened to unravel.

Two policies introduced by Communist officials were particularly intolerable and ultimately motivated the people of Darra-i Nur to rebel. The first was the introduction of Communist ideology and the debunking of Muslim beliefs in the primary schools. When young schoolchildren informed their parents of what the new school officials were teaching, violent feelings against the local Communist government boiled to the surface. The new curriculum undermined the foundation of the central government's legitimacy, which stemmed (as we have seen) from the integration of judicial processes with Muslim beliefs and practices.

The second policy was to increase military conscription. As fighting spread throughout the country, government casualties grew, and it was necessary to draft replacements for the army. The reaction of the people of Darra-i Nur to the demand for conscripts was predictable: they found it intolerable. As an informant stated, "We could not let our sons fight for the *kafirs* [infidels] against Islam." It was at this time that Mir Beg organized the men of Kashmund Qala and the rebellion began.

---

*Although bribery was attacked verbally by Communist officials, in many areas of Afghanistan it remained an integral part of the administrative system.

POLITICAL IDEOLOGY AND SYMBOLISM

As noted, the military success of the people of Darra-i Nur lay in the cooperation of groups previously antagonistic toward one another. Islam played a crucial role in this cooperation. By attacking Islam, the government had not only significantly weakened its own legitimacy, but it had also threatened core values. Islam provides a sense of self; as Abner Cohen argues, selfhood, or the "I," the oneness of an integrated psyche, is necessary for all people. It is attained both in the course of social interaction and in continual participation in symbolic activities provided by social groups. The political aims of social groups cannot be accomplished unless there is political unity. Unity is achieved "not by contractual mechanisms that operate on the individual from the outside through reward and punishment, but by moral and ritual obligations, by 'oughts,' operating from the inside and involving the total self" (Cohen 1979: 101). In Darra-i Nur it was possible for Mir Beg to motivate individuals to put aside ancient antagonisms and present a united political front to the Communist enemy because cooperative behavior *sui generis* came to symbolize the Islamic moral and ideological orders which have always been the sources of the sense of self for the inhabitants of the valley.

The symbolic linking of Islam with unified political opposition to the government probably would not have occurred if either the Communist government had retained the Muslim judicial system which symbolically identified previous regimes with Islam, or government teachers and officials in Darra-i Nur had at least publicly supported basic Islamic tenets. However, because the government both secularized the system of justice and publicly attacked Islamic beliefs, it became identified with kafirism.

The notion of kafirism was very powerful in Darra-i Nur (as in many parts of Afghanistan) and aroused strong emotions among the valley's inhabitants. In essence it stood for moral bankruptcy and inherent evil. The belief that the Communist regime was a kafir government *required* that the inhabitants, as devout Muslims, oppose it. Since opposition could best be accomplished through political unity, putting aside ancient tribal antagonisms became an Islamic moral imperative, and this imperative was skillfully utilized by Mir Beg.

In order to ascertain why a highland leader was successful not only in forging a political alliance, but assuming command of it as well, we must first understand the differing ecological and social structural patterns of the lower and upper areas of the valley. In the process we shall understand why the particular skills of highland leaders were especially suitable for the task of uniting the disparate groups in the valley under the conditions which followed the Saur Revolution and why those of lowland leaders were not.

ECOLOGY, SOCIAL STRUCTURE, AND POLITICAL LEADERSHIP

During the Muhammadzai period cultivatable land was both relatively rich and extensive in the lower parts of Darra-i Nur. The valley bottom was wide, and although some terracing was necessary, the entire bottom land could be cultivated. In this part of the valley the elevation was low and the climate mild. Rainfall was not particularly high, but in most years melt from extensive snow fields in the surrounding high mountains provided ample water for irrigation. This combination of factors permitted intensive cultivation of rice with high crop yields. Of added importance to the lower valley's economic system was a motorable road that transversed Darra-i Nur for about eight miles from its mouth. This road connected the lower valley to Shewa and Jalalabad, thus permitting crop surpluses to be transported to markets in these towns. As a result, rice farming was highly lucrative for those who controlled sizable landholdings, and it is not surprising that it was the most important economic activity in that part of the valley.

The form of local-level politics in the lower valley was closely related to the nature of the economic system. Political competition generally took place between khans (each of whom was supported by his tenant clients). Land was of key political importance, since (through the cultivation of rice 'as a cash crop) it provided wealth that could be used to subvert an enemy's followers, solidify alliances, bribe government officials, and allow one to live in a style necessary for acceptance among the Pashtun-dominated Afghan elite. Land was also important in determining the number of supporters a khan could mobilize in confrontations with his enemies because the number of tenants obligated to support him was in direct proportion to the size of his holdings. Because land was of such importance, most political confrontations concerned it in one way or another; political fortunes rose or fell in relation to success or failure in land disputes, and where land was at issue, each khan was the potential rival of all others. Some khans allied with one another when threatened by a common enemy, but the political factions formed by such alliances tended to be of short duration. In general khans were suspicious of one another and perceived themselves as relatively isolated in a sea of potential enemies.

Settlement and kinship patterns in the lower valley reflected political organization. Settlements were often scattered and comprised of easily defended fortresses, or *qalas*, located in the midst of each khan's holdings. These fortresses were inhabited by khans, their families, and various servants, guards, and lackeys. A khan, his unmarried children, married sons, daughters-in-law, and paternal grandchildren usually lived in the same qala, while his adult married brothers usually inhabited separate qalas. Tenants inhabited scattered small houses or tiny hamlets located close to their landlord's fortress. In the lower valley corporate patrilineages were not an important aspect of political organization, and tribal membership was not politically relevant.

In the upper section of the valley and in the small tributary valleys that reach into higher elevations, there were significant differences in ecological patterns. For one thing, the terrain was considerably more rugged and therefore more difficult to cultivate. The valley floor was often too narrow and rocky to cultivate at all; as a result, most fields were located on mountainsides where the slope was relatively gentle. These areas were not always contiguous, but often scattered throughout the mountains. The size of fields was also affected by the rugged terrain. In general, fields were significantly smaller and narrower than in the lower valley. The transportation system was different as well. Because of the highland terrain, the construction of motorable roads connecting settlements in the highlands to outside market centers was too difficult and expensive. As a result, highland villages were interconnected in many places by paths not negotiable by burden animals. Differences in the irrigation system also related to the terrain. In the highlands a particularly intricate system of irrigation channels fed water to terraced fields, many of which were high above the bottom of the valley. In certain places wooden viaducts were built to carry water along steep mountainsides and across narrow chasms. Finally, the climate in the highlands was too cold for rice cultivation; the staples were winter wheat and maize. Both the lack of cultivatable land and the cold climate limited yields of the staple crops.

These differences had several important consequences. Because crop yields were small in the highlands, agriculture was primarily for subsistence. Moreover, agriculture alone could not provide an adequate base; thus goat herding was as significant an economic endeavor as the cultivation of wheat and maize.

Differences in social and political organization related to these ecological differences. Because cultivatable land was so scarce in the highlands, families built their residences huddled together in compact settlements on land too steep and rocky for agriculture. In some instances these settlements had as many as one thousand or fifteen hundred people. To keep peace within these villages—and especially to deal with potential disputes over scarce natural resources—councils of descent group representatives enforced complex rules regarding agricultural and herding activities. Furthermore, because significant crop surpluses could be neither accumulated nor transported to market centers for sale, the amassing of land beyond subsistence needs was not a viable strategy. Thus there were few large landowners and few tenant clients in the highlands, and the competition for land did not politically isolate neighboring landowners from one another. In fact, the environment necessitated cooperation—for example, for the construction and maintenance of the irrigation system. Furthermore, since fields were scattered in different locations, landowners had to cooperate with different individuals in the various locations where they owned fields. Disputes occasionally arose between the owners of adjacent fields over the distribution of irrigation water, but because disputants had to cooperate to maintain the irrigation system itself, they were generally willing to allow their differences to be adjudicated without bloodshed.

It is clear that the ecological system of the highlands linked villagers in relationships of economic dependency. These relationships were further strengthened by the requirements of animal husbandry in the high mountains. Because of the difficult terrain, goats, who are particularly sure-footed in the mountains, comprised the majority of domesticated animals. However, grazing goats are difficult to control and are fully capable of destroying carefully cultivated fields. Therefore, village councils strongly enforced rules specifying the movement of goat herds. The animals were not allowed near cultivated fields from early spring until late fall. This rule created serious problems for herd owners. First, in the spring the herds had to be driven long distances to high mountain pastures and in the fall had to be returned to pastures near the villages. Generally one individual alone could not accomplish this; therefore, herdsmen usually combined their labor. Second, the herds had to be watched carefully while in the high mountain pastures. To free a majority of the men from having to stay in the pastures away from their villages, most herdsmen formed cooperative companies whose members rotated herding responsibilities. This rotation allowed each member to spend a considerable portion of the spring-summer herding season in his village attending to his other affairs. Herding, like farming, created economic bonds between highland villagers that did not exist among the inhabitants of the lower valley.

Not only did ties of economic dependency link villagers in the highlands, but these ties also crosscut one another. Thus the members of one household cooperated with some households for herding activities and other households for the various agricultural activities. Such crosscutting relationships did not exist in lowland settlements. While disputes of one kind or another constantly occurred in both areas, highlanders had better economic reasons for peacefully resolving them because of the need to cooperate with so many others in economic ventures.* It is not surprising, therefore, that settlements in the highlands took the form of compact villages, while lowland settlements were largely isolated forts and scattered homesteads.

Even more important for our argument here is that the need for peacefully settling disputes in the highlands affected the forms of traditional leadership. Although no institutionalized leadership positions existed in the highlands—the office of chief did not exist—various individuals did have reputations for leadership, and these reputations were at least partially based on the individual's ability to make peace and reconcile opponents in disputes.[†] In contrast, influential leaders

---

*I do not wish to imply that all crosscutting ties in highland villages were based on the need for economic cooperation. In other writings (Keiser 1971, 1981) I have analyzed how the structure of kinship generated crosscutting ties in Oygul, a highland village in Darra-i Nur.

[†]Ovesen (1981: 230-33) gives a particularly interesting account of the *marat*, the traditional peacemaking institution in Darra-i Nur, which clearly shows the importance of arbitration skills to the political success of highland leaders. In

in the lowlands were those who defeated their enemies in disputes and thus furthered their own economic fortunes.

The economic importance of herding was another cause for differences in traditional political leadership between the two parts of the valley. Tribes were an important aspect of highland but not lowland social structure. Their importance in the highlands can be understood when the goat herding is analyzed in greater detail. Goat herding in Darra-i Nur created a potential for conflict, as well as a requirement for cooperation. Herding was a chancy operation at best. Natural disasters struck at random and often resulted in high animal casualties. Theft then became a viable means of recouping losses, and a potential for conflict was created. The scarcity of pasturage in the high mountains further exacerbated this potential. However, because of the many ties of cooperation which linked members of the same village, conflicts usually involved members of different villages. But individual villages were not pitted against all other villages. Rather they were joined together into tribes and village confederations (Ovesen 1981: 223-30), and it was these units which opposed one another over rival claims.

The political relevancy of tribes and confederations (as opposed to villages) in the highlands was linked to the nature of herding itself. It was difficult to successfully steal animals from herds pastured close to one's own. Herders knew each of their animals individually, and it would have been a simple matter for them to identify any stolen animals in nearby pastures—and then plan retaliatory raids. Constant raiding and counter-raiding between neighboring camps would have made it difficult to successfully carry out the necessary herding tasks. Therefore, members of neighboring pastures did not usually steal from one another; instead they cooperated in organizing and carrying out raids against distant rivals. In general, the ideological basis for this cooperation was membership in units of perceived common kinship. This common kinship provided the moral underpinnings for the trust on which such cooperation was predicated.

The importance of tribes and intertribal conflict had as much effect on political leadership in the highlands as did the necessity for

Nuristan the political importance of peacemaking for successful leadership is even greater than it is in Darra-i Nur. In Keiser (1971) I analyze some of the reasons for this.

economic cooperation among village members. In the years preceding the incorporation of Darra-i Nur and neighboring areas into the Afghan state, instances of full-scale intertribal warfare often occurred. After the Afghan conquest of the area in the late nineteenth century such warfare was not tolerated by the central government, and the government was generally strong enough to suppress most of it. Thus in the decades between the conquest and the Communist coup intertribal antagonism most often took the form of small-scale animal raids and counter-raids. (Sometimes, when face-to-face encounters occurred, these resulted in fighting.) Successful raids depended upon knowledge, resourcefulness, and courage. It was necessary to travel stealthily over difficult mountain terrain, strike enemy camps quickly, and retreat rapidly. The personal qualities necessary for organizing and leading successful animal raids were highly valued, and many influential leaders first emerged as the organizers of such raids.

Intertribal conflicts also fostered leaders able to conduct complicated negotiations. Before the Saur Revolution, the highlands of all the valleys in the region formed an arena in which intertribal alliances and rivalries constantly shifted. In this arena tribal leaders often took part in complex negotiations with leaders of other tribes. Therefore, highland leaders had a great deal of experience in dealing with other tribal groups, and the most successful were highly skilled in melding a threat of force with a willingness to compromise so as to reach agreements acceptable to both parties to a dispute.

The different ecology in the lower valley did not require as much cooperation as in the highlands, and the reputation of lowland leaders was not usually contingent on successfully negotiating peaceful settlements. Rather their reputation depended upon accumulating land, money, and tenants by adeptly manipulating allies in a field of shifting political alliances, subtly threatening and using force against vulnerable neighbors, and skillfully utilizing bribery and personal connections to influence Afghan court decisions.

AFTERMATH OF THE SAUR REVOLUTION: RESPONSES TO CHANGE

Conditions in Darra-i Nur after the Saur Revolution created organizational problems that demanded new kinds of social arrangements and political skills. For the first time a motivation to overcome past political enmities, a need to form a viable military alliance, and a compulsion to rebel against the central government existed together. In response, a new pattern of political leadership was born—a pattern connected, however, to older values and previous forms of political organization.

Although a number of men in Darra-i Nur were potential leaders of the rebellion, those from the highlands of the valley had skills which placed them at a distinct advantage over those from the lowlands for at least three reasons. First, highland leaders knew how to organize and lead guerrilla warfare. During lifetimes of herding in the mountains, organizing successful animal raids had been an important qualification for leadership. A knowledge of the mountains, resourcefulness, and courage—all of which were required in animal raiding—were exactly the qualifications needed to organize successful guerrilla warfare against the government forces and their Soviet allies.

Second, highland leaders were skillful at negotiating village disputes. Because they possessed no physical or legal sanctions to enforce agreements, they learned to manipulate symbols that stood for general moral values. Thus they had the necessary skills for utilizing powerful Islamic symbols to effectively unite opposing groups and factions in the valley against the Communist government and its Soviet allies.

Finally, during the Muhammadzai period highland leaders had a great deal of experience in negotiating with leaders of other tribes and confederacies. The skill of combining threats of force with a willingness to compromise was useful in dealing with the potentially divisive groups and factions within the new Darra-i Nur alliance.

In contrast, politics in the lower valley had been confrontational rather than conciliatory, and lowland khans had not needed mediational skills. Thus they were not as well equipped to effectively mediate potentially divisive conflicts or to create and maintain a politically viable alliance. Further, the knowledge and ability to successfully operate in the Afghan legal system so important for khans in the Muhammadzai period were useless following the Saur Revolution since the courts were now part of the very system the inhabitants of the valley were rebelling against. Finally, and perhaps most important, khans had never developed the skills to successfully organize and lead guerrilla warfare in the mountains.

BEYOND THE REBELLION: FURTHER QUESTIONS

In addition to the questions discussed above, three equally, if not more important questions stand out: (1) What can an understanding of the rebellion in Darra-i Nur tell us about rebellions in other areas of Afghanistan? (2) What relevancy does such an understanding have for theoretical issues in political anthropology? and (3) What are the implications of the rebellion in Darra-i Nur for the current theoretical debate among social scientists concerning the nature and causes of peasant insurrections in agrarian societies? Answering such questions in detail would take us beyond the limits of this essay, but I feel that the analysis developed here makes a start. I have argued for the importance of understanding how symbols motivate people to act in terms of moral imperatives. The relationship between the operation of symbols in ritual contexts and the need to achieve a sense of self (as argued by Cohen) is particularly important. Such a perspective could be extremely useful in understanding popular uprisings not only in Darra-i Nur, but in other areas of Afghanistan as well. For example, as Strand reports in his essay on the insurrection in Nuristan above, the refusal of local government officials to allow personnel under their authority to participate in the traditional ritual of nightly prayers was a crucial factor in instigating rebellion. It seems clear that a symbolic interactionalist analysis could be fruitfully applied here.

In regard to the more general theoretical questions, for some time political anthropology has been dominated by an approach based on the assumption that political behavior is primarily motivated by considerations of individual self-interest. This approach, argued persuasively by Fredrik Barth (1966), among others, has provided an explanation for phenomena not satisfactorily dealt with by earlier anthropologists. Yet more recently political anthropologists have begun to question the power of this theoretical approach to explain many aspects of political behavior. Our analysis of the Darra-i Nur rebellion is relevant because it argues for the importance of symbols and moral imperatives in understanding political phenomena. A more general study of the Afghan rebellion could help in understanding the particular manner in which self-interest and moral imperatives are intertwined in political situations.

Finally, in the current debate on peasant insurrections, various Marxist and neo-Marxist (or perhaps more accurately semi-Marxist) approaches have been developed. *Social Origins of Dictatorship and Democracy* (Moore 1966), *Peasant Wars of the Twentieth Century* (Wolf 1969), and *States and Social Revolutions* (Skocpol 1979) all utilize Marxist notions of class conflict, political domination, and control over the means of production to explain why peasant insurrections occur. At least on the surface such approaches do not satisfactorily explain the rebellion in either Darra-i Nur or other areas of Afghanistan. As we have seen, before the April coup the inhabitants of Darra-i Nur viewed the central government as an instrument of Muhammadzai domination. While they suffered for years under this domination, they chose to rebel against a Communist regime that publicly denounced the Muhammadzai, jailed and executed members of the old elite, and embarked on an ambitious land reform policy which broke up estates and distributed the land to previous tenants. It is obvious that focusing an analysis of the Afghan rebellion on this current debate would not only be theoretically enlightening, but might result in a deeper understanding of other peasant rebellions as well.

PART III

QATAGHAN

AND

BADAKHSHAN

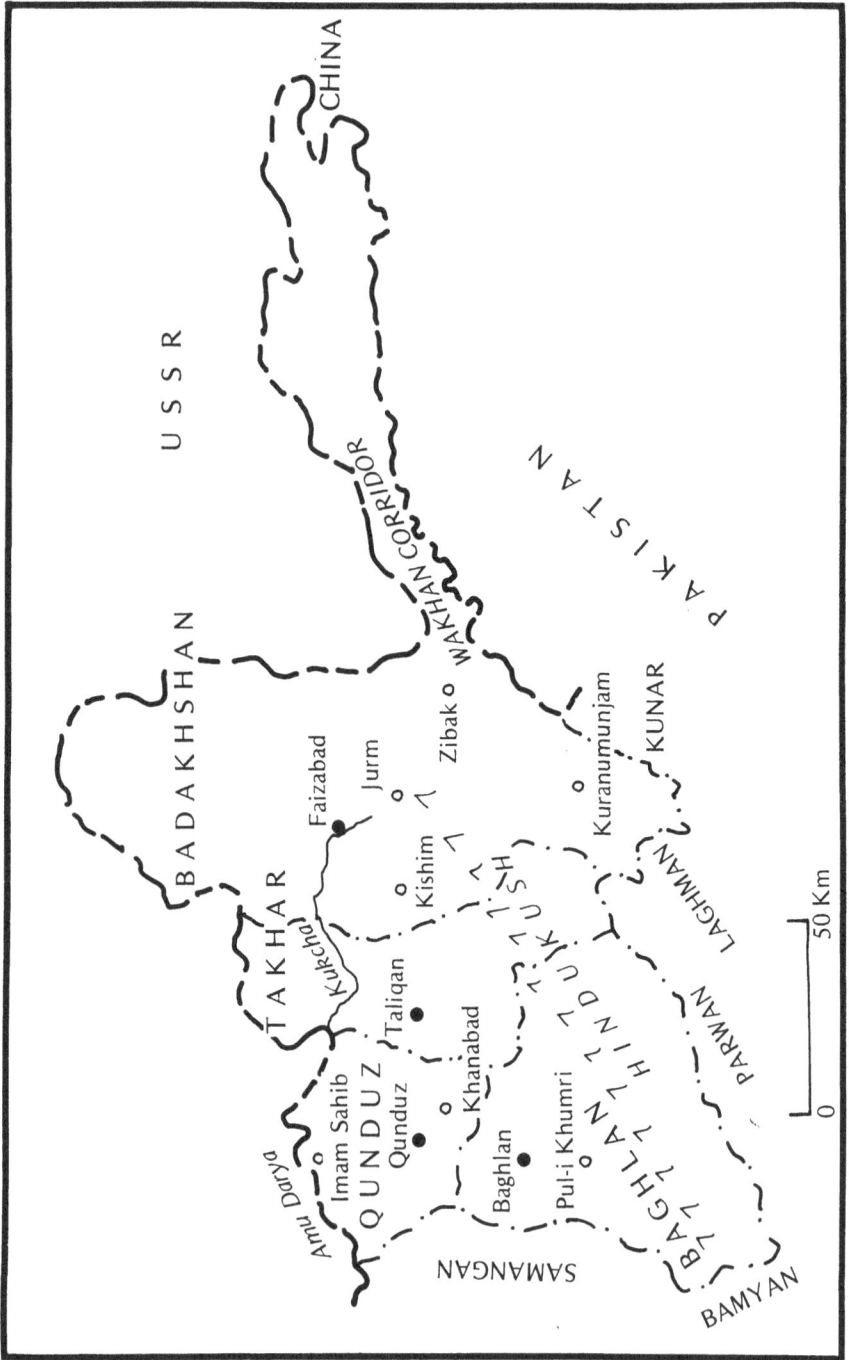

QATAGHAN AND BADAKHSHAN

Chapter 6

CAUSES AND CONTEXT OF RESPONSES TO THE
SAUR REVOLUTION IN BADAKHSHAN

M. Nazif Shahrani

Like in most other parts of Afghanistan, the responses of the peoples of Badakhshan, the extreme northeastern province, to the Soviet-inspired military coup of 7 Saur 1357 A.H. (27 April 1978) and to the December 1979 military invasion and occupation by the Red Army have been far from uniform.* The responses range from active support of the Communist government in Kabul, to passive acceptance of its rule, to an exodus from the area, to armed uprisings challenging the legitimacy of the Marxist regime. It is crucial to our analysis that one understand the causes and motivations behind the different decisions made by various segments of Badakhshan's population in response to national political developments. Particularly important is an explanation of the armed resistance which has flared in Badakhshan against three Kabul governments since 1978. For the first time in nearly one hundred years—i.e., since the consolidation of Kabul rule over Badakhshan—the people of this remote province have taken up arms against the state.[†]

It is argued in this chapter that the responses of the peoples of Badakhshan cannot be explained satisfactorily by focusing solely

---

*The bulk of the information for this chapter was collected through interviews with a large number of *mujahidin* (Islamic freedom fighters) from Badakhshan during a trip to Peshawar and Gilgit, Pakistan, June-August 1980. Also used are data from my earlier field work in Badakhshan (1972-74 and summer 1975) and my personal knowledge.

[†]Before 1979 the last battle in Badakhshan against the central government was fought in 1880 by Mir Alam Khan, the last independent ruler of the province, and lost to Amir 'Abdur Rahman (Alibek 1907: 217-20; Kushkaki 1923: 172; Dupree 1973: 419).

either on current events or on a regional or provincial context; an historical consideration of national political developments is necessary. By focusing only on current events, recent literature has defined the conflict in Afghanistan solely in terms of the *intentions* of the Marxist government (e.g., rapid modernization through radical land reform) or the presumed intentions of the opposition (fighting to retain tribal, ethnic, and regional autonomy or personal wealth and privileges, defense of Islam, etc.).* By so doing, it has obscured what Roderick Aya calls the "political crux of revolutions: namely, an open-ended situation of violent struggle wherein one set of contenders attempts (successfully or unsuccessfully) to displace another from state power" (1979: 40). Therefore, Aya argues that

> intentions and outcomes should be regarded as what they actually are—historical variables—and [one must focus] . . . on the occurrence of revolutionary *situations* of "dual power" or "multiple sovereignty." This means placing the weight of the analysis on, not "states of mind" [or intentions] but basic political processes, social power balances, and contests for control of the state (1979: 40; emphasis in original).†

Viewed in light of Aya's political model, it becomes clear that the conflict in Afghanistan involves, above all else, competition between the ruling party—the Khalq-Parcham, a coalition which came to power with the 1978 coup—and its many opponents for the exclusive control of state power.** In accord with this model, we maintain the following: first, the Afghan resistance movements are primarily

*In politics, Aya states, "Neither the outbreaks nor outcomes are reducible to intentions, both because . . . intentions are notoriously variable in response to changing conditions, and because politics in history is a game with many players, no one of whom calls all the shots all the time" (1979: 48). These assertions certainly ring true of the changing policies of the Afghan Marxist government since 1978.

†The concepts of "dual power" and "multiple sovereignty" come from Leon Trotsky via Charles Tilly and Aya, who defines them as "the fragmentation of governmental authority into two (or more) epicenters, each of which claims exclusive legitimacy, in a territory where only one such violence and taxation monopoly had previously operated" (1979: 44).

**The evolution of the Khalq-Parcham party is discussed by Hugh Beattie in this volume. Khalq is the popular name for the People's Democratic Party of Afghanistan (PDPA).

Islamic political movements and not simply "religious" in nature (see the introduction above); second, the initial force behind the armed resistance and its leadership originated in the major urban centers (*not* the rural areas, as has been frequently claimed), but for tactical reasons the resistance—considered by Afghans to be an Islamic war of liberation, or *jihad*—has been fought to a large extent in the country-side; finally, the principal actors in the struggle for control of political power in this conflict are the newly educated elite (urban and rural, religious and secular), *not* the agrarian tribesmen, peasants, and nomads fighting a central government for their own narrow interests. The role of the peasantry and nomadic populations is crucial insofar as these groups can support or reject the positions of the contending educated elite in the struggle. Within this framework we shall examine and analyze the responses of the peoples of Badakhshan to the Saur Revolution and the Soviet invasion and occupation of Afghanistan.

BADAKHSHAN: HISTORICAL, SOCIETAL, AND POLITICAL CONTEXT

For a comprehensive analysis of responses in Badakhshan we must first briefly examine the following: (a) the geopolitical history of Badakhshan in its regional and national context; (b) the spatial distribution of ethnic groups and the structure of the local political economy; and (c) the local political power structure and shifts within it.

A BRIEF GEOPOLITICAL HISTORY

In the national context Badakhshan is a relatively marginal territory, covering an area of about 40,886 sq. km., much of which is dominated by extremely rough mountainous terrain, interspersed by a large number of deep and narrow river valleys. It is among the least developed areas of Afghanistan—a fact the people of Badakhshan attribute to willful and calculated neglect of the province by the Pashtun-dominated central governments. Badakhshan lacks a modern transportation infrastructure and as a result remains relatively isolated from other parts of the country. In the entire province there are virtually no roads which are usable year round. Motorable roads are limited for the most part to the central areas of the province and generally built and maintained by the local population through corvee labor levied by the government.

There is practically no modern industry in Badakhshan, and no effort has been made to improve either agriculture or animal husbandry. Deposits of gold, iron ore, rubies, sulfur, salt, and lapis lazuli have been reported (Sarwari 1353-54 A.H.: 717-18); however, with the exception of lapis lazuli, none has been commercially exploited to date. Despite the abundance of rivers, no steps have been taken to tap this potential resource for generating hydroelectric power. Instead a limited amount of electricity for the use of government offices in the provincial center is provided by a diesel-run generator.

The best record of central-government service in Badakhshan has been in the field of education. In 1974 the government reported that there were 197 schools for boys and 27 schools for girls in the province—remarkable figures indeed! (Sarwari 1353-54 A.H.: 718).* The government record in the field of health care, however, has been very poor. There is only 1 small hospital and 3 so-called health centers serving an estimated 194,000 (or 170,000) people (Afghan Demographic Studies 1975: 658).† These health-care facilities suffer chronic shortages of both trained personnel and supplies.

Badakhshan is the only province of Afghanistan which borders the Soviet Union (Tajik SSR), the People's Republic of China—PRC (Xinjiang), and Pakistan. Historically the people of Badakhshan have had strong socioeconomic and cultural ties to the Muslim peoples of Russian and Chinese Turkistan, with whom they shared a common cultural history and economic interests. A number of trade and

---

*Of the boys' schools 5 were for grades 1-12, 8 for grades 1-9, 26 for grades 1-6, 21 village schools with 2 teachers each, and 120 village schools with 1 teacher each. Of the girls' schools 1 was for grades 1-12, 4 for grades 1-6, 2 village schools with 2 teachers each, and 18 village schools with 1 teacher each (Sarwari 1353-54 A.H.: 718).

†Population figures reported by the Afghan Demographic Studies are generally based on separate estimates by the Ministries of Agriculture and Interior. These estimates are made in different years for different localities and different purposes. Throughout this chapter I shall first cite the figures of the Ministry of Agriculture and then those of the Ministry of the Interior in parentheses. Adamec (1972) gives a population estimate of 353,000 for Badakhshan, and Ghobar (1967: 11) gives a figure of 316,574.

communication routes passed through Badakhshan to the cities of Bukhara, Samarqand, and Tashkand in Russian Turkistan and to the urban centers of Chinese Turkistan such as Yarkand, Kashghar, and Khutan, as well as to Chitral (Pakistan) and the Indian subcontinent. Large numbers of merchants from urban as well as rural areas of Badakhshan participated in the trade caravans, and some spent many months—or even years—in these and other Central Asian cities. In addition, many young people went to these cities to attend Islamic centers of religious learning, the *madrasah*. In return, Turkistani merchants visited Badakhshan, and many of their pilgrims passed through the province on their way to Mecca. The Bolshevik reconquest of Western Turkistan following the Russian revolution of 1917 and the Chinese Communist takeover of Muslim Eastern Turkistan in 1949, followed by closed border policies of the USSR and PRC in the 1920s and 1950s respectively, have had a significant impact upon the peoples of Badakhshan.

The social, economic, and political consequences of the USSR's and PRC's new policies upon the peoples of Badakhshan varied depending upon the people's degree of involvement in the caravan trade, their educational plans, and their spatial proximity to the two Communist states. The merchant families involved in long-distance trade, religious students, and the communities along the Amu Darya (Oxus River) and in the Wakhan Corridor were most directly affected because the new policies caused them substantial economic and opportunity losses, as well as emotional suffering resulting from the severance of social ties with friends and relatives across the frontiers (for details see Shahrani 1979a). More significant for our purposes is that a very strong and almost universal resentment developed toward the Soviet and Chinese Communists because of what people came to consider their extremely repressive and anti-Islamic policies and activities in Muslim Turkistan. This resentment grew into a bitter hatred—particularly of the Soviets—and was enhanced by two related factors: First, a protracted armed resistance was staged by the Central Asian Muslims during the 1920s and 1930s against Soviet communism (the so-called Basmachi Movement), and some people from Badakhshan and other areas of northern Afghanistan took an active part. Second, sizable communities of Turkistani *muhajirin* (refugees), most of them strongly religious (some *'ulama*—learned religious leaders) came to live in Badakhshan and other northern provinces after fleeing from the Soviets in the 1920s and 1930s (see Shalinsky 1979a). Furthermore, in the early 1960s the people of Badakhshan witnessed the influx of some seven thousand Muslim refugees from Xinjiang province, some of them relatives of Badakhshani caravan traders who had been trapped in the area after the Communist take-over and allowed to leave China only after an agreement had been ne-gotiated between the Chinese and Afghan governments. Most refugees have stressed that there has been a destruction of Islamic institutions in the USSR and PRC and that they had suffered considerably under the Soviet and Chinese Communist regimes.

Many people in Badakhshan feel a strong personal loss over the Soviet occupation of Muslim Turkistan, and their feelings have been strengthened and perpetuated by stories, myths, and proverbs which have become an essential part of the local folklore. For example, it is commonly accepted in many parts of northern Afghanistan that in an effort to indoctrinate Muslim children, the Soviet Communists withheld food and water from them for a long time. When the hungry and thirsty children asked for food and water, their captors told them to ask Allah for them. The children did so, but nothing materi-alized. The Soviets then told them to make the same request of Marx and Lenin. When the children did so, they were given food and water. Moreover, it is commonly believed that as atheists, the Soviets do not recognize any threshold of incest and sleep with their sisters and mothers, and that they have no notion of morality or family propri-ety. Worse yet, they kill old people who are no longer capable of productive work, and from their corpses make soap—a useful product. Local sentiments are best expressed in the Kirghiz saying *"Orustan atang bolsa janingda paltang bolsun"* (If your father was a Russian, carry an axe with you)—i.e., Never trust a Russian, even if he is your father. There is no doubt that the invasion of Afghanistan by the Soviet army has reinforced the worst fears of the people of Badakh-shan.

In short, in geopolitical terms the central government has for the most part extended only perfunctory services to Badakhshan—a treatment which has compounded the province's economic, social, and cultural setbacks following the imposition of the Soviet and Chinese closed border policies. Such treatment has given the people of Badakhshan ample reasons for holding grievances against the gov-ernment in Kabul.

ETHNICITY AND LOCAL POLITICAL ECONOMY

The population of Badakhshan is ethnically very heterogeneous and for the most part spatially defined on the basis of linguistic and/ or sectarian membership. The major linguistic groups are the Uzbeks and Tajiks, together accounting for 166,000 (86 percent)/152,000 (89 percent) of the population. (No breakdown for each group alone is available.) There are six other smaller linguistic groups: 7,000 Wakhi;* 6,000 Shughni; 2,750 Ishkashimi; 2,350 (or 6,480) Kurani and Munjani combined; and 2,000 Zibaki. The Uzbeks are all Sunni. Most Tajiks are adherents to Sunni Islam; a very small number are Shi'a (Imami) believers. With the exception of Kurani, who are Sunni, the so-called "Mountain Tajiks"—the Wakhi, Shughni, Ishkashimi, Zibaki, and Munjani—are followers of the Isma'ili sect of Shi'a Islam.

Two other linguistic minority groups in Badakhshan are the Kirghiz and Pashtun, both of whom are Sunni. The Kirghiz (about 2,000 people) occupy the agriculturally marginal high Pamir valleys in the Wakhan Corridor. The Pashtun (no population estimate available) are a powerful minority who have traditionally either enjoyed the support of the central government, or have represented it in the area. There are two types of Pashtun communities: nomads, who bring their herds to graze in parts of Badakhshan's highlands every summer, and colonies in major towns and administrative centers consisting of landed nouveau riche, a few shopkeepers, and military and civilian government officials.†

Ecologically the central districts and subdistricts (*wuluswali* and *alaqadari*)—Jurm, Baharak, Faizabad, Kishim, Shahri Buzurg, Ragh, and (to a lesser extent) Khawhan and Darwaz—are relatively fertile. In these areas the river valleys are wider and range in elevation from

*Figure based on my field observations. The Afghan Demographic Studies give figures of 4,293 and 1,965. Total figures for the province include small populations of Kirghiz and Pashtun (discussed below).

†Despite Newell and Newell's claim that "Faizabad, the capital of Badakhshan province, had become largely a Pashtun settlement in the twentieth century" (1981: 101), no town in Badakhshan—or village, for that matter—is numerically dominated by the Pashtun. Demographically their numbers in Badakhshan are insignificant. They are powerful only in the political scheme of things and only in circumstances that involve government.

about 3,500 feet in the valley bottoms to 7,000-8,000 feet on the upper reaches. There is sufficient precipitation in these areas for *lalmi* (dry farming) and often river and stream water for irrigated cultivation. Higher mountain reaches provide pasture for sheep and goats. Thus mixed agriculture and herding are the bases of a subsistence economy. These central areas are occupied by the Sunni Uzbek and Tajik majority, living in about 680 compact villages and a few small towns (see Afghan Demographic Studies 1975: 658-719). The few Shiʻa Tajiks are generally found in the same area, but often tucked away in the less favorable upper reaches of the river valleys. With the exception of occasional droughts, agriculture is reliable, and productivity, even in lalmi areas, reasonably good. There is very little concentration of land in the hands of landlords, either absentee or in situ. By far the greatest majority of farmers are freeholders of the type often referred to as the middle peasantry.*

In contrast to the central areas, the peripheral districts and subdistricts of Badakhshan, such as Kuranumunjan, Zibak, Ishkashim, Shughnan, and Wakhan, are extremely marginal agricultural areas and less favorable for human habitation. These areas are high valley environments, ranging for the most part well above 8,000 feet at the valley bottoms to about 11,500 feet at the upper limits of cultivation. In these areas dry farming is not possible and laborious irrigation farming in meager, terraced areas with porous soil is always hampered by a short growing season and frost damage. It is in these areas, in about 180 scattered hamlets along the upland streams, that the various

---

*The size of landholdings varies considerably from region to region in Afghanistan. In the absence of reliable statistics, even the estimates on what may be considered a small or large holding differ among the specialists. Roy (1981) has suggested the following breakdowns on landholdings (see also Etienne 1972):

Category of Landowner	Size of Landholding	Percent of Population
Large landholder	500 jiribs (250 acres)[a]	Less than .01%
Rich peasant	50 jiribs (25 acres)	25
Middle peasant	10-20 jiribs (5-10 acres)	50
Poor and landless peasant	10 jiribs (5 acres) or less	25

[a]I assume this refers to irrigated single-crop land or its equivalent.

In Badakhshan the middle peasantry would make up more than 70 percent of the population, while the rich and poor may be represented equally in the province. Large landholders are unheard of. For a somewhat different distribution of land ownership, see H. Smith et al. 1973: xxxvi.

Mountain Tajiks live. They are barely able to eke out a living from the barren land and suffer greatly from the long, harsh winters. While most households own land, they are very often unable to earn enough from mixed cultivation and herding to satisfy their needs. As a result, many of them serve as seasonal agricultural laborers in the central areas of the province (for details on Wakhan, see Shahrani 1979a).

In addition to the hardships of land and climate, the Mountain Tajiks have suffered from isolation, discrimination, and exploitation by the majority Sunni Uzbek and Tajik groups, as well as by the larger Sunni Afghan society. With minor exceptions the minimal help extended by the central government to the province has not penetrated beyond the central districts. (One exception is the presence of schools in these areas—a recent development except in Shughnan, which has had a school for a long time.)* Discrimination against these groups is rampant in every conceivable area of social interaction. Moreover, they are exploited through their seasonal labor, in trade and exchange of goods and services, by credit terms in the markets, and—most commonly—through the sale of opium because these groups are habitual users.

The Sunni majority in central Badakhshan self-righteously argues that its discriminatory attitudes toward the Isma'ilis are justified since the Isma'ilis are not true Muslims, having no 'ulama, madrasahs, or (worst of all) mosques—i.e., places of public worship with *azan* and *iqamat* (calls for prayers).† Sunni accusations against the Isma'ilis

---

*A primary school was established in Shughnan at about the same time as in the central districts of the province—very probably owing to help from some influential Shughnis in Kabul. During the later part of the nineteenth century the entire family of Yusuf Ali Shah, the *mir* (local chief) of Shughnan, was forcibly moved and resettled in Kabul. Later some Shughni youth were sent to the Kabul court as *ghulam bachas* (page boys) by Shughni elders. These boys were educated (often in the military academy), and some were appointed to influential positions in Kabul. Indeed a descendent of one of them, General Muhammad Ali, served as the Chief Commander of Kabul Police in the 1960s (see Kushkaki 1923: 336-41).

†While it is true that there are no Ismaili-maintained mosques in the Isma'ili territories, there is a Sunni-maintained mosque in each district center which serves the needs of the local government administrators and traders. Given the dispersed settlement pattern necessitated by the local ecology, it is impossible for each community to either build or maintain such an establishment. This fact, I believe, is either not understood by the Sunni majority, or conveniently overlooked.

are neither totally false nor entirely accurate, but the sociological outcome is the same. Needless to say, accusations and feelings of contempt are reciprocated by the Isma'ili communities.

LOCAL POLITICAL POWER STRUCTURE

Before 1880 Badakhshan was an independent, strife-torn area where numerous *mirs* (local chiefs; Tajik word) claimed domain over different valleys and fought each other incessantly. For the most part, they were forced to pay tribute in slaves and goods and services to the mirs of Faizabad (now the capital of Badakhshan) or to khans (local chiefs; Uzbek word) of Central Asia to the north of the Amu Darya. In addition, Badakhshan was under attack from the Uzbek khans of Qataghan, and on occasion the local mirs were made vassals of the Khanate of Qunduz.

During the reign of 'Abdur Rahman (1880-1901), Badakhshan was conquered and incorporated into Afghanistan. Most of the powerful mirs were either killed or taken to Kabul as prisoners. The population of the province was disarmed and its weapons confiscated by the amir. For the first few years after the conquest, a few weak but loyal mirs were appointed as *hakims* (district officers) of their own or neighboring territories, while others were given military ranks and annual salaries. Long before the end of the amir's reign, however, all of the local mirs were stripped of their privileges, and their government positions were given to both Pashtun and non-Pashtun officials sent from Kabul (see Kushkaki 1923). Many other local leaders were eliminated from the scene by means of imprisonment or internal exile—a practice continued by later regimes until well into the 1950s. Therefore, by the turn of the century the local aristocracy had been completely neutralized and replaced by a centrally appointed bureaucracy or eliminated. Like many other parts of Afghanistan, Badakhshan was left without any effective traditional local leadership above the village level.

At the village level the central government introduced the institution of *arbab* or *qaryadar* (village headman), who was elected by the adult males of a village; upon approval of the hakim, the arbab represented the village to the local administration. Until the early 1970s the principal attraction of the office of arbab in Badakhshan villages was *chiqin*, small amounts of cash or goods collected by the arbab either from village households to provide hospitality to visiting officials (with unused goods going to the arbab), or from individuals who used his services in dealing with the government. Frequently when either a village as a whole or a large number of its households engaged in an illicit activity—such as growing opium poppies—the arbab, in collusion with local officials, could demand large sums of money to keep the illicit activity a "secret." However, opportunities for abuse were usually limited, and the job of arbab was considered less than pleasant or honorable by most villagers. By the early 1970s some villages had difficulty finding people to run for the position, so they were forced to hire an arbab at an annual salary, like they hired the village *mirab* (water watchman) or *padawan* (cattle herder). The loyalties of a salaried arbab are to his village; thus the state's links to Badakhshan villages have become very tenuous. (For another account of arbabs, see the chapter by Thomas Barfield in this volume.)

The government treats the villages as important only for such purposes as tax collection, conscription, and corvee labor, and this treatment has strengthened the internal cohesion and cooperation of the villages. As a collective entity, one village rarely has formal political ties with another such entity, although a great many individual kinship and economic ties exist among members of neighboring villages. Most villages in Badakhshan are essentially kin-based communities. As a result, a more important village leadership structure than that of the arbab is operative. Based on kinships, it is headed by village elders called *aqsaqal* or *rish safed* (literally "white beard" in Uzbek and Tajik respectively). Achieving the status of village elder generally entails a certain amount of wealth, good moral standing, and a sense of justice and fairness (among other things), as well as seniority within a kinship group. Most village disputes never leave the village and are resolved or managed with the help of the aqsaqal.*

The religious establishment in Badakhshan, as in other parts of the country, consists of the 'ulama (*mawlawis* and *mullahs*) and the *ruhani* (religious dignitaries), locally referred to as *pir, shah, hazrat, makhdum,* and *ishan.* Unlike in the areas to the south of the Hindu Kush, the religious establishment in Badakhshan did not gain significant political power during the nineteenth century—probably because

---

*One of the major complaints I heard from government officials during my research in Wakhan was that there was very little for them to do.

the area was not under a direct threat of Western colonial penetration, and hence did not need a jihad. The religious establishment in Badakhshan was spared 'Abdur Rahman's wrath since it was weak and nonthreatening.

Both the structure and organization of the religious establishment and relations between religious leaders and followers vary substantially among Isma'ili and Sunni communities in Badakhshan. As mentioned above, the Isma'ili communities have no 'ulama and lack such religious establishments as mosques and madrasahs. However, they have important ruhani whom they call shahs (or pirs). The shahs claim to be either *sayyids* (those who claim descent from the Prophet Muhammad) or *khujahs* (those who claim descent from one of the first three caliphs of Islam—Abu Bakr, Umar, or Usman), and as such they form a distinct group whose members intermarry only with each other and acknowledge a rank order among themselves. In principle they acknowledge the supreme authority of the Isma'ili world leader, the Aga Khan. Each shah appoints his own *khalifah* (representative) in villages where he has followers. The khalifah officiates in village rituals and collects *'ushr*, a tithe paid annually by the disciples of a shah on all forms of income (including harvest, livestock, wages, and even labor). Through their khalifahs, the shahs exercise enormous influence over the daily lives of their followers. Their moral authority is absolute and pervasive. In addition, like the aqsaqals, they are instrumental in resolving village disputes. Yet despite their enormous moral authority and economic power, the shahs have been politically very timid and nonassertive in their relations with state officials. In many instances the shahs themselves have become prey to greedy and corrupt hakims, *qazis* (judges), and the military officers (*kamisars* and *sarhadars*) of the frontier guard detachments (which are independent of district administration).

Nothing comparable to the theocratic organization of the Isma'ili communities can be found among the Sunni Uzbeks and Tajiks, although these groups recognize at least two categories of religious dignitaries. The first comprises what are variously called ishan, hazrat, or pir. These individuals or families are considered to be descendants of a famous *wali* (an accomplished Sufi, a "saint.").* They generally

---

*For a brief history of the Sufis, see the chapter by Robert Canfield, p. 217n. below.

live in towns, district centers, or the provincial capital. The tomb of their great Sufi ancestor is located either in the family compound or nearby and is considered a *ziyarat* or *mazar* (holy shrine). Usually a male member of the household is believed to be endowed with special powers to cure illnesses and may be approached for amulets. Members of the family make an annual round of the mosques in villages where they have traditional followings to collect contributions (*nazr*). One of their main services to their village disciples is to maintain a large guest house where the villagers are always welcome during their visits to a town, district center, or provincial capital. Since they live in the vicinity of government offices, some members of these families make a point of establishing good relations with officials and assume the role of mediators or powerbrokers between the officials and their village followers. The strength of their ties with the rural population varies, but their influence and moral authority over them is undeniable. Ishans, hazrats, and pirs often intermarry and cooperate with each other, so the potential exists for them to form coalitions. However, there is no evidence that they are linked with other such dignitaries outside of Badakhshan.

The second category consists of important living walis of the Naqshbandi order. These individuals live in both towns and villages, and in most cases they are trained Islamic scholars—mullahs or mawlawis. Some of these walis are also called pirs, and these are sought out by *murids* (disciples) from both villages and towns. Murids include a wide spectrum of the population—for example, peasants, artisans, merchants, teachers, students, and some government officials. The pirs' relations with their murids are strictly religious and spiritual and strictly diadic. As a matter of principle both the leaders and followers stay clear of local political issues. Unlike the historically militant Naqshbandi movements to the north of the Amu Darya, the Sufi orders of Badakhshan have been neither militant nor political. Unlike the pirs of the first category, these pirs do not dabble in mediation or powerbrokerage, and as a rule political problems are not taken to them. The size of a pir's following varies depending upon his fame for spiritual achievements and the amount of *fayz* or *barakat* (grace) one is likely to be embued with in his presence. Most pirs acknowledge each other, and some may have leader-follower ties with each other. In some instances murids of the same pir may form mutual help groups. In such instances factors of residence, kinship, and the like may be instrumental rather than their ties to the pir. Despite the strong spiritual content of the networks of pirs and murids, their potential for political mobilization for a common goal is undeniable. (For a different description of pir networks, see Robert Canfield's chapter in this volume.)

A group of religious leaders which is far more active educationally and politically at the local level is the mawlawis and mullahs (the 'ulama), anchored in the mosques, madrasahs, and government schools. Badakhshan has had a very strong tradition of religious education among the Sunni Uzbeks and Tajiks. Madrasahs and mawlawis are regarded by most authorities on Afghanistan as urban phenomena, while village mosques are manned by either "illiterate mullahs" or an "old man with no special training who has achieved his position [as mullah] because of piety" (Roy 1981: 49; see also L. Dupree 1966: 270 and 1967). Whatever truth these statements may have elsewhere in Afghanistan, they are not strictly true in Badakhshan. For example, both madrasahs and mawlawis are found in a large number of villages. In one small valley containing 12 villages with some 600 households, there are 6 mawlawis and 3 madrasahs with a total of 40 students in residence at a given time. Such figures are not unusual in comparable Sunni areas of the province. Most large villages (over 150 households) have mosques which offer Friday prayers and have a madrasah attached to them. In many village mosques a mawlawi is hired as *mullah imam* (prayer leader).

The educational role of the 'ulama is by no means limited to madrasahs. Their main educational role is as teachers to the adult males of their community. As a rule village mullahs are not highly educated—most have about five years of traditional Islamic education—but they are as competent in their field as the village schoolteachers are in theirs. In fact, contrary to Richard Newell's contention (1980: 253) that the creation of government schools reduced the educational role of the rural mullah, many mullahs were hired as teachers in the new secular schools; during the winter months, when the government schools are in recess, the village mullahs continue to instruct the youth in traditional Islamic courses.

Politically mawlawis and mullahs act in concert with village aqsaqals to resolve local disputes. Even in cases where disputes are taken to qazis in the government courts, the disputants will consult mawlawis in madrasahs at the administrative centers. As noted, on many occasions the religious and secular powerbrokers will attempt to settle cases out of court. Generally the intervention of such mediators is preferred for two reasons: in most instances they do not expect payment, and the court system is corrupt and run by "outsiders"—mostly Pashtuns.

Relationships between the mawlawis and mullahs and the general public are respectful and very intimate. Contrary to the assertions of many Afghan specialists, only the very poorly educated mullahs are the object of jokes. The 'ulama exert considerable influence in local political processes by virtue of their moral standing in the community. Although government bureaucracy has systematically attempted to exclude them from taking part in public issues, the attempts have been only partially successful. The power of the mawlawis and mullahs, although very diffused and very much localized, remains potent.

SHIFTS IN THE LOCAL POWER STRUCTURE: THE EFFECTS OF EDUCATION

Traditional political leaders, both religious and secular, had usually chosen a strategy of avoidance rather than confrontation regarding the state. However, the introduction of government schools in the province began to alter not only the structure of local politics, but also the attitudes toward the state itself. The first modern school was established in Faizabad in the latter part of 1930. In the early 1940s others were opened in Kishim, Jurm, Baharak, Shahran-i Khash, Darwaz, and Shughnan. All these schools had very modest beginnings, but by the 1950s, when foreign aid money became available, the school at Faizabad was elevated to a *mutawasitah* (grades 1-9) and the others to *ibtidaiya* (grades 1-6). The graduates of these schools were sent to Kabul, mainly to vocational boarding schools for teacher training, agriculture, Islamic studies, technology, and industrial arts and crafts.* Beginning in 1958 students from Badakhshan were admitted to the military high school in Kabul as well. Vocational high schools compared very poorly in respect to educational facilities with

*The government eventually provided high school education in most of the district centers and several large villages. In addition, a teacher-training high school with boarding facilities was opened in Faizabad in the early 1970s.

the elitist high schools in Kabul. Thus the great majority of graduates from these vocational schools were not allowed to attend the university; the few who were were admitted to only a limited number of colleges and departments.

The composition of students from Badakhshan who attended schools in Kabul was mixed economically and to a degree ethnically, with the largest proportion being Sunni Uzbeks and Tajiks from towns and villages in the central districts. A substantial number of these students returned to Badakhshan to teach in the expanding educational system during the 1960s and 1970s. Some entered the lower ranks of the government bureaucracy, and a few who went to the university remained in Kabul.

By the early 1960s there were several hundred students, teachers, professors, and bureaucrats from Badakhshan living in Kabul. Many of them became actively involved in the national political movements of the 1960s and 1970s, and soon political ideologies and organizations were taken into the province. Three such individuals—Mansur Hashimi, Tahir Badakhshi, and Burhanuddin Rabbani—played leading roles in both the national and provincial movements. These three individuals and their followers represent the full spectrum of political ideologies and organizational developments in Badakhshan, both before and after the 1978 coup. Hashimi, Badakhshi, and Rabbani each have a significantly different perception of provincial and national problems, and (not surprisingly) their proposed solutions vary markedly. Their particular social and economic backgrounds and educational and career experiences are highly instructive, not only as sources of their personal ideological commitment, but as a reflection of the dilemma that the educated elite in Afghanistan—particularly the provincial and rural elite—has come to experience. A brief biographical discussion of each of these men will illustrate the development of political groups in Badakhshan as well as the nature of their ties with national movements.

Mansur Hashimi is the son of a wealthy Sunni Tajik farmer from a village in Jurm district. He was among the early graduates of an ibtidaija school who was sent to Kabul to continue his education. Upon graduating from Kabul Teachers Training High School, he was admitted to the Faculty of Science at Kabul University. During his freshman year he was given a scholarship by the government to study physics at the American University in Beirut (AUB)—the first student from Badakhshan to go overseas for higher education. He studied at AUB from 1955-60, then returned to the Faculty of Science at Kabul University and completed a B.S. degree. He was appointed a physics teacher at the Kabul Teachers Training High School at the time Hafizullah Amin, who became president of Afghanistan in 1979, was principal.* In 1961 he was transferred to the newly created Institute of Education, which was organized and maintained by the U.S. Agency for International Development (AID). Through the institute he was sent in 1963 to Columbia Teachers College, where he completed an M.A. program in science education in 1965. In the United States Hashimi and Amin met again and began to develop a friendship based on a common leftist ideology (see Adamec 1979).

On his return from the United States Hashimi joined the Khalq party and began actively recruiting among high school and university students and low-level bureaucrats from the northern provinces in general and Badakhshan in particular. He married the daughter of a mawlawi from Jurm who had been a deputy minister of justice in Kabul. His political activities met with nominal success among students from Faizabad, a few of his relatives by marriage, several teachers and students from Shughnan district, and some individuals from his own village. In 1965 and 1969 he made bids for election to the Wulusi Jirgah, the Afghan Lower House of Parliament, as representative of Jurm district, but his ideological interest in communism and his membership in the Khalq party were against him, and he was overwhelmingly defeated both times by a candidate with little education but from an influential Hazrat family. Hashimi remained faithful to Amin and the Khalq party even though the party was torn by dissension and splintering, but the great majority of his early recruits from Badakhshan and the northern provinces did not. Overall he kept few followers, mostly in Kabul. There were only four or five known Khalq party members in Badakhshan—all teachers. Neither Hashimi nor his followers were taken seriously in Badakhshan, where they were frequently the object of jokes. Hashimi lacked both leadership qualities and ideological sophistication. His only redeeming

*At that time I was a student at Kabul Teachers Training High School, and I believe Hashimi and Amin then had very little in common: Amin was a strong supporter of the government and an avid, blatant Pashtun chauvinist.

quality—loyalty—paid off when he was appointed Minister of Water and Power (1978-79) in the governments of Nur M. Taraki and Amin.

Tahir Badakhshi is from Faizabad. His father was a former *wakil* (deputy to the provincial council), and the family owned considerable land and had strong rural connections. Badakhshi attended the muta-wasitah school at Faizabad and after finishing it was sent by his family to Kabul to attend one of the most elite non-vocational high schools (Habibiah). During his years in Kabul (in the late 1950s) he chose to express his strong ethnic and regional identity by wearing clothing made only in Badakhshan and strictly avoiding the use of foreign goods. He conducted himself with a high degree of religiosity. He married a girl from Faizabad when he was still in high school.

After finishing high school, Badakhshi entered the Faculty of Law and Political Science at Kabul University. There, in the early 1960s, he abandoned his self-imposed restrictions on foreign products and began wearing foreign clothes and using foreign goods. However, he did not abandon his strong ethnic and regional identity. Instead he began to question the backwardness of Badakhshan, and in social gatherings of students from the province in Kabul he enthusiastically discussed the need to change the lot of the people of Badakhshan. In 1965 Badakhshi joined the Khalq party—it is not clear whether Hashimi was instrumental in his recruitment—and soon thereafter was a member of the Central Committee of the PDPA (Halliday 1978: 28). When the initial split occurred between the Khalq and Parcham factions in 1967, Badakhshi sided with the Parcham faction of Babrak Karmal rather than the Khalq faction of Taraki and Amin—perhaps for both personal and ideological reasons. For one thing, he had divorced his wife—an act that cost him a good number of friends—and married a sister of Sultan Ali Kishtmand, a high-ranking Hazarah member of the Parcham faction and prime minister in the Karmal regime (1979-present). For another, he found the composition of the Parcham faction more acceptable because it had fewer Pashtuns and less of the Pashtun chauvinism so obvious in Amin and the Khalq faction.

By the late 1960s Badakhshi had drifted away from the Parcham faction, accusing both it and the Khalq of being "agents of the Pashtun ruling class." He formed his own party, the Sitami Milli

(Against National Oppression), whose main ideological emphases were a Maoist-type revolution, in which the peasants would be given local power in the countryside, and on countrywide mobilization of minority populations to combat internal colonialism by the Pashtuns (particularly in the northern provinces). Badakhshi considered that the Soviets were aiding Pashtun dominance and exploitation of the non-Pashtuns; hence his dislike of the Soviets. Another national Communist faction, Shu'la-i Jawid, already held a Maoist line, but Sitami Milli's stance against Pashtun colonialism was new, so the group caught on quickly. By all accounts, it had established a remarkably good organization in Kabul, with branches in most provinces in the north—particularly Qunduz, Baghlan, Takhar, and Badakhshan. In Badakhshan it found its strongest support in Faizabad, Darwaz, and (to a lesser extent) the towns of Jurm and Baharak. Its membership of educated people increased considerably during the later years of the presidency of Muhammad Daoud. Prior to the 1978 coup its active members were estimated at over three hundred, with large numbers of sympathizers among shopkeepers and townspeople.*

Burhanuddin Rabbani, also from Faizabad, is a Sunni Tajik from a respectable religious household. He attended school in Faizabad, very probably as a classmate of Badakhshi's. However, his family is not as affluent as Badakhshi's, so after finishing the ninth grade, Rabbani was sent to Paghman, a small town near Kabul, to attend a government-run madrasah and then to the Faculty of Islamic Law and Theology at Kabul University. Upon graduating in 1963, he was hired by the faculty for the teaching staff and later sent to Al-Azhar University in Cairo, where he earned an M.A. degree in Islamic

*Halliday claims that during a worsening of Afghan-Pakistan and Chinese-Soviet relations after Daoud's rise to power in 1973, "a group of Settami Melli [sic.] militants were given military training by [Prime Minister Zulfikar Ali] Bhutto in Peshawar . . . and sent back to Afghanistan," where they staged sporadic military attacks against government installations in Panjsher and Badakhshan in summer 1975 (1978: 28). Whether or not Sitami Milli members received military training in Peshawar, they certainly were not the instigators of attacks in Panjsher in 1975. Credit for those attacks is claimed by Gulbudin Hikmatyar's Hizb-i Islami group. The incident in Badakhshan to which Halliday refers occurred in Darwaz and was the outcome of a personal grudge held by a Sitami Milli member against a district officer; it was not politically motivated (personal information).

philosophy (1966-68). On his return to Kabul he resumed his teaching position at the faculty.

Rabbani is a prolific writer and translator. His articles and translations from Arabic sources—particularly those of Sayyid Qutb, an Egyptian Islamic revolutionary scholar—were published continuously in the late 1960s and early 1970s in several journals of various government ministries and colleges of Kabul University. In addition, he was a regular contributor to the newspaper *Badakhshan*. In 1970, when Rabbani was teaching at the Faculty of Islamic Law and Theology, it inaugurated its own monthly journal, *Shara'iyat*, with Rabbani as editor.

Most of Rabbani's writing is politically motivated. In recent biographies on him, it has been stated that a small number of professors of the Faculty of Islamic Law and Theology had formed the nucleus of an Islamic movement as early as 1957 and that Rabbani became a member of this group at its inception (see Jamiat-i Islami [JIA] N.D.f.: 10, and Editors of *Mirror of Jehad* 1982b: 16-18). Whatever his earlier political involvements in Afghanistan, his two years at Al-Azhar University, at a time when Egyptian Ikhwan al-Muslimin (Muslim Brotherhood) groups were under attack by President Gamal Abdul Nasser under the influence of the USSR, heightened his awareness and political commitment. By 1968 Kabul University was extremely politicized, and Communist political groups were hard at work. Alarmed by the Communist agitations and the government's lack of response, Rabbani and a number of his colleagues began to organize an Islamic opposition. By 1969 an Islamic political action group had been formed with one of Rabbani's senior colleagues, Professor Ghulam Muhammad Niyazi, as nominal leader (*amir*).[*] Called Jawanani Musulman (Muslim Youth), the organization was better known as Ikhwan al-Muslimin.[†] Many students in the university and high schools were recruited and committees organized. Rabbani is said to have gone to Badakhshan in 1969 and organized the initial cell of the group there with fifteen recruits from Faizabad—mostly teachers and high school students. Indeed substantial membership

---

[*]For details of Niyazi and his role as founder of the Islamic movement in Afghanistan, see a series of articles in JIA 1359-60 A.H. Also see Rahman and Qureshi 1981: 71-78.

[†]Jawanan-i Musulman changed its name to Jamiat-i Islami in 1978.

gains were made among the educated elite—students, teachers, administrators—throughout the Sunni central area of Badakhshan.

From the beginning Jawanani Musulman's opposition was directed against both the state and Communist groups. It staged numerous demonstrations against the Khalq-Parcham and other leftist groups. In 1972 Rabbani was elected amir, apparently with Niyazi's blessing. The group increased its political opposition to the government especially after a coup in 1973, when Daoud came to power with the help of the Parcham faction. Daoud retaliated harshly and sent many of the group's leaders to jail. Some, including Rabbani, went underground and reemerged outside the country. The group's organization among educated youth in Badakhshan apparently continued; Rabbani maintained mail contact with them from a self-imposed exile, first in Saudi Arabia and later in Pakistan.

Before the 1978 coup the educated youth of Badakhshan, like those of Kabul, were highly politicized and factionalized, both in school and outside. In schools relations among members of different political groups had become very tense in the 1970s. Within the school administration, promotions, course assignments, and teacher placement were all affected by political allegiances. Even student grades were influenced. The local population was aware of these political differences among the educated youth but for the most part ignored them, believing the power of the state to be indestructible. The situation changed substantially, however, when the Marxists took power.

RESPONSES IN BADAKHSHAN TO THE SAUR REVOLUTION

The initial reaction in Badakhshan to the Khalq-Parcham coup was no different than in other parts of the country: jubiliation on the part of the leftists, dismay on the part of the Islamic activists, and little reaction from the majority. The coalition in Kabul apparently carried over into the countryside, and for a time Khalqis, Parchamis, and Sitami Milli (who joined the coalition after the coup) worked together. During the first few months the Khalq party membership rose to about two hundred among the educated Badakhshanis. The new members were mostly urbanites from district centers, a few with rural backgrounds from the central districts, and substantial numbers from the peripheries, especially Shughnan, where peasants reportedly joined as well. During this period, Tahir Badakhshi was appointed president of the Publications Department of the Ministry of Education, and several other Badakshanis were given middle-rank bureaucratic positions in various ministries, especially the Ministry of Water and Power, which (as noted) was headed by Mansur Hashimi.

The first passive but symbolically significant negative reaction in the province came from the Kirghiz. In June 1978 Haji Rahman Qul, the Kirghiz khan, sent his eldest son to Faizabad to get news. His son returned with the message that the government was Communist and under the influence of the Soviets. With this information and his own analysis of radio news reports, Haji Rahman Qul, together with some elders of the Kirghiz, decided in mid-August to take refuge in Pakistan. By the end of August their exodus was complete. Probably the first Afghan refugees from the Saur Revolution, they were motivated by what they perceived as a direct Soviet threat from across the border rather than a serious threat from within Afghanistan.*

The first major armed disturbance in Badakhshan did not occur until almost a year after the 1978 coup and was directly linked to a purge of Parchami and Sitami Milli members from the government by the Khalq faction. In April 1979 about seventy or eighty Sitami Milli—mostly educated youth from Badakhshan and a few from Takhar province—attacked the army post in Baharak. Apparently they had contacts inside the army base: their attack was successful, and they captured the Baharak subdistrict center, taking some arms and ammunition. The army retaliated brutally: some forty members of the group were quickly captured and killed, and others were caught later and executed as *ashrar* (riffraff or reactionaries), a term used in reference to all anti-government forces.

This initial armed rebellion increased repression in the province by the Khalq regime. The government appointed Hashimi "Commander of the Revolutionary Defense Forces" in the northern provinces, and he set up three types of defense units:

---

*The Kirghiz exodus was justified on the same grounds as their earlier flights from the USSR and PRC (see Shahrani 1979a and 1981a).

1. Sazman (Organization)—largely middle school and high school students serving as police and intelligence units;

2. Watan Parast (Patriots)—recruited from among the illiterate masses by means of draft or levy on villages; given large quantities of small arms and some basic training to defend their own areas;

3. Defa-i Inqilab (Defense of the Revolution)—mainly teachers who coordinated the activities of the other two units.

These defense efforts were accompanied by mass imprisonments, torture, and murder of suspected "enemies" of the revolution. Hundreds of respected local 'ulama, ruhani, teachers, and pious individuals were drowned in the Kukcha River, a major tributary of the Amu Darya. In August 1980 the number of executions alone was estimated by many mujahidin from Badakhshan to be as high as three thousand. Hashimi is said to have ordered all of the executions and to have witnessed some of them. He publicly accused and ridiculed very respected, pious men, calling them (for example) agents of imperialism.

In parts of Badakhshan a great deal of repression accompanied the heavy-handed implementation of the Khalq government's programs for land reform and adult education. The alleged land reform apparently benefited only the relatives and friends of Hashimi and other party officials, while people were angered by demands that older women attend adult education classes. Furthermore, the impact of the reform efforts was magnified by a rather ill-timed census effort by the government. Much of the conduct of Hashimi and Communist officials shocked the Badakhshanis, yet they took no immediate action.

Members of Jawanani Musulman—now Jamiat-i Islami (JIA)—had begun to organize outside the towns and establish ties with the traditional 'ulama and villagers. Many group members were schoolteachers in remote villages; they were assigned by the government to take the census as well as to teach adult education classes—situations which provided them ample opportunities to raise the awareness of the villagers as to the nature and intent of the government in Kabul. By early 1979 the group had reestablished contact with Rabbani in Peshawar and had sent some members to meet with him. Peshawar had become JIA's headquarters.

The conditions for rebellion were ripe, and the rebellion began when a member of JIA, 'Abdul Basir, who was teaching in the Kuran subdistrict—which has lapis lazuli mines—organized a group of 'ulama and peasants and initiated an armed uprising on 2 Saratan 1358 A.H. (23 June 1979) that spread through the province in a matter of weeks.* The uprising was successful; the *alaqadar* (subdistrict officer) was killed and some arms and ammunition taken. It is important to note that the decision to initiate the rebellion in Kuran was a well-calculated tactical move. The area has no motorable roads and therefore is not readily accessible to the government's mechanized forces. More significantly, the people of Kuran are the best armed in Badakhshan because they have been smuggling lapis lazuli for several decades, and the possession of arms has been essential to their activities.

News of the attack was sent to Peshawar, and JIA dispatched seventy mujahidin to Kuran, mostly Badakhshanis and Nuristanis. As the mujahidin began to move toward Jurm, they met with success against both the regular army and a militia Hashimi had mobilized. (He had been able to garner recruits from only two areas in the province—the Khash Valley between Jurm and Faizabad, where his own native village lies, and from the Isma'ili Shi'a areas.) Large numbers of the militia were apparently wiped out in a series of confrontations, and in less than ten days the mujahidin captured Jurm, swelling their ranks, heightening morale, and acquiring quantities of arms and ammunition from the Communists. Within days after the capture of Jurm, there were armed attacks on government facilities in every part of the province. In every instance the local members of JIA took charge of organizing armed units and led them into battle. In addition, they established local committees for the administration of justice and maintenance of order in liberated areas.

Very early in the rebellion the battle lines in Badakhshan were drawn rather clearly on the basis of linguistic/sectarian allegiances. Armed rebellion against the Khalq regime and the Sitami Milli was pervasive throughout the central Uzbek and Tajik areas, but there was virtually no uprising in the peripheral areas of the Isma'ili minority groups. The militia recruited by Hashimi quickly disintegrated. I was

---

*In September 1981 JIA (1981) reported that 'Abdul Basir was commander of the mujahidin forces in Badakhshan.

told by mujahidin from the Khash Valley that most of the people who joined the militia were convinced they were going to fight foreign soldiers (American, Chinese, Pakistani) who were about to invade their villages—only to find themselves confronting people from the next valley.

Since the beginning of the rebellion, the battle lines have not changed. The Isma'ili population near the Soviet borders has either sided with the government or accepted the new order without resistance. For this reason the media have reported that the Wakhan Corridor has been annexed by the Soviet Union. Most of the Kirghiz who could leave the area have done so, the Wakhi have not rebelled, and the Soviets are thus peacefully installed in at least this small area of Afghanistan.

In the central areas of Badakhshan the mujahidin were in virtual control (with the exception of the garrison and airstrip in Faizabad) from September 1979 to June 1980, when the Soviets began an air offensive and began sending armored divisions through Ishkashim and the Warduj Valley to the embattled areas. In July 1980 the mujahidin estimated a combined Soviet and Afghan force of 12,000 in the province.* They also estimated human losses to be between 15,000 and 20,000. Up to 90 percent of the Sitami Milli in the province are believed to have been killed—not only by the mujahidin, but by the Khalqis and Parchamis as well. The remainder are thought to be in hiding in larger cities, including Kabul. Badakhshi was killed during Amin's rule. After the Soviet invasion Hashimi was imprisoned and as of this writing remains in jail.

Since the Saur Revolution the people of Badakhshan have been transformed from a generally passive and servile peasantry into a highly assertive, armed revolutionary force. Their organization is best at the local level, where a number of villages within a valley or adjacent valleys have organized themselves into military units (*jabha*—

---

*Since the USSR's invasion, the Soviets have established a large military garrison in Faizabad and carried out many large-scale operations against various mujahidin strongholds in central Badakhshan. However, their gains have been temporary; with the exception of Faizabad, they have been unable to control any parts of the province. Reports in summer 1983 indicated that the Soviets have closed off some of the more easily accessible passes connecting Badakhshan with Nuristan and Pakistan. Thus Badakhshani mujahidin have been forced to use higher and more difficult access routes to deliver weapons and ammunition.

fronts) and created basic administrative structures. These local units involve individuals from all strata of society, and leadership is determined by the consensus of its armed members. The new educated elite and the traditional religious establishment have created an unusually strong alliance which has drawn respect, support, and admiration from the masses. In addition, there is a loose regional hierarchy of command in the province. No more than a dozen families have left the central areas of the province for Pakistan, and there is a strong determination on the part of the Badakhshanis to stay and fight. As of summer 1980 the mujahidin claimed an armed force of about 30,000 under three regional commands in the central area.* All of the mujahidin in the province express allegiance to JIA and Rabbani.

CONCLUSIONS

The current conflict between the ruling Khalq-Parcham government of Afghanistan and its opponents differs from all previous political upheavals involving the central government (e.g., the Civil War of 1929, Safi Revolt of 1947-49, Qandahar riots of 1959) in at least three major ways. First, the political focus of the conflict centers on the issue of the legitimacy of the central government. Therefore, the minimal objective of the Islamic resistance is to replace it with a completely new state organization based on entirely different principles. Second, the current resistance originated in the urban centers. Finally, the leadership of the resistance emerged entirely from among the newly educated elite and not from the ranks of the tribal chiefs, rural landlords, or traditional religious and aristocratic establishments. Instead traditional local leaders and the peasantry have been successfully mobilized by the political and military efforts of young, educated Afghans.

The most important reason for the resistance is disagreement as to what constitutes legitimacy of state authority. The plurality of groups involved in the conflict is a function of different perceptions

*Recent information (August 1983) indicates that Badakhshani mujahidin have maintained control of the rural areas in central Badakhshan. Faizabad is still held by the Soviets, and a great deal of the fighting is concentrated around district centers and roads. The Soviets continue to bomb and strafe suspect villages.

of the concept of legitimate authority. The first to define the concept had been 'Abdur Rahman, who described the Kingdom of Afghanistan as an *Islamic state* charged with the defense of Islam and Muslim territory. Obedience to the king, "whether just or despot," was proclaimed obligatory *"provided his command does not violate the Shari'a"* (Ashraf Ghani 1978: 282; emphasis added). Thus the Afghan monarchy communicated one thing effectively to its people (whether by means of the traditional 'ulama or the modern media): the Islamic foundation of state authority.

'Abdur Rahman's successors gave lip service to Islam, but they were nevertheless determined to create a secular and "modernized" nation-state, patterned after Western models. In the 1920s King Amanullah (1919-29) made a disastrous attempt at the secularization and rationalization of state organization, so the process was slowed down, but systematic attempts at undermining Islamic institutions and values in favor of Western ideas of secular nationalism through secular education continued. The government was able to manage any threat from the traditional religious leadership by use of military force or cooption. Much to the government's surprise, challenges to its authority came from those it considered its allies—the secular educated elite. The first organized opposition was lodged by the secularized left—both Marxist-Leninist and Maoist—who questioned the legitimacy of the state on the bases of "class interests" and "scientific materialism." The government offered only half-hearted Islamic rhetoric to check the leftist claims and did not convince those of the educated elite with Islamic commitments that it was fulfilling its responsibilities to safeguard Islam and Islamic values. Its legitimacy was brought into question, giving rise to the emergence of an Islamic political opposition. The coups of 1973 and 1978, as well as the current conflict, are the results of such challenges, counterchallenges, and the continuation of competition by the Afghan elite for the establishment and control of what each political group considers to be legitimate state power and authority.

The conflict in Badakhshan is directly linked to national political developments through the Badakhshani educated elite who have been active at the national, provincial, and local levels. The Khalq-Parcham ruling group represented by Mansur Hashimi, the anti-Pashtun Maoist Sitami Milli led by Tahir Badakhshi, and the JIA of Burhanuddin Rabbani—all have their origins in the national political arena in Kabul.

The initiators of the well-planned armed uprising against the Khalq-Parcham government in Badakhshan were the Sitami Milli, followed by JIA. No spontaneous tribal revolt led by local khans or mullahs has occurred in Badakhshan—not for a lack of grievances against the state, for (as we have indicated) there were many, but because isolation, discrimination, and exploitation, no matter how pervasive, had not provided a sufficient and necessary motive for rebellion. Furthermore, the state had effectively neutralized the traditional local aristocracy of mirs, while religious leaders in the province had never before had occasion to coalesce above the village or town levels. Most important, Badakhshanis had been disarmed and most of their weapons confiscated by the state at the turn of the century. Kushkaki (1923: 174-381) estimated the total number of matchlocks (*tufangi filtai*) in the entire province at about 1,500 in 1921. As Eric Wolf points out, "A rebellion cannot start from a situation of complete impotence; the powerless are easy victims" (1969: 290). Wolf further asserts that "the decisive factor in making a peasant rebellion possible lies in the relation of the peasantry to the field of power which surrounds it" (1969: 290).

In Badakhshan the fields of power with clear political motive for rebellion—who at the same time had access to tactical means—were the Sitami Milli and JIA groups. The Sitamis had arms and training; like the Khalqis, they had assured the success of their initial armed venture by infiltrating the local army garrison in Baharak. JIA launched its armed uprising by attacking Kuran, a remote and indefensible government outpost in the only area in the province where the local population owned arms, and it was thus able to capture more weapons to expand its military activities.

The success or failure of the three contending political groups in mobilizing support in Badakhshan has depended on at least three factors: first, their notions of what constitutes legitimate authority—i.e., their political ideology; second, the effectiveness of their means and methods of communicating their objectives; finally—and most important—the perceptions of their ideologies and objectives by both the local masses and the groups' elite adherents. Such perceptions are of course influenced significantly by primordial sentiments of kinship, friendship, residence, ethnicity, and religious-sectarian allegiances.

The reasons for the failure of the Khalq-Parcham government are amply discussed elsewhere in this volume; here we need only emphasize the major ones: the alien and anti-Islamic nature of the Khalq-Parcham ideology, its haphazard policies of reform and heavy-handed implementation, and its close identification with the Soviet occupation forces. The Khalq-Parcham's greatest problem, aside from a lack of understanding of rural Afghanistan, has been its total inability to communicate with the people. As Roy has pointed out,

> It's no exaggeration to say that ... no revolutionary political speech is comprehensible to the Afghan peasant even if he happens to possess a solid classical culture. He may know Sa'di's *Rose Garden* by heart and still understand not one syllable of the news given over the Afghan radio (1981: 51).

In Badakhshan the Khalq-Parcham drew practically no support from among the Uzbeks and Tajiks of the central areas. Here the presence of refugees from Soviet and Chinese Turkistan and their preconceptions about communism and the Soviet invaders (whether correct or incorrect) have been crucial in the decision not to support the Marxist government. In addition, the atrocities and indignities committed by Hashimi seriously affected the credibility of the regime. Moreover, the appointment of a former schoolteacher from Shughnan (an Isma'ili area) as Governor of Badakhshan did not help the image of the regime.

The passive acceptance of the Khalq regime by the minority Isma'ili groups in the province may have several reasons: (1) They had no reason to join with the Sunni majority of central Badakhshan—who has oppressed the Isma'ilis—in opposition to the state; (2) While the Khalq government was in distant Kabul, its Soviet protectors and their guns were poised only a few hundred yards from Isma'ili lands across the Amu Darya; (3) Most Isma'ilis in the Amu Darya valley have for decades witnessed visible material improvements on the Soviet side, while their own situation has deteriorated. For the educated Shughni who joined the Khalq party, witnessing the improvements in local conditions on the Soviet side was without doubt a major consideration.

The relative success of Sitami Milli recruiting efforts was undoubtedly the result of the group's anti-Pashtun stance rather than its Maoist ideology. Indeed its membership and appeal were strongest in the two largest areas of Pashtun concentration in Badakhshan—Faizabad and Darwaz, an area frequented every summer by Pashtun

167

nomads (see Barfield 1981). The almost total annihilation of Sitami Milli—mostly by Islamic groups—is an indication of the thinness of its support among the general population, probably due to its Communist orientation.

The success of JIA among the educated youth as well as among the peasantry in the central areas of the province is due partly to the insensitive treatment of the masses by the Khalq government. However, a more significant reason for its success is the Islamic basis of its notion of legitimate authority and the Islamic content of its revolutionary objectives. The political ideology of JIA is not only familiar to the masses, but it is also well understood by them. Furthermore, JIA has been able to recruit large numbers of religious leaders to its ranks throughout the Sunni areas, making the communication of its objectives most effective. Soon after the armed uprisings started, the Badakhshani 'ulama began to take a leading role alongside teachers and students in the battlefield. In the summer of 1980 at least one of the major regional mujahidin guerrilla units (in Yaftal) was led by a mawlawi, 'Abdur Rahman.* With the elimination of the Sitami Milli, the opposition in Badakhshan to the Soviet occupation forces and the puppet regime of Karmal was left in the hands of JIA.

Whatever JIA's standing elsewhere in Afghanistan, in Badakhshan it has proved to be an effective Islamic revolutionary movement. It has provided "potential followers the one thing they seem to need most: an escape from powerlessness" (Lewis 1974: 15; see also McClelland 1970). It provides not only leadership, but also weapons. With increasingly effective use of recently acquired arms, Badakhshani youth are transformed into a formidable guerrilla force. Therefore, guerrilla warfare, which has been called "the latest weapon in the Communist arsenal" is being used against the Communists (Ahmad 1971: 138). Ironically leftist revolutionary literature is extremely informative as to the nature of Islamic movements in Afghanistan. For example, Ahmad states the following:

A revolutionary guerrilla movement seeks not simply to inflict military losses on the enemy but to destroy the legitimacy of its

---

*Additional evidence of active participation by Badakhshani 'ulama in the resistance at both the provincial and national levels is the participation of six mawlawis in drafting a charter for the Islamic Unity of Afghanistan Mujahidin, which successfully brought together seven major resistance groups in a coalition.

government and to establish a rival regime through the creation of "parallel hierarchies" (1971: 142).

Ahmad's statement is as applicable to the mujahidin movement in Afghanistan today as it was to Communist movements in China, Cuba, or (for that matter) Russia a few decades ago.* In contrast, it is worth noting that the Islamic revolutionary movements in Afghanistan strike at the heart of a pronouncement made by Maxime Rodinson, an outstanding Marxist scholar, in 1958 that "religions in their traditional forms no longer inspire the great movements of today" (quoted in Ansari 1981: 65).

The changes in the reform policies of one contender in the conflict, the Khalq-Parcham party, certainly support Aya's contention that "the genesis and course of revolutions cannot be defined (much less explained) by the conscious intentions of any single contender" (1979: 47) and my reason for deliberately avoiding a detailed discussion of the ideologies or programs of the contenders. Only one thing can be stated with certainty: the politicized and armed Islamic youth and peasantry will have to be either silenced or satisfied before the current brutal and tragic war the Soviets are waging against the Muslim peoples of Afghanistan can be terminated.

*There is a major difference between the current situation in Afghanistan and earlier Communist-inspired wars of liberation in Asia. In the earlier instances the Communists were waging a war with the help of the poor, weak, and exploited against powerful exploiters. In Afghanistan, ironically, the Communists have (intentionally or unintentionally) served either the interests of the rich, the aristocratic, and the oppressors of the peasantry, or those of Soviet colonialists. Most of the wealthy, urban, well-educated, and merchant class and former high government officials have been allowed to buy their way out of the country and have made their way to either Europe or the United States. At the same time, many rural landlords and rural rich have taken refuge in Kabul, where the Khalq-Parcham government and Soviets protect them. It would appear, therefore, that the enemies of the Communist regime in Afghanistan are the very Afghan peasants the Communists profess to be protecting.

Chapter 7

WEAK LINKS ON A RUSTY CHAIN: STRUCTURAL WEAKNESSES IN AFGHANISTAN'S PROVINCIAL GOVERNMENT ADMINISTRATION

Thomas J. Barfield

In April 1978 the People's Democratic Party of Afghanistan (PDPA) seized power in Kabul with the help of sympathetic units in the Afghan military in what has come to be known as the Saur Revolution. Although the PDPA quickly announced a program of sweeping change for the country, the "revolution" itself was merely a coup that placed a new party at the head of the old political structure. This structure was the product of fifty years of conservative dynastic rule of the Musahiban royal lineage that had begun with the installation of Nadir Shah as king in 1929 and ended with Muhammad Daoud as president of a nominal republic. Yet the PDPA, backed by the military, tried to use this structure as a vehicle for radical change— a decision which showed that the PDPA had fundamentally misunderstood the nature of the power structure it had inherited. In particular, the provincial administration under the Musahibans had not been designed to carry out change, and when opposition to PDPA policies arose, the struggle took place at the local level, where its opponents were strongest. To understand why opposition both began at the local level and was strongest there, we must turn to an analysis of provincial government before 1978. We shall focus our analysis on Qunduz province, where I did field work in 1974-76.

PROVINCIAL ADMINISTRATION BEFORE THE PDPA: QUNDUZ PROVINCE

In most of Afghanistan there have traditionally been two power structures: the local government administration, which was an arm of the central government, and tribal or village structures indigenous to each region. In the nineteenth and early twentieth centuries the two often coexisted. The central government recognized the legitimacy of tribal leadership at the local level and used it in a form of indirect rule. However, with the reign of Amir 'Abdur Rahman (1880-1901) the government in Kabul began to implement a policy of direct government rule wherever possible. Over time the central government gained sole legitimacy over provincial areas except for some Pashtun areas along the Pakistan border. Officially this meant that Afghan citizens now stood as individuals in their relationship with the Afghan state and that tribal or ethnic groups had no legal status. In practice this was not so. Nonetheless, to make the point the government of the Republic of Afghanistan (1973-78) demanded that all surnames (of recent origin in Afghanistan) which marked tribal, ethnic, or regional membership be changed to ones with no such significance. This order was widely ignored even within the government.

The central government was effective in expanding its power, but it did not completely displace older tribal structures. It was satisfied to encapsulate them and keep them from causing trouble. At the local level tribal groups still provided their members with important support outside the official government channels. The strength of tribal ties varied considerably throughout the country—strongest in Pashtun areas in the south and in the remote mountainous parts of Afghanistan, and weakest in urban areas and on the northern plains, where the government was better established. Even where the government administration was entrenched, tribal groups still played an important role in daily life.

In Qunduz province (in northeastern Afghanistan) the Imam Sahib Valley of the Amu River was an important subdistrict (the lowest level of government administration). Until 1930 it was a sparsely populated malarial swamp inhabited by Uzbeks and nomadic Arabs. (The details I present below on local government will be drawn primarily from the Arab communities, with which I am most familiar.) In the 1930s, as part of a provincial development project, extensive amounts of land were reclaimed for the cultivation of cotton and rice.* The population rose sharply and included such new groups

*Cotton cultivation was under the control of the Spinzar Cotton Company, which had sponsored the development and which maintained a monopoly on the

as Pashtuns from the south, Turkmens from the west, and Uzbeks from the Soviet Union (Barfield 1978). The national government in Imam Sahib was represented by the usual provincial administration, divided between the subgovernor and the police commandant. In addition, because it is located along the Soviet frontier, Imam Sahib was the headquarters of the regional border patrol under the command of a commissar.

Imam Sahib would seem to provide a case where the government should have displaced local tribal organizations. In spite of its pervasive presence in the town, however, the government seemed remote to the local villagers because there was no organic connection between the subprovincial administration and the people it ruled over. The subprovincial government was the lowest administrative unit in a national hierarchy whose center was in Kabul. Enforcement of decisions below this point depended ultimately on force because the tribesmen and peasants in the subdistrict did not see themselves as objects of that administration. Their alienation from the administration was due in part to feelings that under the Musahibans the government was always a predominantly Pashtun organization, and in part to a wide psychological distance between government officials and the rural population.

The most striking aspect of provincial administration was its domination by Pashtuns. In Qunduz province almost all the officials were Pashtuns. Although the province contained a large number of Turkic speakers, they were never government officials. These were almost always outsiders—usually Pashtuns from the south—and they were frequently transferred to prevent them from developing personal power bases. As a result, they had little knowledge of the areas under their jurisdiction, and they had little interest in creating close ties with local leaders.* In addition, administrative distance was encouraged by the centralized government organization. All major decisions were referred to higher officials in Kabul. All provincial recruitment

buying and processing of raw cotton. Spinzar had its headquarters in Qunduz and branch factories in all the towns of the region. In 1976 the sale of raw cotton brought over $3 million to the farmers of the Imam Sahib Valley alone.

*This was in sharp contrast to Spinzar officials, who expected to spend their entire careers in the region and who often developed very elaborate local political networks.

and staffing were done through the ministries in Kabul, and each ministry maintained a separate chain of command that precluded easy cooperation at the local level. In general, an official was more concerned with keeping good communications with his superiors in Kabul than in having good relations within his district.

The psychological gap between government officials and the village people was based on urban/rural differences. Officials were urban people who disliked service in the provinces and who constantly schemed to be transferred to Kabul or at least a bigger town. They dressed in Western suits, which set them off from the turban-wearing residents of rural Afghanistan. Indeed, with few exceptions, government officials were embarrassed by rural Afghanistan, stating that it was a backward place full of backward people. Such contempt was fully reciprocated by the local population, which found the officials overweight and overbearing and declared them to be congenitally corrupt. Moreover, villagers expressed doubts about the religiosity of the officials, particularly over such matters as drinking alcohol and making regular prayers. Each group viewed the other as a tricky adversary. Like oil and water, the two never mixed unless shaken together by some conflict or dispute.

Administration at the local level was carried out by intermediaries. Each village had an *arbab*, who was the official link between the village and the local administration. Arbabs were not part of the government, although they were supposed to be important local leaders. In many cases, however, an arbab was important by virtue of his appointment and not because of indigenous support. Real tribal leaders often had no official connections with the government, but they were continually sought out by their people to resolve disputes and mediate problems—especially with other ethnic groups. Thus in practice two sets of leaders existed in a village: indigenous leaders with local support, and the arbab, the village's official leader. (Among the Arabs of Imam Sahib indigenous leaders were known as *bays*.)

The Arabs in Imam Sahib are pastoral nomads who were granted land in the valley by Nadir Shah in 1920, when he reorganized the region as war minister for King Amanullah. At that time the Arabs had a strong clan organization, and their tribal groups were linked to the government by an *ilbegi* for the Arabs as a whole and a *ming bashi* for each clan. With the advent of more direct provincial administration, formal clan organization disappeared. After 1920 the government took charge of justice, distributed individual (instead of clan or tribe) titles to land and pasture, and no longer recognized the Arabs as a political unit. Nevertheless, the local government did not replace tribal leadership because the Arabs viewed government as a source of trouble. The average Arab came into contact with the government only in criminal cases, for conscription, or when he had to pay a bribe to use pasture along the USSR border. In general, it was thought best to avoid government officials whenever possible.

In order to avoid the government at the local level, the Arabs sought out a bay when they had problems. Traditionally a bay was not only a man with substantial animal wealth, but he was also a political figure who had to have a reputation for good judgment and honesty. A bay's authority was informal and flowed from the willingness of people to defer to him. For example, Arabs feared being caught up in formal court cases because these inevitably resulted in demands for bribes or at the very least brought unwanted scrutiny on individuals who wished to remain anonymous. This fear was enough to give a bay power to resolve disputes informally. Moreover, unlike government officials, a bay was able to get background on the cases brought before him and thereby deliver a verdict that would meet with the approval of the community at large. His resolution of minor but often acrimonious disputes at the village level helped to insulate the Arabs from the government, keeping their villages concealed from outside observation. Very little of what went on in the Arab community ever reached the attention of local government officials.

By custom the arbab was chosen by the people and confirmed by the government. In 'many cases, however, the arbab was simply appointed by the government without consultation. As noted, the position was not inherently powerful. An arbab could command power only when he acted on behalf of the government as its agent. When he tried to command action on his own, he could be safely ignored. Arbabs were usually literate men with business interests outside of the village; often they held urban property. Links to a larger world were important because dealing with government officials required a greater sophistication than most Arabs acquired in the course of sheep-raising. The position had a poor reputation because it was associated with trouble and because many arbabs were known to be corrupt.

There were two radically different role models an arbab could follow. In the first, a bay would take the position of arbab out of a sense of responsibility to his fellow villagers. Although he would hold the position, he would never use the title of arbab. For a bay to be called an arbab was considered undignified and indirectly a stain on his honor. In the second model, an opportunist could use the position of arbab to advance his own interests. In sharp contrast to the bay, such a person often insisted upon being addressed as arbab. Publicly flattered, he was privately despised.* However, this type of arbab served a function by handling criminal cases. A bay acting in the capacity of arbab defended a village's collective interests, but he would not handle individual criminal cases because it was considered dirty work. Criminal cases and influence peddling therefore became the stock in trade of the venal opportunist arbabs. For example, when a nomad was caught stealing sheep and faced criminal charges, he would seek out the services of an arbab to bribe the police to drop the charges. The arbab would extort as much as possible from the hapless thief and pay as little to the police as necessary, pocketing the difference as his fee.

In sum the weakest link in the government chain of command was between the subprovincial administration and the villages, where the government was faced with indigenous political structures and where its own agents were not well respected. Under such conditions the government was effective only when it had a specific target for punitive action. Its intermediaries were useless as enforcers of general policy. A bay arbab would put the interests of his people before those of the government, while a venal arbab had no independent political support. The defects in the weakest link were not critical under the Musahiban dynasty because it required provincial officials only to keep the peace, administer justice, see that conscription went smoothly, and collect small amounts of taxes. They were not expected to engage in social action projects that might require greater local co-operation than the government was able to muster. By the time of Daoud's republic the national government was not dependent on the

*It was this kind of arbab that gave the position its bad reputation. According to one local proverb

The pig is in the jungle,
The arbab is in the village.

Needless to say, a comparison with a pig is hardly flattering in an Islamic society.

political, financial, or ideological support of the provincial population to carry out its policies. Local government officials were charged with maintaining the status quo with as little effort as possible. National politics and programs were largely divorced from rural areas.

MUSAHIBAN STRATEGY TO REDUCE PROVINCIAL INFLUENCE

The Musahiban government policy toward provincial Afghanistan had its roots in a reactionary civil war that overthrew King Amanullah (1919-29). Amanullah had tried to create a more centralized state along the lines of Ataturk in Turkey and Reza Shah in Iran. To this end he had increased taxation, made social reforms, and moved to push the Islamic clergy out of government. His policies alienated a wide variety of Afghans for different reasons. Complaints about rising taxes were coupled with conservative ideological issues about the status of women and the role of the clergy in government to produce a formidable coalition against him. In 1924, Amanullah's social and political reforms sparked the Khost Rebellion. The Afghan army proved incapable of quelling the trouble, and Amanullah was forced to seek the aid of tribal levies. With this move he succeeded in ending the revolt, but the cost to the government's prestige was high. Amanullah was forced to rescind a number of his reforms. In 1928, after taking a world tour, Amanullah tried to reinstitute his reform program. This time opposition was more widespread, and the Afghan army crumbled in the face of numerous attacks, forcing Amanullah to flee Afghanistan after abdicating the throne. Following a period of anarchy, Nadir Shah was placed on the throne by an army of Pashtun tribesmen, who also took the opportunity to loot Kabul (Gregorian 1969: 227-92).

The lesson of the civil war was not lost on Nadir Shah and his Musahiban successors: the security of the government was to be paramount. No reforms, modernizations, or political actions were to be undertaken if they would destabilize the government. At the same time, the dynasty sought to increase the power of the central government at the expense of local tribal leaders.

The Musahiban dynasty developed a tripartite strategy. Its first objective was to rebuild and reorganize the Afghan army. With modern weapons the army would protect the government from the dangers of isolated rebellions and enable it to carry out its policies even when they were unpopular. The army became the government's most effective national institution, with a professional officer corp leading a force of conscripts. However, conscription had been one of the policies found objectionable during Amanullah's reign; in consequence, the Musahiban dynasty exempted a number of Pashtun tribes from service and allowed others to select the conscripts themselves.

The government's second objective was to reduce its dependence on the rural economy. Traditionally Afghan governments relied heavily on land and animal taxes for revenue. Taxes of as much as one fifth of a crop were not uncommon. Amanullah had been the first to change collection of taxes in kind into cash payments. In order to raise money for his new projects, he then increased the tax rate, especially on stockbreeders (Abdul Ghani 1921: 124-30). When he did so, land and animal taxes amounted to almost two thirds of government revenue (Fry 1974: 155-56).

Amanullah's fiscal dependence on the rural areas to pay for his projects made him vulnerable to opposition from the provinces. The Musahiban rulers saw such a dependence as a basic weakness and began to cut their financial ties to the rural areas. They encouraged the emergence of a national bank and the creation of a modern sector in the Afghan economy, which they first taxed and then nationalized. The tax burden was shifted from taxes on land and animals to taxes on imports and exports that included a complex set of currency exchange rates. By the early 1950s the extraction of taxes from provincial areas was well into decline, and the revenue brought in barely covered local administrative expenses (Schurmann 1962: 234-35). By 1972 land and animal taxes accounted for less than one percent of total government revenue (Fry 1974: 155-56). The cost of government had been transferred from direct taxes on the rural economy to indirect taxes raised through government monopolies and by greater direct taxation of the merchant class, which was not politically powerful. For large-scale development projects the government did not rely on taxation at all, but began to depend on foreign aid in the form of grants and loans which soon made Afghanistan one of the largest recipients of aid for its size anywhere.

The government's third objective was to make social and economic reforms gradually. The policy of gradualism depended on the government's other policies—i.e., the army was prepared to meet local opposition (if any), and the government did not have to finance new programs from the rural economy. Amanullah's reforms had raised tremendous opposition in spite of the fact that they had been implemented only on a small scale. The Musahiban dynasty attempted to work around conservative opposition or confront it only over specific issues.

The strategy for reforms was to introduce them first in Kabul and then in other cities. The government would defend its programs in these limited areas, but it would not attempt to implement them in the countryside. The abolition of a legal requirement that women be veiled in public provides a good example. This law was not dropped until 1959—and then only when there was pressure in Kabul to do so. It was dropped without fanfare, but the government let it be known that it would protect women who chose to go unveiled. This it did, putting down riots in Kandahar (which had more to do with taxes than veils) and arresting conservative clerics who assaulted unveiled women (L. Dupree 1973: 530-36). The government did not go further and demand that women not use the veil. In fact, the use of the veil, which was an urban custom, began to spread in some of the more prosperous provincial areas as a sign of sophistication when it was rapidly falling out of favor in Kabul. As with other changes, the government judged that opposition could be fairly easily overcome, and that by limited, quiet action it could avoid creating ideological issues that would arouse more general opposition.

The tripartite strategy effectively insulated national policies from rural opposition. As they became first militarily and then financially more secure, successive Musahiban rulers felt freer to act. However, they were still careful not to deliberately provoke provincial Afghans by demanding any great changes in the way they lived; furthermore, government reforms were always justified as being in line with orthodox Islamic values. One consequence of this strategy was to increase the distance between the values held by Afghanistan's small literate urban population and the tribal village populations. It was the literate urban class, many of whom were in the civil service, military, or schools, that wanted to see greater and faster change. The left wing political parties in particular drew their strength from this urban base in Kabul. Their ideas were attractive to a growing number of unemployed high school and university graduates, as well as many junior officials in the government and military.

This urban class was largely a creation of the Musahiban governments. While the dynasty had developed a large number of structural defenses against conservative opposition, it was quite vulnerable to attacks by the left, which was centered largely in the capital and within many important government institutions. It is ironic that the dynasty fell to this element after spending most of its political energy insulating itself from the conservative forces that had brought down Amanullah. When the 1978 PDPA coup took place, a more radical version of the progressive urban ideology which the Musahiban dynasty had helped foster became the PDPA's program for changing the whole country—including the provincial areas so carefully excluded before.

THE PDPA AND THE IMPLEMENTATION OF SOCIOECONOMIC CHANGE

The PDPA victory took place entirely at the national level—that is, in Kabul. Both the Khalq and Parcham parties that had combined to create the PDPA were urban-based and had few members living in rural areas. Nonetheless, their program for a new Afghanistan focused great attention on radically restructuring the lives of provincial Afghans. It was sweeping in scope: it called for land reform, the abolition of brideprice, and the reduction of many types of rural debts, and it included a thirty-point outline of Afghanistan's future economic, political, and social policies (Charpentier 1979). This program was bound to raise issues that had been buried since the fall of Amanullah, yet the PDPA did not see provincial opposition or difficulties in implementation as insurmountable obstacles.

The PDPA's confidence was based on its control of the military and on a belief that its opponents had no power—a belief that had validity largely because of the Musahiban dynasty's success in reducing the influence of tribal and religious groups in national politics. However, the PDPA did not recognize that the Musahiban governments had brought fifty years of peace by making concessions to the rural areas. Social and economic reforms had only marginally involved the rural population, and the government had not challenged traditional beliefs or economic patterns. In contrast, changes in provincial Afghanistan were the centerpiece of the PDPA program because rural Afghanistan was the source of what the new government most objected to. Lacking its own rural organization, the PDPA planned to use the old provincial administration inherited from the Musahibans to carry out its reforms—after staffing the upper levels with party members.

Whether the civil and military bureaucracies, which had been designed only to preserve the status quo, were adequate for a new role of implementing radical change was not immediately clear. When the PDPA tried to carry out its program, it discovered that neither institution was as strong as it had anticipated. The provincial administration soon proved incapable of making major changes in the face of local opposition, and the military proved unable to put down this opposition when confronted with armed rebellion.

The PDPA failed to implement its reforms in large part owing to three basic problems: (1) It was unable to win the acceptance of its program because its arguments were alien to the bulk of the Afghan population—i.e., it was unable to win the ideological struggle; (2) It tried to use the Musahiban administrative structure as a vehicle to implement radical change when that structure was ill equipped for any positive action; (3) At the local level, where the PDPA's programs were to be carried out, tribal and religious leadership was better organized than the government.

The PDPA failed not only to analyze the objective state of Afghanistan's economic and social development, but also to put the party's propaganda in a form that would attract a broader base of support outside the party itself. The Afghan economy was almost exclusively agricultural. People supported themselves by farming, raising livestock, or producing traditional handicrafts. Afghan society was both bound and divided by ties of kinship and religion. The modern sector of the economy was tiny and employed few workers, and even these had ties (through kinsmen) to the traditional economy. In spite of these objective conditions, the PDPA declared that the Saur Revolution was proletarian in nature, when in fact no genuine proletariat had yet emerged in Afghanistan. As a result, it appealed consistently to class interests in a country where the political idiom was still tribal or religious. In any village ties of kinship usually overrode class interests. In Imam Sahib, where a cash economy was firmly established, a poor Arab would support a rich Arab in a dispute with a Tajik. Ironically, what class consciousness existed was found among the wealthy, who saw the PDPA program as a threat to their interests. The PDPA therefore found it difficult to attract rural supporters.

The PDPA also failed to consider the ramifications of many of its actions. Many of the issues it considered purely economic had social components, and many of its social reforms affected such basic values as family honor. For example, when the PDPA declared initially that its government was established on a secular base, it undercut its legitimacy in the eyes of the rural population. In Imam Sahib nothing was ever completely secular: slaughtering a sheep, praying to finalize a contract, or giving money in thanks for good fortune—all had some religious overtone. There was a strong belief that a non-Islamic government had no legal authority, and that a Muslim had the right— even the duty—to rebel against such a government. The PDPA thought that its land reform policy would bring it the immediate support of the rural poor. It did not—because land ownership was part of a web of social relations that included much more than a mere title to land. People in Imam Sahib were divided along linguistic, tribal, and religious lines that made the implementation of any such policy difficult even if the government had full control.* Other problems existed because a sharecropper needed not only land, but also seed, animals, and credit, which were supplied by the landlord in many cases. Even the rhetoric of land reform engendered fear in the north, where it was associated with Stalinist policies of collectivization. Social reforms like the abolition of brideprice did not take into account the importance these payments had in reflecting the honor of the families involved. While previous Afghan governments had occasionally tried to regulate marriage payments, they had been acutely aware that government authority was not recognized in family matters. Wittingly or not, the PDPA was raising the same issues that brought about the downfall of Amanullah.

The implementation of the PDPA program was the responsibility of the new government's officials who were appointed to the

---

*In the past an Arab village had successfully forced the removal of a small government project to settle Turkmens in Imam Sahib too near to what the Arabs considered their own territory.

top positions in the old government hierarchy. They served a dual purpose, acting as heads of the local administration and cadres for pushing the new policies. Since rural Afghans looked upon the government as a source of trouble, the association of the PDPA's new policies with the old provincial administration did the PDPA no good. Moreover, except for the top ranks, the staffing of the new government remained much the same as it had been under the Republic because the PDPA did not have enough members to fully staff the provincial administration. Most important (as noted), the administrative structure had been designed by the Musahibans to keep order, not to implement change. Links between the local government and the villages had always been brittle; they broke when provincial PDPA officials tried to run the reform program and found that their writ ran only to the edge of town. In the face of general opposition, sparked by different incidents in each region, the PDPA responded with military force. While the PDPA had the support of the military at the upper levels, most of the army and police force consisted of conscripts drawn from the rural areas who were more in sympathy with the conservative opposition than with the government. As civil war broke out, the Afghan army was depleted by massive desertions.

Perhaps the most basic difficulty faced by the national government was its own weakness at the provincial and subprovincial levels. Under the Musahiban dynasty traditional tribal and religious leadership had grown weaker in the face of growing government authority. Nevertheless, villagers still sought out nongovernmental leaders when they wanted solutions to many problems. The existence of such an alternative power structure, while of minor importance in normal times, provided a ready-made political structure to organize against the new government (Salzman 1978). At the local level traditional leaders had the ability to bring their neighbors together using kinship ties and personal contacts. Unlike the PDPA, opposition leaders used the old political language of Afghanistan, calling on their followers to defend the faith of Islam, the honor of their families and country, and their property. The parochial nature of this type of opposition made it pervasive but noncentralized, resulting in the seeming paradox of the PDPA government becoming weakened to the point of near collapse without having an easily identifiable enemy at the national or international levels.

THE PDPA AND AMANULLAH: SOME STRUCTURAL SIMILARITIES

In the longer view of Afghan history the PDPA's attempts to make socioeconomic changes in Afghanistan were faced with problems similar to those that confronted Amanullah. This was not surprising since the Musahiban dynasty had designed its policies in response to Amanullah's defeat. It had worked around conservative opposition, but it had never destroyed it. In addition, the structural similarities between the regimes and the policies of the PDPA and Amanullah were striking. Both inherited peaceful states—the PDPA from the Musahibans, Amanullah from the work of his grandfather, Amir 'Abdur Rahman. Both soon announced programs of sweeping change for Afghanistan, and both were supported by a young, educated urban class which planned to use the old government structure as an instrument for change. In announcing such programs, both the PDPA and Amanullah showed that they misunderstood the power structure of the states they had inherited. The old structures were fundamentally conservative, and they combined the threat of military force with political accommodation to maintain the peace. At the provincial level they had encapsulated indigenous tribal, village, and religious organizations but had never fully replaced them. The people saw themselves as subjects of the state but not participating members of it. The weaknesses of local administration were disguised because its limits were rarely tested. Amanullah and the PDPA soon discovered these weaknesses when they tried to implement change from the top and found them fatal to their programs. Neither regime was capable of dealing with the simultaneous but undirected rebellions that occurred in response to their attempts at change, although the PDPA had inherited a far greater military force than that available to Amanullah.

Amanullah fell. The PDPA was saved from a similar fate by the armed invasion of the Soviet Union, which removed the Khalq party faction from power and replaced it with its Parcham rival. While this prevented the collapse of the national government in Kabul, it changed the nature of the rebellion from a domestic affair into one based on resistance against foreign occupation. The roots of the rebellion still remain buried in Afghan history.

Chapter 8

EFFECTS OF THE SAUR REVOLUTION IN THE NAHRIN AREA OF NORTHERN AFGHANISTAN

Hugh Beattie

On 27 April 1978, a military coup in Afghanistan brought to power the leaders of the People's Democratic Party of Afghanistan (PDPA)—an event to which the government subsequently referred as the Saur Revolution after the month in which it occurred (the second month of the Afghan calendar). The PDPA was divided into two principal factions, Khalq ("people") and Parcham ("flag"). Within two or three months of the coup the former faction had gained the upper hand over the latter and was to be largely responsible for the policies pursued by the new regime until the Soviet invasion in December 1979 (L. Dupree 1979b:1-3). By looking in some detail at the effects of the Saur Revolution in one part of the country, I hope to illustrate some of the ways in which the political aspirations of the Khalq government were out of step with those of ordinary Afghans.[*] In doing so, I shall attempt to shed more light on the question of why the Khalq government, despite its claim to represent the will of the Afghan people, failed to win much popular support.

Shortly after taking power, the new government embarked upon a string of ambitious reforms which it hoped would transform Afghan society. Using material collected in the late summer and autumn of 1978, I shall describe the way in which these reforms were implemented in the small town of Nahrin in northern Afghanistan and explore local reactions to them. Some of the social and economic problems which the reforms were intended to solve will be briefly outlined, and the reforms themselves will be analyzed and placed in

---

[*]For details of left-wing groups in Afghanistan and their history, see Halliday (1978:20-32) and Khalid (1980:209-13).

historical context. In conclusion, the causes of the revolts which broke out against the Khalq government will be compared with those of the rebellion which led in 1929 to the downfall of King Amanullah, an earlier advocate of rapid and intensive modernization.

THE TOWN AND SUBPROVINCE OF NAHRIN

The town of Nahrin is situated about one hundred miles north of Kabul in the northern foothills of the Hindu Kush mountains. Though it has a population of less than two thousand, at the time of my visit the town had a flourishing bazaar with over three hundred small shops and a number of teahouses and modest eating places. The bazaar drew its customers from a military training camp which was a mile or two away, as well as from the numerous villages in the area (Centlivres 1976c:133). The town contains the administrative headquarters of the *wuluswali* (subprovince) of Nahrin, which forms part of the province of Baghlan. The town lies at the southeastern end of a valley some fifteen miles long and five miles wide at its greatest extent. A river runs through this valley as well as through the Yarm (or Jilga) Valley in the southeast of the subprovince, making possible some irrigated agriculture. Loess hills around the valley and the plateau of Burqa to the north are used for dry-farming. The inhabitants of the subprovince are mostly settled cultivators, though groups of pastoral nomads pass through on their way to and from summer pastures in the mountains.*

The total population of the subprovince was estimated in 1974 at 70,000 (Centlivres 1976b:264); it comprises members of several different ethnic groups. As late as the first decades of the twentieth century, there appear to have been a large majority of Uzbeks and a small Tajik minority. Nowadays Pashtun immigrants from the south own much of the irrigable land in the valley, and the Uzbeks have retreated to Burqa. The Tajik population has been considerably swelled by immigration, while an area to the southwest of the town is inhabited largely by Hazarahs, who, like the Pashtuns, seem to have moved into the subprovince fairly recently. A few villages near the

---

*Some pastoral nomads have begun to buy land in the Nahrin area—for example, the Lakan Khel group, who were the subject of a recent film by Asen Balikci, *Sons of Hadji Omar*.

185

town, in the Yarm Valley and along the road to the provincial capital of Baghlan, are inhabited by people who call themselves Absarinas and say that they are one of the Chahar Aymaq or "four tribes" of Qataghan (Jarring 1939:19; Centlivres 1976b). In addition, there are some Tajik and Hazarah villages in the Yarm Valley; as well as a small community of non-Uzbek Turks, while pastoral Gujars have been moving into the area fairly recently (Centlivres 1976b:264). (Nahrin is shown on the map on p. 138.)

PRINCIPAL KHALQ SOCIAL AND ECONOMIC REFORMS AND THEIR IMPLEMENTATION IN NAHRIN

Three decrees—Nos. 6, 7, and 8—were the main planks of the Khalq program of social and economic reform. Decree No. 6 was intended to put an end to land mortgage and indebtedness; No. 7 was designed to stop the payment of brideprice and give women more freedom of choice in marriage; No. 8 consisted of rules and regulations for the confiscation and redistribution of land. Here I shall present the main points of these decrees.*

DECREE NO. 6

It is worth emphasizing that Decree No. 6 was one of the few really original features of the Khalq program. Nothing like it had been attempted in Afghanistan before, whereas (as we shall see below) this is not true of most of the other Khalq policies. The decree was announced in July 1978; its aim was said to be the freeing of "millions of toiling peasants from the yoke of exploiters" (*Kabul Times*, 7/17/78). As far as mortgages are concerned, land which had been mortgaged before 1353 A.H. (21 March 1974) by people who owned outright no more than 10 *jiribs* of first-grade land or its equivalent (1 jirib = 0.2 hectares [ha]) was simply to be returned to them after any crops planted on it had been harvested. Land mortgaged in or after 1353 was also to be returned to its original owners, but they were to repay a percentage of the original mortgage. The percentage increased as the date of the transaction of the mortgage approached

---

*Full texts of these decrees can be found in the newsletters of the Afghanistan Council of the Asia Society.

the date of the announcement of the decree. Thus people who had mortgaged their land in 1353 were to repay 20 percent of the mortgage principal during the second year after the issue of the decree, whereas those who had mortgaged their land in 1356 were to repay 90 percent of the principal over five years beginning in the second year after the issue of the decree (Articles 1 and 2).

As regards debts, the wording of the decree is somewhat confusing. "Debts due to landowners and usurers" which had been incurred by those who owned no land were canceled completely (Article 3). However, for other debts—for example, debts incurred as a result of the advancement of credit to those who were landless or who owned 10 jiribs or less of first-grade land or its equivalent—a procedure similar to the one described in connection with mortgage repayment was to be adopted. Loans taken out before 1353 A.H. were canceled outright. For loans contracted in or after 1353 different proportions were to be repaid, up to a maximum of 90 percent for those taken out in 1357 (Articles 4 and 5). In order to oversee the implementation of these complex regulations, a "Committee for the Solution of the Problems of the Peasantry" was to be set up in each subprovince, consisting of the subgovernor, the "official in charge of properties," and representatives of the judicial, educational, and agricultural departments and the peasantry (Appendix 1, Article 5).

One of the causes of indebtedness—loans for agricultural improvements—was to be removed through the provision of credit for such improvements by the Agricultural Development Bank (Appendix 1, Article 8). (The bank had been founded in 1970 with a grant from the United Nations [Fry 1974:91].) However, the decree did not indicate how the repayment of the specified percentages of mortgages or loans was to be financed.* The provision of credit for nonproductive purposes does not seem to have been one of the functions of the Agricultural Development Bank, which in any case had not opened a branch in Nahrin by December 1978. The only institution which the Khalq government created in Nahrin to advance

---

*It may be because of such practical flaws that Halliday asserts that Decree No. 6 "did not touch . . . the main area of rural debt, viz. debts to bazaar merchants and moneylenders" (1980a:24). Otherwise it is difficult to see what he means since the provisions of the decree certainly applied to debts to bazaar merchants and moneylenders (provided that they had been incurred by people who met the specified criteria).

nonagricultural credit was referred to as the *sanduq* (box or chest). People paid a membership fee of 50 afs. and then made monthly payments of 30 afs.; in return they could borrow small amounts and repay them in installments. (In 1978 one af. was worth about $.025.)

Accurate statistics are not available, but there is little doubt that in the late 1970s indebtedness was a serious and widespread problem in the Afghan countryside. In a survey of 17 villages in 8 provinces carried out in 1968-69, 56.8 percent of the families interviewed had debts on average of 16,316 afs. (about $400) (Toepfer 1972:101). In 57 percent of the cases the money had been borrowed to cover everyday living expenses, and in 30.5 percent to meet the costs of marriages and funerals. Interest rates varied enormously; although it could happen that no interest was charged at all, a rate of 50 percent or more was common (Toepfer 1976:77). Toepfer found that relatively little land was mortgaged—about 8.5 percent (1972:100). However, a severe drought in the early 1970s evidently compelled more people to mortgage their land or fall into debt (for example, see Poulton et al. 1973, pt. 3:53). Moreover, it seems that more land was alienated through indebtedness than through actual mortgage. As I have indicated, the practice of advancing loans to peasants at very high rates of interest was common. The peasants were forced to use their land as security for these loans, and when (as often happened) they were unable to repay them, the security fell to the creditor. According to Grötzbach, indebtedness and mortgage arose in the first place from the fact that incomes were too low to meet the expenses of marriages, funerals, and unexpected crises such as illness. In addition, they were often insufficient to meet the overhead costs of running a small farm, and the absence of institutions providing credit on reasonable terms compounded the problem (Grötzbach 1972:208; see also Ferdinand 1962:132).

No instances of the cancellation or partial repayment of loans according to the terms of Decree No. 6 came to my attention in Nahrin, but I heard of several cases involving mortgaged land. Land which had been mortgaged within the last ten or fifteen years was generally returned to its owners without much difficulty. Complications arose mainly in connection with claims that land which had supposedly been sold thirty or forty years ago had really only been mortgaged. Since in all but a few cases people had not registered their title to their land when they bought it, it was often very difficult for them to prove that it had been purchased outright and not mortgaged. My impression was that some people tried to take advantage of this.

A typical case occurred in a village a few miles from the town. A Pashtun who owned about 35 jiribs of land was faced with a claim that some of this land had only been mortgaged and should therefore be returned immediately. He maintained that his father had bought the land nearly half a century ago. The local Committee for the Solution of the Problems of the Peasantry dismissed the claim, but the plaintiff took the case to the provincial committee in Baghlan. It caused the Pashtun and his family a great deal of worry; though he made several trips to Baghlan to try and sort things out, the matter had still not been settled by the time I left Nahrin.

Another case involved a group of buildings which included a few shops, a restaurant, and some rooms for rent; they stood on about 2.5 jiribs of land, and land and buildings together were said to be worth at least 250,000 afs. (about $6,400), which made them a very valuable property by local standards. The owner of the land and proprietor of the restaurant, a Tajik named Sharif Jan, had neglected to register his title to the land when he bought it many years ago, so that it was still officially registered in the name of the man from whom he had purchased it—his father-in-law Jamal. Following the promulgation of Decree No. 6, one of Jamal's sons went to the local committee and claimed that the land had only been mortgaged all along and should now be returned to him. The committee upheld his claim. The case seems to have turned on the discovery of an old letter written by Sharif Jan. When Jamal died about twenty-five years ago, Sharif Jan's title to the land had been challenged by the man who had originally sold it to Jamal. In order to disprove the man's claim to the land, Sharif Jan had written to the subgovernor stating that the land belonged to Jamal's family and had been mortgaged to him, since at least the family's title to it was incontestable. In November 1978 Sharif Jan and his family were evicted and the restaurant was locked up. Sharif Jan's sons went to Kabul to appeal to the Ministry of Justice against the decision.

DECREE NO. 7

Decree No. 7, issued in October 1978, had three main provisions. First, it prohibited the transfer of money and goods from a groom's family to a bride's in connection with marriage, apart from 300 afs. *mahr* (wedding gift) (Articles 1, 2, and 3). By doing so the decree's intended effect was not only to prohibit payment of brideprice, but also to force people to spend less on their wedding celebrations. For example, in Nahrin and apparently elsewhere (e.g., see Schurmann 1962:211) the family of the groom paid for the food which the bride's family prepared and served at the wedding feast. Second, it granted freedom of choice in marriage (Article 4), and third, it fixed minimum ages for engagement and marriage (sixteen for women, eighteen for men—Article 5). Anyone infringing these regulations was liable to a period of imprisonment of from six months to three years (Article 6).

By contrast with indebtedness and mortgage, Afghan rulers have for a long time regarded high brideprice payments and costly wedding celebrations as problems worthy of attention. As far back as 1884, Amir 'Abdur Rahman had fixed what Kakar calls "the very low figure of 30 rupees" as the maximum brideprice (1979:170), but his ruling had little effect. Another attempt to limit the heavy expenditure connected with marriage was made by 'Abdur Rahman's successor Habibullah in 1911, when he laid down maximum amounts that could be spent on marriage according to class (Gregorian 1969:198). The Family Code introduced by Habibullah's successor, Amanullah, placed limits on wedding expenses and brideprice payments (Gregorian 1969:243-44; Poullada 1973:71). In addition, Amanullah tried to give women the right to marry whom they pleased and to fix minimum ages for marriage. These attempts at reform were ignored by the population as a whole (Poullada 1973:145). Since the reign of 'Abdur Rahman marriage in particular has remained an expensive undertaking for the groom's family. In and around the town of Nahrin average brideprice payments in 1978 were about 50,000 afs. (approximately $1,250), though some of the money was usually spent on the bride's trousseaus. (Payments were probably somewhat lower in the remoter and poorer villages.) Brideprice of this order amounted to two or three years' average income and (as noted) was frequently a cause of indebtedness.

Following the promulgation of Decree No. 7 in the autumn of 1978, it looked as though people in Nahrin would try to observe its provisions. They held less elaborate wedding celebrations, and it was rumored that one or two people in Baghlan had been prosecuted for breaking the new rules. In the Yarm Valley, where there were no administrative officers, the senior teacher in the local school, an enthusiastic Khalq supporter, did his best to enforce the decree.

On the whole the new rules were not popular, however. People with unmarried daughters resented the decree most because they could no longer expect to receive brideprice payments for them when they were married. Moreover, families which had a male member betrothed but not yet married at the time the decree was issued were also directly affected by it because the usual practice was for half the brideprice to be paid at the time of the betrothal and the other half at the wedding. In one case, a man had betrothed his younger brother before the decree was announced, handing over cash and goods to the value of about 25,000 afs. The decree was issued before the marriage could take place; nonetheless, the girl's family demanded the remainder of the brideprice before it would permit the wedding to go ahead, threatening otherwise to call the whole thing off. It could easily have done so by saying that the girl no longer wanted to marry since the decree stipulated that no one could be forced to marry against his or her will, and there was no way in which it could have been made to return the half of the brideprice it had received at the time of the betrothal. The same kind of problem was faced by a young man who had agreed to pay a brideprice of 70,000 afs. The betrothal had taken place, and he had given the girl's family nearly two thirds of the money. He was not in a position to pay the remainder, but when the decree was issued, he could see no reason why the marriage should not take place. However, the girl's family hoped to obtain the rest of the brideprice, and said that as the girl was not yet sixteen, according to the new rules she was too young to be married.

In particular Decree No. 7 was unpopular in Nahrin because it represented a threat to male honor. By banning brideprice—and especially by declaring that women could marry whom they pleased—it threatened to undermine the strict control over women on which the maintenance of male honor depended. In addition, men resented the decree because they generally believed that it was Islam and not just local custom which encouraged the payment of brideprice and demanded that women live in purdah (Beattie 1982:47).*

[*]Nancy Tapper (in this volume) deals in greater detail with problems arising from the implementation of Decree No. 6. See also the chapter by Nancy Dupree.

DECREE NO. 8

Decree No. 8 was issued in December 1978, and its implementation began shortly afterwards. It had two main provisions: (1) In future no family could own more than 30 jiribs of first-grade land or its equivalent; larger amounts of poorer quality land could be retained in inverse relation to the land's productivity (Article 3).* Holdings in excess of the amounts specified were to be confiscated by the Land Reforms Department (Article 9). (2) Expropriated land and state land were to be distributed free of charge to "deserving persons" in units of 5 jiribs of first-grade land, 6 jiribs of second-grade land, and so on to a maximum of 50 jiribs of seventh-grade land (Article 12).

At several points the decree referred to agricultural cooperatives, but it is an exaggeration to say, as L. Dupree does (1979b:3), that the decree encouraged their formation.† Unlike the Iranian land

*The decree gave the following coefficients so that amounts of poorer quality land could be converted to their equivalents in first-grade land: First-grade land—1.00: orchard and vineyard land; double-crop irrigated farmland; Second-grade land—0.85: double-crop irrigated land; Third-grade land—0.67: single-crop irrigated land, half or more of which is cultivated annually; Fourth-grade land—0.40: single-crop irrigated land, less than half of which is cultivated annually; Fifth-grade land—0.20: dry-farming land cultivated annually; Sixth- and Seventh-grade land—0.15: dry-farming land cultivated every two years or less. Halliday notes that the Khalq land reform was not based on any cadastral survey of the Afghan countryside (1980a:24). In Nahrin it seems that landowners themselves were ordered to declare the size of their holdings and that their figures were used as the basis for the confiscation and redistribution of land. Article 31 of Decree No. 8 made it compulsory for all landowners to register their holdings within one year after the announcement of the decree. A margin of error in the declaration was permitted, but a landowner was to be penalized if more than 20 percent of the information he supplied was incorrect.

†The Khalq government issued a number of other laws and regulations to assist in the creation of agricultural cooperatives and, agricultural credit and loan facilities, but these were quite separate from Decree No. 8 (L. Dupree 1979b:3-4). For example, a regulation dealing with the formation and management of agricultural cooperatives was issued in August 1978 (*Kabul Times*, 8/24/78). During the autumn of 1978 the local administration in Nahrin began setting up a cooperative to make fertilizer, seed, and machinery available to the farmers and to help with marketing their produce. There was to be an initial scaled membership fee. People owning between 1 and 5 jiribs would pay 50 afs. per jirib, and the fee would go up with the size of the holding to 200 afs. per jirib for those owning between 15 and 20 jiribs; those who owned more than 120 jiribs were ineligible for membership. The first cooperative in Afghanistan had been founded in the

reforms of the early 1960s, Decree No. 8 did not stipulate that everyone receiving land should join a cooperative (Lambton 1969:63). However, it did state that various agencies such as the Afghan Chemical Fertilizer Company and the Agricultural Development Bank should open offices in areas where land reform was being carried out and "provide necessary facilities . . . under easy terms to persons who have acquired land" (Article 36). Furthermore, special committees were to be set up at provincial and subprovincial levels to settle disputes arising from the decree's implementation (Article 26).

Land reform has a much shorter history in Afghanistan than do attempts to limit marriage and funeral expenses. According to Poullada (1973:135), King Amanullah carried out the only major land reform program in Afghan history in the 1920s by selling off large tracts of public land at 10 afs. per jirib. However, Grötzbach asserts that this land was mostly sold to large proprietors and that Amanullah's agricultural policies, which included a switch to the collection of land tax entirely in cash, favored large landownership (1972:59). Indeed considerable inequalities in land ownership persisted until 1978, although the absence of reliable statistics makes it impossible to be very precise about them. Afghanistan is often said to have been predominantly a country of small owner-operated holdings (for example, see Wilber 1962:226); according to L. Dupree (1977b:5) over 60 percent of farms were of this kind. In fact there seems to have been considerable regional variation, with large holdings being more common in the south and west. North of the Hindu Kush, and to some extent in Nahrin, large and small properties were found side by side. Nevertheless, throughout the country as a whole it appears that between 40 and 50 percent of the rural population were landless (Toepfer 1976:24; Halliday 1978:33), though land ownership was much less concentrated than in Iran before land reform (Toepfer 1972:101; Grötzbach 1972:209).

In August 1975 the government of President Muhammad Daoud announced a land reform law, but it appears never to have been implemented. In a number of ways it was less radical than Decree No. 8. For example, it would have permitted landowners to retain more land than did the decree: 100 jiribs of double-crop irrigated or orchard land, 150 jiribs of single-crop irrigated land, or 200 jiribs of

Koh Daman in the late 1960s with the assistance of the United Nations and the Swedish government, and in 1971 a second was set up in Baghlan (Fry 1974:92).

dry-farming land (Article II).* However, when it came to the redistribution of expropriated land, the 1975 law was as radical as the decree; it gave first priority to "the farmer, who, prior to the promulgation of the law has been toiling in agricultural work on distributable land" (Article I). (Decree No. 8 stated that land would be redistributed first to "the landless peasant who is busy working on the distributable land" [Article 24].) In both cases, as with the first stage of the Iranian land reform (Lambton 1969:73), it was envisaged that land would mainly be given to those who were already working it as sharecroppers. Halliday asserts that the Iranian reforms were deliberately designed to distribute land only to the richer farmers (the sharecroppers) who at least had access to cultivable land and to exclude the remainder of the rural population—the *khushneshin*, or landless casual laborers (1979:117). At first it may seem surprising that the Khalq government pursued a strategy of redistribution similar to that adopted by the Shah of Iran. However, as in Iran, most of the land belonging to large owners in Afghanistan was cultivated by sharecroppers or tenant farmers. Short of collectivization or bringing new land under cultivation, there was no alternative to giving the sharecroppers title to the land they were already cultivating, even if the casual laborers did not receive any land as a consequence.

There were, however, features of Decree No. 8 that made the Khalq land reform program much more radical than its counterparts in neighboring countries. In particular these were the absence of compensation for those whose excess holdings were confiscated, and the small amount of land a family was allowed to retain in its possession. A second land reform law in Pakistan, implemented in 1972, only reduced the maximum individual (not family) holding of irrigated land to 60 ha and of unirrigated land to 120 ha (Urff et al. 1974:180). The Iranian land reforms permitted a landowner to retain one village or 6 *dangs* of land in different villages in his possession (the ploughland of an Iranian village is usually divided into 6 dangs; Lambton 1969:64).

---

*By contrast with Decree No. 8, compensation was to be paid to the owners of land which was expropriated over a period of twenty-five years at 2 percent interest (Article X). Those among whom the land was redistributed were to pay for it in annual installments (Article XXXIV).

Decree No. 8 was not implemented until after I had left Nahrin; thus I can only hazard a guess at its possible effects.* These are unlikely to have been substantial for two main reasons. First, landholdings in the area were smaller than in many other parts of Afghanistan—for instance, in places like Khanabad and Taliqan in the plains to the north of Nahrin. In those areas there were numerous estates between one and six hundred ha (Grotzbach 1972:209). In the vicinity of the town of Nahrin it appears that only a handful of people owned substantially more than the maximum holding permitted under the terms of the decree. Some people had probably seen the writing on the wall after the coup in April 1978 and reduced the size of their estates by either transferring title to parts of them to relatives or simply selling them. In March 1979, following the implementation of the decree in Nahrin, I heard that portions of the holdings of three people who lived in or near the town had been confiscated and redistributed. Second, the redistribution is unlikely to have benefitted the very poor—i.e., the landless casual laborers— because the larger estates were mostly cultivated by sharecroppers, not managed as single units worked by wage-earning laborers, and, as noted above, it was the sharecroppers who were to be given priority when land was redistributed.

OTHER POLICIES OF THE KHALQ GOVERNMENT AND THEIR IMPLEMENTATION IN NAHRIN

Various other policies which were pursued by the Khalq government were not formally expressed in numbered decrees. Here I shall look at five of these—policies to encourage female education, put a halt to the use of *arbabs* (village leaders—see below) as instruments of indirect rule and speed up the workings of the local administration, control prices, attack corruption, and rally the population with a

---

*As far as the country as a whole is concerned, the *Kabul Times* (6/18/79) reported that the land reform program was 85 percent complete in the summer of 1979 and that 2,700,000 jiribs had been redistributed to 233,000 families. In February 1980 the International Wheat Council forecast a "record low" for Afghan wheat production—2.3 million tons, compared with the previous year's 2.8 million (*Middle Eastern Economic Digest* 24, 7). The speed with which land was confiscated and redistributed is likely to have played a big part in this drop in production.

vigorous propaganda campaign.* It is fair to say that in these respects Khalq policy did not on the whole represent a departure from previous policies, but rather was an intensification of existing trends.

Efforts to give women a modern education in Afghanistan began with King Amanullah, but the results were confined to Kabul, where it is said that by 1928 eight hundred girls were attending government schools (Gregorian 1969:243). The schools were closed during Bacha-i Saqaw's interregnum in 1929, but female education received further encouragement during the reign of Zahir Shah and the presidency of Daoud. Attempts to make an education on modern lines available to girls in Nahrin had begun with the opening of a girls' primary school in the late 1960s. By 1978 the school had nearly three hundred pupils, and two others girls' schools had been opened in villages in the area. However, very few girls went on to study at the local secondary school, partly perhaps because it was coeducational.

Primarily, the Khalq government wanted more girls to attend secondary schools. The director of the secondary school in Nahrin, a Pashtun from Kunar, was a member of the Khalq party who had been given the post after the Saur Revolution. He said he deplored the reluctance of people in Nahrin to allow their daughters to be educated beyond the primary level. He also told me that he and the other party members in Nahrin were looking for a suitable woman to set up a Khalq women's committee, one of whose tasks would be to persuade more girls to stay on at school. Secondarily the government wanted more girls to attend the primary schools. In Nahrin pressure was sometimes put on their parents to allow them to do so, but the tactic was unpopular. Many men said that as good Muslims, they did not want their daughters to be exposed to the influence of school, and they complained of the high cost of books and uniforms.

The government's attempt to reduce the importance of arbabs can be seen as one of a series of efforts—going back at least as far as the reign of 'Abdur Rahman—to strengthen the direct authority of the central government and reduce the power of local leaders. 'Abdur

---

*The government is also said to have launched "massive literacy campaigns throughout the country" (Charpentier 1979:118). I did not hear much about these in Nahrin, but according to the *Kabul Times* (2/5/79), they were going on throughout the subprovince.

Rahman invited "various feudal chieftains" to Kabul, granted them subsidies, destroyed their strongholds and fortifications, and took hostages from among their families (Gregorian 1969:133). King Amanullah abolished the ranks and titles of what Poullada calls the "tribal aristocracy" and curtailed their other privileges (1973:108).

The arbab in Nahrin in the late 1970s was a much humbler creature than members of the "tribal aristocracy" had been. He was a kind of village headman who acted as a link between the villagers and the local administration. Among his duties were drawing up lists of men of the age for military service, assisting with tax collection, and generally representing the villagers when they had dealings with the government. In Nahrin arbabs sometimes enjoyed considerable influence, which they used at times to take advantage of the members of their own communities.* In 1978 the new Khalq subgovernor of Nahrin explained that the arbabs no longer acted as intermediaries and that the ordinary villagers were now free to approach the local administration in person; thus one source of *istismar* (exploitation) had been removed.

Undoubtedly it was easy enough to take away the duties and privileges entrusted to the arbabs by previous governments. It was not such a simple matter to stop people going to them for authoritative advice as they had done before. On the whole, the new subgovernor seemed to be succeeding in his aim of encouraging people to bring their problems to the local administration and no longer to expect the officials automatically to take the arbab's side in a dispute (as they had tended to do in the past). Whether the members of the arbab's own community continued to seek his advice and treat him with respect depended largely on the reputation he had established previously. In one Pashtun village some miles from the town, I heard people heaping scorn on their former arbab and saying he had been so corrupt that they were glad he no longer possessed any authority. In contrast, in an Absarina village nearer the town, people were con-

---

*The position of arbab seems to have been hereditary in Nahrin, though people said that before 1978 the administration would replace an arbab if it could prove that he had been abusing his position. With reference to a village south of Mazar-i Sharif, Poulton et al. (1973, pt. 3:42) reports that the arbab (or *malik*) was in principle elected every year, but I did not hear of annual elections in Nahrin. See also the chapter by Thomas Barfield in this volume.

tinuing to ask their arbab for advice on such matters as disputes over inheritance.

As part of a campaign to discredit the arbabs, the Khalq sub-governor tried to stop people using the word arbab except as a term of abuse. During a game of *buzkashi* which the subgovernor happened to attend, one of the players, a former arbab named Jabar, succeeded in winning a round.* When the spectators started to applaud him and shout "Arbab Jabar!," the subgovernor angrily responded, "Not arbab Jabar, *pahlawan* (hero, champion) Jabar!" In the government's propaganda campaign, the arbabs were denounced as *arbabha-i rishwat khur* — bribe-eating arbabs.

In addition to the success of the attack on traditional local political arrangements, the new subgovernor was very pleased with the way he had speeded up the adjudication of minor disputes. He dealt with these personally rather than passing them over to a properly constituted court. He adopted the procedure of frequent recourse to oath-taking. (In this respect the procedure was surprisingly similar to one followed by the local administration in the Andarab Valley to the south of Nahrin twenty years earlier [Uberoi 1968:76-80].) The sub-governor would begin with the *sih sang-i zanush* (literally the "three stones of his wife"), which is said to be part of traditional divorce procedure (L. Dupree 1973:205). A man taking the oath has to throw three small stones on the ground, saying as he does so that if he is not telling the truth, his wife is not his wife and he is no longer married to her. If the subgovernor felt that he had not arrived at the truth by this means, he would take the office copy of the Quran (reverently wrapped in a special cloth and tied with ribbon) down from its shelf by his desk. He would ask the defendant, or sometimes the plaintiff, to place his right hand on it and swear that he had told the absolute truth. If either party prevaricated, the subgovernor, a large, well-built man, would slap his face vigorously or pull him around the room by his ear before deciding on a suitable punishment or dismissing the case.

In one typical case a laborer had had an *ariza* (petition) written in which he claimed that a landowner had refused to pay him properly

---

*Buzkashi is the most popular sport in northern Afghanistan. Mounted on horseback, the players struggle to gain possession of the carcass of a calf or goat (e.g., see Azoy 1982).

for some work he had done for him.* When the matter came before the subgovernor, the landowner insisted that he had paid the laborer all the money he owed him. The subgovernor then asked the laborer whether he would testify to the truth of his claim by taking an oath on the Quran. The laborer said he would do so willingly. At this point, the landowner announced that perhaps he had been mistaken after all and agreed that he probably did owe the laborer some money. The subgovernor ordered him to settle the debt immediately. While people in Nahrin did not always like the subgovernor's heavy-handed methods, on the whole they seemed to approve of the fact that minor disputes were being settled more quickly—and apparently more fairly—than in the past.

In an effort to regulate prices, in June 1978 the Khalq government declared that shopkeepers could raise their prices by only 8 percent above their level on 27 April 1978 (the date of the coup which brought the Khalq government to power) (L. Dupree 1980d: 4). Regulating prices and trying to control the quality of goods had been common practices in Afghanistan before 1978 (for instance, see Centlivres 1972:47). In Nahrin, in an effort to comply with the spirit of the new law, the new subgovernor set out by having a number of prices lowered. For example, the bus fare from Nahrin to Baghlan was reduced from 40 to 35 afs., while the most popular *ariza nawis* in the bazaar had his shop closed on several occasions in the autumn of 1978 (on the subgovernor's orders) for failing to reduce his charges. A number of restaurants were fined for serving food of poor quality. More important was an attempt to fix the prices of staple commodities; for example, the price of wheat was fixed at 53 afs. per *ser* (7 kilos), that of sugar at 30 afs. a kilo. Such moves were generally popular with the consumers.

The Khalq attack on corruption had precedents in the anti-corruption campaigns conducted by King Amanullah (Poullada 1973:75) and similar efforts by subsequent rulers. Under President Daoud, for instance, teams of jurists were "regularly dispatched to the provinces to ferret out ineptitude and corruption" (Weinbaum 1980:52). In Nahrin the subgovernor's attempts to eradicate bribery were well received by most people, though it is difficult to say how

*All approaches to the local administration had first to be made in the form of written petitions drawn up by an *ariza nawis* (petition writer).

effective they really were. In one case, a clerk in one of the departments of the local administration lost his job and was imprisoned for two years after it was discovered that he had demanded several hundred afs. from a member of the public for performing a service that was part of his normal duties. Wealthy young men could no longer buy their way out of military service. People said that although bribery still went on in the local administration, it was less prevalent than before. Considering how deeply rooted the custom was, even this was something of an achievement (for example, see Uberoi 1968: 82-84).

Regarding the Khalq government's use of propaganda, it is important to note that previous Afghan governments had also tried to influence public opinion by whatever means were available. 'Abdur Rahman, for example, had published pamphlets in which he invoked the concept of the divine right of kings—in effect becoming the first Afghan ruler to do so (Kakar 1979:8). The press and radio (and now television) have been controlled by the state since their inception. Even a new flag introduced with great ceremony by the Khalq government in October 1978 had its counterpart in a new flag introduced in 1928 by King Amanullah, the design of which reflected nationalist and Islamic ideals (Poullada 1973:76). However, the scale of the Khalq government's efforts to win popular support, involving modern communications and techniques of agit-prop, was new.

The aim of Khalq propaganda was to rally support for the government and its policies and to discredit its predecessors. In Nahrin crude cartoons from *Anis* and other national newspapers, caricaturing the late President Daoud in particular, were pinned to a board in the center of the bazaar. Every shop and teahouse displayed a photograph of President Nur M. Taraki. More important, the subgovernor organized demonstrations of support for the government every two or three weeks. These usually consisted of a procession from the local government offices to the secondary school or to the army barracks. The schoolchildren, their teachers, and the officials in the local administration formed the great majority of those taking part. They carried red banners covered with slogans wishing a long life to President Taraki and death to feudalists and imperialists. After the procession there would be a speech by the subgovernor or perhaps a visiting dignitary from Baghlan. In a typical speech a speaker would begin by reminding his listeners how lucky they were. "*Khush bashen*" (be happy), he would shout; *"watan az shumast"* (the country is yours); *"watanfurushha raftand"* (the sellers of the country have gone). He would then usually refer to the reforms being carried out by the new government, to the exploitative practices of President Daoud and his predecessors, and to their unholy alliance with Western imperialism (British in particular) and with feudal interests within Afghanistan.* The Ikhwan, or Muslim Brothers, were another favorite target. Maj. Gen. 'Abdul Qadir, ex-Minister of Defense, was not only attacked verbally, but also burned in effigy at one demonstration in late August 1978 — soon after he and two other members of the cabinet, Col. Muhammad Rafi (Minister of Communications) and Sultan Ali Kishtmand (Minister of Planning), had been arrested, allegedly for plotting to overthrow the government (see L. Dupree 1979b:3). A demonstration in late October commemorated the anniversary of demonstrations in Kabul on 3 Aqrab (25 October) 1965 which had resulted in the deaths of three students. The demonstrations usually ended with the shouting of revolutionary slogans (for example, see *Kabul Times*, 7/26/78).

Early in November the subgovernor planned to hold a demonstration — or what he referred to as a "conference" — to celebrate the implementation of Decree No. 7 — it was to have included dramatic sketches illustrating the themes of the decree performed by the schoolchildren — but it was cancelled owing to an unseasonably early snowfall. Apart from the demonstrations, buzkashi games were sometimes sponsored by the local administration since they attracted large

---

*The Khalq government strongly identified itself with King Amanullah and his efforts to modernize Afghan society and strenuously propagated the Soviet historians' view (see Gregorian 1969:266-27) that Amanullah's downfall was largely due to British intrigues with the tribes living along the frontier with British India. For example, a great deal was made of the fact that T.E. Lawrence, under the pseudonym of Shaw, happened to be stationed at the time at an RAF base in the North-West Frontier Province. The Soviet view is not on the whole shared by Western historians (for example, see Poullada 1973:259). As resistance to the Khalq government increased, the speeches of Taraki and other members of the government increasingly referred to the nefarious role being played by "maulanas ... mullahs ... and ... other clergymen made in London" (*Kabul Times*, 3/11/79). They appear primarily to have been referring to Sibghatullah Mujadidi, who leads the National Liberation Front, one of the resistance groups based in Peshawar (Khalid 1980:203). The Mujadidi family traditionally enjoyed high religious status in Afghanistan and played a large part in triggering the revolt against Amanullah (Poullada 1973:126-29).

crowds which formed captive audiences for speechmaking. All in all, however, my impression was that this propaganda campaign was having very little effect. As noted, the demonstrations essentially attracted only people who were employed by the government, and the jargon used in the speeches tended to confuse rather than to enlighten. Understandably terms such as "feudalist," "imperialist," and even "democratic" did not mean very much to most people, and the traditional wariness and mistrust of government were not going to be overcome by rhetoric alone.

Under Khalq rule the local administration in Nahrin seems to have become somewhat more accessible to the poor and uneducated villagers of the subprovince. In other ways, however, it seems to have become more autocratic than before. Although the new Khalq subgovernor came from a much poorer and less sophisticated background than his predecessor, his outlook was equally authoritarian.* Younger and much more energetic, he was a Pashtun from Kunar who had attended the Teacher Training College in Jalalabad. He had worked in the administration of the Jabal ul-Siraj cement factory near Charikar before being appointed subgovernor of Nahrin in the spring of 1978. Early in 1979 I heard that he had been transferred to the cement factory at Pul-i Khumri and that a local man had been appointed in his place.

The autocratic style of the local administration was shown in a number of ways. To obtain poles for a new telephone line to Baghlan, it simply took materials without payment from privately owned orchards and stands of trees throughout the area. After Id-i Qurban, a religious festival in which animals are sacrificed, the municipality of Nahrin was ordered to collect the hides of the animals which had been slaughtered, whereas people had been accustomed to selling them or using them as they wished. The subgovernor's residence became the Khalq party headquarters in Nahrin, but little effort was made to enroll people into the ranks. My impression is that this was the case in the country as a whole and that the Khalq organization was intended to be an elite party with restricted membership on the Soviet model.

---

*The subgovernor's predecessor seems to have been the only high-ranking official in Nahrin to be replaced by the Khalq government when it first took power. The *commandant* (security chief), the head secretary in the local administration, and the *sharwal* (mayor) of Nahrin remained in their posts.

ATTITUDES TOWARD KHALQ POLICIES IN NAHRIN

It goes without saying that the larger landowners objected to the expropriation of much of their land without compensation and the shopkeepers disliked the more rigorous attempts to control prices. While some people benefited from the provisions of Decree No. 6 and regained control of their land, others found themselves defending their title to land they had been using for decades, and they sometimes lost it altogether. In particular, incidents such as the closure of Sharif Jan's restaurant created anxiety among those who owned property, however small. People arranging marriages were faced with the awkward problem of reconciling the new rules in Decree No. 7 with traditional norms. At the same time, the attempt to speed up the adjudication of minor disputes was welcomed by many people, as was the attack on bribery. The abolition of the arbabs' responsibilities and privileges was on the whole popular; in any case it was unlikely to offend anyone except the arbabs themselves. There was nothing to stop people from consulting their former arbab if they wanted to.

Taken together, the Khalq government's reforms and the manner in which they were implemented in Nahrin amounted to a vigorous if not always well-conceived attempt to change existing economic and political relationships and to alter many patterns of customary behavior. As noted above, many of the policies had precedents in modern Afghan history, but the energy and speed with which they were introduced were original. Thus in spite of the popularity of one or two of the new policies, it is hardly surprising that the overall reaction was one of irritation and anger at the extent to which the new government was interfering in people's lives.

The irritation and anger were compounded by the fact that most people in Nahrin felt a deeper loyalty to Islam than to the Afghan state. Islam, it was believed, sanctioned most if not all of their cherished customs, particularly those concerning the status of women and marriage. Hence it was felt that in trying to change these, the Khalq government was attacking Islam. As the pro-Soviet leanings of the government became more apparent, people began to fear that this was the thin end of the wedge. Regarding the Russians as *kafirs* (pagans), they were well aware that across the northern border the practice of Islam was not encouraged. Furthermore, older people were anxious lest the chaos and insecurity of the late 1920s, when Bacha-i-Saqaw had forced King Amanullah to abdicate and leave the country, be repeated. They recalled that at that time Ibrahim Beg and his followers had taken advantage of this breakdown in the central government's authority to cross the border from Soviet Turkistan into northern Afghanistan. Ibrahim Beg was one of the last survivors of the Muslim guerrillas who had resisted the Soviet reconquest of the tsarist Central Asian empire in the 1920s. (The Soviets referred to the guerrillas as *basmachi*—bandits.) Ibrahim Beg passed through Nahrin, where he is said to have robbed and murdered some of the local people (Sattar Khan 1353 A.H.:54; see also Gregorian 1969:332).*

My impression is that there was hostility toward the new government among the great majority of the local population, irrespective of economic position and ethnic identities. This may seem surprising in view of the ethnic diversity of the inhabitants of the area. However, ethnicity does not appear to have been of great political significance in Nahrin, at least by comparison with some other parts of northern Afghanistan, such as Rustaq (Centlivres-Demont 1976:269) or Saripul.[†] Nor were disparities in wealth as marked as in some other regions.

After the coup in April 1978 soldiers began patrolling the bazaar at night, and as the year wore on the atmosphere became more tense as reports of fighting in the southeast along the Pakistani frontier began to filter through. Meanwhile, the national struggles between the Khalq and Parcham factions of the PDPA had local counterparts in Nahrin. For example, the Parcham head teacher of the girls' school lost his post in the aftermath of the alleged conspiracy led by the Minister of Defense, 'Abdul Qadir, who had Parcham connections (see p. 201 above). Opposition to the Khalq government led to violent incidents in Baghlan and to an uprising in Pul-i Khumri early in 1979. The presence of the army base near the town helped

---

[*]Ibrahim Beg was expelled from Afghan Turkistan in 1931 by Amanullah's successor, Nadir Shah (1930-33) and returned to the Soviet Union, where he was quickly captured and executed (Gregorian 1969:332).

[†]According to Centlivres-Demont, support in Nahrin for candidates in the parliamentary elections in 1969 reflected local solidarity rather than ethnic loyalties (1976:276-77). For Saripul, see Richard Tapper's chapter in this volume.

to keep things more or less peaceful in Nahrin for a while, but fighting seems to have spread to the area subsequently.* For example, in December 1980 Radio Kabul reported that "a group of rebels who had for some time been engaged in robbery and murder in the district of Nahrin, Baghlan province, were recently crushed by the security forces and party activists" (*BBC Summary of World Broadcasts*, 12/18/80).

KING AMANULLAH AND THE KHALQ GOVERNMENT: AFGHAN PERCEPTIONS

One view of King Amanullah's economic and social policies is that they alienated the urban and rural population in general and the tribes and the religious establishment in particular and hence were largely responsible for his downfall (for example, Gregorian 1969:263). On the other hand, Poullada has suggested that in the towns Amanullah's reforms affected only the upper classes and that his agricultural policies minimized peasant dissatisfaction (1973:135). As noted above, there remains some doubt as to the extent to which Amanullah's agricultural policies benefited the peasantry. Nevertheless, Poullada argues convincingly that Amanullah failed to take sufficient account of the traditional antagonism of the Pashtun tribes in the east and south of the country toward the central government, and that the rebellion which led to his downfall was largely caused by tribal separatism. The stresses and strains of modernization were "tangential to the basic conflict" (p. 159). It does seem that Amanullah's reform program created comparatively little resentment in the towns and did not lead to significant urban protests.

In contrast, what happened in Nahrin suggests that the Khalq government's reforms upset most of the nontribal urban and rural population, as well as the tribally organized groups.† While revolts

---

*Early in 1979 I heard that the army base was to be turned into a center for counterinsurgency operations.

†Afghanistan's new rulers have obviously reached this same conclusion. The government of Babrak Karmal is said to have almost completely halted the land reform program, abandoned efforts to educate women in rural areas, and given up the attempt to abolish the payment of brideprice (Halliday 1980c: 10). The *Guardian* reports that the land reform decrees were substantially modi-

first broke out in Nuristan, Khost, and the Hazarajat—that is, the remoter parts of the country where the government's control has never been strong—uprisings and demonstrations soon followed in a number of towns and cities, most notably in Herat in March 1979 (for example, see Griffiths 1981:185).* The fact that there was considerable hostility in the towns as well as the tribal areas to the Khalq government shows that opposition to it cannot be attributed merely to the same spirit of tribal independence which brought down Amanullah. The causes of urban unrest are likely to have been in principle much the same as those of rural discontent. Almost certainly they centered on the unprecedented degree of control the new government was trying to exercise over every section of the population, largely through the implementation of its modernization program. As noted, it was widely felt that in this way the government was attacking Islam as well as encroaching upon individual liberties.

Poullada (1973:274) suggests that Amanullah had been seriously handicapped by failing to use propaganda to rally the people behind his modernization program. In the Khalq case it is difficult to avoid the conclusion that its propaganda campaign was often counterproductive. Public reaction to the new flag is a good example. The flag was red; people were fully aware that red was a color associated with the Soviet Union and drew the appropriate conclusions. Because the Khalq government came to power by means of a military coup rather than a popular uprising or a "war of liberation," it lacked popular support from the beginning. Nevertheless, there was considerable dissatisfaction with the previous government, and many people were ready to give its successor the benefit of the doubt. Had it presented itself and its reforms as inspired by nationalism or Islam, the Khalq government might have generated enough support to survive. Instead

fied during the summer of 1981: Religious leaders and landowners who agree to mechanize and sell their crops to the state are now permitted to own more than the maximum of land permitted by Decree No. 8. Tribal chiefs whose land was confiscated by the Khalq government are being allowed to repossess some of it on condition that they support the government. Some of the land belonging to army officers which was expropriated under the terms of Decree No. 8 is being returned to them as well (*Guardian*, 11/10/81).

*Other instances of urban protest were riots among the Hazarahs in Kabul in June 1979 (*Le Monde*, 6/28/79) and the shooting of a number of Soviets in Kandahar three months later (*Daily Telegraph*, 9/16/79).

it chose to talk in socialist terms, to identify itself closely with the Soviet Union, and to rely on coercion when opposition began to surface. It did not repeat the mistake Amanullah made when he reduced both the size of the army and its pay (Poullada 1973:76).

CONCLUSION

Most of the domestic policies pursued by the Khalq government rapidly to modernize Afghan society were not particularly original and did not differ significantly from the attempts at social and economic reform of various rulers during the last one hundred years. For instance, 'Abdur Rahman had attempted to limit marriage expenses in 1884, setting the first of several precedents for the Khalq government's Decree No. 7. Only Decree No. 6 can be considered an innovation.

Nevertheless, the evidence from Nahrin makes it clear that never in Afghan history has there been such a ruthless attempt to push through so many fundamental changes in such a short time. The implementation of the Khalq reforms undoubtedly involved unprecedented interference in the lives of ordinary people. Some had their marriage arrangements upset, others found their land titles challenged by those clever and unscrupulous enough to manipulate the provisions of Decree No. 6. The few large landowners naturally resented the confiscation of large parts of their estates, and shopkeepers objected to being told to lower their prices, but it was often the poorer men who bridled at being bullied into sending their daughters to school. Most important, people tended to believe that many of the customs which the government was attacking were sanctioned by Islam, to which their loyalties were stronger than to the Afghan state. The government's evident leanings toward the Soviet Union — symbolized by the switch to a red flag — created further antagonism.

Nahrin may not be entirely representative of northern Afghanistan in that ethnic and sectarian rivalries do not seem to have been strong enough there to have enabled the government to win support by favoring one group at the expense of another — as may have happened in some other areas. Nevertheless, there is no doubt that throughout the north, and indeed the country as a whole, the Khalq reforms and the way in which they were implemented caused intense hostility. The rebellion which brought down King Amanullah in 1929 may plausibly be attributed to tribal separatism, but tribal separatism was not primarily responsible for opposition to the Khalq government, though it doubtless played a part in some cases. Rather I would suggest that it was the implementation of the government's reform program, coupled with its increasingly visible dependence on the Soviet Union, which was the principal source of the antagonism the great majority of Afghans rapidly came to feel toward the Khalq regime.

PART IV

BAMYAN

AND

TURKISTAN

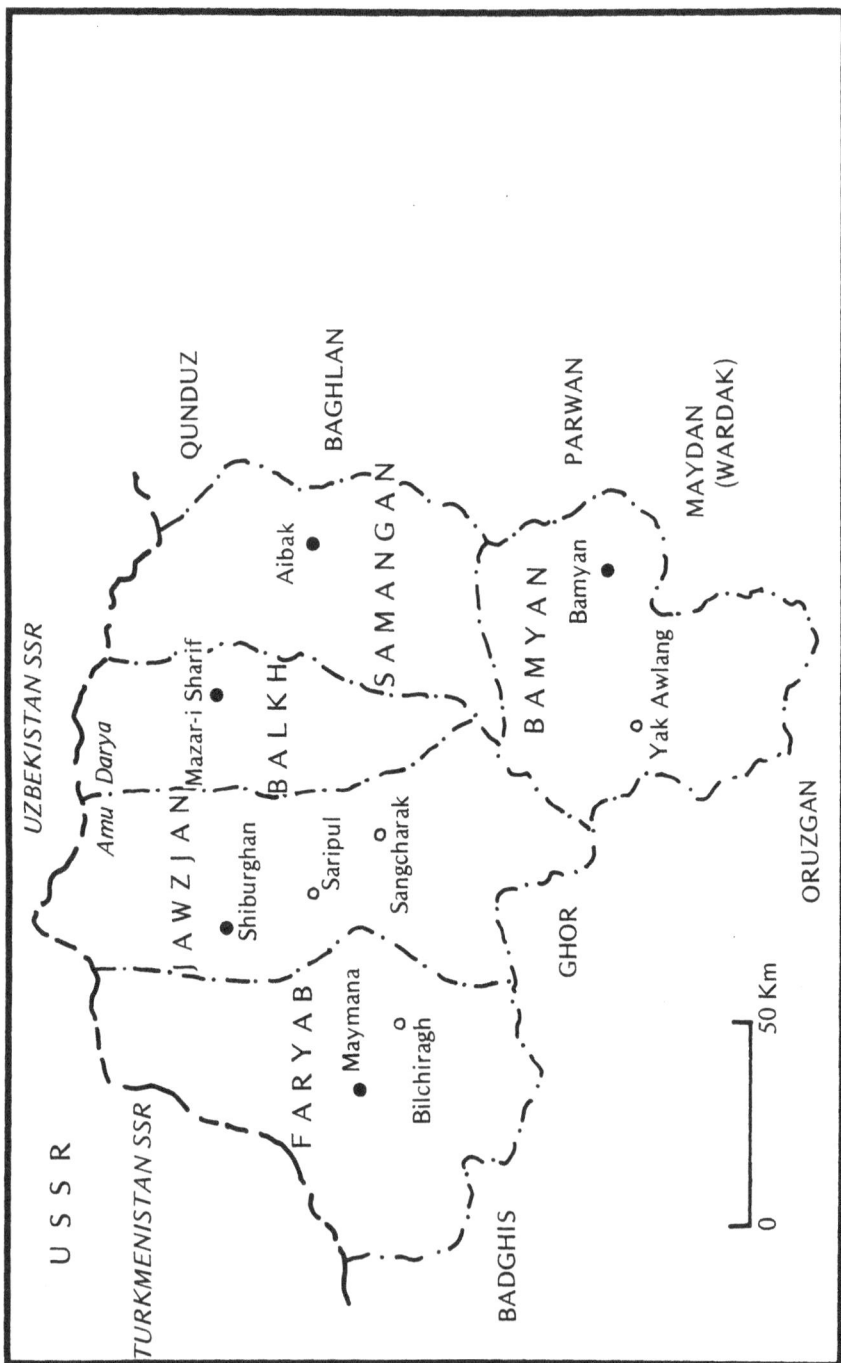

USSR

UZBEKISTAN SSR

TURKMENISTAN SSR

Amu Darya

QUNDUZ

BAGHLAN

Aibak

SAMANGAN

BALKH

Mazar-i Sharif

JAWZJAN

Shiburghan

Saripul

Sangcharak

BAMYAN

Bamyan

PARWAN

MAYDAN
(WARDAK)

Yak Awlang

GHOR

ORUZGAN

FARYAB

Maymana

Bilchiragh

BADGHIS

50 Km

0

BAMYAN AND TURKISTAN

Chapter 9

ISLAMIC COALITIONS IN BAMYAN:
A PROBLEM IN TRANSLATING AFGHAN POLITICAL CULTURE

Robert L. Canfield

THE SIGNIFICANCE OF ISLAMIC COALITIONS

The term "Islamic coalition" implies a certain alignment of people, a certain type of leadership within this alignment, and a certain set of moral understandings that give a sense of meaning and significance to the people who form such an alignment. In this chapter I shall explain the specific qualities of Islamic coalitions in one region of Afghanistan—Bamyan—where the coalitions may be similar to those elsewhere in the country, and suggest how they may relate to the current *mujahidin* (holy war fighters') resistance movement.

PREVAILING IDEAS ABOUT HOW ISLAM FIGURES IN
AFGHANISTAN POLITICS

It has long been accepted that Islamic authorities—commonly called "mullahs"—have had a great deal of influence on traditional affairs in Afghanistan. Studies of Afghanistan's political history frequently mention the significant role that religious authorities have exerted in the country's affairs.* Most analysts of Afghanistan social affairs have noted their social and political influence. For example,

*See especially Caroe (1965), Gregorian (1974), Kakar (1971, 1979), Stewart (1973), and Wilbur (1955).

I am grateful to Jon Anderson for several interchanges (orally and in correspondence) on this paper, and to Hugh Beattie and Stephen Sellers, who offered helpful comments on earlier drafts.

Elphinstone reported that Meer Wauez, a mullah, had become so popular with the Afghans that he used his influence to dethrone Shah Mahmood (1972, vol. 1: 281). More than half a century later, Sultan Muhammad Khan wrote the following:

> At the time of the accession of the present Amir ['Abdur Rahman] to the throne of Kabul, he found the most arbitrary and fantastic powers being exercised in the administration of the state by the clergy of Islam .... The uneducated fanatic community of the so-called Ghazis [Islamic Victors] ... [was] entirely under their influence. In many rebellions and insurrections which endangered the Amir's work, the mullahs took a large share.... Mullah Mushk-i-Alim and his son stirred up the most dangerous rebellion against the Amir (1900: 86).

Khan believed that the amir had diminished the power of the mullahs: "In the present day it is impossible for the most powerful mullah to stir up the feelings of the populace" (1900: 87) A quarter of a century later Iqbal Ali Shah wrote in similar terms:

> Until quite recently the religious thraldom of the priests in Afghanistan was quite complete.... Incidents are not unknown when the throne had felt that its security to a very large extent lay in being favorably disposed toward fanatical mullahs. The influence that the clergy exercise over the people centers around the proclamation of holy war or jehad (1928: 210).

Shah concedes that

> the active cooperation of the mullahs, or clergy, is of great significance [for the newly formed government]. As the bulk of the people still are under the spell of the clergy, through the agencies of the mullahs the king at Kabul can add to his power, and through their instigations too he can very materially suffer in his prestige and control.... The frowns of the clergy of Afghanistan can imperil the safety of the Afghan King and threaten his throne, as their blessings can consolidate his strength.... The preaching of the mullahs keeps up the martial spirit of the Afghans at white heat (1928: 216).*

*Stewart (1973) frequently mentions the activity of mullahs during the 1920s; in her index see "Akhunzada, Mahmud"; "Chaknawar Mullah"; "Gul

Even though the social and political strength of the religious leaders is generally noted, social analysts have not given much attention to the structural arrangements through which these leaders have exerted their influence. The usual focus has been on the kinds of sociopolitical units that are generally considered important in the political affairs of Third World countries: tribes, peasant communities, ethnic groups, regional groups, and national units such as political parties and governments. Coalitions based on religious ideals which could exert a strong influence on public affairs have not received much serious attention.

The three most important books on politics in Afghanistan have given little attention to such coalitions. Richard Newell (1972) focused on national institutions, mainly in the Zahir Shah period (1933-73). He brushed past the political influence of *pirs* ("saints") and mullahs in the introductory chapter in order to get to the political topics he considered important: government policy, international affairs, economic development, and political parties.* Louis Dupree (1980a), in his encyclopedic work on Afghanistan, devoted one chapter to religion but said little about the sorts of religious alignments that have borne upon public affairs. Like Newell, the political units that he explained with greatest cogency were secular: tribes, ethnic groups, regional groups, political parties, and of course government. Poullada (1973) explicitly sought to deal with one prominent example of the influence of religious authorities on Afghanistan politics—the popular uprising in 1929 against King Amanullah which was reputedly instigated by religious authorities and motivated by religious concerns. Poullada concluded that it was not the opposition of the religious authorities to the king or concern about religious matters that brought forth such a general uprising, but "tribal power." The religious authorities only "legitimated" the insurrection; the real motives for it were political. In addition to these important works on political processes and alignments in Afghanistan as a whole, a

Agha"; "Hadda Mullah"; "Hazrats of Shor Bazaar"; "Lame Mullah"; "Masum"; "Mullahs"; "Shah Agha"; "Sher Agha"; and "Tagao Mullah."

*In a recent shorter work R. Newell (1980) speaks more directly to the problem of the influence of Islam in Afghanistan. N. Newell and R. Newell (1981) mention the pervasive role that Islam as an ideology and Islamic coalitions as organizational networks have played in the recent uprisings against the Marxist Afghan government and its Soviet sponsors.

number of anthropologists have written about politics in local or re-gional contexts,* but few have had much to say about religious or sectarian groupings on the local or regional level.[†]

The cumulative effect of this attention to secular alignments has been that scarcely anyone seems to doubt that they are the impor-tant units of political action in the country. As the consensus of the current sociological literature now has it, religious coalitions are not important political units in Afghanistan.

ISLAMIC COALITIONS AS SOCIOPOLITICAL UNITS

In Bamyan, where I did field research between 1966 and 1968, I found that religious coalitions—or rather Islamic coalitions (a better term, for reasons to be explained below)—exerted a significant in-fluence on social and political affairs; furthermore, these coalitions linked up in national arenas in such ways as to convince me that they could have a similar bearing on public affairs in other parts of the nation. I shall outline the characteristic features of the coalitions of Bamyan, explaining how they have political as well as religious qualities. I shall emphasize that the Islamic coalition is one type of social unit that bears upon local affairs in Afghanistan and so acts— at least in certain contexts—as a political force. This point seems especially significant at this time, when the various localized resistance groups in the country identify themselves as mujahidin. Islamic co-alitions like those in Bamyan seem to be an important type of orga-nizational structure through which many of these local groups have coalesced in order to resist the Marxist Afghan government and its

*See L. Dupree (1976a) for a comprehensive review covering most anthropo-logical studies done in Afghanistan up to 1976. Several valuable studies have been done since, many of them by contributors to this volume (see bibliography). Some others are Balland (1974), Centlivres (1976b, 1979, 1980), Centlivres-Demont (1976), Einzmann (1977), Glatzer (1977), Gronhaug (1973), Shalinsky (1980), and Snoy (1972).

[†]Einzmann (1977) and Gronhaug (1973) are exceptions. Centlivres (1972: 42, 165, 166) briefly describes craft guilds led by Islamic authorities (pirs) in Tash-qurghan, but Charpentier (1972) does not mention them. Hallet and Samizay (1980) mention that such guilds exist in Kandahar. Because craft guilds have had an influence on political affairs elsewhere (see Miner 1965), I assume that they do in Afghanistan as well.

Soviet sponsors.* To explain how a religious unit can act as a political force, we shall need to consider a more general question of how subtle nuances of understanding in one culture can best be represented in another, for the fact that social alignments defined as "Islamic" may have political qualities raises the question—at least to Western "secular" minds—of whether "religious" aspects of public groupings can be distinguished from "political" aspects.

Thus the focus of this study will be on the structure of a certain kind of organization. The approach will be causal-functional: we want to examine the organizational features of Islamic coalitions in Afghanistan. As a result, we will treat rather too lightly the cultural understandings, the "logico-meaningful" structures that inform the lives of the people who form these coalitions.†

THE STRUCTURE OF ISLAMIC COALITIONS

By Islamic coalition I mean a network of people that are brought together as an Islamic body for collective public action. It is a network in that it is a "relevant series of linkages existing between individuals which may form a basis for the mobilization of people for specific purposes, under specific conditions" (Whitten and Wolfe 1973: 720). In this section I shall describe the Islamic coalition first in its minimal form and then in its expanded and maximal forms as I observed them in Bamyan in 1966-68. In succeeding sections I shall explain more precisely the coalitions' political qualities.**

*Virtually all the groups active in the resistance have an explicitly Islamic quality. The following sources describe the resistance groups in Afghanistan: *Afghanistan Times* 1, 1 (1980, pp. 1ff.), Chaffetz (1980), Dastarac and Levant (1980), L. Dupree (1979a, 1980a), Gage (1980), Halliday (1980a), Howe (1980), and N. Newell and R. Newell (1981).

†The terminology here is that used by Geertz (1959) and developed much earlier by Sorokin (1937). The "logico-meaningful" structures—i.e., the shared understandings that inform people's lives—cannot be treated fully from a causal-functional approach.

**There have been a few studies of Islamic networks and coalitions elsewhere in the Islamic world. Some prominent ones have concerned Morocco: Gellner (1969), Eickelman (1976), and Crapanzano (1973). Some useful studies of Islamic leaders elsewhere are Siegel (1969), Gilsenan (1973), and Mayer (1967).

THE MINIMAL UNIT: THE PIR NETWORK

In its minimal form in Bamyan the Islamic coalition was a grouping of people aligned, usually rather loosely, to a pir; this might be called a pir network. The pir network was essentially a collectivity of dyadic relations between the pir and each of his followers or clients (*murids*), but secondarily it entailed a number of other cross-cutting ties as well.

The pir was the pivotal figure—for various reasons: (1) The pir was relatively wealthy, at least in land, and often in other ways as well. One pir I knew owned several financial enterprises, the most lucrative of which was an export-import business. (2) The pir was generous and thereby had many social "debtors." A pir provided hospitality to his clients, feeding them generously when they came to visit; when the pir visited them, he occasionally gave some of them presents. (3) The pir had many personal connections with prominent individuals in Bamyan and elsewhere in the country; he and his family—in fact more his close relatives than the pir himself, who normally was occupied with worship and meditation—served as patrons or sponsors for his clients when they needed the special attention of prominent people or (especially) government officials. A note from a pir or a member of his family asking that a client receive special attention sometimes made the difference between the client's receiving rough or deferential treatment in a government office. (4) The major reason for the pir's pivotal role in the pir network was that he was thought to possess special spiritual or moral qualities. By definition a pir was a person who had *karamat*, a spiritual or moral essence attributed to people especially close to God.* The understanding of how a person happened to have karamat varied somewhat according to the teachings of the different sects—Sunni, Imami Shi'ite (the Ayatolla Khomeini kind; also known as "Twelvers"),† or Isma'ili Shi'ite (the Aga Khan kind). However, all the sects generally shared the belief that God's favor was passed to believers through his *walis*, "friends" or "vice regents" (i.e., the pirs); indeed without walis there would be no blessing at all in the world. These views were

---

*Karamat comes from the same Greek word as the English term charisma. In Islamic tradition it is a somewhat more concrete, materially beneficial entity.

†For an explanation of the term "Twelvers," see note on pp. 220-21 below.

expressed in the eleventh century by Hujwiri, an influential Sufi mystic from Ghazni:

God has saints [awliya] whom He has specifically distinguished by his friendship [wilayat] and whom He has chosen to be the governors of His kingdom and has marked out to manifest His actions and has peculiarly favoured with diverse kinds of miracles [karamat] and has purged of natural corruptions and has delivered from subjection to their lower soul and passion, so that all their thoughts are of Him and their intimacy is with Him alone. Such have been in past ages, and are now, and shall be hereafter until the Day of Resurrection (1910: 212-13).*

Many Afghans still believe that the power of walis is present in the world (although many people I knew in Bamyan acknowledged with regret that the great pirs were all gone now, or at least were not so evident). This belief in walis was the ultimate cultural basis for the pirs' influence. It was because the pirs were held in awe by the people that they acquired their wealth in the first place, for their followers gave them "gifts"—pirs were never paid for their services—to acknowledge that they were in some sense "governors of God's kingdom" and to express their loyalty and gratitude for the favors the pirs had bestowed upon them.

As mentioned already, the dyadic tie between the pir and each of his clients was not the only relationship of importance in the pir network. The clients themselves were bound together by many other ties. Some of these were by locality, for most members of a community were united by ties of descent, intermarriage, and cooperative contracts (see Canfield 1973b). Such ties tended to make the members of a locality also members of the same pir network. In addition, many clients of a pir in different communities intermarried, so that

*The word pir and the concept of wali are used by all three Islamic sects. However, the wali concept was absorbed within the Shi'ite traditions and became intrinsic to Shi'ite theology. It developed outside the main juridical tradition of Sunnism as part of Sufi thought. Sufism, a mystical tradition that became a conscious movement after the ninth century, although for a time opposed by Sunni jurists, was eventually legitimated theologically and incorporated into Sunnism. The Shi'ites strongly opposed formal Sufism (perhaps because they recognized in it a threat to the core of Shi'ite piety?), but they did not in principal reject the concept of wilayat (see Hodgson 1974, vol. 2, index).

the affinal bonds that formed among people of different regions normally fell within the membership of one pir network. Furthermore, the members of a single ethnic type frequently occupied a particular territory and intermarried; thus the members of a pir's network mostly belonged to the same ethnic type. These ties therefore held the members of a pir coalition together in a kind of corporate association, and the result was that the pir network was interlaced with many kinds of ties beyond those between the pir and his clients.

In effect most of the ties in the pir network had both "sacred" and "secular" qualities. The religious flavor of the ties was evident in the rituals that contributed to community and tribal and ethnic group solidarity. These rituals were regarded as mainly Islamic; in fact the more important ones (e.g., Friday prayers, Id celebrations, and month of fast) were regarded as essentially Islamic. The ties of affinity as well were strongly suffused with Islamic implications; for example, marriages were always joined according to rules stipulated by Islam, and sometimes they were further sanctified by the special blessings of the pir. Moreover, the ties of affines joined by Islamic marital rituals were reinforced by the visiting and sharing activities that took place on Islamic holidays, supposedly according to the requirements of Islam.

The ties of community, affinity, and common descent were therefore not solely secular. The Islamic quality inherent in the relation of people to their pir lent to their social, economic, and political relationships a religious and even sectarian cast (for the pir was always identified with an Islamic sect). The pir network, even though it focused on the pir himself, was more than a composite of the many individual ties between a pir and each of his clients; it was a corporate body joined by interlacing ties. These provided many grounds for trust, loyalty, and cooperation among the pir's clients.

Included within a pir network were the mullahs who acknowledged the karamat of the network's pir. In Bamyan a mullah was simply anyone who was learned to any unspecified degree. In rural areas some people were called mullah simply because they were able to read, even if only barely—such was the esteem among the rural people for literacy. Other mullahs were truly learned, and a few were extremely well educated. The esteem of people for mullahs varied according to the mullahs' learning, the more learned being the more esteemed. It also varied along other lines, such as according to the renown of the mullahs as preachers and as healers—for their ritual knowledge was believed possibly to include ways to cure and deliver the afflicted. Unlike pirs, mullahs were paid—and some were paid very well. They normally had regular allowances for teaching children and leading prayers, and they received extra remuneration for offi- ciating at deaths, marriages, and circumcisions. The knowledge of mullahs therefore served as a basis for their prestige and wealth, and the "big" mullahs developed a significant influence over the people they served. Mullahs had prestige and often wealth even though, be- cause of their bookish ways, they had become a stereotype and were sometimes the butt of jokes (behind their backs of course).

The mullahs in Bamyan (and I think elsewhere also) were not so influential as the pirs, however, because even though learning was not a requisite for pirship, the pirs had augmented their karamat by studying and writing, thus acquiring reputations for much Islamic learning. Having both the sacred power of a pir and the superior learning of a mullah gave them great prestige. In popular cognizance the great pirs were also great mullahs. As is well known (see Fazlur Rahman 1966), mullahs all over the Islamic world have opposed or at least distrusted pirs and the Sufi tradition which provides the concep- tual bases for the pirs' authority. In theory, mullahs are supposed to point out the authentic pirs and denounce the false ones so that the common people will not be misled (Fazlur Rahman 1966; Hodgson 1974). In practice, the mullahs in Bamyan were not especially learned, and they deferred to the pirs, who were usually more learned and certainly more highly esteemed by the common people. The Shi'ite pirs in fact sent out client mullahs to teach their followers on their behalf, and these mullahs of course extolled the superior karamat of their commissioning pirs.

Many Isma'ili and Imami pirs exerted great influence over their clients—a general characteristic of Shi'ite coalitions for dogmatic rea- sons—but this seemed less true of the Sunni pirs. Unlike the Shi'ites, the Sunni pirs did not have well-organized administrative networks. Most of them did their own teaching and collecting of gifts and/or contributions, for example, whereas the Shi'ite pirs had intermediary mullahs (*khalifahs*) who visited local communities on the pirs' behalf; they taught, officiated in prayers, and collected the gifts and contri- butions for the pirs. The Sunni peoples regarded these pirs as less powerful than certain Sunni pirs who did not come into the valley, such as the Hazrat of Shor Bazaar, whom they might have visited in Kabul if they had had a pressing need. Moreover, among the few educated men among the Sunnis, most of whom were not native to Bamyan, some did not acknowledge any pir.*

WIDER CONNECTIONS AND THE EXPANDED COALITION

The pir and his clients (including the mullahs who acknowledged and supported his pirship) formed the minimal unit of religious coalition. This minimal unit never stood alone, however. The pir and his network had ties with other pirs and their networks. They were united through two kinds of association—one horizontal and the other vertical. In the horizontal association pirs who acknowledged each other's legitimacy developed informal ties, especially through the intermarriage of their families. Indeed many families of pirs had intermarried for several generations. Such connections served as the basis for fellowship and cooperation among the pirs and their networks, as occasions required.

In addition to the horizontal associations, the pirs of the Isma-'ilis and Imamis acknowledged higher authorities outside of Afghanistan. The Isma'ili pirs acknowledged the superior authority of the Aga Khan, Prince Karim Khan, the living Imam of the Isma'ilis.† The

---

*The difference in the strength of the dedication of Sunnis to their pirs may have had to do with Sunni dogma, which has been ambivalent (to say the least) about the Sufi teachings about walis, which underlie the concept of pirship (see Fazlur Rahman 1966). Sunnism does not now deny that walis exist, but most Sunni mullahs severely question the claims of all but the most powerful pretenders; in essence they demand additional credentials—that is, those of learning. The Sunni pirs that are regarded highly (the ones who have large and loyal followings) are noted for their learning. Using learning as a measure, the Sunnis of Bamyan could venerate one Sunni pir but regard another one as even greater. Moreover, I think it is because of this measure that the great Sunni pirs are mostly known (especially among outsiders) as mullahs—that is, as learned authorities rather than as pirs.

†The Shi'ites use the term "Imam" to refer to the person who has (or had) the right to lead the Islamic community. The Imams are related through a chain of descent from Ali, the Prophet's son-in-law, and thus from the Prophet himself (although for some Shi'ites, Ali is more significant than Muhammad). But the Shi'ite sects differ over which descendants are the rightful heirs to the Imamate.

Imami pirs similarly acknowledged higher authorities in Iraq and Iran.* Both the Imami and Isma'ili pirs sent or carried contributions on behalf of themselves and their followers to the higher authorities. The Sunni pirs did not link up into such a formalized hierarchy, but they claimed lineal connections with prominent families in other countries, the relationships often putatively going back through a line of religious authorities to the close associates of Muhammad, if not to Muhammad himself. Moreover, Sunni pirs took great stock in the relationships they had with prominent teachers and fellow students they had met while studying abroad.

MAXIMAL LIMITS OF THE COALITION

The maximal unit of Islamic coalition in Bamyan was the sect. I know of no association of any kind between people of different sects, be they pirs, mullahs, or commoners. That is, only pirs who belonged to the same sect would acknowledge each others' claims to pirship and maintain social or affinal ties with each other; they and their mullahs and other followers maintained a sharp distance from members of other sects. The leaders of a maximal coalition—the pirs and mullahs of a sect—have at times come together to evaluate accusations against one of their peers for teaching false doctrine, but this apparently has happened rarely. The Isma'ilis tell of a time when one of their mullahs was brought before an assemblage of Sunni authorities. Shah (1928: 213-15) records an instance of this kind that took place during the reign of Habibullah (1901-19).

The Imamis follow a line that ended with an Imam, the Twelfth, who disappeared, and they await his reappearance, which will herald the approach of the end of time. The Isma'ilis follow a line of Imams that diverged from the Imami line at the Seventh Imam (thus they are sometimes called "Seveners") but continues to the present. Since the nineteenth century their Imam has been known in the West as the Aga Khan.

*The Imami pirs of Afghanistan were sometimes called *mujtahids* (learned enough to make innovative interpretations), but most people acknowledged that they were not true mujtahids; all of the true mujtahids, people told me, were in Iraq and Iran. Since the Iranian Revolution, Khomeini may be regarded as the most prominent mujtahid of the Imamis. I have heard from some Afghans that he is in any case highly admired by many Afghans, even some that are not Imamis.

In Bamyan, therefore, there were three maximal Islamic coalitions—that is, the Sunni, Isma'ili, and Imami sect groups. However, the members of one sect seldom formed a united bloc; they did so only when threatened by a similar bloc—that is, by the maximal coalition of another sect. For example, the pir networks of the Hazarah Shi'ites joined forces under the headship of a single Imami pir when confronted with a Sunni army in the Hazarah-Afghan war in the nineteenth century (Kakar 1971).

THE SPATIAL PATTERN OF ISLAMIC COALITIONS

As already noted, Islamic coalitions spilled out beyond the boundaries of Bamyan; how they are situated spatially in Bamyan remains to be explained. As is discussed in other publications (Canfield 1973a, 1973b), the Sunni populations occupy the central lowlands of the Bamyan Valley, the Imami Shi'ites occupy the highlands to the west, south, and east of the valley (the northern side is mostly uninhabitable), and the Isma'ili Shi'ites are interspersed among the Imamis in highland valleys of the east of the region. All of the pirs on whom the Islamic coalitions of Bamyan focused lived outside the Bamyan Valley. The pir of the Isma'ilis lived in Kayan, some distance to the northeast. He was pir for all the Isma'ili people in Bamyan, although there were some disputes about his pirship (which I shall discuss below). There was one other Isma'ili pir in Afghanistan, recognized by the pir of Kayan and his clients, and he lived in Shughnan, a region in Qataghan (see Shahrani 1979a). There were two Imami pirs for Bamyan: one lived in Kabul in the Shi'ite district of Chindawul; the other lived in Yak Awlang, a region to the west of Bamyan. There were two Sunni pirs; both lived in Kabul province— one in the city of Kabul and the other in Paghman.

POLITICAL ACTIVITY IN ISLAMIC COALITIONS

I found the pir networks of Bamyan to be highly politicized— especially those of the Shi'ites. The political dimensions of these networks can be shown by a brief summary of some of the public issues that in 1967-68 concerned the members of one pir coalition of the

Isma'ili sect, most of whose members lived in Bamyan. In any other context, these issues would have been recognized as political, but in these cases they implicitly entailed some religious elements as well.

A major issue that unsettled all of the pir's clients was a dispute between the pir—specifically his sons, who were his heirs—and his nephew. The nephew was the son of the former pir; he had been only a child at the time of his father's death, and his father's brother had become the new pir. This nephew felt that he should have received a greater share of his father's wealth. The issue was exacerbated by the fact that the current pir was very old and would surely die soon, and his property would then have to be divided. Explicitly the issue was concerned with who would inherit the pir's wealth, but implicitly it represented another claim—namely, that the nephew was in fact the proper heir, and thus the rightful pir, because his father had been the previous pir. As Shi'ites, these people favored passing the pirship in a line of descent. Thus, in theory at least, the nephew felt he had a better claim to the pirship than the actual pir. The fact that the nephew claimed a large share of the inheritance revealed that he felt he was in a position to challenge the pirship—not by challenging the present pir directly, but by challenging the right of one of the pir's sons to succeed to the pirship.

A second issue of major political importance was the death of a woman in a village a day's walk from the village of the pir and his nephew. The causes of her death were in dispute: her family claimed that she had been hit with a shovel by a neighbor; the neighbor and the rest of the village claimed that she had been killed by falling rocks. The woman and her neighbor belonged to the Isma'ili sect, and hence to the same pir network; thus the conflicting claims generated much interest among the pir's clients generally. But this interest was heightened by the fact that the woman and her family were known to be sympathetic to the claims of the pir's nephew, whereas the rest of the village was not. The division within the network over the pir's dispute with his nephew was thus intensified by a lively division over the causes of the woman's death. The woman's family eventually took the case to court—a procedure that was seldom resorted to by the followers of the pir. The appeal to the court revealed that the community had been torn in two.

A third major issue involved a dispute between a mullah and the members of a village that had invited him to come and teach their children. In order to entice him they had offered him some land. But when the dispute between the pir and his nephew broke out, the mullah (who came from an area loyal to the nephew) sided with the nephew. The members of the village, loyal to the pir, then tried to get the mullah out of the community and to recover the land they had given him. However, the mullah had already registered the land with the government, so (at the time I left) the villagers had been unable to recover it.

Finally, one of the pir's sons was accused of molesting the wife of his neighbor, and the neighbor (who was being supported by followers of the pir's nephew) went to court for redress. The neighbor's complaint provided an occasion for a general who had long held a grudge against the pir to persecute the pir and his clients. The court case extended over many months and involved many other complicating events.

There were thus three court cases generated by disputes within this pir network, and all of them were in some way complicated by the nephew's claim to a large portion of the pir's wealth and his implied claim to the pirship. These cases generated much discussion and disagreement among the members of the pir's network. There were debates; there were intrigues; there were superficial arguments and underlying personal antagonisms; and there were of course tempting bribes offered to the court officials. In sum, the pir network was clearly not solely a ritual or sectarian association. It had some important sociopolitical dimensions: the behavior of the people in the network entailed conflict and maneuverings such as one would find in political groups elsewhere.

TRANSLATING THE STRUCTURE OF ISLAMIC COALITIONS INTO WESTERN CONCEPTS

It should be apparent that the Islamic coalition, as I saw it in Bamyan, was not a religious unit; it was an Islamic unit. The term "Islamic" here implies a broader range of meanings than are normally associated with the term "religious" in Western contexts. It connotes an association of ritual, social, and political qualities in a single entity.*

*Other authors in this volume have referred to the permeation of Afghanistan social affairs with Islamic values. For example, see Barfield's comments on Imam

THE MUJAHIDIN: FIGHTERS FOR A HOLY WAR OR FREEDOM?

The association of ritual and political qualities is implicit in a term that the resistance groups in Afghanistan now use in referring to themselves: mujahidin. The word itself represents the particular association of meanings that I believe is entailed in the meaning of Islamic coalitions. However, it has been difficult to translate the word into Western terms because it suggests an association of qualities not familiar to most Westerners. As is widely known and as indicated above, in a strict sense mujahidin means "holy war fighters." Yet many journalists and some scholars have persisted in translating the term as "freedom fighters." Until recently that translation has seemed to me especially unfortunate, for it secularizes a genuinely religious term. I have come to realize, however, that in a loose sense the term freedom fighters may in fact better convey to the Western public the true content of the resistance fighters' motives.

Consider what the literal meaning of the term "holy war fighters" implies. Most Westerners would normally assume that anyone who calls himself a holy war fighter is a fanatic. If he is willing to kill and die for a religious cause, he must be narrow-minded, bigoted, intractable, insensitive, and possibly even cruel. There are, in fact, some newcomers to the study of Afghanistan who have taken the mujahidin to be disagreeable and undesirable in ways suggested by our word "fanatic." For example, one of these has called the resistance fighters "primitive fundamentalist Moslem tribesmen who would make Khomeini look like a graduate student at M. I. T." (Halliday 1980b: 71). Another, cited as an authority on contemporary Afghanistan, is quoted as saying that the Afghan resistance fighters "are medieval. . . . They're absolutely barbarians. . . . They don't even pretend to stand for anything enlightened, anything good for the people. . . . These are medieval people who are criminally exploiting the name of Islam" (quoted in Paul 1980: 14). That is not the image of the resistance

Sahib (p. 181) and Keiser's on Darra-i Nur (p. 124; see also p. 126). Tavakolian's central point is that indigenous religious and political authority merge to help maintain local political autonomy among subtribes of Durrani nomads (p. 249). Katz emphasizes the links between government service, national defense, and Islam for the people of Nuristan (p. 109). Shalinsky has noted that "Islam is . . . explicitly linked to politics in the hostility toward the Russians" (1980; see also Shalinsky 1979b).

fighters that most scholars would consider most accurate, so even though some of them know otherwise, they translate the word mujahidin as freedom fighters.

In addition to not carrying a negative connotation, the term freedom fighters has the merit of capturing well for the Western mind a dimension of the moral sensibility of the people of Afghanistan. It indicates that the resisters are fighting for a legitimately sacred cause, for if there remains anything sacred in Western consciousness it is the concept of freedom. Within Western consciousness one of the inalienable rights of the human being is freedom. Freedom is a cause for which an honorable person may justifiably kill and die. Thus the looser, freer rendition of mujahidin makes the motives of the resistance fighters understandable and respectable to Westerners.*

While this loose translation effectively conveys the moral sensibility of the mujahidin to the Western public, however, it unfortunately loses an important element of it. For the sincere Muslim in Afghanistan takes it for granted that freedom entails the right and responsibility to command good and oppose evil according to the truth of God as it has been revealed in Islam. If the quest for freedom is the mujahid's motive, it is for the freedom to obey God and direct others to obey God.† For this reason, I prefer the stricter, more literal translation of the word mujahidin; it preserves the religious qualities of the term without seriously detracting from its political qualities. In any case, implicit within the word is a merging of religious and political concepts.

---

*The Afghanistan Marxists and Soviets have another term for the mujahidin: bandits. It is interesting to note that the Russians called the anti-Bolshevik Muslim rebels of Central Asia in the 1920s by the Turkish equivalent: *basmachis* (see d'Encausse 1967 and Shalinsky 1980).

†The quest for the freedom to obey God and to direct others to obey God is explicit in the literature of some of the resistance groups. In a pamphlet outlining its aims, the Hizb-i Islami (Islamic Party) included the following statement: "Justice in human society is impossible unless it is based on belief in God, life after death and the guidance of prophets. Afghanistan fell into miseries as it departed from the rule set above, though its population is entirely Muslim. . . . We, therefore, believe in (i) faithful adherence to the principles of Islam, (ii) eradication [of] tyranny and exploitation, (iii) fostering virtues, (iv) introduction of law and (v) reawakening of religious feelings and sentiments, (vi) spreading the divine message throughout the world. . . . Afghanistan is fundamentally an Islamic state where Un Islamic ideas and practices should not exist" (*sic.*; N.D.a: 7-9).

To say that political and religious concepts are "merged" in the mujahidin groups—and especially in the Islamic coalition—is to consider the terms from a Western point of view. Westerners assume that a clear distinction can be made between religion and politics, and they tend to regard the merging of these two separate qualities as unusual. However, this assumption is in fact a historically recent development even in the West. The distinction between religion and politics became important in the seventeenth century, when the word "religious," meaning the worshipful appreciation of God, changed to mean adherence to a system of beliefs defined by a church. By the end of the century many people had come to feel that the beliefs and practices associated with a particular church differed from those associated with the affairs of state (see W. C. Smith 1963: ch. 2).*

*Apparently the distinction between a sacred and a profane domain was already in evidence as early as the fourteenth or fifteenth centuries; Hugh Beattie has pointed out that it was implicit in the position of Marsiglio of Padua (personal communication). The distinction took a precise form as the philosophes (Diderot, D'Holbach, Rousseau) and others such as Voltaire and Hume sought to distance themselves from the sectarian antagonisms of their time. They viewed the medieval church as a drag against the accelerating intellectual advances of their time, and they identified instead with the classical Greeks, who were agnostic. The church and the sectarian quarrels of their time were "religious," they said, and they wanted no part of them. The distinction appealed, for other reasons, to the Erasmians and later the Puritans.

Some scholars trace the development of the separation of church and state in the West to a different source. According to Verduin, the idea that church and state should be separate was sown by first-century Christians. By preaching a voluntary repentance and faith, they presented to the world "a new and very revolutionary concept of society, namely, that men can get along peacefully in the market place even though they do not worship at the same shrine" (1964: 21). The early Christians took it for granted that the willingness to conform to the rules of public intercourse (those of "the market place") and the rules of worship ("the shrine") were separable. "In the New Testament vision, that which we today call the State and that which we now call the Church are agencies that cater to different loyalties" (Verduin 1964: 22). In the fourth century, when Constantine embraced Christianity, he made it the cult of Rome in place of the old Roman cult. For Rome this constituted little structural change. For Christianity it constituted a radical shift in its relation to the public sector; its pristine emphasis on voluntary repentance and faith gave way to an emphasis on formal compliance to church regulations. Thus Christianity became alien to its essence by its being made into law. This Constantinian fusion was the legacy

Assuming a precise distinction between church and state, between religion and politics, many scholars of Afghanistan affairs have tended to distinguish between political and religious entities there. They suppose that the essence of a public movement in Afghanistan, inasmuch as it is public, is political; whatever religious qualities it has are only a facade. Religious emphases in political situations have been treated as mere "propaganda." Declared religious motives for cooperative public actions have been regarded as "politically" motivated—that is, based on self-interest. The tendency to regard political movements as ipso facto nonreligious or insincerely religious seems to arise from the Western belief that people can be impelled by either political or religious motives but not both at once.

THE INTRINSIC UNITY OF POLITICAL AND RELIGIOUS CONCERNS IN THE ISLAMIC COALITION

In Afghanistan public affairs religious concerns are not always separable from political and material interests. Western biases tend to mask that fact, so Westerners may miss the full range of moral implications entailed in Afghanistan's Islamic coalitions. As noted, in the Islamic coalition political and social ideals are merged. To be sure, there are some strong social or political reasons why religious categories have often come to stand for the public interests of large masses of people in Afghanistan—as in the case of the two Anglo-Afghan wars in the nineteenth century, for example—but inherent in those reasons are cultural reasons as well: the moral framework that informs public affairs does not clearly distinguish religious obligations from political ones.* In Anderson's words, it appeals to "the same

of medieval Christianity and (after some hesitation) was swallowed whole by the Protestant reformers. Throughout the medieval and Reformation period, however, there was a "heretical" fringe who rejected the fusion. Gradually their voices were more widely heard, and eventually their position was endorsed by Protestantism. This took form in the Constitution of the United States, which disallowed a public cult. (For more on this see Verduin 1976.) An excellent discourse on Islam as both a "political" and "religious" entity is Watt (1968).

It may be argued that in the West as well the concept of freedom is as sacred as any concept and is indeed intrinsic to many political movements. However, in the West the fact that freedom is a sacred notion, a kind of religious concept, overall evaluative structure" (p. 286 below). This is why, from our point of view, many public movements in Afghanistan have seemed so "religious." They have seemed religious because they in fact were— without being any less "political" in their impact. As has often been said, Islam is a way of life. As Muslims see it, it entails an understanding not only of the nature of family obligation, but also of economic and social obligation; and because economic and social relations are the stuff of politics, Islam is inherent in the business of politics. The Islamic coalition in Afghanistan is a specific social manifestation of that. It is as political as a tribe, peasant community, or ethnic group.

ISLAMIC COALITIONS AS ORGANIZATIONS FOR GRASS-ROOTS RESISTANCE

We do not know much about how the peoples of Afghanistan have formed resistance groups against the current Marxist government and its Soviet sponsors, but resistance groups of some sort have clearly sprung up, without centralized coordination, all over the country. It seems likely that the preexisting Islamic coalitions have been involved in the mobilization of these groups—just as they have been involved in resistance groups in generations past. No doubt the Soviet invasion has caused important adjustments in the relationships among people and groups. But the ties that connect people in the Islamic coalitions are well-traveled avenues of trust, and the power of traditional relationships, well established by years of practice and local customs, will likely have channeled the new arrangements along familiar lines.

has to be pointed out; its religious or sacred implications are not explicit; people are not conscious of the "sacred" or "religious" implications of their politics. The mujahid *knows* that his religious values are coterminous with his political causes. He knows that his values derive from religious (that is, divine) sources and that this religion, as originally given, has political (i.e., public and moral) implications.

*Many works on Islam refer to the unity of religious, social, economic, and political qualities in Islam. See Eickelman (1981), Fischer (1980), and R. Tapper (1979).

Chapter 10

ETHNICITY AND CLASS: DIMENSIONS OF INTERGROUP
CONFLICT IN NORTH-CENTRAL AFGHANISTAN

Richard Tapper

Few reports of events in the north-central region of Afghanistan
have appeared since the Soviet invasion of 1979, but they all indicate
that resistance there has been as strong and implacable as anywhere
in the country. In order to provide an essential background to the
current resistance and future developments, I shall attempt to analyse
the interaction of ethnicity and class in a region characterized by
both extreme ethnic diversity and extreme disparities in ownership
of the means of production, outline the development of intergroup
conflicts in the region, and elucidate changing local perceptions of
these conflicts. In the absence of specific information, I shall suggest
the probable reactions of the local population to the 1978 Saur Revolution, on the one hand, and to an increasing Soviet presence, on the
other.

Although this chapter has little to offer to general theories of
ethnicity and class, a few preliminary remarks are necessary.* Ethnicity is taken to refer to subjective or cultural notions of kinship,
common culture, and origins; class refers to material interests—i.e.,
objective relations to the means of production. In these terms a
tension between ethnicity and class as alternative frameworks of
identity, modes of social organization, or dimensions of social differentiation and conflict is a common theme in most parts of the world.
Ethnic groups not inherently related to each other may, through
competition for scarce resources, become stratified as status groups,

*For relevant discussions, see Despres (1975), especially the article by van
den Berghe. See also Beck and McArthur (forthcoming). For discussions of ethnicity in northern Afghanistan, see particularly Centlivres (e.g., 1976a, 1976b,
1979, 1980). See also Barfield (1978).

if not as classes; classes, inherently stratified and unequal in terms of power, acquire cultural and ideological attributes and may be perceived by members in ethnic terms.

In some cases—perhaps rarely—ethnicity and class coincide to the extent that all members of a particular class are considered to have common ethnic origins, or all members of a particular ethnic group have a similar class position (relation to the means of production). In such cases it is sociologically interesting to investigate how far and how explicitly ethnicity and symbols of ethnic differentiation are used—and by whom—to perpetuate or to change the class situation. More often (as in the case to be analysed) class divisions cut across ethnic boundaries: members of an ethnic group have different relations to the means of production, while members of a class have different ethnic affiliations. The problem then is to investigate the nature of people's perceptions and understandings of interests, identities, differentiation and conflict, and the degree to which—and why—ethnic ascriptions and loyalties give way to class consciousness.

The material for this exposition derives from field research carried out in north-central Afghanistan between 1968 and 1972—the year of the "ethnographic present" below; I have little information on developments since then.* The research centered on the Saripul district (*wuluswali*) of Jawzjan province and focused mainly on the nomads based there, who also pass through the neighboring districts of Sangcharak (also in Jawzjan) and Lal-o-Sarjangal (in the central province of Ghor); other data were also collected in these districts, as well as in the province of Faryab to the west. Saripul district is named after its administrative center, a market town of about 20,000 people and the seat of a subgovernor (*hakim* or *wuluswal*) whose jurisdiction extends officially over 10-12,000 square kilometers of rough country inhabited by a population of some 150,000.

*Fieldwork in north-central Afghanistan in 1970-71 and 1972 was conducted jointly with Nancy Tapper as a Social Science Research Council project (HR 1141/1) and was also supported by the School of Oriental and African Studies (SOAS); a survey trip in 1968 was financed by a grant from the Nuffield Foundation. An early draft of this paper was presented at a seminar in SOAS in 1971; it was revised for the 1980 AAA panel in Washington, and later presented at a seminar in the Centre for Middle East Studies in Durham University. I am grateful to participants in those seminars and the panel, and particularly to Nancy Tapper, for helpful comments.

RICHARD TAPPER

NORTH-CENTRAL AFGHANISTAN: ECOLOGICAL, ETHNIC, AND POLITICAL STRUCTURE

The western part of Afghan Turkistan, falling within the provinces of Jawzjan and Faryab, is both fertile and ethnically diverse. From the steppes and sandy deserts of low elevation near the Soviet frontier, the land rises in loess hills southward towards the Band-i Turkistan mountains, with peaks up to thirty-five hundred meters. Higher mountain chains lie further to the south in the provinces of Ghor and Bamyan. Springs and snow runoff from these ranges feed streams and rivers flowing north, cutting deep, spectacular gorges across the mountains and then disappearing soon after reaching the Turkistan steppes. Summers and winters in Turkistan are extreme; in the mountains the summers are pleasant but short, snow often lying in the valleys for over six months of the year.

In the mountain valleys at fifteen hundred to two thousand meters, a limited amount of wheat and barley can be irrigated by the fast-flowing streams, while precarious crops of wheat are raised on the slopes above. Otherwise the slopes above three thousand meters provide good if rocky pasturage after the snows melt, and flocks of hardy mountain sheep can be raised as long as much of the irrigated valley land is devoted to fodder crops for use in the long winter. In the scattered settlements, houses are closely packed for protection against the extreme cold.

As the mountain ranges and valleys decrease in altitude towards the north, the climate becomes less harsh and settlements are more frequent. Dry and irrigated cultivation are more productive, while the mountain slopes still offer good seasonal pastures. Closer to the urban market centers of Saripul, Sangcharak, Gurziwan, Bilchiragh, and Maymana, fruit orchards and vineyards predominate in the valleys and dry-farming on the mountain slopes at up to two thousand meters. Still further north the mountains give way to rolling hills and steppes—fine winter and spring grazing; cultivation is normally restricted to the broad valleys of the Saripul, Shur Darya, and Shirin Tagaw rivers.

The steppes and foothills of Afghan Turkistan are traditionally the lands of the Uzbek Turks, people closely related to the populations of Bukhara, Samarqand, Tashkand, and elsewhere in Central Asia. Until the consolidation of Afghanistan under Amir 'Abdur

Rahman (1880-1901) the towns of the area (Maymana, Andkhoy, Aqcha, Shiburghan, Saripul) were seats of small semi-independent Uzbek khanates, and the population surrounding them was primarily Turkic-speaking. Uzbeks used to be organized on a tribal basis, though this is now largely forgotten; formerly too they included semi-nomadic pastoralists, but now they are entirely settled—in this region at least. Though there are no longer any Uzbek nomads, many families, particularly the better-off, continue to live during summer months in traditional round, felt-covered tents set up in orchards near their houses. Uzbek farmers produce grain and fruit; in the towns the craftsmen and tradesmen are predominantly Uzbek. In Saripul a number of powerful Uzbek families, descendants of former chiefs, are looked to by all local Uzbeks for political and religious guidance.

Small enclaves of other Turkic groups are found in the region, mostly refugees from the Soviet Union. Turkmens are numerous in the districts of Shiburghan and Andkhoy but few in Saripul. Linguistically and culturally related to the Uzbeks, but distinct and seen as such by all, the Turkmens are still tribally organized and largely pastoralists, though they do not normally practice long-range transhumances. A dominant feature of Turkmen economic organization is big livestock corporations, headed by chiefs and producing karakul lambskins. In addition, they are prominent in the carpet-weaving industry for which western Turkistan is noted.

There are several scattered communities of Arabs in the Saripul vicinity with little political unity. They too are mainly pastoralists, specializing in the *arabi* breed of sheep, producing lambs and yearlings for the local and national markets. They claim descent from Arab tribes of the original Islamic conquests, but they now speak Persian and have assimilated some features of both Uzbek and Turkmen cultures.

Moving south out of Turkistan and into the mountains, one finds discrete groups of Hazarahs, Tajiks, and Aymaqs. The Hazarahs long defended their independence as a nation of about one million people. They are supposedly descendants of Gengis Khan's Mongol hordes; although they speak a Persian dialect, some have retained Mongol elements. The characteristic always used to distinguish them is that they are Shi'ite Muslims, whereas the vast majority of Afghans are Sunnis. Since the conquest of their territory by 'Abdur Rahman in the 1890s, small groups of Hazarahs have scattered over the country, several settling in the Saripul vicinity, where they are industrious cultivators and have a chief of some influence. Here they are in close economic and social contact with people of other ethnic groups but they retain their distinctive identity and maintain ties with their relatives in the mountains of the western Hazarajat. The latter are still organized under powerful local chiefs and practice mixed farming, cultivating wheat and barley and raising *hazaragi* sheep, which have a high milk output and hence contribute much of the ghee which forms an important item in the diet of all groups in the region.

The Tajiks in this region appear to be a residual category of Persian-speakers with no other tribal or ethnic affiliations. They are often confused—and confuse themselves—with Aymaqs. The Aymaqs are of various groups. In the Saripul region there are outposts of two of the main Chahar Aymaq of western Afghanistan, the Firuzkuhi and the Taymani. These have lost contact with their home culture; most have forgotten which group they belonged to and now call themselves Tajik. Other peoples who call themselves Aymaq—especially in the Kachan valley and in Sangcharak—are suspected (probably correctly) of being Hazarahs recently converted to Sunni Islam; Kachani "Aymaqs" have marriage links with the Hazarahs to the south of them. Tajiks, Aymaqs, and Kachanis are mixed farmers, cultivating grain and fodder crops but exporting little except fruit. They also raise sheep and cattle, and during summer many of them move into tent camps not far from their villages.

The ethnic groups mentioned so far are territorially quite well defined. Aymaq and Hazarah groups are often quite isolated—two to three days' journey even in good weather from the nearest town or road. These mountaineers rarely leave their valleys, let alone the region; they rely for information of the outside world on military conscripts, on the few locals who travel to market, and on the nomads who pass through their lands in spring and summer.

Scattered through the area are small distinct communities such as Sayyids, Khujahs, and Ishans, claimants to holy descent who for the most part live like their neighbors but get religious dues from them and sometimes specialize in providing religious education and services. Two kinds of gypsies are found in the region, Jats and Juggis, considered by the other groups as blots on the ethnic landscape. Jats, living in small settled pariah groups, offer musical services and circumcision. The nomadic Juggis, who are rarely in one place for more than a few days, are said to be based in India; their women are beggars, while the men do odd repairs and make household goods. These Juggis are particularly feared for their magical powers.

Pashtun immigration in the north of Afghanistan began on a large scale with the pacification of the area and its inclusion in a unified Afghan state under 'Abdur Rahman in the late 1880s (see N. Tapper 1973 and 1983). The amir was anxious to colonize the heavily depopulated but fertile tracts of Afghan Turkistan and the northwest and also to bulwark the frontiers against possible incursions from the north. For these purposes he chose his own people, Pashtun tribesmen. The colonization came from two directions. First, members of the Ghilzai/Ghiljai tribal confederation and other tribes from eastern Afghanistan—often the amir's political opponents—were sent north in exile in large numbers to settle and farm (most of them were farmers by origin). Some of these immigrants gradually moved west to Shiburghan and Maymana. Secondly, several thousand families of the amir's own tribal confederation, the Durrani and their associated tribes from Kandahar and the southwest, were sent to the northwest as frontier guards. Many of these later moved eastward to Maymana and Turkistan. All of them were long-range pastoral nomads by origin, but they were granted land rights in favored spots and given advances to help them settle and cultivate, though few of them did so at first.

A third group of Pashtuns passes through the region. Since the opening of the Hazarajat to them in the 1890s, trader nomads of various eastern Pashtun tribes have penetrated the mountains in summer, where they set up large tented bazaars and sell goods brought from India and Pakistan to the locals and to pastoral nomads from the south, west, and north. On the closure of these bazaars in late summer, some of the traders move north to continue trading in the Saripul region, returning east and south in autumn.

Before 1900 only small groups of Pashtuns had arrived in the Saripul region, where they occupied vacant lands and settled with little local opposition. Then large numbers of nomads began arriving from the west and southwest, ousting Arab and Turkmen pastoralists from the local grazing lands. These nomads were largely Durrani of the Ishaqzai tribe, led by one small subtribe, the Nazarzai, which by 1910 had seized control of all vacant productive lands in Saripul and acquired tax-farming and other lucrative posts.

Various Pashtun groups are found today in Jawzjan province. By far the most numerous of the Durrani tribes from the southwest is the Ishaqzai, of which some fourteen subtribes (averaging 150-200 families) have villages and winter quarters in Jawzjan, mostly in the vicinity of Saripul town. There are a few small groups of Alizai and Nurzai. Non-Durrani tribes from the southwest include Bakhtyari, Baburi (in Shiburghan), Baluch (whose non-Pashtun origins are known but no longer relevant), Maliki, Baruti, and Moghol. Most of these groups have important local khans. The Ghilzai confederation is represented in Saripul by small numbers of Hotaki and Tokhi, who came with the Durrani from the southwest, while there is a powerful group of Ahmadzai from Kabul in Shiburghan and a smaller group in Sangcharak. In Shiburghan and Aqcha there are Shinwari and Kakar from the east and southeast. In Faryab province there are Ishaqzai, large numbers of Alizai, Nurzai, Barakzai, Popalzai, and Atsakzai Durrani, and Shishpar, Tahiri, and Moghol groups, as well as Taraki and Tokhi Ghilzai from the west. In the town of Pashtunkot near Maymana there is a large colony of eastern Pashtuns, mainly Ghilzai. In both Jawzjan and Faryab provinces there are scattered colonies of rich landowning Wardak and Muhmand from the east.

The Saripul region as a whole is dominated politically and economically by members of the Nazarzai subtribe of the Ishaqzai Durrani, leading members of which—the Khans—are near descendants of Sayf Akhundzada, whose sons (headed by the eldest, Ghulam Rasul Khan) led the Ishaqzai migration to the region at the turn of the century. Nazarzai Khans conduct extensive pastoral activities but base their power partly on control of immense areas of farmland and partly on privileges granted them by successive Afghan governments. Ghulam Rasul Khan's son, 'Abdul Ghafur Khan, was for many years subgovernor at Saripul, and until his death in 1969, he directed a lucrative business at Mazar-i Sharif. In recent years the family has controlled regional affairs informally through the subgovernors, who are now appointed from Kabul. In the 1965 and 1969 parliamentary elections a brother of 'Abdul Ghafur Khan managed by devious means to win the Saripul seat against the votes of the majority. Haji Khayr Muhammad Khan, son of 'Abdul Ghafur Khan and present head of the Khan family, lives in Saripul town. Other branches of the family live on and supervise their estates, which are scattered throughout the region, including one each in Sangcharak, Shiburghan, and Ismaydan in the mountains.

POPULATION PRESSURE, THE ETHNIC MOSAIC,
AND EMERGENT CLASSES

In the basic ecological, ethnic, and political structure of the region outlined above, the main force of change during the twentieth century has probably been an increase in population. Until a generation or two ago, the region was underpopulated, while the writ of government did not extend far outside the administrative centers, being concerned mainly with the collection of taxes from the peasants. Farming was confined almost entirely to the irrigated river valleys, and many parts of these were uncultivated "jungle." Recently government control and public security have improved, taxation has lightened, the population has increased, and a land rush has occurred as a result. Now the river valleys near Saripul are cultivated to the full; moreover, dry-farming of the surrounding steppe and mountain slopes has spread rapidly at the expense of pasture, although in many places this new farming is a very risky enterprise. Like Afghanistan as a whole, the region now depends for survival on a successful dry-farmed wheat crop. In a good year Saripul can export a surplus, but after bad years, like 1970 and 1971, famine threatens as wheat prices are grossly inflated, not only because of the bad local harvest, but also as a result of speculation and of the immigration of destitute peoples from even less fortunate areas to the west. By 1970 there was a population saturation in the region, given the water resources available. Both crafts and trades have expanded, as has employment in government service; there has also been a small amount of employment in new industry, particularly associated with Soviet gas and oil exploration and exploitation, mainly in Mazar-i Sharif and Shiburghan but in the Saripul vicinity as well. However, there is now a continual emigration to the supposedly less crowded and developing provinces of the northeast.

The population pressure in the vicinity of Saripul in 1970 was reflected in the ethnically complex settlement pattern. For instance, on the road between Saripul and Shiburghan, one passed in quick succession communities of the following ethnic groups: Uzbek, Durrani, Maliki, Durrani, Uzbek, Hazarah, Durrani, Baluch, Arab, Sayyid, Durrani, Ghilzai, Durrani. With the acute pressure on resources and the dominant position of the Pashtun khans, competition and hostility tend to develop into a common opposition to the Pashtuns on the

237

part of the rest. Few Pashtuns have settled south of Saripul, however, and settlement in the mountains remains comparatively homogeneous, Uzbek, Aymaq, and Hazarah territories being still distinct. Table 1 gives rough estimates for the membership of ethnic groups in the Saripul district as a whole.

A further reflection of the growth of population was the emergence by the early 1970s of a fourfold class structure: a traditional elite of landowners, tribal chiefs, wealthy merchants, and other regional leaders; a "bourgeoisie" of independent propertied tribesmen and peasants and established traders and artisans; a propertyless and dependent rural and urban "proletariat"; and a new "intelligentsia" of young, educated townspeople, especially teachers and some officials (including some educated and even employed in Kabul). This class structure did not coincide with the ethnic divisions, nor do standard local occupational categories have any ethnic implications—e.g., *maldar* (pastoralist), *mulkdar* (landowner), *gharibkar* (laborer, usually casual), *dukandar* (shopkeeper), *dihqan* (farmworker). Although most pastoral nomads are Pashtun and most townspeople and educated youth are Uzbek, both these groups and most of the others contribute significant numbers to each of the four emergent classes. (There are besides a number of officials and a few traders who come from outside the region, sometimes from ethnic groups not otherwise represented in the region.)

Table 1

ETHNIC GROUPS IN SARIPUL DISTRICT, 1970

Ethnic Group	Religious Affiliation	Number of Households	Percent of Total
Uzbek and Turkmen	Sunni	10,000	40%
Aymaq, Tajik, Kachani	Sunni	5,000	20
Hazarah	Shi'ite	2,500-3,000	10
Durrani Pashtuns	Sunni	2,500	10
Other Southwestern Pashtuns	Sunni	2,500	10
Arab and Sayyid	Sunni	1,000-1,500	5
Ghilzai and eastern Pashtuns	Sunni	1,000	4
Total		25,000	100

LOCAL PERCEPTIONS OF ETHNIC IDENTITY

Not surprisingly, people have widely differing perceptions of the cultural complexity of the Saripul region and of their own role within it. Objectively language might be thought the most obvious criterion for distinguishing each group—for example, Uzbek from Turkmen varieties of Turkish; western from eastern Pashto; Aymaqi, Hazaragi, and Arab dialects of Persian. In most cases, however, language is not seen as a critical mark of ethnic identity. In Saripul town and surroundings, Uzbek is the mother tongue of the majority; few non-Uzbeks learn the language except, oddly enough, some of the Nazarzai khans. Persian is the lingua franca, widely spoken by members of all groups. Virtually all Turkish- and Pashto-speakers— particularly those such as the nomads who are in regular contact with other groups—speak Persian more or less fluently; both men and women need it for dealing with hired servants and herdsmen and the traders who visit throughout the year. Pashto, the language of the dominant group, is officially promoted as a national language, but this policy has had little effect in Saripul as yet. Another aspect of the policy—the promotion of the concept of Afghan nationality—has been more successful, though hindered by the fact that "Afghan" (locally "Awghan") is the term used by all groups for the Pashtuns, and "Afghani" ("Awghani") for their language. Pashto-speakers generally call themselves "Pashtuns," but often in the north they too refer to themselves as "Afghans," particularly when speaking Persian. To Durrani tribesmen in Saripul the terms "Durrani," "Pashtun," and "Afghan" are practically synonymous, and they use them interchangeably to identify Durrani as opposed to all other groups, including non-Durrani Pashto-speakers.

The criteria for marking and maintaining ethnic boundaries vary with the boundary and the group, and their relevance changes according to context. On the one hand, in the political context (as mentioned above) competition between groups over resources leads to major alignments—especially between Pashtuns and the rest—seen as an opposition of Afghan versus Uzbek. On the other hand, in interpersonal exchanges of goods, services, and information, ethnic barriers are normally lowered. Members of all groups meet in the marketplace, though there is a tendency to localization. Generally, although outsiders rarely venture into the mountains alone, in the Saripul vicinity

there is considerable mobility of trade and labor among different
ethnic groups. Moreover, the Pashtun pastoral nomads passing the
length of the region maintain a complex chain of transactions involving goods and information. Most important, each nomad household has a series of "friends" in Uzbek, Aymaq, and Hazarah villages
along the route—usually debtors who take cash advances, animals,
and wool from them, to be redeemed in local produce and fodder
supplies over a number of years. Nomads regard these "friendships"
as important, interest-bearing investments akin to the lands some of
them own in the same villages. Although the villagers have recently
sometimes withheld their dues, relations between the participants to
these friendships are always cordial, despite obvious latent tensions
and frequent backbiting. In the religious context, the Shi'ite/Sunni
dichotomy is so absolute that members of the two sects often discuss
their differences dispassionately together. However, between Sunni
groups—especially Uzbek and Pashtun—there may well be acrimony,
phrased in terms of disparagement of the other's orthodoxy, cleanli-
ness, piety, and so forth.

For some groups—for example, Aymaqs, Tajiks, and Uzbeks,
among whom descent is not ideologically important—locality and territorial ties appear to be critical; there is some evidence that a change
of residence by a member of one of these groups into the territory
of another leads quickly to a change of ethnic identity. However,
Hazarahs, whether in the Hazarajat or near Saripul, are distinguished
primarily by their Shi'ism. Any convert to Shi'ism becomes to outsiders a Hazarah, while a Hazarah genuinely converted to Sunnism,
though he may not for some time be accepted into any other ethnic
group, ceases to be a regular Hazarah. In contrast, among Pashtuns,
Arabs, Sayyids, and Turkmens, descent and marriage practices are
crucial criteria for recruitment to the group. While none of the
groups in the region objects strongly to taking wives from elsewhere,
these four claim they never give women outside the ethnic group.*
Furthermore, Aymaqs or Uzbeks cannot become Arabs, Turkmens,
or Pashtuns, although the opposite is possible.

It is among Pashtuns that the most complex criteria of ethnic
identity are used. To be recognized as a Pashtun in this region, one
must speak Pashto, practice Sunni Islam, trace descent to the apical

*See Nancy Tapper's chapter in this volume.

ancestor Qays 'Abdur Rashid, and not allow one's sisters or daughters to marry non-Pashtuns. Ethnic identity with the khans who dominate the region and with the rulers of the country allows even the poorest Pashtun nomad to conceive an ethnic status hierarchy with his own group at the top. However, other groups, apart from their resentment of Pashtun political dominance, speak with contempt for the ordinary Pashtun nomads and peasants as primitive, unclean, impious, and speakers of a barbaric language. Turkic-speakers class Pashtuns with Aymaqs, Tajiks, and others as "Parsiwan" (literally Persian-speakers), while Pashtuns use this same term for all non-Pashto-speakers.

Durrani usage differs from that of other Pashtuns. They often discriminate only two main ethnic categories: "Uzbek" includes all non-Pashtuns (i.e., Tajiks, Hazarahs, and Aymaqs, as well as Turkic-speakers), while "Parsiwan" refers specifically to non-Durrani Pashtuns from the southwest.* Durrani (other than the khans) get on reasonably well with most "Uzbeks," both in terms of exchanges of goods, services, and information and in terms of personal friendships. Cultural differences between them are either taken for granted or brought out into the open; the common bond of Islam is frequently brought up, even with Hazarahs, for interested and objective discussion. Apart from sharing the region's general uncompromising aversion to the godless Russians, Durrani reserve their greatest ethnic hostilities for the "Parsiwan," who not only are their main rivals for pastures and farmlands, but also share Durrani culture and ideology and can easily "pass" as Durrani and thereby gain the extra status of close association with—and access to the services of—the Nazarzai khans.

OPPOSITION TO THE KHANS

The domination of the Nazarzai khans has not remained unopposed. In the first years after their arrival in the region, they oppressed the local Uzbek and Aymaq population, as well as previous Pashtun arrivals, forcing many of these to emigrate from the region. In 1929-30—during what has come to be known as the "Saqawi"

---

*Another term used by Durrani for "Parsiwans" is "Opra"; see N. Tapper (1973: 67, n. 62).

revolution—the Uzbeks, Turkmens, and Aymaqs of Saripul rose against the Nazarzai khans and drove them into the mountains, setting up a supporter of Bacha-i Saqaw as governor in the town. Nadir Shah terminated the revolt in 1930, restoring Durrani rule in Kabul, and reigning himself until his assassination in 1933. Meanwhile, the Nazarzai khans regained power in Saripul and commenced reprisals. They recovered their former lands and seized more—even lands belonging to Hazarahs and Arabs, the only local ethnic groups to have sided with the Pashtuns against the supporters of Bacha-i Saqaw. But as a result of complaints by leading Uzbeks, Ghulam Rasul Khan, head of the Nazarzai khans, was placed in house arrest in Kabul, where he later died.

A number of other Nazarzai khans were arrested and placed in temporary custody in the early 1930s, when government control was being reestablished in Turkistan by the minister Muhammad Gul Khan Muhmand. Despite fiercely pro-Pashtun sentiments, Muhammad Gul Khan refused to countenance the oppression perpetrated by the khans. He balanced the domination of Durranis from Kandahar by introducing many more eastern Pashtuns to the area (especially as landowners between Aqcha and Balkh), and he appears to have dealt fairly with petitions against the Nazarzai brought by Uzbeks and Aymaqs from throughout the Saripul region and its hinterland.

During the following decades, however, local authorities turned a blind eye to the oppression of minority groups, in conformity with what was essentially a tacit central government policy of political and cultural discrimination against non-Pashtuns. Ethnic divisions were manipulated at both local and national levels. In the Saripul region there were numerous further revolts against the sons of Ghulam Rasul Khan. In the mountainous hinterland the Hazarahs of Kashan and the Aymaqs of Chiras and the upper Saripul river valleys drove out most of the Nazarzai khans by abandoning their villages and lands or threatening to do so, appealing to the central government over the heads of the local officials, and on occasion resorting to armed resistance; they tolerated only one or two khans for what good they could do in the role of patrons.

Confrontations have also occurred in and around Saripul, usually between Uzbeks and Pashtuns. Typically one of the khans would seize property (land or flocks) belonging to an Uzbek peasant (sometimes a village leader); the latter would complain to government, but might then suffer violence—often murder—by agents of the khan, whose complicity could not be proved. However, in one notorious case in 1970 a khan personally shot dead seven Uzbek farmers who had come to his house to complain; he was said then to have had their bodies desecrated. He was arrested and sentenced to four years in jail, but after having served a few months in considerable comfort, he was released on payment of 100 *jiribs* of land to each of the bereaved families;* a public peacemaking ceremony in Saripul followed, accompanied by a two-day *buzkashi* tournament (see Azoy 1982). The outcome of this case was generally reckoned to be a victory for the Uzbeks and dishonor for the Pashtun khans; many Pashtuns, however, maintained that by their standards the acceptance of compensation was dishonorable. Nonetheless, the Uzbeks would probably not have achieved even this limited success if they had not been represented by their own powerful leaders. By the early 1970s Uzbeks, Hazarahs, and Aymaqs of the region had such leaders, often able to defend their followers' interests effectively when threatened.

THE SHIFT FROM ETHNICITY TO CLASS

Confrontations such as those described above have generally been perceived as interethnic disputes (*dawa*) and as evidence of a polarization of "Afghan" versus "Uzbek" in local political affairs. In recent years, however, there has been a shift in perception, resulting mainly from the increase in population, the scarcity of resources, and a growth of material inequality. The shift has been accompanied by new forms of confrontation. First, the Nazarzai khans have had a series of disputes with "Parsiwans" (i.e., non-Durrani Pashtuns from the southwest). There have been numerous incidents of violence; in two notorious cases, the murders of Baluch and Maliki tribesmen by thugs said to have been hired by Nazarzai khans were followed by unsuccessful efforts by the khans of the victims' groups to exact justice from the government.[†] Secondly, the Nazarzai have met resistance

---

*For a Western equivalent of jirib, see p. 186 above.

[†]In the case of the Baluch killings, it was not until a Baluch representative from the southwest spoke up in parliament in summer 1971 that a team of enquiry was sent to Saripul, but even then the results were inconclusive.

from their Ishaqzai fellow tribesmen (though not from their immediate followers).

Violence in such cases may be perceived as part of intratribal, factional vendettas (*badi*), but the major regional conflict is increasingly recognized as oppression (*zulm*) by Pashtun khans of Uzbek peasants. Pashtun peasants and tribesmen face a growing contradiction between their ethnic loyalties and their class position—particularly when they find themselves liable to oppression by the Nazarzai, either through theft of their property by the khans' thugs (accompanied by the threat of murder), or through extortionate demands for "fees" for political and judicial representation. Wealthy Uzbek urban leaders clearly face a similar contradiction, having much in common in terms of interests, lifestyle, and even friendship with the Pashtun khans who have so blatantly oppressed their ethnic followers.

In the 1960s and early 1970s ethnic and tribal identity (*qawmi*) still provided the basic framework and language of social and political interaction in the region. The qawmi mode of association and of conducting political business was contrasted with the *rasmi* (official) mode. "Class" as a concept was not explicitly recognized except by newly educated urban youth. There was no term equivalent to "class" in common speech, though other terms for collectivities and statuses had strong class connotations—for example, *khan* and *bay* (wealthy and influential men) and *rayat* (economic and political dependants of khans and bays). Among Pashtun nomads and villagers *wulus* (originally "people"—a Turkic term) was constantly in use to describe the power of united community effort, especially against the oppression of both khans and the government. Maxims such as *Da wulus zur da Khuday zur* (The people's power is God's power—or perhaps *Vox populi vox Dei*) were commonly quoted to explain the success achieved when a community collected a *lashkar* (army) to carry out its purposes.

During the 1960s the majority-supported Uzbek candidate in the Saripul elections to parliament was twice defeated by a Nazarzai khan, yet there were several significant indicators of change. First (as noted above), the khan had had to resort to devious means to gain victory. Secondly, numbers of local people who had passed through school and even university in Kabul, and had experienced personally the discrimination against minority groups, were beginning to express support for Soviet- or Maoist-oriented socialist groups. Prominent among them was the defeated Saripul candidate, 'Abdul Hakim Shar'i, who, though himself from a leading Uzbek family, appealed to the class interests of ordinary townsmen and villagers; his aim was said to be "to waken the people." (Shar'i later became Minister of Justice under Nur M. Taraki and Hafizullah Amin.) Thirdly, the traditional leaders of the Uzbeks, Pashtuns, and other local groups were increasingly seen to be colluding to control land and the administration—though they did not do so obviously, given that their power still rested to a great extent on the support of their ethnic and tribal followers. However, ordinary Pashtuns were becoming aware of their economic class interests and weakening in their ethnic and tribal political allegiances; in 1969 many Pashtuns voted for Shar'i and many more wanted to. Class consciousness appeared to be particularly evident among some of the propertyless, who were used to travelling throughout the region as petty traders and laborers. Nonetheless, the notion of class unity, other than that based on common resistance to oppression, had not emerged strongly. Confusion was clearly felt especially among peasants who owned land; for many of them the weakening of ethnic loyalties paralleled a breakup of family ties and a general decline in religiosity and seemed to forecast the end of the world. As one Durrani village headman said in summer 1972 (while Zahir Shah was still on the throne):

> In our history books it says we shall not reach the year 1400 [A.H.]. Shortly before it is due, the end of time will arrive. The mullahs can't agree . . . they are no use, and we have no sheikhs or prophets now to guide us. Those we do have are not straight; they say one thing but have another in their hearts. God knows what is in their hearts. The world is coming to an end. . . . Our books say that at the end of time, truth will be lies, people will abandon right and do wrong, brothers and fathers and sons will fight together. That is the way things *will* be, they say—but look around now! Not one person in ten prays. The world is coming to an end.

The year 1400 (A.H.) began in late 1979—shortly before the Soviet invasion of Afghanistan.

The policies of the regime of Muhammad Daoud (though I have no information on their effects in Saripul) must have further accelerated the transformation of local intergroup confrontations, in popular perception, from ethnic into class conflict, and possibly into an opposition between government (and its supporters and beneficiaries) and the mass of the populace. Governments since April 1978 have promoted the idea of a revolution of the masses against feudal and tribal oppression and reaction, while the ethnic heterogeneity of the country was formally recognized in Decree No. 4 of May 1978. If the Taraki regime had promoted its reforms—even those affecting land tenure and marriage—under an ideology of Islamic socialism, it could have won much popular support in the Saripul area. The popularity of the regime and its successors was greatly reduced, however, by the continual preference shown in both public statements and practice to Pashtun and Baluch tribesmen and by the increasing influence of the Soviets. The latter, for the thirty years of their presence in the north as advisers and technicians, together with their families, did nothing to promote an acceptable public image—or even to show a sensitivity to possible Afghan antipathy to them. What the vast majority of people from all the ethnic groups and classes in the Saripul region saw and heard of the Soviets and their eating, drinking, and sexual habits simply confirmed their stereotype of the Soviet way of life as antithetical to every value they hold dear.

PART V

WESTERN AND

SOUTHERN AFGHANISTAN

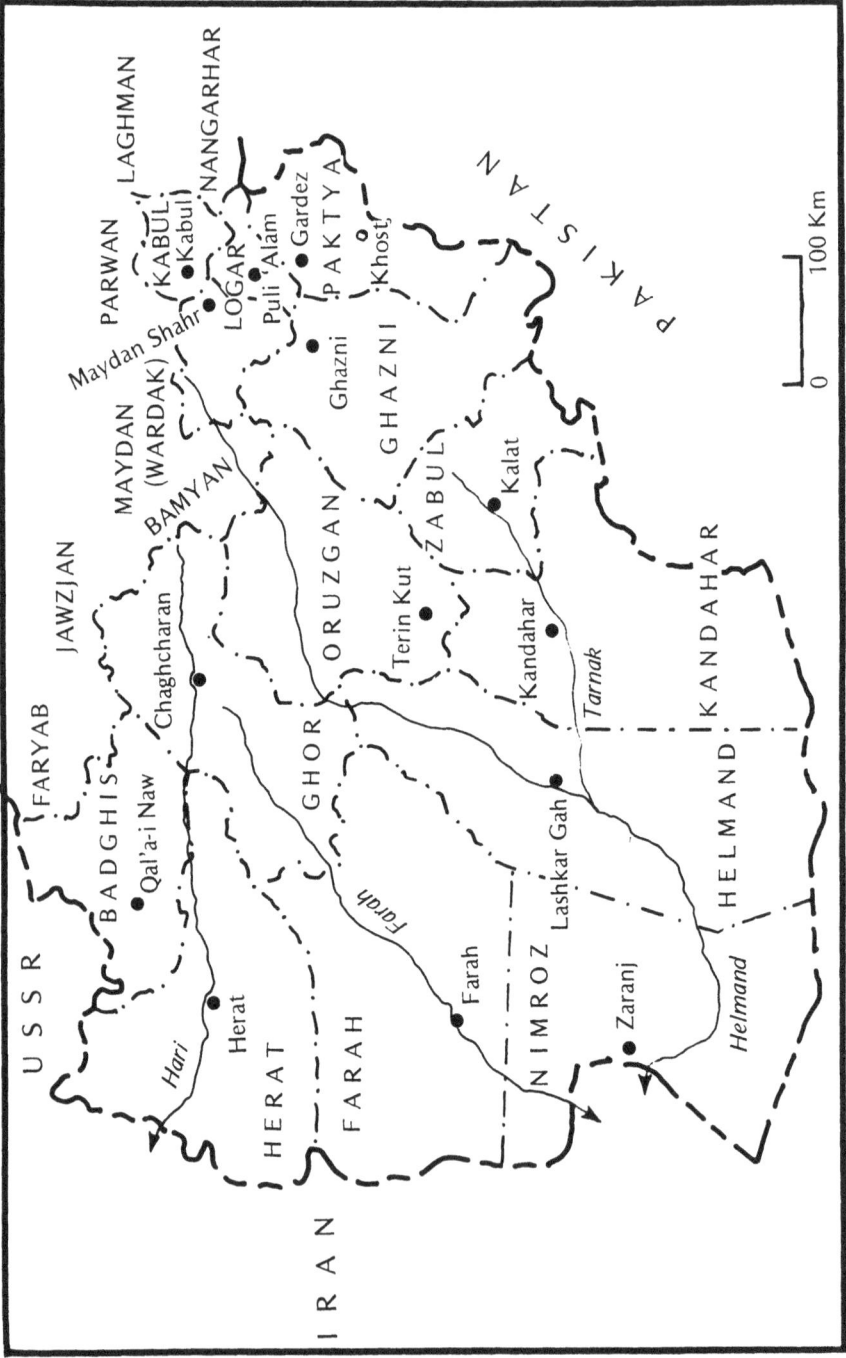

WESTERN AND SOUTHERN AFGHANISTAN

Chapter 11

SHEIKHANZAI NOMADS AND THE AFGHAN STATE:
A STUDY OF INDIGENOUS AUTHORITY AND FOREIGN RULE

Bahram Tavakolian

There has been an interesting turnabout in recent discussions of Islam in rural Afghanistan. After a long—and unwarranted—history of denigration by Afghan urban elites and the international scholarly community of religious piety and fervor among rural Pashtun populations, there has been an equally unwarranted turn toward an exaggeration of the significance of Islamic fundamentalism as the source of rural opposition to the central government of the Democratic Republic of Afghanistan (DRA). In this essay I propose to question both positions by using an historical and ecological perspective to show how indigenous religious and political authority merge to help maintain local political autonomy among subtribes of Durrani nomads, and to suggest that the political conflicts between these subtribes and the central state are not limited to hostilities with governments which are patently atheistic, communistic, or puppets of the Soviet Union.

My discussion will focus on one of the subtribes of Durrani Pashtun nomads, the Sheikhanzai, among whom I conducted field research in 1976-77. I shall present the view that Sheikhanzai religious beliefs and practices have traditionally provided moral and ideological justifications for their political autonomy, egalitarian and kinship-based social structure, and ecological adaptations. However, Islam is not a determinant, but an expressive and integrative symbol of their cultural identity and of their political opposition to the constraints of foreign rule. Most important, to the Sheikhanzai foreign rule is represented by *any* central government, and any central government presents potential threats to the stability and continuity of traditional forms of social and economic behavior. The Sheikhanzai's fears have been frequently realized in recent years, as in past experience, and their responses are neither the simple expression of tribal resistance to change or hostility to outsiders, nor a "tribesman's paranoiac conviction that no good was intended toward him" (Poullada 1973: 34).

The Sheikhanzai presently number approximately eight thousand pastoral nomads in a total population of two hundred thousand Ishaqzai lineage members in the provinces of Herat, Badghis, and Ghor of northwest Afghanistan. The herding of sheep and goats is their main basis for subsistence, and their migratory cycle takes them from winter pastures near the Iranian and Soviet borders to summer pastures at an altitude of over ten thousand feet in the western Hindu Kush. While originally from regions of Pashtun preeminence such as Kandahar, Girishk, and Farah, the Ishaqzai and other Durrani nomads began to occupy pastures in northern Afghanistan in the mid-1880s. There was a threat of Russian expansion into the area, and Amir 'Abdur Rahman needed a population to entrust with the responsibility of maintaining the region under at least the nominal control of the Afghan government. According to Hasan Kakar

In late 1882 the amir decided to settle nomads . . . in the depopulated northwestern areas. The purpose of the colonization program was essentially defensive, but increase in government revenue, the prosperity of the land, the decrease of pressure among the inhabitants of densely populated areas, and finally the weakening of tribal power were also goals (1979:131).

The amir stated in 1886 that "It is proper that as the king is an Afghan, his tribesmen, the Afghans should guard the frontiers" (quoted in Kakar 1979:132). However, demonstrating his ambivalent views toward his fellow Durrani tribesmen, in August 1885 the amir had expressed other motives for wishing to relocate them:

There was an extensive plain in Turkistan which was lying waste. I had a great mind to make it a cultivated and inhabited place. I devised a plan to root out from Afghanistan the enmity of cousinship and domestic quarrels, which are mixed up in the nature of

250

this people. So I gave *takavi* [advances] and road expenses to such people, and sent them to that direction. Up to this time, 18,000 families have settled there (quoted in N. Tapper 1973:60).

Abundant and fertile land was made available to potential colonizers, and loans did not have to be paid back for two years nor tax revenues collected for the first three years; nonetheless, other circumstances reduced the attractiveness of 'Abdur Rahman's plan. For one thing, the predatory raids by Turkmen in the region were one of the major reasons why the area had been left largely vacant. In addition, the lands which the colonizers left behind were confiscated by the government, depriving the migrants of guarantees of economic gain or even security. Finally, it was among the amir's intentions to encourage Durrani nomads to take on a sedentary and cultivating way of life in place of pastoralism. As Nancy Tapper has pointed out, part of 'Abdur Rahman's preference for cultivation in the northern regions was based on the need for permanent settlements (as opposed to seasonal camps) to protect the frontier from Russian advances. However, she adds that 'Abdur Rahman

> does not seem to have appreciated the degree to which pastoralism and cultivation were economically complementary and both necessary if the waste-lands were to be exploited with maximum benefit. He lacked sympathy with the nomadic way of life and moreover was unaware of the difficulties entailed by his insistence that maldar [nomadic pastoralist] immigrants to the north should settle and start cultivation (1973:62).

> The Amir clearly intended the maldars to become self-sufficient economically, by growing their own grain in the future. This was essential in order to avoid further drains on Government resources and increased hostility on the part of local inhabitants. It is not clear, however, whether he expected the maldars themselves to become settled cultivators, or to engage labourers or tenants to work for them, or to adopt a semi-nomadic existence (66).

While the resettlement was partially successful and some of the Durrani nomads took up cultivation in the northern regions (N. Tapper 1973:66), there was governmental support by late 1886 for use of the lands for grazing purposes as well from Gulran in the west to Badakhshan in the east (62). Tapper points out that this change of policy initiated a "wholesale northward migration of Durrani" (62), and Kakar notes that "This migration became the beginning of a north-ward movement that has continued over the years until recently" (1979:131). With the government's change of policy and with a reduction of the problems of dryness, mosquitoes and flies, and Turkmen raids, which had plagued settlers in the earlier years of colonization, there were eight thousand families of Kandaharis in the region by 1890 and eleven thousand families of Durranis by 1907 (N. Tapper 1973:71-72). That this migration has indeed been con-tinuous is attested to by reports from my Sheikhanzai informants that some of them switched their winter pasture locations from Farah northward to Gulran as recently as the early 1960s.

It is significant that certain patterns which were characteristic of the relations between the Ishaqzai nomads and the central state almost a century ago are still prevalent today. For example, there has long been a governmental desire to break down patterns of local authority and political autonomy among the Durrani subtribes and to replace them with the jurisdiction of the central government. Under 'Abdur Rahman, Taju Khan Ishaqzai, an Ishaqzai leader, was responsible for the direction of Durrani affairs until 1889, when he was dismissed as a result of disputes about taxation (N. Tapper 1973: 72). Under Habibullah (successor to 'Abdur Rahman) a more formal hierarchy was established involving a governmental administrator and revenue administrators in charge of political and economic dealings with the nomadic population. Although such attempts to integrate nomads into the governmental processes of the central state have been only minimally successful, the intent has been clear and unwavering.

During the period of my field research, the Sheikhanzai remained largely outside the control of the central government. They failed to register births or to obtain identification cards; they paid no taxes and did no military service; they did not send their children to gov-ernment schools or take their internal legal disputes to government officials for resolution. In addition, they crossed the Iranian border essentially at will, both to sell animals at prices higher than those obtainable in Afghan markets and to work as temporary wage laborers in Iran. Nonetheless, they were forced into dealings with the central government as a result of land disputes and accusations of crop dam-age by sedentary villagers, who went to government officials for redress. Without identity cards, the Sheikhanzai were frequently also without legal rights, even to pasture areas they had occupied for generations. Furthermore, without permanent affiliation in areas administered by government personnel, Sheikhanzai rights and claims were ignored in favor of those of the sedentary population. In effect, sedentary villagers, whether more loyal to the central state or not, gained the support of the government at the expense of nomads, who through their avoidance of the agents and institutions of the central government saw the local balance of political power shift steadily away from them.

Another dimension in the relationship between the nomads and the central state has been a recurrent attempt to use the Pashtun ethnicity of Durrani nomads to establish Afghan claims to areas of ethnic heterogeneity and jurisdictional ambiguity. As Poullada points out, this policy offers the dual blessing to the central government of diluting "the power of both the settlers and those into whose area they were transplanted" (1973:16). By selecting the Durrani for resettlement in the northern regions—a task which he had temporarily assigned to the Farsiwan (Dari-speaking) Jamshidi—'Abdur Rahman established a basis for formal Pashtun political superiority and informal privilege and economic advantage in those regions (N. Tapper 1973:78). In addition, the Pashtun character of the central government was thus advanced at the expense of the other ethnic groups of Afghanistan. Meanwhile, the Durrani themselves were split up between the geographically disparate zones of Kandahar in the south and Badghis in the north, and they therefore represented less of a consolidated political threat to the central regime.

More recently the government has appointed Farsiwan administrators (both Aymaq and Tajik) to positions as provincial governors, subprovince heads (*wuluswals*) and subdistrict officials (*alaqadars*); as a result, Pashtun nomads have suffered further losses in local power. Their perception of the government as a tool of the sedentary Farsiwan population has been heightened, and the likelihood of any acknowledgment of common bonds with the Pashtun central government has decreased.

Finally, despite the willingness of the central state to take full advantage of the economic contributions of pastoral nomads, it has demonstrated a consistent ignorance and disapproval of the techno-economic and social demands of their lifestyle. Richard Tapper points out the following:

In official view, the nomads, with their wandering habits, their unruly behavior, and their primitive way of life, are anachronistic, the epitome of backwardness, survivals of a past that Afghanistan as a developing nation is struggling to leave behind. In all respects—social, economic, political, and administrative—the dogma runs, nomads are obstacles to modernization ... [and] their obvious particularist interests attract the blame for failures of modernization schemes, where these are more likely due to the persistence of tribal and ethnic loyalties within the modernizing elite (1974:136-37).

By no means are such relations between nomads and the central state unique to Afghanistan, of course. Bates has discussed similar kinds of government policies of the Ottoman central state for tribal populations:

In those border regions which were difficult to control, Ottoman policy was aimed continually at shifting support among ethnic groups, allowing none to achieve supremacy or to establish stable exercise of authority which might jeopardize the claims of sovereignty of the state. ... Such support was rarely consistent because the ultimate objective was always complete control. At the same time the government strived to prevent any tribe or ethnic group from setting up a reliable power base which could not be destroyed by shifting alliances (1971:118).

Prior to the arrival of the Yörük [into southeastern Turkey], the forced sedentarization of Kurdish and Türkmen tribes starting in 1865, had been largely accomplished, a project which arose from the government's desire to bring politically threatening tribes under control. ... The Yörük, when they came into the region, filled an economic niche of pastoral nomadism which had been vacated for strictly political reasons. ... The Yörük were permitted to enter the region and to remain nomadic as they were never the threat to the state that the more powerful Türkmen and Kurdish tribes had been. The Yörük are in many ways representative of the adaptation of a politically weaker entity to the demands of a stronger one (125-26).

Similarly, Stauffer (1965), Salzman (1971), and Irons (1974) discuss the economic and political controls exercised by the central state over the pastoral nomadic populations of Iran, and Cole (1975) describes the relationship between Al Murrah Bedouin and the Saudi Arabian state. In each of these cases, a recurrent theme is the attempt of the central government to increase its direct control over nomadic tribes through sedentarization and detribalization. Thus far the Sheikhanzai of Afghanistan have countered such attempts by their ability to maintain political autonomy and a high degree of economic independence (though not self-sufficiency) through pastoral nomadism, segmentary lineage organization, and a merger of religious and political authority at the local level.

SHEIKHANZAI SOCIAL ORGANIZATION AND THE CENTRAL STATE

The tribal political organization of the Sheikhanzai is based on the principle of patrilineal segmentary lineages and an absence of a centralized decision-making and leadership structure. These groupings are the bases for descent and inheritance; however, they are not residential units, and individual camp groups of Sheikhanzai may be, and generally are, composed of members belonging to different lineage segments. Marriage is almost exclusively endogamous within the parent tribe of Ishaqzai, but not necessarily within the Sheikhanzai lineages alone; thus affinal ties reinforce extra-lineage relations and economic and political cooperation between the Sheikhanzai and camps and lineages of their more distant Ishaqzai cousins—i.e., a total population of over two hundred thousand pastoral nomads.

Each lineage segment, clan, or subtribe—indeed each individual camp group or household—may act as an economically autonomous unit. Each may negotiate its own rights to pasture and water, execute exchanges of surplus animals and animal and dairy products for grain from villagers and urban merchants, or purchase necessary commodities such as tea, sugar, candy, and salt and manufactured goods such as guns, cooking utensils, radios, watches, and clothing. This economic independence is limited by only one constraint: all the sheep and goats owned by camp members must be herded on a collective basis. Furthermore, political authority is at the local level as well, typically expressed in the immediate relationship between a camp headman and camp members. Yet the camp is not the smallest unit of political authority. Through extended kinship ties, the possibility exists for individual tent-households to be encamped in a variety of locations and with diverse relatives. Hence the leadership of a camp headman is insufficient to direct the actions of camp members, who may easily flout his authority by moving to more hospitable camps.

The political autonomy and structural flexibility of Sheikhanzai camp groups and lineages are crucial for their herding lifestyle — especially in an ecological zone of desert and highland valley pastures, in an environment which offers an average of only ten inches of precipitation each year, where rainfall is unreliable, where communication and transportation facilities are inadequate, and where narrow migratory routes and tenuous ties to pasture land are under increasing pressures from village cultivators. Indeed the ability of camp groups to negotiate their individual migration and settlement schedules and locate adequate and relatively inexpensive grazing for their livestock is a prerequisite to economic strength and continuity.

It should not be concluded, however, that Sheikhanzai pastoralism is simply a matter of economic maximization and pragmatism, or that raw economic self-interest operates devoid of social responsibility and control. Kinship obligations are ideologically and socially enforced to promote solidarity, corporate identity, and mutual and reciprocal economic assistance. Contrary to Louis Dupree's (1973: 190-91) assertion that the last century has seen a major reduction in the importance of tribal genealogies, the Sheikhanzai continue to trace their ancestry over a five- to seven-generation period. More important, this ideological emphasis on kinship relations is translated into collective social behavior in the form of tribal councils, common rights to pasturage, and group responsibility for compensation and retribution.

Indigenous political authority is not at odds with or in control over individual self-interest but is a means by which that self-interest is defined, coordinated, expressed, and mobilized for the common good. Headmen, mullahs, and *pirs* (saints) are the representatives of the collective body to the outside world;* however, all political and economic decisions which touch upon the lives of group members

*Mullahs and pirs are discussed in some detail in Robert Canfield's chapter in this volume.

are the consequences of community will expressed through the general consensus of tribal elders. There is no subjugation or rule by an elite, or even by a majority because unanimity of opinion is the objective of tribal assemblies. Anyone displeased with the results retains the option of moving into another camp. A consistent pattern of inter-personal domination is rejected as an affront to personal integrity and to a Pashtun sense of honor.

Foreign—i.e., centralized—rule is implemented in Afghanistan through power, coercion, and oppression, which contrast sharply with the voluntary and participatory nature of legitimate local govern-ment. People like the Sheikhanzai are certainly not without leaders, decisionmakers, and individuals who wield legitimate—especially sacred—authority; they are, however, without tyrants. In the tribal lineage structure based on ties of kinship, coresidence, and mutual assistance, allegiance to the social unit is not understood as subor-dination of the individual to the group, but as recognition of a social self with both responsibilities and privileges as a group member.

In essence the Sheikhanzai conception of political authority is based on the principle of egalitarian and participatory democracy and the rejection of hierarchy and centralization. The authority of the Afghan state, on the other hand, is conceived as illegitimate, usurped, totalitarian, and infidel. The mountain and desert barriers of the north-west region provide nomads such as the Sheikhanzai, and other rural populations as well, with refuge from governmental control and intervention in their lives, and they impede the coercive centralized programs of sedentarization, conscription, and assimilation which have been more successfully implemented in other Middle Eastern countries.

Certainly one major reason for the Sheikhanzai ability to retain political autonomy lies in the weakness of the governmental infra-structure—a weakness that even the Soviet troops and puppets have not yet remedied. In addition, however, I believe that we must under-stand the moral basis for Sheikhanzai political authority in contrast with that of the central state, and this requires that attention be given to Sheikhanzai concepts of religiosity and religious authority.

BAHRAM TAVAKOLIAN

SHEIKHANZAI RELIGIOUS AUTHORITY

Quite unlike the stereotypes maintained about them by urban and sedentary populations, and unlike accounts of nomads in other portions of the Muslim world (e.g., Barth 1964), the Sheikhanzai demonstrate a great respect for mullahs and for religious knowledge and participation. In contrast with Dupree's discussion of "religious non-literacy" and his suggestion that "The Islam practiced in Afghan villages, nomad camps, and most urban areas ... would be almost unrecognizable to a sophisticated Muslim scholar " (L. Dupree 1973: 104), the Sheikhanzai adhere closely to the tenets of the Hanafi school of Islam. Dupree states that "[Pashtuns] believe but seldom worship; they are ruggedly irreligious unless an outsider challenges their beliefs" (126). However, among the Sheikhanzai even temporary camp sites include areas marked off with stones for collective prayer, and in winter camps underground *masjids* (mosques) have been constructed to house mullahs and children who are taught to read the Quran. While regular prayer five times a day is by no means universal—any more than it is among any other Muslim population—prayer is common among both young and old men, and even among women, who say their prayers in their tents.

Almost every camp group includes individuals who have made the hajj to Mecca, and all who are physically able strictly observe the fast during the month of Ramazan. *Zakat* (almsgiving) gifts are made directly to the poor and to travellers—they were offered even to me— as well as through the giving of sacrificial animals to individuals in other camps who are attributed to have special religious knowledge and abilities. Sacrifices during Id-i-Qurban (a feast celebrating the end of the ritual of pilgrimage to Mecca each year) are mandatory, and sacrificial animals are regularly offered for *khayrat* (blessing) to remember the dead, to ask Allah to make the sick well, to help the barren bear children, and to bring rain to the pastures.

Such practices are at sharp variance with the conventional wisdom among sedentary peoples about nomad religiosity, and the Sheikhanzai return the compliment by saying that villagers and city folk may have more substantial masjids and more educated mullahs, but they do not think and act like Muslims. Although their education in orthodox Islam comes exclusively from their own religious specialists, the beliefs and practices of the Sheikhanzai are religiously neither lax nor insincere.

How do the Sheikhanzai's beliefs and practices affect religious authority or its merger with political authority? For one thing it is the haji and the mullah who command the greatest respect and exert the greatest influence over camp affairs—not other camp members who may be more wealthy but less religious. Second, the more wealthy camp members typically enhance their social standing and their political influence through the sponsorship of religious activity. They provide economic support to mullahs, encourage their sons to take on religious training and specialization, and marry off their daughters to mullahs in their own and in other camp groups. Furthermore, their supplementary alms to poorer kinsmen and clients are understood as acts of religious devotion, as is their use of surplus wealth for religious pilgrimage and ritual sacrifice.

A similar blending of sacred and secular authority is discussed by Salzman (1975) for Iranian Baluchistan, but there is a major difference: among the Sheikhanzai sacred authority does not merely support political authority; it *is* political authority. By and large camp headmen and their immediate relatives—brothers, sons, and sons-in-law—are hajis and mullahs. The only formally educated Sheikhanzai, according to all my informants, was the son of a headman, and he was sent by his family to become a *mawlawi* (religious scholar) through Quranic instruction in Peshawar, Pakistan. The most devout men of all, aghas and pirs of the Naqshbandi order of Sufism, serve as political mediators and economic redistributors who through their *murids* (devotees) in different lineages and camps help to consolidate the tribal political organization and to equalize regional and individual differences in wealth.

A specific example of the significance of sacred authority can be informative in understanding the direction of local affairs by religious leaders. The wealth and power of Tawakkul, an upstart *malik* (regional headman) were rejected in favor of the leadership provided by a Sufi agha, Aghajan, noted for all-night devotionals to Allah and for the redistribution of wealth. Tawakkul, a wealthy, thirty-five year old Sheikhanzai, attempted through his personal ownership of two *ramah* (over one thousand sheep) to serve as a mediator in relations between four client camp groups and a local government official. In a dispute between the Sheikhanzai and

Firuzkuhi villagers, Tawakkul successfully bribed the official to demand that cultivated lands be returned to pastoral usage. That is, he sought central government intervention in local political affairs with a rival ethnic group; he hoped through this action to consolidate local support for his political leadership by demonstrating to the Sheikhanzai that he could deal with the government and demonstrating to the government that he represented the Sheikhanzai.

Aghajan, twice Tawakkul's age but with a fraction of his wealth, insisted that the newly reacquired pasture lands not be used by the Sheikhanzai for fear of the strings that might later be attached to this victory through a continued dependency on the government official—not only in terms of further bribes which would be necessary to maintain support for the Sheikhanzai cause, but also in terms of a loss of political autonomy. Despite the economic sacrifice of much needed pasture lands, the camp groups supported Aghajan in a council meeting and left the lands vacant. They dismissed Tawakkul as "but a boy" and not a leader. To be sure, his age worked against him, but the basic error he made in the Sheikhanzai perspective was his attempt to go beyond indigenous forms of authority, thus violating the perceived need for continued autonomy from non-Sheikhanzai sources of political authority.

In contrast with Barth's (1959) view of the maximizing, individualistic, and entrepreneurial Pashtun, the apparently less pragmatic sacred leadersip of Aghajan was followed. Tawakkul was seen as manipulative and self-interested and Aghajan as an altruistic saint. However, Aghajan was considerably less than a saint. Although he did indeed give away much wealth from sacrificial donations, a considerable portion of it also found its way to his sons. Moreover, in persuading the Sheikhanzai of the necessity for continued separation from the central government, he in essence guaranteed a continued flow of sacrificial donations to him, or at the minimum to his redistributive control. He was able to use his sacred position to block Tawakkul's attempt to establish a basis for secular political influence.

This kind of example of a religious basis for authority was frequently repeated during the period of my field research, and it is typically religious leadership that provides the basis for inter-camp and inter-lineage negotiation and collective effort. In addition, religious leaders are the most common representatives of the Sheikhanzai in relations with other Pashtun nomadic tribes, with other ethnic groups, and with nomads in other pasture territories. Murids come from as far away as two hundred miles to receive amulets (ta'wiz) from pirs and other saints. Although above I emphasized the adherence of Sheikhanzai to Islamic orthodoxy, Dupree is quite correct in noting that "To reinforce his beliefs, the rural Afghan localizes his religion" (L. Dupree 1973:114). This localization of belief and ritual reinforces indigenous authority at the expense of a wider conception of the "brotherhood of Islam."

A consequence of such localization is that despite the predominance of Hanafi Muslims throughout the northwest area, the Sheikhanzai claim that Farsiwan villagers and townspeople are Muslims in name only. Ironically, Hazarah, who are Shi'a Muslims, but with whom the Sheikhanzai have almost no regular contact, are considered devout—if mistaken—while Taymani and other Aymaq Hanafi villagers are considered disreputable hypocrites. It is important to note two functional values, internal and external, of these views. Internally, localization of religion promotes the expression of values and behavior which support kinship obligations and tribal solidarity and inhibit the use of individual wealth as a basis for personal power and relatively permanent stratification. Aghajan's authority derived from his religious position and his ability to demonstrate the characteristics and capacities identified with a saint, traits which by definition promote the social and moral good for all. There is no equivalent formalization of the properties of a secular leader; in defining Tawakkul as an upstart, the Sheikhanzai were rejecting the self-seeking and ambitious nature of his personal attempt at leadership, his lack of responsibility to the moral underpinnings of the social group, and, by extension (in contrast to the meaning of his name—"unquestioning follower of the Prophet"), his form of piety.

Egalitarian economic relations and kinship-based cooperation and reciprocity are not merely practically necessary to the Sheikhanzai (as noted above), but also they are morally right and "Muslim" in character. Those outside of the circle of mutual support are "non-Muslim" in their identities and behavior. In addition, the relative economic independence enjoyed by the Sheikhanzai is reinforced through their economic and social controls against out-migration and sedentarization. A constant labor supply is kept intact, animal wealth is not converted into landholdings, and an absence of anticipatory inheritance contributes to an abundance of patrilineal extended households which include fathers and their married sons. Pastoralism and filial obedience are more than economic and social custom; they are moral imperatives, and they are ecologically adaptive.

In external relations, Sheikhanzai religious ideology and authority present a view of villagers, merchants, and bureaucrats as corrupt and exploitative. Such a view is realistically applied to villagers who encroach upon ancestral pasture areas, merchants who try to cheat Skeikhanzai in marketing activities, and civil servants who accept double bribes from both villagers and nomads. The religious orientation of the Sheikhanzai impedes intermarriage and economic symbiosis with Farsiwan cultivators and provides positive sanctions for social isolation and local autonomy. Through their self-identification as "true Muslims," the Sheikhanzai lend support to their distinctive ethnicity, economic cooperation, and self-rule in the face of ever increasing village cultivation and the expansion of central governmental powers.

Even during the relatively tranquil period of 1976-77, Sheikhanzai condemned the government of Muhammad Daoud as a foreign government, in spite of its (as well as its predecessors') openly pro-Pashtun leanings and policies. "Foreign rule" exercised by the Afghan central state was explicitly rejected on historical, religious, and political grounds. However, the specific political character of the Daoud government mattered less than its real and perceived threats to Sheikhanzai political structure and economic viability. The avoidance of external political authority and of the "obligations of citizenship" such as military service, compulsory education, birth registration, land registration, and taxation was ecologically necessary—especially under conditions of mounting pressures from ethnically distinct villagers—in order to fulfill labor needs, obtain flexible and ample access to pasturage, and carry out diverse strategies of stock accumulation, movement, distribution, and exchange.

The typical central government view of nomadic pastoralism as an anachronistic and irrational pattern of land use, economy, and society has brought about major changes in the ecological context of Sheikhanzai pastoralism. In particular, various attempts to consolidate the power of the central state and to diminish tribal political autonomy are evident: government support for increased cultivation in pasture areas, the development of mixed economies among village populations, attempts at centralization of the livestock market, and an aborted attempt to establish a program for the "rationalization" (a frequent euphemism for "sedentarization") of pastoralism.

In this context Sheikhanzai religious authority has served as a metaphor for resistance—not to change per se, but to external domination. For the Sheikhanzai, religious belief and practice provide ideological and structural reinforcement for their internal solidarity and their collective strength against foreign interference. It is my contention that we are witnessing a similar process in the nationwide rebellion of the people of Afghanistan against the DRA. Both in microcosm and in whole, Afghanistan is not experiencing a jihad against atheism, but a political struggle against usurped authority. In this struggle Islam serves as a convenient and morally powerful unifying symbol for otherwise disparate and antagonistic groups.

THE SAUR REVOLUTION AND THE SHEIKHANZAI

In the preceding discussion I have attempted to establish that conflicts between ethnic and tribal minorities and the Afghan central government do not date simply from the Communist takeover of April 1978 or the Soviet intrusion of December 1979. Anyone familiar with Afghan history is already well aware of this. But the geopolitical domino theory has been resuscitated, transported to the Muslim world, and applied to Afghanistan by Zbigniew Brzezinski and others, and such an analysis has generally taken precedence over a concern for local-level politics and adaptation. In response, I have concentrated on Sheikhanzai opposition to nominally Muslim and pro-Pashtun central governments—those of Daoud and his predecessors—and I have tried to demonstrate the ecological basis for this opposition, stressing that to a Sheikhanzai tribesman or tribeswoman the concept of foreign rule applies to the authority of indigenous foreigners—people of different ethnic groups, different levels of education, and different lifestyles—as well as to rule by non-Afghans. In this view the central government, since its formation by Ahmad Shah Durrani in 1747, has always been a foreign government representing a relatively Persianized, less religiously oriented, urban, educated, elite population which is both culturally distinct and politically separated from the tribal and rural masses of Afghanistan.

I have had to refrain from discussing the Sheikhanzai participation in the ongoing rebellion because I have no information on
what the level or nature of their participation has been. I can only
speculate, with self-evident justification, that the decrees of the DRA
having to do with marriage transactions, land ownership, and governmental control of the economy have been particularly offensive to
the rural population. Of course even this speculation assumes that
the DRA attempted to implement its proposals among the Sheikhanzai, and this may never have been the case. Even in 1977 the
Sheikhanzai were not uniformly aware that Zahir Shah had been
ousted in 1973 or that they were no longer living in a monarchy but
in a republic. Thus the initial effects of the DRA may simply have
bypassed the Sheikhanzai.

At the same time, it would be inconceivable to me that the
Sheikhanzai are not presently involved in the struggle. There is quite
obviously—and tragically—no unified and coordinated rebel opposition to the central government and to the Soviet troops, and there
is certainly nothing at all which resembles a potentially successful
national liberation movement. There is only a very loose collection
of as many as sixty different regional pockets of insurgents with
common objectives such as political and economic independence and
(perhaps) an ideological emphasis on the preservation of traditional
Islamic culture, but with few direct linkages among them. Because of
the Sheikhanzai's need for seasonal pasturage, their reliance on sedentary peoples for the wheat which is a staple in their diet, and the
likelihood of attempts to conscript their sons, I can only assume that
they have been among the insurgent groups.

Paradoxically the disparateness, and even the disunity, of the
various rebel factions is the reason why the insurgents are unlikely to
overthrow the Communist government in Kabul but why they may
succeed in maintaining their unique cultural identities and local political autonomy after the major fighting is over and the Soviet troops
withdraw. In their self-imposed geographical isolation and ethnic
segregation, they may be able to maintain indigenous authority and
to evade "foreign rule" as they have during previous assaults by imperialist powers and despite the effects of internal colonialism.
However, there is little chance of their being able to shift the balance
of power back to rural and tribal populations.

Were the institutions of secular authority more firmly entrenched among tribal populations such as the Sheikhanzai, it is likely that more of a competitive and opportunistic form of leadership would have emerged. These institutions are more typical of many Afghan villages, as well as of many of the nomadic populations of Iran. It is instructive that in both of the latter instances, the extension of central governmental rule has been facilitated by the cooptation, or simple replacement, of tribal leaders by government representatives. In contrast, the moral context of Sheikhanzai political authority has successfully retarded such developments and has preserved both the ideology and the practice of widely diffused authority, morally earned and expressed.

As I have stressed, the merger of indigenous religious and political authority has been ecologically adaptive as a means of promoting internal cohesion and collective action along with a pattern of ethnic distinctiveness. It is both ironic and fitting that an ecological process which has for centuries drawn diverse ethnic groups apart and forced them to rely on their particularistic identities and objectives to combat the power and threat of the central state is now encouraging the adoption of a common moral basis for an essentially local, but extensive and multifarious, revolutionary opposition to external political authority. Presently nomads, villagers, and townspeople in Afghanistan are united in their opposition to state domination over their lives, and are at the same time able to express a common identity in symbolic terms through their allegiance to Islam. Such is the legacy of the Afghan central state.

Chapter 12

HOW AFGHANS DEFINE THEMSELVES
IN RELATION TO ISLAM

Jon W. Anderson

Islam provides powerful motives and a central discourse for mobilizing political action in Afghanistan which often remain opaque in more strictly political analyses. Afghan identifications with Islam have obscurities for observers who frequently, sometimes explicitly, attribute the obscurity to Afghans themselves as insincere or fanatical or both by highlighting the more accessible fact that Afghans make such charges against each other. Summary treatments, in particular, tend to generalize portions of such discourse apart from its contexts or the capacities in which it is addressed. Thus does Louis Dupree's depiction of "religious non-literacy" (1973:95ff.) echo views of those *shari'a*-minded portions of the population for whom learning legitimates their own mediations of Islam, and Leon Poullada's characterization of "demands couched largely in religious terminology but transparently political in nature" (1973:171) in his otherwise penetrating analysis of the tribal revolt which drove Amir Amanullah from his throne in 1929 does not comprehend how tribalism is for Afghans a primary manifestation of their identity as Muslims. Slightly farther afield, Ahmed's (1976) revisionist interpretation of political consolidation in Swat as an essentially Islamic project

For comments on an earlier version of this chapter and on portions of my argument presented at the Universities of Bergen and Copenhagen, I am grateful to T.O. Beidelman, Robert Canfield, Dale F. Eickelman, Reidar Grønhaug, M. Jamil Hanifi, Michael E. Meeker, and Bo Utas. Fieldwork in Afghanistan between 1971 and 1974 was financially supported by U.S. National Science Foundation grant no. GS-30275 and archival research at the India Office Library, London, in 1980 by the Etnografisk Museum of the University of Oslo. Parts of this chapter were written at the Südasien-Institut of Heidelberg University with the support of the Alexander von Humboldt Foundation (Bonn).

proceeds from a similarly arguable (but in this case opposed) inter-pretation which is itself part of the data. Equivocal findings are not in themselves false, and these are among the more nuanced apprecia-tions of the settings of Islam among Afghans. But missing from such partial, implicitly partisan accounts of Afghan views are additional data which lie more in the background than in the foreground of their discourse about the configuration of Muslim capacities, and analytically subordinating specific structural properties to general functions of "religion" as an institution or process underestimates more telling data about how Islam operates in conjunction with other local aspects of identities rather than as a univalent partisan interest.

Variously implicit or self-evident for Afghans, such data can be elusive, and not only because their expression is often allusive. Many do not appear to be about religion at all. Yet very little in which Afghans engage is not explored for Islamic significance. No important initiative—and especially no social one—is undertaken without dedication "in the name of God" (*bismillah*); "infidel!" (*kafir*, one who denies or rejects God's revelation) is among the commonest charges exchanged in Afghan disputes. It is not the point of departure but of escalation from which there is no turning back by placing opposition beyond the ultimate mortal pale, until opposi-tion is resolved in mutual submission to a larger interest. Popularly, the generic designation for such submission of temporalizing to enlarging interests is *sunnat*, or the practice of one of God's prophets and thereby vouchsafed as "Islamic." As a counterpoint to the direct revelation of the Quran, sunnat, of which the most embracive within mortal grasp is the dedication/invocation "bismillah," popularly cir-cumscribes the widest range of Islamic solemnity. The Islamic character of identities tends to be lost when particular aspects of life are considered separately, for their interrelations are what matter and why Afghans so readily dispute over the conjunction of Muslim capacities with the overall configuration of social relationships.

That conjunction is found in mediations of Islam through *shari'at* (law, in the keeping of *'ulama* or religious scholars), *tariqat* (spiritual exemplars, often Sufi), and *qawm* (tribe, and more generally relations of codescent). These institutions have counterparts through-out the Muslim Near East (see Gilsenan 1982; Keddie 1962), and their particular configuration among Ghilzai/Ghiljai tribesmen in

eastern Afghanistan is the subject of this analysis. Ghilzai and their sub-
divisions in the region between Kabul and Kandahar are a portion of
the population of southern Afghanistan and western Pakistan who
are the locally called "Afghans" (avghan). Although nationalist governments of Afghanistan in this century have appropriated this
designation for the citizens of that country, in popular usage it is applied only to Pakhtun/Pashtun tribesmen and implies an autonomous
political identity. For Ghilzai, it has overtones of their relations to
each other as autochthones, to non-tribesmen as variously displaced,
and to the state as both Afghan and Muslim. Examining the grounds
of these relations which unite generally found problems of Ghilzai
self-identifications as Muslims will serve to place the somewhat
equivocal regard they enjoy back into the perspectives from which
such views derive and are put forth, above all by Ghilzai themselves.

"AFGHANS" IN A MUSLIM STATE

Islam in Afghanistan encompasses virtually all the population
and, defining the social universe as Muslim, frames many differences
as differences between kinds of Muslims. Robert Canfield (1973a,
1978) in particular has documented how infusing sectarian (mazhab)
affiliations with the political significance of communities over-
determines those as identities. Although part of a more abstract
sociological problem, this infusion is also found in a specific historical
process. Politics of national integration and liberation have long been
embedded in moral, even eschatological, matters of identity as each
ruler of Afghanistan has pressed his project as essentially Islamic.
Afghan domination of the country to which they have given their
name is in particular closely identified with Islam. For Ghilzai, this
has been significantly the case since they played leading roles against
British invasions in two Anglo-Afghan wars of the nineteenth century,
and since they provided levies for conquering and converting to Islam
the formerly non-Muslim population of what is now Nuristan during
the reign of Amir 'Abdur Rahman (1880-1901). Also, under 'Abdur
Rahman, the effective incorporation of Shi'a Hazarah to the west of
Ghilzai country, for which Ghilzai provided levies and then took the
opportunity to expand their own realm (see Ferdinand 1962; Kakar

1971:83ff.), likewise went beyond tribal aggrandizement as the *mission islamique* of an officially Sunni state.

While supporting or at least tolerating this state as Sunni and as avghan like themselves, many Ghilzai often opposed the specific dominion that was established by Durrani Pashtun from the south in the eighteenth century after Ghilzai had overthrown Safawid (Persian and Shi'a) rule, and particularly during the reign of 'Abdur Rahman.* Before and after their campaigns for the amir against non-avghan, armed resistance to Durrani government among Ghilzai was often led by religious figures, including a serious revolt in 1883 under Mushk-i Alam, a Sayyid mullah with marital connections among Andar Ghilzai (*Biographical Accounts* 1888:145), and again under his son in 1886-87. Likewise resisting government interference in the local autonomy which Ghilzai took to be their share in the avghan dominion, many joined a rebellion of Pakhtun in neighboring Khost in 1924, also led by a mullah, until the then amir, Amanullah, secured a *jihad* against it from "Kabul mullahs" (*Military Reports* 1941:151ff.) and practical assistance from other tribes. Similar events continued to occur on a diminishing scale throughout the 1930s, after the influential Sher Agha Hazrat of Shor Bazar in Kabul refused to repeat an earlier mediation which had initially secured Ghilzai acquiescence to Nadir Shah's campaign for the throne, usurped after the revolts of 1929 toppled Amir Amanullah; or his mediation was refused by Ghilzai on account of his service to the new monarchy (*Military Reports* 1941:216). Because of the diverse mix of capacities in which such events are joined, they can be murky, but the pattern in each case began with resistance to exercises of police powers by the state in tribal areas, to taxation and conscription proposals, or to innovations, which encroached on Ghilzai exemptions that were the substance of their nominal partnership as avghan in the Durrani-dominated state. After conflict had escalated into government demands for submission and tribal demands for rescension — each in the name of Islam and often voiced through mullahs—it would usually

---

*To date, the most detailed analysis of Ghilzai relations to the state can be found in Yapp (1962, 1963, 1964) for the critical period of 1840-42; Kakar's (1971) treatment of 'Abdur Rahman's consolidation of Afghanistan in the 1890s contains extensive material on state relations with Ghilzai which is drawn from British sources.

be resolved through other religious intermediaries who, also in the name of Islam, would secure the minimum requirements of each side.

Although evidence is sketchy, it appears that these intermediaries, lumped with "mullahs" in British reports of the period, were in fact acting in other capacities.* Sher Agha was a *sheikh* of a Sufi order (*tariqa*) which was reputed to have "wide" adherence among Ghilzai. Sheikhs, with *pir* and *miyan* ("saints"), in general have a reputation as men of peace whose interest in God makes them disinterested in mundane conflicts—in contrast to mullahs who, as purveyors of learning, often involve themselves in escalating conflicts into Islamic ones. Mullahs also tend to depend on a more continuous utility to their congregations, and there are many more mullahs than pir or miyan in Ghilzai country. Pir and miyan tend to be found outside or between tribal cores; but as mullahs are necessary for religious instruction, nearly every settlement has one or more. Pir have reputations for learning as well as for inspiration, which distinguishes them from *malang* or *faqir*, whose entire identity is focused on inspiration and whose characteristic poverty is a measure of being out of this world. Forced to take positive stands in ordinary affairs by having to pronounce on "what the Book [Quran] says," mullahs are easily drawn into conflicts, while pir and miyan, for a passivity which comes from focusing their identity on God, find their major social role in mediating settlements. Mediators in larger tribal conflicts with the government were always pir rather than mullahs.

In conflicts with the government, as well as in local intertribal conflicts that tended to attract government interest in monopolizing law and order and therefore escalated into tribe-government conflicts, Ghilzai do not appear to have acted as a unit. Their support for the government, usually passive, was in narrower local and often subtribal capacities, either in not joining the fray or in joining for local reasons. For instance, Ghilzai are reported to have refused to assist Amir Amanullah when he was driven from the throne, and some even

---

*Histories of the modern period concentrate on the politics of state-building (e.g., Gregorian 1969; R. Newell 1972), although none in the detail of Kakar's (1979) account of the regime of 'Abdur Rahman. For the tribal side of this process, I draw on the extensive British intelligence reports to the India Office, London (L/P&S/12 nos. 1738, 1739, 1740, 1568, and R/12/126), which extend into the 1940s and are particularly detailed for the 1930s.

attacked his troops (*Military Reports* 1941:195). The Durrani restoration under Nadir Shah was initially supported by Ahmadzai Ghilzai, some of whom had been punished with exile to northern Afghanistan by Amanullah for taking part in a revolt against him in 1924; but Nadir's claims were resisted by many Ghilzai. Throughout the 1930s various "troubles" occurred, though diminishing in scope as the longer-term consolidation of the new government more effectively kept conflicts local and ungeneralized. By 1939 all Ghilzai tribes had formally accepted the Durrani restoration, although until 1973 certain groups enjoyed de jure exemptions from conscription and taxation and de facto freedom from having officials stationed in much of their territory.

One means for securing Ghilzai acquiescence and diluting their autonomy was the cooptation of religious figures into the state sector. While 'Abdur Rahman attempted to assume personally the function of the 'ulama,* the restoration government was more subtle. It granted or acknowledged 'ulama oversight of legal administration and much of education; in practice this authority would have meant positive intervention in tribal affairs, and many Ghilzai came to feel that if mullahs were not working directly for the state — many were, as were all judges (*qazi*) in the reestablished shari'a courts — they were at least doing the government's work of weakening the tribes. In such measures they recognized a diverging institutional interest for religious functionaries implied in the financial support of mullahs by the state. Even if government favor did not join 'ulama interest to that of the state or (as observers often interpret it) give influence to the government through them over the tribes (see Gregorian 1969: 305ff.), it did provide for a general institutional focus for 'ulama, of which the establishment of a Jamiat-i'ulama in 1931 is only the tip of a process manifest in rural areas in which mullahs became no longer so much the clients of tribesmen as played against tribalism in a triangular but unequal relationship.

Any such institutionalization in Afghanistan marks an initiation rather than a culmination and, moreover, differs significantly between national and local levels, as well as between different localities. At any given time, there are diverse identifications and obligations

---

*Kakar (1979:154-56) discusses 'Abdur Rahman's "testing" of mullahs, and Ashraf Ghani (1978) provides a glimpse from Afghan sources of the amir's efforts to project himself as an *'alim* through publishing commentaries in his own name.

within the 'ulama, whose capacities are self-assumed and popularly, hence variably, acknowledged. The same is true of the tribes and the government, which are each in a continuous internal dialectic that touches on social relations far beyond their immediate interactions and are not all consistent. Government, for instance, is locally manifest in its various organs pursuing different levels of policies whose combined effects are realized locally as piecemeal contests between national and other consolidations. From a local point of view, these are penetrations in the form first of extensions of police power and the associated machinery of officialdom, and subsequently of services which draw tribesmen in more immediate capacities into diverse extratribal spheres of relations as individuals. These services include schools (established at many constabulary posts), government monopolies for "assuring" certain supplies (often in competition with nomad-borne trade of Ghilzai who brought cloth, sugar, and industrial products back from their winter migrations to India), the expansion of roads and bazaars (served by road traffic, which made caravans obsolete), and (recently) development projects. All combine to effect multiple and piecemeal cooptations, prominently of local leaders who cooperate, but also of ordinary tribesmen (see Anderson 1978a). Moreover, government came increasingly to provide alternative fora for expressing and mediating local conflicts through officials, courts, and (until 1973) parliamentary representatives, who often provided a local-interest lobby in Kabul.

It is significant for the evolution of this complex set of relations that government seems increasingly to have managed to avoid relying on religious figures for mediating disputes with the tribes over the past thirty years, in contrast to its reliance on such mediation in the 1930s. Between 'Abdur Rahman's attempts to assume personally the ulamid function and the later institutional isolation of ulamid interests, a longer-term shifting balance of influences is suggested in the observation by Kakar:

> The position of the mullas was strengthened very much in the nineteenth century, especially during the Second Anglo-Afghan War when some mullas for the first time in many centuries emerged as leaders of the campaigns and in many cases offered more sound military opposition to the British than either the sardars or tribal elders did (1979:153).

It would seem that the situation confronted by 'Abdur Rahman and in the Durrani restoration of the 1930s was not, therefore, straight-forwardly "traditional," but rather there was a radical prominence of Muslim functionaries in the political field. Nor can it be said that Nadir's restoration of the Durrani monarchy effected a return to a status quo ante in defusing a situation prevailing at his assumption of the kingship. In order to put these pieces better into perspective, it is necessary to consider the tribal context in which religious figures directly act—sometimes but not necessarily—as leaders.

TRIBAL CONTEXTS OF ISLAM

The structure of avghan tribes is remarkably continuous over time and throughout a population estimated to be upwards of ten million and perhaps as much as sixteen million between the Hindu Kush mountains, the deserts of Baluchistan, and the Indus Valley. In spite of demographic and political flux, the account of tribal distributions given by Elphinstone over a century and a half ago remains a good guide, especially to those of the Ghilzai homelands (see Anderson 1975). Tribal structure may even have been enhanced in recent years by a diminution of its functions to local relevance for land tenure and to generalized communal identifications. Formations such as "Ghilzai" and its component tribes and sections endure as frameworks of orientation rather than of action. They are not mo-bilized as such, but define fields of local political activity, in which their normal tendency is to divide politically into factions focused on the followings of would-be leaders (see Barth 1959). They are not normally the agencies but the frames of party interests, expressing in themselves a larger, more problematic interest for which parties com-pete. Their significance is as an image of history in constituting a record and an episteme of collective continuity as a joint heritage. Formally tribe (qawm) is formulated as the "sons" of one "father," whose landed estate is divided among them and whose "character" (*huy*) is shared by them as a body which is localized in continuous segments, replicating this form and called variously *khel* or **-zai*, as in Sulayman Khel or Ghilzai. Patrilineal inheritance of land by males only assures the association of any segment with a territory, which is thought of as a subsidiary portion of the overall homeland (*watan*).

In a scheme of ramifying patrilineal descent, successively wider ranges of agnatic codescendants are grouped under successively remoter fathers back to Qays, the notional ancestor of all avghan. By holding that Qays went to Mecca and received Islam directly from Muhammad, who called him 'Abdur Rashid, avghan deny having any pre-Islamic past or equivocal history of conversion. Conceiving of their existence as wholly within the *dar al-Islam* and temporally coterminous with it, their apprehensions of themselves, as Barth (1969a) noted in other settings, join patrilineal descent and Islam, and Ghilzai assert that being Muslim is literally inseparable from their heritage. Qays symbolizes this sense of linkage between avghan with the most solemn form of Islam without intermediaries other than the Prophet himself. This genitive and original link is, in its conception, what makes them a body, both for sharing it undifferentiatedly and in the implication that there were no avghan in the non-Muslim realm prior to the revelation of the Quran. Their claim is not to holy descent — they receive rather than participate in revelation — but to an exemplary Islam and an exemplary possession of Islam which places them on a par with Arabs in this respect and before all others except Sayyid descendants of the Prophet.* The most that Ghilzai will claim for Qays is a kind of companionship with Muhammad and that they are therefore Muslim as a qawm, which is thus a kind of sunnat. Qawm is thereby represented as a Muslim project and mediation of Islam to avghan.

This conception is for the most part taken for granted, as a fact of the first instance which explains rather than having to be explained. It underwrites more summary notions that what avghan do must be Muslim since it is not possible to be more Muslim. Jettmar (1961) has noted, for instance, the spread in Indus Kohistan of their tribal forms, especially of land tenure and council government, as part of the practice of Islam; and a century of British expe-

---

*Tribesmen will casuistically raise questions about whether *all* Arabs are on this par on the grounds that not all Arabs accepted Muhammad's prophecy in the positive fashion of Qays's seeking him out, nor even during the Prophet's lifetime. In such arguments, Sayyid are said to constitute a qawm from Muhammad, in contrast to the larger qawm of all Arabs. The comparison is sometimes drawn to complete arguments for the irrelevancy of what came before Qays — tribesmen do not share dynasts' interests in connections to the kings of Judae — and sometimes to emphasize that Sayyid are, after all, also a qawm in the world.

rience following the First Anglo-Afghan War showed how quickly defense of those forms could escalate into defense of the Faith. The claim for a unique mediation of Islam, analytically speaking, is an identification of Pakhtunness with Islam, but it is limited by other mediations through shari'at and tariqat, which diminish a common sense of being "already" Muslim. While to be avghan (a Pakhtun tribesman) is to be Muslim, the reverse is not true, and the truth that one can still be Muslim provides the basis for critiquing Pakhtunness as sunnat in comparison to the mediation of Islam through learning and through personal identification with the divine.

Truly to be Pakhtun is (in a Ghilzai idiom which seems common throughout the North-West Frontier Pakhtun as well) to "do Pakhto" (*pakhto kewul*). This refers to following a tribal code of conduct known in eastern Afghanistan and in Pakistan as *pakhtunwali, nangiy pakhtanah*, or just *pakhtanah*. Pakhtanah is the plural-cumulative form; nangiy pakhtanah means "Pakhtuns' honor" in an active sense, and pakhtunwali is one of a number of compounds which designate the inhabitants of a place, the possessors of some skill or knowledge, or participants in a joint activity who are thereby constituted as a group with a property.* The notion of "doing Pakhto" is explicitly superordinate to speaking Pakhto language (*pakhtu wayul*—to talk in Pakhto) and similar to the abstraction in sunnat of action or practice as a defining attribute. Manifest in personal conduct, tort law, demeanor, and general stance before the world, it locates one with respect to the world in complement to Islam and qawm as the configuring components of avghan identity.

British analyses from the North-West Frontier tend to treat pakhtunwali, as it is called there, as primitive law, from which derive the commonly cited "injunctions" to revenge, hospitality, asylum, and council government (see Spain 1963; Berry 1966; Barth 1969a). Ghilzai agree that those are significantly pakhtanah, but insist that it is about what one must do in order properly to be Pakhtun and

---

*Pakhtunwali is not universally presented in the normative fashion claimed by Ahmed (1980), whose description is based on Frontier tribes. The term itself is not used in western Afghanistan, although Pashtun there can decipher it to refer to their custom (Glatzer, personal communication). The fullest discussion of its composition from an area where it does not serve as a claim to distinction, as on the North-West Frontier, is provided in Steul's (1981) study of Khost, to the east of Ghilzai country.

commonly summarize it in positive terms as treating all persons alike and without distinction from oneself. They describe it as holistic ethic and emphasize that it is not merely a body of rules. Its ethical activation is through *ghayrat*, a notion of altruistic bravery and self-determination, including respect for the integrity of others as one's honor. It joins wife, home, and territory as parts of the patrimony secured by fathers for their sons (see Anderson 1983b).

Ghilzai hold pakhtunwali in its broadest sense to be an improvement in relation to tariqat and shari'at for securing a dar al-Islam, for being both communal and immediate; shari'at is mediated through learning and thus through the persons of mullahs and qazi who are its keepers, and tariqat is mediated through personal identification and focus on the self. Ghilzai will freely admit to being, in their words, "bad Muslims" and to "not following the religion (*din*)" for avoiding the shari'a courts and disrespecting men of religion (*diniy khaluk*) in the persons not only of mullahs and qazi but also in some respects Sayyid, pir, and miyan, and the lesser figures of *akhundzadah* (descendants of religious leaders). They also point to violations of the shari'a in pakhtunwali. Punishments (*hadd*) prescribed in the Quran are not applied, nor is the eye-for-eye doctrine of *qisas*, although both are known to be reforms of revenge, which they claim a right to pursue. Women are systematically disinherited of real property and in marriage lose rights in their natal lineages. Divorce, which is a law of God specified in the Quran, is virtually impossible, while marriage which is lesser custom (sunnat) is binding, and widow-inheritance is common. Generally speaking, personal law is based on self-determination (ghayrat) and on the revenge of degradations of personal integrity rather than on the precise punishment of delicts laid down in the shari'a and its definitions of punishment as communal interests. All of this is summed up in common proverbs such as "there are things which are required but are not done, and things which are done that are forbidden," and said especially of remoter districts which symbolize ghayrat pakhtanah and "genuine" (*rasti*; also means correct) Pakhtun.

Many Ghilzai argue for or against qawm or some other form of Islam in view of these ambiguities. Others regard such argument as either disingenuously ignorant (*napokha*—literally, undercooked) or mischievous (*shaytani*—divisive; literally, devilish). To more subtle minds, the contradictions between pakhtunwali and shari'at or, to a

276

lesser extent, tariqat take the form of conflicting allegiances to tribe, law, and personalism, and the conflict dissolves if those are kept apart, as in separate contexts. Ghilzai represent this as the ideal case and hold that others "need" the mediations of Islam in shari'at and tariqat more than Pakhtun do, or that those are more suitable for dealing with others as Muslims than for dealing among avghan, who are "already" Muslims. But this must be understood to be continuously at issue both in principle and in the particular case, especially as these mediations of Islam are presented as alternatives to each other.

CONFLICTING IDENTITIES

In broad terms, there emerge tensions between shari'at, tariqat, and qawm as complementaries, on the one hand, and as alternatives for which there are interested spokesmen, on the other, out of what those do not share as mediations of Islam. Ghilzai often assert that they do not "need" mullahs or have no "work" (*kar*) for them beyond teaching Quranic recitation and reciting at rites of passage at birth, circumcision, weddings, and funerals, for witnessing oaths, divisions of harvests, the making of contracts and other joint undertakings. It is in deference to their learning—often to their assumption of learnedness—that mullahs are invited to lead prayers or to perform other services, for which any Muslim is fit and customarily the "most" Muslim of those present is chosen. Mullahs themselves are not all alike in respect to learning; considerable pride attaches to employing those with formal education, called *mawlawi* (who are recognized teachers), while derision is heaped upon those whose presumptions exceed their abilities. Considerable effort goes into confining mullahs to their "proper" role where tribal feeling is strong enough to be mobilized and perceived to be under pressures which necessitate that mobilization. While this feeling may be heightened by the alienation of mullahs from their clientele—and many Ghilzai complain that "the mullahs are not ours any more"—this is not only a modern phenomenon. It is always potentially present in the relations of mullahs to the communities which employ them. More fundamentally, it is a recognition that other mediations of Islam diverge from their own when contexts are not definable exclusively by *qawmwali* (tribalism, in the sense of possessing "tribe").

Conflicts of interpretation are what, in the first instance, admit mullahs into their frequently reported roles in articulating, even instigating, disputes and issues among tribesmen and are not confined to proclamations of jihad. Ghilzai point to the mingling of mullahs in factional conflicts and routine disputes, where charges of kafir against opponents that mullahs are seen as all too ready to make either destroy qawm as the framework for resolution or, as on tribal boundaries, work against the mobilization of more encompassing qawm, which is the positive project of khans (see Anderson 1983a). Entree is provided in their presumption to pronounce on "what the book says," which refers not only to the Quran—many tribesmen can recite the text—but to its legal interpretation embodied in shari'at. As keepers of that sunnat, mullahs are accounted quick to take anything not in their interests as non-Islamic, even anti-Islamic, and thus tend to escalate conflicts beyond their originating settings. In contrast, pir, miyan, and others usually identified as "saints," including the descendants of such men (akhundzadah, *pirzadah*), and sometimes Sayyid, stand not only apart from most intra-Ghilzai conflicts, including those with authorities, but essentially stand for reconciliation represented in personal identification with God. These identifications are flexible and are accounted ambiguously for embracing a range that is formally similar to that of the mullahs' and overlaps with it as well as with what is pakhtanah.

Sayyid enjoy an ambivalent regard, for while their descent from the Prophet embodies his submission to God ahead of other men, they are nevertheless a qawm with worldly interests in Ghilzai views. Some may be individually devoted to God and thus merge into a broader category with pir, miyan, and akhundzadah; some are mullahs of an otherwise ordinary sort, although the less ordinary among them tend to merge with the Shi'a hierarchy in the estimation of many Ghilzai. On the whole, they are left alone as passive men of peace who, in their whole identification with God's purpose, embody that reconciliation that has been "forgotten," as it is put, or willfully set aside in mundane competitions among men.

Persons who thoroughly manifest this kind of transcendence are few, and for the most part are found outside or on the margins of Ghilzai country proper.* But their prototype is found everywhere in

*There are few seats of saints in Ghilzai country; although a few minor akhundzadah farmers have settled and there are a few shrines, they are mostly

the marginal figures of malang or faqir who are, socially speaking, nowhere. Malang or faqir wander about or "live in graveyards," especially in those containing shrines to *shahid* (martyrs), of which they are sometimes notional keepers. Taking no other identity than that of diniy khalek (persons of religion), they are as far beyond the mortal pale as humans can be in Ghilzai estimations and, having given up home, kin, possessions, and occupation in the world (*dunya*) for religion (din), provide a point of comparison for what it means to devote one's entire being to God. To assist such persons, as to give freewill offerings to Sayyid, is accounted a holy act—for God; there is no other reciprocation, and such persons are not intermediaries among men. Individually, their motives may be suspect or they may be considered crazy (*leyweney*), but as a type they represent how being diniy khalek means to be very nearly out of this world.

Pir and miyan, akhundzadah and Sufi sheikhs differ from malang insofar as their identifications with Islam are routinized through learning, or at least a presumption of being learned, without resting their identity on learning as mullahs do. Practically speaking, they tend to accumulate various degrees of following for making godliness accessible in fashions which are continuous with those available through Sufism. Around such figures form networks of loyalties whose most organized expression is the Sufi tariqa. Thus, as an approximation of the malang's way, some ordinary tribesmen, particularly second sons and younger brothers who have reason to feel shortchanged in tribal society, may be more or less secretly or occasionally drawn to Sufi devotions. Whether or not they formally join a lodge, or only attend exercises (*dhikr*) when in the cities where these are held, theirs is a halfway step in the direction taken by malang which does not so much transcend qawm as it transcends the most mundane tendency of it to become a frame of conflict. In this respect, Ghilzai view Sufi and malang as directly embracing religion in one's person in contrast to merging into a social whole represented in shari'at as an alternative to qawm.

Sufi devotion provides a means which fits the situation in which many partially alienated tribesmen find themselves, but for others it

located along margins between tribal watan. Far more are found in the surrounding cities; an exhaustive account of the shrines around Kabul, some of which are visited by Ghilzai, including the seats of important pir, is provided by Einzmann (1977).

279

is a bridge to alienation. It may be seen as a complement to the mediation of Islam represented in qawm, as is learning to cite the Quran, when those are viewed as means rather than as accomplished facts. It is more often pursued where tariqa are found and the bonds of qawm loosen their comprehensive character. But Sufism tends to become an alternative to qawm when qawm is reckoned a failure for securing the comprehensive totality which sunnat implies, to fail as *umma*, or a specifically Muslim community, or to have become too much of the world by unraveling in individual pursuits. Those who are dedicated to qawm as synthesizing sunnat/umma for securing Islamic brotherhood may express suspicion of too much devotion to tariqat, or of devotion which goes on too long, as posing just that unraveling, but they reserve greater suspicion in this respect for shari'at.

Like Sufis, religious functionaries such as mullahs and qazi straddle categories, but in an opposite direction which is often seen as "using" religion for or in corrupt pursuits. This view depends very much on their perceived relations to avghan and on whether shari'at and tariqat complement or displace qawm as a medium of Muslim identity. What is imagined is a divergence of institutional forms that reflects tendencies of individuals to be incompletely Muslim, and thus to introduce forms of self-authorization in competing spokesman-ships for Islam, threatening the social order of qawm as a resolution of the immediate and transcendental aspects of humanity into a kind of "natural" community. In Ghilzai terms, nominal brothers enjoy an original equality with respect to each other that is defined by an abstracted ancestor, in whom they are united, just as the equality of Muslims rests on their mutual subsumption under God as His crea-tion. By this reckoning, tribalism becomes a this-worldly counterpart of creation and, when Muslim—as avghan tribes are presumed to be—a form of salvation. Undoing qawm correspondingly compares to repeated failures of revelation prior to Muhammad and is in very literal views of many Ghilzai the work of Satan. Accordingly, mullahs and qazi are freely referred to as "devils" (*shaytan*) for meddling in tribal affairs or interjecting themselves between tribesmen by mis-chievously taking things into their own hands. This last is to make *jama'a* (society—an undifferentiated community and, in narrowest terms, the gathering for prayer) into an association which is volun-tary only, rather than to reinforce qawm as primordial jama'a.

Given the relative rise of religious figures in the late nineteenth century and subsequent efforts by government to coopt at least some and to neutralize others, salutary examples abound in which tribesmen can point to religious functionaries interjecting themselves into factional disputes and exacerbating—sometimes creating—conflict through their own rivalries for congregations, influence, and endowments. They point to places where many mullahs and their *taliban* (pupils training to be mullahs) compete with each other or with tribal notables as exemplifying the dangers that religious functionaries pose in their combinations of religion (din) and politics (*siyasi* — competition for worldly power). Some point to the seamy reputations of towns for drug-dealing, illicit sex, excitement, sharp practice, and many fervent "hot" mullahs drawn to large mosques and shrine centers, where they compete for attention and place in the world. Others are more bothered by pressures from ambitious mullahs to expand rural mosques and shrines, mostly found outside villages or by villages on tribal margins, into seminaries with autonomous clienteles for themselves. Whether or not such reputations are deserved, they are current among tribesmen, who constitute in such stereotypes a kind of object lesson about how mullahs especially interact with confused social environments as creatures and creators of chaos, and are part of common ideas that tribesmen do not "need" shari'at and that it, in turn, is only appropriate among non-avghan Muslims. In practice, there are degrees of activity and interference on the part of shari'at functionaries, but that merely confirms the problematic status of such persons. Those who are "hot" in their fervor must necessarily disrupt a social order with which they do not identity, while those who are "tamed" are so accounted as captives of the wills, variously, of tribal khans or of government officials perverting religion into the service of their own purposes. The "tame" and "hot," in Ghilzai estimations, both "deny religion" by coming between men who are "already" Muslims, while entrée is provided by their own failures as Muslims.

Many tribesmen would prefer to dispense altogether with mullahs and qazi and to keep pir out of tribal affairs as species, albeit ambiguously, of aliens. The case is clearer with qazi, who are government officials, but more problematic with mullahs because they are more present and their lack of provenance is more immediate. Most say that their fathers were mullahs, and "his father before him."

Such claims mirror those of Sayyid and of pirzadah and akhundzadah families to a genetic legitimacy which parallels that claimed for qawm; on a more practical level, few mullahs practice in the place of their birth, and Ghilzai routinely take mullahs to have no Pakhtun ancestry, even though they speak Pakhto, because they do not "do Pakhto." In a fundamental sense, they cannot. The combined effect of such rejections of and by avghan underwrites an aversion on the part of ordinary tribesmen to their sons becoming mullahs and to having fully fledged seminaries in rural mosques, which conflicts with the otherwise acknowledged value, even necessity, of religious instruction that is not resolved by holding Quranic recitation to suffice. Clericalization is seen as a characteristically Shi'a heresy and a mark of religion gone bad. Irrespective of their personal rectitude — and many mullahs and qazi are individually adjudged to be moral men — it is their relation as a heterogeneous class that is corrupting. The dilemma is resolved, but not really solved, by emphasizing the divergence between pakhtunwali and shari'at to be contextual in condemning one or the other as divisive. Even insisting that shari'at is only appropriate among other Muslims, who lack primordial identification with Islam, is seen to open a door which can only be closed by advocating either an explicit constitution of society as umma, which would be "mullah rule" in some cynical tribalist interpretations, or one that excludes mullahs and qazi, even to some extent pir and Sayyid, from Pakhtun society altogether.

CONTEXT AND VARIATION

Both the shari'at/tariqat and qawm options are available, are continuously discussed, and both occur to some extent. It is always possible to find persons disgruntled with their lot or situations that are inadequately met in one or the other terms which make the alternative attractive and a constant subject as organizations for the mediation of Islam; so in relation to each other they emerge as alternatives whose relative value shifts according to context. Idealized as complementaries, the mediations of Islam through shari'at and, even more, through tariqat, improve on that through qawm in socially heterogeneous settings by maintaining that diversity is a false perception akin to the chaos of misbelief in the time before Muhammad. That is, perceptions that something very like the pre-Muslim condition obtains beyond the tribal realm shift to include tribalism in relation to larger contexts, in which shari'at is more suitable, and to smaller ones, for which tariqat appeals. Contained in each is a version of a conception of the moral community as jama'a, constituted through sunnat, in which all submit equally and totally in a seamless whole which precludes the authorization of one person by another. Tribalism, in the form of pakhtunwali, secures this community through its most direct expression in *jirgah*, which are councils of the whole community for deciding some case between its members or for undertaking a course of joint action. For that, jirgah are omnicompetent and define the community insofar as any residual disagreement can only be resolved by expulsion of the recalcitrants. This conflicts absolutely with shari'at specifications of individual rights and duties as well as with the privilege of qazi to render decisions, as Ghilzai are well aware. So as the community of Islam is made to encompass the community of Pakhtun, Islam is made to identify a universe of contention.

Paradoxically, although it is less an intellectual paradox than a lived dilemma, the impact of association that is *only* Muslim is, in this instance, particularizing for randomizing association and personalizing continuously the exercise of will. It recalls an issue "already" solved. To realize a community of cobelievers only supposes a diverse social environment. For Ghilzai, this has been found quintessentially in cities with their cosmopolitan assemblages of diversely originating peoples or, nearer home, in those parts of the countryside not tribally organized, where among otherwise disconnected individuals other mediations of Islam than qawm appeal directly by appealing over the temporality of diversity.

It is on the appeal of this highly abstract and thereby not altogether convincing feeling that periodic, somewhat ambiguously religious uprisings have proceeded. Opposition to British encroachments throughout the nineteenth century consistently took a religious idiom under at least putatively religious leadership from every amir of Afghanistan down to the various so-called "mad mullahs" on the North-West Frontier. The latter were neither merely so fanatic as the British often depicted them (see Davies 1932), nor so single-mindedly millenarian as recent interpretation (e.g., Ahmed 1976) would have it. At least in Afghanistan, there are continuities between malang and pir and between pir and mullahs that rest on the same evaluative structure. There is a continuity between the individual tribesman who becomes in some measure, either temporarily or partially, Sufi or who drops out altogether as malang in a personal *jihad al-'aql*, the larger collective undertaking of jihad against heretics (traditionally, for Ghilzai, the Shi'a Hazara, but also usurpatory governments) and unbelievers such as the former Kafir of what is now Nuristan, and opposition to British suzerainty on the North-West Frontier led by a series of mullahs, faqir and akhund. But there is nothing in Afghan experience quite like the maraboutic state of Morocco, nor religious leaders quite like the Sudanese Mahdi for reasons which lie in how at least some Afghans identify themselves as Muslims.

Mediations of Islam through shari'at and tariqat differ from that in qawm, whether as complements or as alternatives, in how they shift the resolution in qawm of equality and hierarchy in one or the other direction for Ghilzai. In tribal experience, shari'at emphasizes hierarchy between Muslims by shifting equality into the ultimate future through continuously problematizing what is "already" resolved in the primordial submission of Qays to the most direct form of revelation available to ordinary humans. Shari'at is in the keeping of mullahs and qazi, who authorize what is sunnat and pronounce on what is kafir—essentially anything they do not stand for, but most immediately any tribalist presumption of privileged access to Islam. Tariqat resolves in the opposite direction by shifting asymmetry to an ultimate God-man relation and emphasizing here-and-now equality through social disengagement. Stress on immediate equality between Muslims and abstracted hierarchy resonates with qawm as an Islamic project and confers influence of a sort on pir-like figures, who may be sought out for mediating conflicts between the already-Muslim, but it does not confer any positive authority. Ghilzai emphases on malang as exemplars of this mediation of Islam and their diminished contact with pir and Sufi sheikhs, who in any case do not so much seek out followers as they are themselves sought out, tend to inten-sify a personalist and retreatist view of tariqat among them as remote in space but personally immediate. By contrast, the organizational expression of shari'at through qazi and mullahs is personally removed but socially immediate, even intrusive, and for that potentially com-petitive in authorizing what is Islamic between Muslims.

Not to put too fine a point on it, the differentiation of these mediations of Islam rests on presuppositions about settings to which they are appropriate, and the problem is that none of these settings are mutually exclusive. Shari'at, which is appropriate for dealing with Muslims outside a tribal context, cannot be confined there; neither can tariqat, which is appropriate for dealing with tribesmen in a Muslim context, be so confined. By their disjunctions, each competes with a tribalism set both in relation to other Muslims and in relation to non-Muslims. So the conjunction which distinguishes pir from malang, on the one hand, and respected mawlawi from "devilish" mullahs on the other hand, similarly unravels in the conflict of disjunctive settings. And in fact this is what happens.

Continuity with all politics is not only potential but has apparently been intensified by governments in Afghanistan emphasizing their Muslim legitimacy through shari'at at least since 'Abdur Rahman (see Ashraf Ghani 1978) and through the reinstitutionalization of Hanafi jurisprudence and establishment of a Jamiat-i ulama under the Musahiban monarchy. What might be intended to place tribe and government (itself based in a tribal ascendancy) on the same side also places them in the same arena; the sanctification of an interest which is defined in conflict with another, whether intratribally or between tribe and government, into which religious figures are drawn does not so much widen that interest as it invites counter-sanctifications that escalate the stakes into moral ones. The result of intensified opposition is to make resolution dependent on the sort of intermediaries for which the quiescent pir and miyan or sheikhs have been traditionally sought out on the basis of their embodying positive symmetry between Muslims in comprehensive, personal, and equivalent subordination of both parties to God. The issue, in practical terms, is what must be surrendered.

Such associations of shari'at with strife and of tariqat with peace on the two flanks of qawm seem to have been the experience of Ghilzai, and of other Pakhtun within the context of Afghanistan. Opponents have been Muslim, and in an important measure avghan, even when they were the government; conflicts have been, if not settled, at least muted by piecemeal relinquishment of issues or climbing down from moral heights to the more mundane origins of disputes in which mullahs escalate and pir deescalate conflict. While this pattern has never been stable, but rather has fluctuated, the (ideally) complementary mediations to qawm seem to have emerged as something more like alternatives to it—shari'at through institutional estrangements from tribal settings and tariqat through estrangements of tribesmen on a personal level. Still, with growing independence of mullahs from tribes as institutions and of tribesmen themselves, which are by no means equal, a basic pattern remained in the counterpoint of initiatives of mullahs, who seek out tribesmen, while pir-like figures are sought out by tribesmen; the difference lies in the former becoming more institutional and the latter more individual with the values of both continuously contingent.

This latter experience, more than its forms which are common, contrasts significantly with that of Pakhtun on the North-West Frontier in an important respect. There, the government was not Muslim before 1947, and mediation of intra-Pakhtun conflicts became continuous with positive programs of self-determination successfully achieved when the ramifying influence of the Wali of Swat over "fractious" tribesmen was recognized by the British as a native "state" in the 1920s (see Ahmed 1976:117-22; also Barth 1959: 128-32). But it also was present in numerous faqir and "mad mullahs" who attempted to impose their mediation between tribesmen and to rally them as, above all, Muslims in defense of their dar al-Islam and whose efforts were *not* "legitimized" by British recognition and thus remained self-limiting to those who would accept their mediation. Something like this situation seems now to have arisen in Afghanistan. With the perception of a regime as fundamentally *anti*-Muslim, the situation is, within the direct experience of contemporary Afghans, new in breaking down a trichotomy into a multifaceted dichotomy whose facets are in competition with each other to articulate Muslim allegiance. It is, moreover, further complicated by rival accretions of experience less widely shared but incorporated within the same overall evaluative structure in which qawm served for many tribesmen as an idealized resolution of what was incomplete in shari'at and tariqat. This is, in fact and increasingly, a complex society in which such dimensions articulate diverging perspectives that become the bases for competitive interests in the same thing. It does not detract from their sincerity as Muslims, nor does it make them fanatics, that these tribesmen do not need mullahs for theirs to be a Muslim combat. Rather, it points to the depth of that sincerity that national liberation can be cast as a combat for religion in extremis because that religion is so essentially a part of what they conceive of themselves fundamentally to be.

PART VI

THE SAUR REVOLUTION

AND THE AFGHAN WOMAN

CHINA

PAKISTAN

USSR

IRAN

Faizabad

BADAKHSHAN

NANGARHAR

Jalalabad

Baghlan

Charikar

Kabul

Gardez

PAKTYA

NAZAR-I
SHARIF

QATAGHAN

PARWAN

KABUL

Bamyan

Ghazni

GHAZNI

Nazar-i Sharif

SHIBURGHAN

Shiburghan

Maymana

MAYMANA

Oruzgan

Chaghcharan

Kandahar

KANDAHAR

HERAT

Lashkar Gah

GIRISHK

Herat

Farah

FARAH

100 Km

0

AFGHANISTAN: PROVINCES AND CAPITALS BEFORE 1964

Chapter 13

CAUSES AND CONSEQUENCES OF THE ABOLITION OF BRIDEPRICE IN AFGHANISTAN

Nancy Tapper

In 1978 the government of Nur M. Taraki, President of the Revolutionary Council in Afghanistan, initiated a wide-ranging program of change and development. Along with land reform and other measures to wrest power from traditional leaders in Afghan society, the government promulgated Decree No. 7, which aimed at fundamental change in the institution of marriage. A prime concern of the decree, which also motivated other reforms of the Taraki government, was to reduce material indebtedness throughout the country; it was also meant to ensure the equal rights of women with men.* In this chapter I shall argue that if reforms such as those embodied in Decree No. 7 were implemented, they would be unlikely to change either the levels of indebtedness or the status of women in any direct way. Rather they would be likely to alter the whole system of economic goals and values throughout much of rural Afghanistan and perhaps in addition lead to fundamental changes in the nature of ethnic relations in the countryside. It is not difficult to suggest how legislative changes might disrupt such traditional systems, but what form a succeeding structure might take depends on the outcome of the national political struggles in general. In any case, although such proposed reforms, casting the issues of poverty and women's status into a basically First World perspective, may be seen

*Thus in a speech on 4 November 1978 President Taraki said that it was "through the issuance of decrees no. 6 and 7, the hard-working peasants were freed from the bonds of oppressors and money-lenders, etc. ending the sale of girls for good as hereafter nobody would be entitled to sell any girl or woman in this country" (Afghanistan, MIC, *DRA Annual* 1979:216).

as a radical improvement from the legislators' point of view, this perspective has many critics in the Third World and elsewhere.

I shall begin with an overview on legal reforms concerning marriage; present a brief discussion of an anthropological perspective on marriage payments, in which I shall offer ethnographic evidence to suggest something of the character and scale of the possible consequences of the implementation of a marriage reform; and conclude with an analysis of ethnicity and marriage in Afghanistan.

LEGAL REFORMS AND THE STATUS OF WOMEN

The first two articles in Decree No. 7 forbid (respectively) the exchange of a woman in marriage for cash or kind and the payment of other prestations customarily due from a bridegroom on festive occasions; the third article sets an upper limit of 300 afs. on the *mahr*, a payment due from groom to bride which is an essential part of the formal Islamic marriage contract.* In addition, the legislation aims to change marriage customs so as to give young women and men independence of their marriage guardians. Thus (albeit somewhat ambiguously) the ages of first engagement and marriage are raised to sixteen for women and eighteen for men. The decree further stipulates that no one, including widows, can be compelled to marry against his or her will; it carries the implication that no one can be prevented from marrying if he or she so desires. The penalties instituted to uphold these measures include the forfeiture of any illegally paid brideprice or other marriage prestations and a prison sentence of between six months and three years (*Anis*, 25 Mizan 1357 A.H. [1978]; Afghanistan, MIC, *DRA Annual* 1979:86-87, 216).[†]

---

*Taraki explained that "we are always taking into consideration and respect the basic principles of Islam. Therefore, we devised that an equivalent of the sum to be paid in advance by the husband to his wife upon the nuptial amounting to 10 'dirhams' [traditional ritual payment] according to 'shari'at' [Islamic canon law] be converted into local currency which is afs. 300. We also decided that marriageable boys and girls should freely choose their future spouses in line with the rules of shari'at" (Afghanistan, MIC, *DRA Annual* 1979:216).

[†]See the interesting discussion of earlier marriage reform in Afghanistan, the political background to Decree No. 7, and some of its implications for the position of Afghan women in N. Dupree (1981:1, 10-12).

Implicit in the thinking behind the decree (and most other reforms of the institution of marriage elsewhere) is the assumption that brideprice payments and other marriage gifts directly cause general indebtedness on the one hand and an inferior status for women vis-a-vis men on the other. If the causality of these relations is taken for granted, any examination of their exact nature is inhibited. Such thinking itself becomes a political dogma; its proponents ignore its historical origins, and, because the dogma is couched in ideal/legalistic terms, they pay little attention to the social practices it attacks. For instance, such thinking directs attention away from the way status inequality generally and thus social and material poverty (as opposed to simple economic indebtedness) are actually created and perpetuated through the institution of marriage as a whole; similarly it leaves unexplored the relation between marriage and the social and cultural construction of gender roles.

The two aims of Decree No. 7 — to reduce material indebtedness associated with marriage and to improve the status of women — are parallel to and historically connected with legislative reforms of the institution of marriage which have occurred throughout the world, not least in the Americas and Europe, over the last one hundred years or so. Clearly the impetus for such reforms derived from changes in the roles of women and the institution of marriage in Western industrial society and the ideological shifts which these entailed; the changes included an increasing "domestication" of women, their marginalization from the modern economy, and a decline in the importance of marriage as an institution articulating values and activities relevant in many areas of social life. However, the changes which led to reform measures in the West did not necessarily occur in societies where the institution of marriage may have continued to occupy a fundamentally different and more important role in articulating persons, resources, and information. But with the expansion of colonial empires and increasing Western ideological dominance, the particular socioeconomic context of marriage reforms in the West was forgotten, and the value system of which they were a part came to be represented as universally valid. The situation described by Sayigh is relevant throughout the Muslim Middle East (as well as elsewhere): by the end of the nineteenth century, the institution of marriage and the status of women in Islamic countries were treated as indicators of the backwardness of Islamic cultures, which might "catch up with the West" only through a process of social evolution and imitative change (1981:263).

Some of the better known examples of the universalizing of the Western value system were marriage reforms introduced into African societies in the 1930s, when colonial administrators particularly attacked brideprices paid in cattle (see Mair 1971:195-96), and certain forms of marriage—such as exchange marriage among the Tiv of West Africa—were prohibited both because they offered women little say in marriage arrangements and because of the web of indebtedness they created (Bohannan 1967). Furthermore, Christian missionary activity throughout the world has usually been based on assumptions about the absolute value of Western institutions. And marriage reforms similar to those in Africa have occurred elsewhere, though in a less direct fashion; see, for example, Croll's discussion of contemporary China (1981).

In Afghanistan previous rulers had introduced reforms relating to marriage and women's status; their aim was to transform Afghanistan into a "modern" society. In this respect Decree No. 7 has much in common with marriage reforms from the time of Amir 'Abdur Rahman Khan (1880-1901). Writing of Amanullah Khan's Family Code of 1921, Gregorian notes the following:

> Some token efforts at reform had been made in this area by Abdur Rahman and Habibullah. but none of their measures were as great in scope or as earnestly applied as those of Amanullah. Child marriage and intermarriage between close kin were outlawed as contrary to Islamic principles. In the new code Amanullah reiterated Abdur Rahman's ruling that a widow was to be free of the domination of her husband's family, followed his father's example and placed tight restrictions on wedding expenses, including dowries, and granted wives the right to appeal to the courts if their husbands did not adhere to Quranic tenets regarding marriage. One source reports that in the fall of 1924, Afghan girls were given the right to choose their husbands, a measure that incensed the traditionalist elements (1969:243-44).

Reforms after Amanullah were similar to his in substance. Louis Dupree notes that a 1950 law banning "ostentatious life-crises ceremonies prohibits many of the expensive aspects of birth, circumcision, marriage and burial rituals" (1973:209), and Knabe gives details of how the Marriage Law of 1971 was a further attempt by lawmakers to curb the indebtedness which arises from the costs of marriage (1977a:164), which "are a burden for Afghan society as a whole" (1977a:149).

Kemali has examined in detail the history of marriage reform in Afghanistan:

> To date the areas conventionally covered by marriage reform [problems of excessive expenditure in marriage ceremonies, child marriage, polygamy, and divorce] are governed by the traditional Hanafi law which, on the whole has remained in its medieval form in Afghanistan. The existent statutory legislation which has been added to the Hanafi law, has introduced no substantial change to the Hanafi traditional doctrines (1976:i).

Only in July 1973, when the conservative nature of the Afghan constitution was one of the issues behind the *coup d'etat* which established Muhammad Daoud's Afghan Republic, did there seem some chance of promulgating more substantial marriage reforms coupled with legal sanctions. Kemali, in response to what he sees as the "social evils emanating from excessive expenditure in marriage" (1976:47), outlines directions the reforms might take to correct the consequences of traditional practices. The continuity is clear between his arguments in favor of marriage reform, those of earlier reformers, and those of the draftees of Decree No. 7: all derive from Western models of social production and reproduction; moreover, they contain a distinct Pashtun ethnic bias in their understanding of the traditional institutions of marriage in Afghanistan. Kemali notes the following:

> Excessive expenditure in marriage undermines the human dignity of women as it tends to render them into a kind of property of the husband or his family. [It] weakens the financial status of the family and tends to bring or worsen poverty. [It] tends to render the adults highly dependent on family resources; this in turn weakens their position in regard to the exercise of their right of consent in marriage as well as their freedom of choice of a life partner. Dependence of the youth on the family resources is enormous even without the stimulus of this additional factor. Marriage

becomes largely dependent on the possession of financial means; this leads to intolerable discriminations against the poor. Excessive expenditure in marriage deprives many of the right to marry (e.g. many women); it also leads to late marriages, and often brings about a wide disparity of age between the spouses. Excessive expenditure in marriage constitutes a source of embitterment and conflict during the course of marital life.... Costly marriages contribute to the continuance of the tradition-bound society and tend to slow down the process of reform.... The practice is self-perpetuating (1976:47-48).

In Afghanistan, as elsewhere in the Muslim Middle East, the legal code relating to marriage and the family is based directly on the Shari'a or canon law of Islam, and reforms in this area have typically provoked extreme reactions, explicitly in the defense of Islamic principles. However, it would seem that the relation between reform legislation and Islamic fundamentalism actually works the other way around. The strength of the reaction clearly depends on the importance of the institutions of marriage and the family in the regulation of daily living and the extent to which they are threatened. Since many Muslims see few discrepancies among customary practices, social identity within a community, and formal Islam, the last can become a source of ideological unity which may be used to defend a traditional social structure.

"Islamic" reaction to marriage and family reforms has often idealized the position of women by taking an extreme legalistic view of Islamic family law. Arguments between political and social progressives and reactionaries crystallize around the issue of "women's status" (a concept which itself conceals a variety of biases which derive from Western male models of gender). Men and women who see themselves as educated and modern can justify attempts to change the customs of those they label tradition-bound and ignorant in terms of raising the status of women. Modernization — implicitly meaning the growth of technological skills, material wealth, and social complexity on a Western model — becomes for the progressive, educated elite an unambiguous goal, and in an area such as the reform of marriage, a direct link is assumed between the nature of the traditional institution and poverty and the assumption left unexamined. In Afghanistan, even in the context of the Saur

Revolution, such complicated associations have continued to be evident in attempts to propound legal reforms which could reconcile Islamic principles with progressive politics and the goal of modernization.*

AN ANTHROPOLOGICAL PERSPECTIVE ON MARRIAGE PAYMENTS

It has long been accepted by anthropologists that marriage prestations in any society do not admit to a simple economic or utilitarian interpretation because, as Comaroff points out, "their utilitarian quality is [itself] a culturally constituted variable" (1980: 41). "Moreover, the way in which actors experience and construe transactions does not itself explain why those transactions occur, or how they relate to an ordered set of values in any socio-cultural system" (11). Comaroff offers a general criticism of previous studies of marriage prestations; his main objection is the "tendency ... to make a functional distinction [between marriage and marriage prestations] in which marriage is seen as structurally prior, and prestations largely as its institutionalized mode of facilitation (35-36). He argues that this misses the point that where marriage payments exist, "they represent a critical element in the symbolic order with reference to which unions are classified and invested with social currency" (36) and that "the meaning of marriage prestations, given their semantic relationship to marriage, depends in large measure upon the location of the latter in any constitutive order" (39).

Such a perspective on brideprice and marriage gifts is particularly important in the case of marriage systems such as those found in rural communities throughout Afghanistan, in which the making of marriages is the central focus of most economic and political activity and the principal means by which status is expressed and validated. This is particularly the case of the marriage system among the Durrani Pashtuns in north-central Afghanistan, among whom (I have argued) "marriage prestations and the transfer of women between households must be seen as part of the wider system of exchange and control of all productive and reproductive resources" (N. Tapper 1979; 1981:387ff.).

---

*In this context see especially N. Dupree (1981).

ETHNOGRAPHIC EVIDENCE ON THE CONSEQUENCES OF MARRIAGE
REFORM

To illustrate, in terms of one Afghan community, the probable short- and longer-term impact of marriage reforms such as Decree No. 7 on communities in rural Afghanistan, I draw on ethnographic material collected by Richard Tapper and myself in 1970-72.* The community of Ishaqzai Durrani—numbered some two hundred households living in villages in the Saripul district of Jawzjan province, where they operated a dual economy based on the ownership of extensive irrigated farmland and flocks which were taken to summer pastures in the Hazarajat.

I argue that for these Durrani the whole structure of social and material poverty as well as the spectrum of relations between the sexes is articulated through the institution of marriage. The heaviest expenses any household has to bear are concerned with marriage. In other words, production is directed largely toward reproduction— toward acquiring wives who will produce sons who will produce labor and political support in defense of productive and reproductive resources, especially land and women. The expense of marriage is considerable among the Durrani. The average value of brideprices in 1971-72 (paid in cash, animals, and other goods) was 65,000 afs., then about $800—several times an average household's annual income. It is important to note that brideprices vary much less between rich and poor Durrani than household wealth or income, so that marriage is much more difficult for the poor than for the rich. At the same time, the poor can aspire to the same kinds of marriages as the rich, and they sometimes compete for the same women.

The marriage arrangements made by a poorer household almost never result in direct indebtedness, but the choice of bride, the agreed brideprice, and the time taken to complete a marriage may visibly

---

*Fieldwork among Durrani Pashtuns of north-central Afghanistan was done jointly with Richard Tapper in 1970-72 as a Social Science Research Council (UK) project; for further information see R. and N. Tapper (1972) and N. Tapper (1977, 1979, 1980, and 1981). The ethnographic present refers to the fieldwork period. Detailed material was collected on only one subtribe; however, many aspects of its culture are common to Durrani throughout Afghan Turkistan, and I am reasonably sure that much of what I have to say is also applicable to the social organization of rural Durrani communities elsewhere in the country.

confirm or indeed increase a household's poverty. However, it is crucial to an understanding of the system to realize that these same elements may also communicate the wealth and high status of a household and indeed increase that household's standing in the community. Through the choice of spouse, the character and amount of the prestations, and the manipulation of ritual symbols, marriage arrangements communicate the real and potential strengths and weaknesses of a household. Evaluations of a household's overall status within the community are made according to its marriage arrangements. While the marriages made by a wealthy household may confirm its strength, they may also reveal weaknesses of which others will take advantage. Furthermore, the complex of meanings associated with marriage arrangements directly affect women inasmuch as women identify themselves, and are almost totally identified with, their household of marriage. In more general terms, gender status as it is represented in relations between the sexes, as well as in relations among women or among men, depends on the way the institution of marriage as a whole is constituted: brideprice and the degree of independence of women are only two dimensions of this whole.

The members of the community discuss control of all resources—especially labor, land, and women—in terms of honor; debt and credit in all contexts, including marriage, are also assessed in these terms. We can view the real inequality in such a system as a spiral whereby the weak lose control of resources of *all* kinds, lose honor, and become weaker still, while the strong gain control of resources, gain honor, and become stronger. Yet honor, as it relates to inequality and competition, is balanced by an alternative Islamic and Pashtun ideology of equality, which is also seen in terms of honor.*

Elsewhere (N. Tapper 1981) I have analyzed Durrani marriage in terms of symmetrical and asymmetrical modes. The first, comprised of direct exchange marriage (primarily sister-exchange), conforms to Durrani egalitarian ideals and defines the ethnic group as a whole; the second, in which women are given for brideprice or in compensation for blood, creates and maintains a status hierarchy among Durrani households. Actors manipulate the ambiguities in each of these alternative modes to make and evaluate status claims. In other

*For a more detailed discussion of this point, see N. Tapper (1979:215ff., and 1981:391-93).

words, both equality and competition are confirmed or denied through the complex institution of marriage and expressed in the language of honor.

The meaning of any Durrani marriage relates ultimately to the exchange system as a whole and to the differential values given to four ranked spheres of exchange (see Firth 1950 and Bohannan 1967). Men are ranked in the first and highest sphere. Direct exchanges between or of them include the most honorable and manly of all activities, and these activities are prime expressions of status equality: vengeance and feud (*badi*), political support and hospitality (*milmastya*), and the practice of sanctuary (*nanawatay*).

Women belong to the second sphere. Durrani women are often treated exclusively as reproducers and pawns in economic and political exchanges. Women accept this ranking of themselves, but they and men see their importance confirmed in the highly valued form of exchange marriage, the most important kind of exchange and a prime expression of status equality within this sphere.

Exchanges of productive resources—especially of land, animals, and valuables—form a third sphere, in which the equivalence of various items has more to do with the social relations between givers and receivers than with market values. The special treatment accorded productive resources and capital goods is perhaps best seen in the composition of a brideprice where, for example, the relation between the value of animals given and their market price is complicated and more indicative of social status than the prices of meat, milk, or wool in the bazaar. Exchanges of land and valuables are also treated in a special way and carry various complex meanings. It is of the greatest importance to Durrani that land should never be sold or mortgaged to outsiders. Similarly the loan or gift of expensive animals such as horses and camels and luxury goods such as guns, rugs, or jewelry is used as a gesture of political support or friendship between households. Land and other valuables are acceptable for inclusion in a brideprice, and the valuables included in a bride's trousseau should not be traded in the local market.

Finally, market values are relevant in direct exchanges of produce in the fourth sphere. The barter of produce is a frequent but low-status activity associated with the poor.

There is only one proper conversion between the first two spheres: two or more women can be given in compensation for the killing or injury of one man. The meaning of this conversion is ambiguous, but usually the honor goes to the killers who have "taken" a man and "give" only two women. Marriage for brideprice is the most obvious form of conversion between the second and third spheres: a woman for productive resources, valuables, and cash. The conversion clearly compromises the honor of the wife-givers, who are very unwilling to take goods from the even lower sphere of produce (e.g., by accepting grain as a substitute for some part of the productive resources or capital goods of the brideprice), while honor redounds to the wife-takers. Such conversions communicate status inequality.

As noted, within the system debt does not result directly from brideprice payments, nor does wealth depend directly on being able to give women and receive productive resources. Rather it is the control (or lack of it) of the complex interactions among resources in all four spheres which leads to wealth (or poverty) — especially to a family's ability to cope with debts which arise in the wider social environment from dealings with the government, tribal leaders, or moneylenders. However they arise, debts to such external agents are greatly feared and can lead to the loss of women in marriage or the loss of male labor through imprisonment, voluntary exile, or the wholesale emigration of families from the region. Mortgages, especially of land or guns for cash or grain, are seen as a short-term strategy to finance such debts and to maintain household self-sufficiency — to stave off hunger and ensure the continued support of the male labor force. However, should such a short-term strategy fail, the household is likely to be left without male labor for production and defense and to be greatly weakened. An alternative and longer-term strategy to cope with the exigencies of the wider environment lies in marriage. Marriage arrangements can be delayed or exchanges arranged; men of any household can find brides and need not incur further debt to do so. Through immediate affinal support, and ultimately through sons, a household can continue to be self-sufficient.

In sum, brideprice is not simply a means to get a wife, such that its abolition would mean anyone is now free to find a wife. For the poor or disabled man there have always been alternative ways of getting wives, while brideprice has always involved a highly complex system of meanings beyond that of simple monetary value. The evidence of the ideology and practice of Durrani marriage has clearly shown that it is a system which encompasses the contradictory values of hierarchy and equality in Durrani society. Marriage provides the context and the motive for the expression of these values—and it does so not only among Durrani, but also between Durrani and other groups in the polyethnic state of Afghanistan. Viewed diachronically, the status and ethnic identity of both individuals and groups may change over time. For example, marriages may be used to achieve and simultaneously confirm Durrani identity and thus provide an effective means of incorporating non-Durrani into the ethnic group. The opposite pattern is also found: ultimately individuals and groups who intermarry with other ethnic groups can lose Durrani status, especially when oppressed and impoverished households leave an area and migrate to a distant part of the country.

ETHNICITY AND MARRIAGE

The evidence presented above suggests that legislative tinkering with marriage prestations, even if fully implemented, could not in any simple way reduce indebtedness or improve the status of women among Durrani; rather it would overturn the whole social construction of marriage and its relation with other aspects of the social order. Moreover, I have hinted at some of the concomitant ethnic implications of Durrani marriage. In this section is a more detailed description of the relations among ethnic groups in northern Afghanistan based on marriage (see also N. Tapper and R. Tapper 1982).

Durrani ethnic identity and their ideals of status equality depend on claims to religiously privileged descent, implying superiority to all other ethnic groups. Much interethnic competition is disguised by Durrani perception of this superiority and by the absolute prohibition on the marriage of Durrani women to men who are not Durrani but are of some "lower" ethnic status. The integrity of the entire Durrani ethnic group depends on the maintenance of this rule, and breaches are dealt with collectively and with great ferocity.

The emphasis on descent and the ban on women marrying "down" (hypogamy) are also found among other groups of Pashto-speakers whom the Durrani loosely call Farsiwans—that is, groups of diverse origins such as Khalili and Maliki from southwest Afghanistan, Ghilzai, and other Eastern Pashtuns (see R. Tapper in this volume). Durrani consider these other Pashto-speakers to pose the greatest

302

threat to their ethnic integrity and security. A relationship of rivalry and hostility between Durrani and Farsiwans is of long standing, and the Durrani ban on women marrying "down" with Farsiwans is an effective means of preventing Farsiwans from gaining access to Durrani resources and identity.

Durrani attitudes and values are different from those of all the non-Pashto speaking ethnic groups in the area. Persian-speaking groups such as Aymaqs, Arabs, Tajiks, and Hazarahs and Turkic-speaking Uzbeks and Turkmens are differentiated from the Durrani by basic features of social organization as well as language, custom, and (in the case of the Hazarahs) religion. The ethnic boundary with such groups is marked for the Durrani by a plethora of criteria, among which the ban on hypogamy, while it remains fundamental from the Durrani point of view, is simply taken for granted. Indeed it is made more or less irrelevant in this context by the other groups' own conceptions of both ethnic identity and marriage. Among the other ethnic groups in the area, there are various criteria of identity; in some cases they are based on economic differences, in other cases on geographical distribution, and so on. However, apart from the Arabs and Turkmen, institutions of descent and marriage do not seem to play a central role in marking ethnic boundaries as they do for the Durrani and Farsiwans.

In the system I have described for the Durrani, the overriding jural responsibilities for the control of a married woman (and the honor she represents) rest with her husband and his agnates. The virtually complete transfer of rights in and duties toward women at marriage is associated with a number of customary features: marriage is very expensive, there is no divorce, affinal ties are relatively unimportant, and women do not in practice inherit property (see N. Tapper 1979:29ff.). As far as I could ascertain, the marriage arrangements are different among the other ethnic groups: a woman is not completely alienated on marriage from her family of birth. She commonly takes her share of the patrimony, and her agnates retain residual rights in her—for example, in her remarriage as a widow. Moreover, marriage does not have the same relation to the control of productive resources and capital for these groups as it does for Durrani (and Farsiwans), and brideprices are usually considerably lower, both absolutely and in relation to wealth. Finally, and perhaps as a consequence of the character of marriage among these other ethnic groups, marriage is apparently not used among them, as it is among the Durrani, as the single most important means of political competition.

In addition to the factors discussed, there are other aspects of the relation between ethnicity and marriage which need consideration. For one thing, there is some intermarriage between all the groups I have mentioned. Indeed there is a network of intermarriage which links all the major ethnic groups in the area, as well as groups farther afield. Thus 10-15 percent of wives of men in the Durrani group were from "inferior" ethnic groups. Among the non-Durrani groups in the north-central part of the country, intermarriage may again account for perhaps 10-15 percent of all marriages. In both cases, a number of these marriage may lead to enduring political and economic ties between the households concerned. Certainly such a network of intermarriage has economic implications, not least in terms of marriage prestations per se.

Unfortunately there is not sufficient information available to elucidate the relation between the economics of brideprice and the movement of women throughout the country, though a countrywide pattern undoubtedly exists. I heard, for instance, that Durrani from Maymana travelled to Sistan to find inexpensive brides; others from the northwest went to Badakhshan for the same reason, while Durrani from the south of Afghanistan would travel north to marry their daughters where brideprices were high. Of course the monetary value of a brideprice is not the only consideration, and the implications of networks of intermarriage must be qualified in certain fundamental ways. The economic implications must be separated first from the motivation for such marriages and second from the meaning such marriages have in terms of ethnicity. As we have seen, at the very least intermarriage has a profound connection for Durrani, Farsiwans, Arabs, and Turkmens with ethnic identity per se, which in turn relates in a very basic way to conceptions of status differences within such ethnic groups. Though relations among marriage, the control of resources and information, and social status are different for other ethnic groups in the region, I think it is fair to assume, if only because of the economic and political power of the Durrani and Turkmen within the region, that any substantial alteration in the meaning of marriage within these groups (perhaps by the implementation of marriage reforms) could lead to a complete restructuring of ethnic relations.

CONCLUSIONS

Marriage reforms such as Decree No. 7 attack symptoms, not conditions of a social order. Nonetheless, they may have many short-term consequences. For example, Beattie has described how marriage arrangements in progress were simply halted by the decree's prohibition of marriage payments (p. 191 above; see also Olesen 1982:117n, 128, 138n). Moreover, women suffer a diminution of value in their own eyes and those of their husbands and brothers by being given away "free" (see N. Tapper 1981). Such reactions occur in terms of the traditional system and are often expressed in terms of formal Islam. If the prohibition on brideprice payments and other expenses of marriage continues to be enforced in the absence of other fundamental changes, one can expect that the traditional function of the institution of marriage in effecting and communicating status changes within a community will be replaced by an alternative system. Such a system, which would probably emerge as a variant on the traditional institutions, would almost certainly continue to use the idiom of honor to express the control of productive and reproductive resources. Social inequality would persist, probably on the same scale as in traditional Afghan society, but would be revealed and manipulated by other means.

In the longer term, however, the underlying goals of the reforms—to reduce material indebtedness throughout the country and to ensure women's rights—could be approached only through the introduction of both an alternative motivation for production and a consistent program of education and other measures which would allow women to gain control of a variety of resources, including information, capital, and their own labor. But given that the marriage reforms are themselves derived by an Afghan elite from a First World ideology of production and gender roles, it is unlikely that these goals will be realized even if linked with substantial reforms in other areas. Rather, given the comparative scarcity of resources within the country, it is more likely that any such transformations of Afghan society would result in an inferior imitation of First World society in which poverty and discrimination against women remain integrally connected.

Chapter 14

REVOLUTIONARY RHETORIC AND AFGHAN WOMEN

Nancy Hatch Dupree

WOMEN AND EMANCIPATION BEFORE THE SAUR REVOLUTION

Afghan leaders have addressed themselves to the subject of reform for women for a hundred years. These spokesmen, predominately male, have held that a nationalist ideology encompassing emancipation for women is essential to the creation of a progressive image for the nation. Yet contradictions between religion, custom, and reform have plagued the feminist movement in Afghanistan since its inception. Amir 'Abdur Rahman (1880-1901) introduced many laws in an attempt to align customary social practices with the prescriptions of Islam. Using the dictates of the Quran, he forbade child marriages, forced marriages, the leverite (forced marriages of widows to brothers of deceased husbands), exorbitant brideprices, and marriage gifts. He upheld hereditary rights for widows and ruled that women could seek divorce. He granted freedom to wives in cases of nonsupport by husbands and authorized the *mahr* (a gift of property or money promised by a groom at the time of marriage; a wife may demand it at any time, particularly when abandoned, separated, or divorced). However, he also imposed the death penalty for adulterous women – which is contrary to the Quran – and decreed that men were entitled to full control over their women because "the honor of the people of Afghanistan consists in the honor of their women" (Kakar 1979:173).

The concept that women should be considered as contributing members of society beyond motherhood was first introduced during the reign of Amir Habibullah (1901-19), the son of 'Abdur Rahman. Mahmud Beg Tarzi (1865-1933), a leading reformer in the early twentieth century, argued against overly protective restrictions on

306

women; in addition, he pleaded for education for women, stressing that egalitarian Islam does not deny women education and that it is an Islamic duty to provide them with opportunities to function fully in the society. Only with educated women in the home, he said, could the family remain strong and the nation progress. To bolster his arguments he published accounts of famous women through history in his newspaper *Siraj al-Akhbar* (Schinasi 1979:212).*

The religious leaders read Tarzi's essays with growing displeasure. They contended that education for women would lead to the breakdown of the family, sexual anarchy, and ultimately degrade women. The honor of the nation would be lost. Conservative aversion increased as Habibullah's son, King Amanullah (1919-29), attempted to institutionalize reforms for women. Despite 'Abdur Rahman's efforts, unjust customary practices persisted. Therefore Amanullah once again pressed to abolish child marriages, forced marriages, and the leverite and to assure widows' rights. He ordered that exorbitant engagement, wedding, and marriage gifts be curtailed. In addition, Amanullah attempted to go further by advocating monogamy, the removal of the veil (*chadari*), the end of seclusion (*purdah*), and compulsory education for girls.[†]

Amanullah's queen, Suraya, and his sister, Siraj ul-Banat, were the first Afghan women to speak out publicly on the subject of equality for women. They had learned their lessons well from the liberal-minded men around them. Speaking in 1923, Siraj ul-Banat said the following:

> Some people are laughing at us, saying that women know only how to eat and drink. Old women discourage young women by saying their mothers never starved to death because they could not read or write. . . . But knowledge is not man's monopoly. Women also deserve to be knowledgeable. We must on the one hand bring up healthy children and, on the other hand, help men in their work. We must read about famous women in this world, to know that women can achieve exactly what men can achieve.**

[*]For a general discussion of women in the early twentieth century and subsequent periods, see N. Dupree 1978.

[†]For the Amanullah period, see Poullada 1973 and Stewart 1973.

[**]Published in the Kabul newspaper *Anis*; quoted in Afghanistan, MIC, *Progress Report* 1977: 9. The MIC publication was banned by the Democratic Republic of Afghanistan (DRA), but one copy is available with this author.

Queen Suraya, the daughter of Mahmud Beg Tarzi, spoke to women during the 1927 Jashn (Independence Celebrations) even more forthrightly:

> Independence has been achieved. It belongs to all of us. . . . Do not think, however, that our nation needs only men to serve it. Women should also take part as women did in the early years of Islam. The valuable services rendered by women are recounted throughout history, from which we learn that women were not created solely for pleasure and comfort. From their examples we learn that we must all contribute toward the development of our nation and that this cannot be done without being equipped with knowledge. So we should all attempt to acquire as much knowledge as possible in order that we may render our services to society in the manner of the women of early Islam (*Anis*; quoted in Afghanistan, MIC, *Progress Report* 1977:9).

In spite of such references to Islamic heroines, the conservatives would have nothing of it, and their opposition erupted into open revolt. The Khost Rebellion (March 1924-January 1925) was their first overt protest. In 1929 conservative religious and tribal leaders spearheaded a rebellion which overthrew King Amanullah. To restore the sanctity of Islam and the honor of the nation, Amanullah's successor, Habibullah Ghazi (Bacha-i-Saqaw; 17 January-13 October 1929), insisted upon a return to reactionary customs regarding women. He demanded that women remain behind the veil under strict male control and that girls' schools, together with all other vestiges of the women's movement, be suspended.

For the next thirty years—that is, until 1959—under Nadir Shah (1929-33) and his son Zahir Shah (1933-73), women remained in seclusion and wore the veil. Nevertheless, the concept that women should participate in national development was reintroduced as a national policy. Separate schools were established, and education for women gradually gained respectability. Women were employed in professions considered appropriate for them—teachers, medical personnel, and administrators in female institutions.* Thus when the government, led by Prime Minister Muhammad Daoud (1953-63), launched a revolution for women in 1959 by announcing its support

---

*For the Nadir Shah period, see Woodsmall 1960:151-96.

of the *voluntary* removal of the veil and an end to seclusion, Afghan women were well prepared to take their place in multifaceted activities. In addition to furthering social justice, the emergence of women onto the public scene enhanced economic development by providing a potential 50 percent increase in the labor force. Conservative elements in the society who protested were jailed and challenged to provide positive Quranic proof —not interpretations—for their objections (L. Dupree 1959 and 1980a:249). None were forthcoming, and the evolutionary processes toward emancipation began. But very few women spoke out publicly on the subject. The egalitarian ideology was still provided by men, who continued to dominate the reform movement.

Women were automatically enfranchised, without a suffragette movement, by the 1964 constitution, which stated that all Afghans "without discrimination or preference, have equal rights and obligations before the law." Among other things this constitution guaranteed women "dignity, compulsory education, and freedom to work."

Over the years increasing numbers of educated women emerged to work in government and business as secretaries and judges, hairdressers and diplomats, entertainers and parliamentarians. They were employed in some factories, including ceramics, fruit packaging, pharmaceuticals, and housing construction. At no time, however, were women expected to engage in public manual labor. Women in Afghanistan have never carried bricks and buckets of cement on their heads at construction sites, nor performed menial tasks in the streets. The direction of change was positive and steady, but because of the government's insistence on voluntary acceptance, the numbers of women who made changes were small in terms of the total female population and largely confined to the middle and upper strata of urban communities. Nonetheless, the society as a whole became gradually reconciled to women's participation in the totality of the society.

Undercurrents of dissent existed. In 1968 conservative members of parliament proposed to enact a law prohibiting Afghan girls from studying abroad. Hundreds of demonstrating girls vociferously brought their constitutional guarantee of equal rights to the attention of the parliamentarians. In 1970 two conservative mullahs (Muslim religious leaders) protested such public evidence of female liberation as miniskirts, women teachers, and schoolgirls by shooting at the legs of women in Western dress and splashing them with acid. In protest five thousand girls, fearful that the legal system (dominated by males, often conservatives) would prove too lenient to the mullahs, spontaneously took to the streets of Kabul. These first demonstrations by women were early indications that a women's consciousness was developing—an initial statement that women should be considered a viable force with potential leadership.

Progress continued without further strident demonstrations, but at the same time age-old beliefs and customs prevailed, even among the enlightened. The government of the Republic of Afghanistan, founded by Daoud on 17 July 1973, attempted to redress specific problems through a Penal Code (1976) and a Civil Law (1977), both of which followed the constitutional injunction that "There can be no law repugnant to the basic principles of the sacred religion of Islam." The Penal Code and Civil Law included the familiar articles against child marriage, forced marriage, and abandonment. They protected inheritance and expressly declared the mahr to be "the property of the wife" (Civil Law: 110). Yet numbers of sex-discriminating social customs favorable to male dominance in matters such as divorce, child custody, adultery, and the defense of honor were perpetuated by their entrenchment in these legal statutes.

Many attitudes reflected in the laws, both positive and negative, had been the subject of argument between Muslim traditionalists and modernists for centuries. Contradictions became most destructive in families which encouraged partial emancipation while insisting on patriarchal control as an ideal. For example, to encourage a girl to seek education and then deny her the right to exercise her choice to work outside the home and select her marriage partner naturally fostered incipient rebellion.

The insistence on patriarchal control arose in part from the fact that in Afghanistan women symbolize honor—of the nation and of the family. Any deviation on the part of women from honorable behavior as it is defined by any given family or group is seen to besmirch the honor of those in authority and cannot therefore be tolerated. It is this attitude which has perpetuated overly protective institutions and customs such as the veil and seclusion. At the same time, if women are placed on an exalted symbolic pinnacle, it behooves men to respect those who behave with honor. Indeed respect for women is a genuine personality trait in Afghan males and a basic element in traditional male-female relationships. Observers from sophisticated Islamic cities such as Tehran have remarked with wonder that attractive, young, unaccompanied females were able to walk through the streets of Kabul without being subjected to abusive stares, vulgar remarks, and jostling.

Few Afghan women wished to destroy their respected status, but many began to ask for a more precise definition, in modern terms, of what constituted honorable behavior on their part. After all, women had been asked to contribute to national development and enhance the image of a progressive Afghanistan. They had responded with distinction, functioning with poise and dignity, with no loss of honor to themselves or to their families, and with much credit to the nation. They had proved the correctness of the modernist contention that there is nothing inconsistent with Islam, or modesty, and full participation. But as they became increasingly aware of the importance of their roles, women began to examine their opportunities as individuals rather than stereotypes or national symbols. They longed to be released from the strictures of family consensus and given the right to determine life-crises decisions as individuals. They began to articulate goals which conflicted with male-oriented ideals.

The government was still unable—and unwilling—to insist on breaking restrictions imposed by the family, which continued to be the single most important institution in Afghan society. Family attitudes, not government guarantees, decided the future of girls. Furthermore, laws favoring women were indifferently enforced, and as more and more women entered the work force, competition caused indifference and resentment to surface. Positions of responsibility and power were occasionally offered to women, but disproportionately to the female work force. Criticisms of sex discrimination and tokenism were raised. Yet women were unwilling to take a militant attitude toward sexism, and they lacked the cohesive leadership necessary to permit them to function as a distinct group with power to force the guarantees pledged to them in legal statutes. By the end of the 1970s skepticism and cynicism were pervasive, and the emancipation movement was labeled by many as a purely cosmetic sham which the power elite espoused for its own aggrandizement and perpetuation.

In truth stagnation had set in and changes were needed. Although all but a few deplored the violence which accompanied the Saur (April) Revolution and the establishment of the leftist Democratic Republic of Afghanistan (DRA) on 27 April 1978 (L. Dupree 1979d), many looked forward with anticipation to new programs unshackled by precedent.

MOBILIZING AFGHAN WOMEN AFTER THE SAUR REVOLUTION: APRIL-JULY 1978

On the women's front a sense of unease set in early regarding the new government. Within twelve days the Revolutionary Council under Prime Minister Nur Muhammad Taraki had presented the "Basic Lines of the Revolutionary Duties of the Government of the DRA" and broadcast it over Radio Afghanistan (Afghanistan, MIC, *DRA Annual* 1979:67-70). Article 12 ensured "equality of rights of women and men in all social, economic, political, cultural, and civil aspects." The abrogated constitutions of 1964 and 1977 had made identical blanket assurances.

Government leaders offered little concrete in the way of articulating expectations or specifying action-oriented programs to implement Article 12, however. Dr. Anahita Ratibzad, member of the Revolutionary Council and Minister of Social Affairs, was among the ablest, most dynamic members of the new leadership. On 10 May she made a major address to her staff and Kabul's teachers, in which she pledged to translate Article 12 into action. She described the "duties of women and mothers, who shape the future of the country . . . to bring up sons and daughters who are sincere and patriotic" and told women to "take steps to consolidate your revolutionary regime as bravely as the heroic and brave men of this country" (*Kabul Times*, 5/11/78).

It was not surprising to find that women were being called to participate in political action, but it was disappointing to note that women were still being assigned primarily culture-bound, stereotyped roles as mothers duty-bound to fulfill supportive roles for family and nation. Afghan history and folklore are replete with idealized accounts and legends of heroic women who provided guidance and inspiration to their menfolk in times of crisis. If the ideal personality type for Afghan men is the warrior-poet, a lauded personality type for Afghan women is the poet-heroine. Many of the Afghan heroines were mothers whose sagacity had inspired their famous sons and whose stirring poems had furthered nationalistic causes – for example, Nazo, mother of Mir Ways Hotak (1709-15), who had removed the yoke of the Persian Safawids, and Zarghunah, mother of Ahmad Shah Durrani (1747-72), who had founded an empire. Women who had defied the customs which proscribed education for women in the harems were also extolled. Zaynab, daughter of Mir Ways Hotak, was a scholar in both Pashto and Dari. She wrote, taught, and acted as political adviser and stood with her brothers at the bastion of Kandahar when the city was besieged in 1738 by Persia's Nadir Afshar. Spina Herawi, Aisha Durrani, Amana Fidawi, and Mastura Ghori were among the accomplished poetesses illuminating the courts and harems of the past. Rabia Balkhi (tenth century), who wrote a poem on her prison wall in her own blood to condemn the injustice of being denied the right to marry the man of her choice, is particularly beloved. Heroines of the battlefield inspired armies both with daring acts and stirring couplets. Malalay, the most often quoted of these fighting heroines, rallied Afghan troops in the battle against the British at Maywand (near Kandahar) in 1880, and Ghazi Adi rescued the flag of a dying *mujahidin* (freedom fighter) opposing the British in Kabul during the Second Anglo-Afghan War (1878-80). These types of poet-heroines have been revered through history for their individuality, patriotism, duty, and courage in transcending the controls imposed upon them.

In an attempt to mobilize Afghan women, the DRA held up these poet-heroines as models, pointing out that "Women have always been prominent in politics and social struggles, like Rabia, Malalay, Zarghunah, and Aisha" (*Kabul Times*, 7/3/78). The rhetoric stressed the obligation of women to identify with these heroines, but the rights due women remained amorphous even though almost daily functions hailing the Saur Revolution were held in girls' schools throughout Kabul.

Lengthy DRA speeches rang with scathing condemnations against the tyranny, injustice, corruption, torture, and lack of attention that had been the "hallmarks of the defunct regime" under which "thousands upon thousands of women had lived in dark homes and humid caves, with no ear to hear their cries of anguish, no heart to beat for them," as Dr. Anahita phrased it (*Kabul Times*, 5/11/78). The defunct regimes, said Sultana Umayd, Director of Kabul Girls' Schools, "had championed women's rights for purely demagogic reasons, flouting the prestige of Afghan women and weakening their creativity through deprivation and oppression" (6/25/78). "Now," said Suraya, President of the Democratic Organization of Afghan Women (DOAW — see below), "all injustices and slavery have been eliminated, and Afghan mothers can rear heroes and heroines like Malalay." "Now," said Ruhafza Kamyar, Principal of the DOAW's Vocational High School, "society belongs to us and we belong to society, and it is up to us to make efforts to our last breath for the realization of the aspirations of the people" (6/5/78). The speakers did not say how the aspirations could be realized. The meetings ended with the chanting of slogans calling "death to the bloody hangmen" (5/22/78).

All revolutionaries must downgrade their predecessors in order to justify their actions. From the beginning, however, the totally negative harangues of the DRA sounded slightly hollow in light of the fact that it was the very women who heaped vituperation on past leaders who had benefited most from the movement those leaders had initiated. The most prominent women speakers during the early months after the Saur Revolution had been active in education and medicine for many years, as principals and administrators with positions of responsibility. The career of Dr. Anahita exemplifies the development of these women. She was born in October 1931, the daughter of Ahmad Ratib, a dissident journalist who opted for exile after he had incurred the disfavor of the authorities. (He died of tuberculosis in Tehran about 1935.) Anahita's mother, a half-sister of Mahmud Beg Tarzi but outside the elitist society, became a nurse-maid in the home of Shah Mahmud, brother of King Nadir. Anahita—whose birthname was Nahidah—was educated at and graduated from the eighth grade at Malalay Girls' School in Kabul in 1945. The next year she entered nursing school. In 1950 she studied nursing in the United States, and on returning to Kabul, she was appointed in 1953 as Director of Nursing at Kabul's Women's Hospital, where she also taught nursing. Joining the newly established Faculty for Women at Kabul University, she went on to enter the Medical College at the university in 1957 and became a member of its teaching staff upon graduation in 1963. Along with three other women, in 1965 Anahita stood for and won election to the Wulusi Jirgah (Lower House of Parliament) as a candidate from Kabul City for the People's Democratic Party of Afghanistan (PDPA). These elections marked the beginning of an experiment in constitutional monarchy when numbers of liberal and leftist newcomers appeared in the political arena. Anahita marched in the vanguard.

Dr. Anahita joined the leftist PDPA when it was founded by Taraki on 1 January 1965. During a period of relatively free press (1965-73) she wrote for the weekly *Parcham* (first published on 14 March 1968) until it was banned in July 1969. Her major assignment within the PDPA, however, was the formation in 1965 of the DOAW to counter the establishment's Women's Welfare Association (established in 1946), a nonpolitical organization offering education and employment opportunities to women (among other supportive activities). The PDPA accused the Welfare Association of being run by aristocratic women for their personal satisfaction without concern for the real issues facing women.*

Dr. Anahita was rewarded for her loyal party work in 1976, when she was elected to the Central Committee of the PDPA; she was reelected in 1977. After the Saur Revolution she was elected to the Revolutionary Council of the DRA and appointed Minister of Social Affairs.

On the one hand, Dr. Anahita symbolizes the success women could achieve after Daoud's emancipation movement was initiated in 1959. On the other hand, one can understand her rancor toward the elitists, for she too had been a victim of the shabby treatment meted out to women by the old society. Because her widowed mother had been taken into the home of the royal family, Anahita had grown up as the plaything of princes, but when it came to marriage, she was married off to the family doctor—some say to pay his bills. Therefore, she also represents those women experiencing the frustrating

*The Welfare Association was called the Afghan Women's Institute during Daoud's Republic of Afghanistan. The DRA claimed that Daoud had been "scared stiff of the growth of the democratic movement of women, using every means to prevent it. The so-called Women's Association, set up by well-known court appointees, tried to deflect women from genuine class struggle" (*Kabul Times*, 3/10/79). The international leftist press, especially in the United States, persists in parroting the DRA contention that no attention was paid to the women's movement prior to the establishment of the DRA and crediting the DRA with the initiation of the emancipation movement. For example, Bechtel states the following: "For long centuries most [women] were treated like slaves . . . sold into marriage and denied the right to participate in social and economic life . . . . Equality for women was proclaimed immediately after the April Revolution" (1981:11). For a counter statement, see N. Dupree 1980:22.

contradictions inherent in an emancipation stymied by family strictures and entrenched social customs.

It is hard to deny Anahita's charm, ability, and enthusiastic energy. From the day of her appointment as Minister of Social Affairs, she was indefatigable, visiting welfare centers, schools, kindergartens, and medical facilities. She received women's delegations from the provinces, and to one and all she articulated the party's concern to eradicate the discriminations of the past.

By the end of May 1978 a few hints as to the direction that women's programs might take began to surface through the DRA rhetoric. The expansion of kindergartens was given first place, and the "democratization of social life" through a restoration of the rights and privileges of women was hailed as a major task:

> Privileges which women, by right, must have are equal education, job security, health services, and free time to rear a healthy generation for building the future of this country . . . . Educating and enlightening women is now the subject of close government attention (Editorial, *Kabul Times*, 5/28/78).

The National Agency for the Campaign Against Illiteracy, accused of ineffectiveness since its establishment in 1969, was slated for reorganization "to teach people the aims of the Revolution and how to meet these goals (*Kabul Times*, 6/26/78). Week-long seminars were held to familiarize teachers with the new literacy and the techniques of "enlightening the masses" (7/9/78). In July 1978 it was reported that 19,672 Afghans were registered in literacy programs, 1,616 of whom were women.

Those who knew Dr. Anahita in the early days of the DRA had confidence in her leadership and great hopes that the Ministry of Social Affairs would provide the necessary means to implement positive programs. However, internal power struggles between two factions within the PDPA, Khalq (Masses) and Parcham (Banner), ended these hopes. Parcham lost the struggles, and on 12 July 1978, only three months after she had come to power, Dr. Anahita left Kabul to become Ambassador to Yugoslavia. Her lover, Babrak Karmal (then Deputy Prime Minister), and other members of the Parcham leadership were similarly dispatched. When they later refused to return home, they were purged from the PDPA and branded as counterrevolutionary conspirators plotting to pervert the

Saur Revolution. Taraki and his First Minister Hafizullah Amin then set out to consolidate Khalq power (L. Dupree 1980e and forthcoming).

MANIPULATING AFGHAN WOMEN IN THE NAME OF REFORM: JULY 1978-DECEMBER 1979

Dr. Anahita's expulsion was a loss. Her Ministry of Social Affairs was dissolved "since the Social Affairs Ministry was not needed right now," according to Taraki (*Kabul Times*, 10/18/78). Women's affairs were relegated to the Ministry of Education. Women prominent in the DOAW no longer made public appearances. No woman was appointed to subsequent cabinets or to any other substantive positions. Mrs. Taraki and Mrs. Amin only rarely appeared at functions. Neither functioned in the forefront of the political scene, and both primarily fulfilled ceremonial roles. Following the patterns set by past regimes, they graciously received flowers and opened exhibitions of needlework.

The Khalq government did not ignore women. Taraki held that "without the participation of the toiling women no great movement relating to the toiling classes has achieved victory, because women form half of the society" (*Kabul Times*, 8/23/78). Furthermore, when speaking to Polish journalists in September 1978, Taraki stated the following: "The people's state not only protects the women's movement but will also carry on intensive and effective struggles to equalize the rights of women with those of men. Afghan women from now on are free in the real sense of the word and have equal rights with men" (9/26/78). Admirable sentiments—but Taraki did not elaborate on how the lot of women had improved since the Saur Revolution, nor did he speculate about the creation or extension of specific programs. However, one avowed PDPA objective—"to awaken the political consciousness of women"—was vigorously promoted. With its promotion begins the purposeful manipulation of the women's movement as an appendage to national politics by a leadership attempting to establish legitimacy and consolidate its power. Public demonstrations were ordered to build up popular support and morale.

The DOAW was renamed the Khalq Organization of Afghan Women (KOAW) with Dilara Mahak, formerly principal of Amana

Fidawi School, as president. Functioning in close association with the Khalq Organization of Afghan Youth (KOAY), the KOAW actively rounded up women to attend "grand functions" or gather in the streets to participate in "grand marches," shouting "Hurrah, hurrah," and slogans condemning "the reactionary plotters," and supporting the "Glorious Saur Revolution" while they waved huge posters of "our Great Leader," Taraki. Frequently these grand marches ended in "volunteer clean-up" sessions, and the people of Kabul were treated for the first time to the sight of girls wielding brooms, sweeping the streets in public in the company of men (*Kabul Times*, 10/29/78). So much time was consumed in meeting, marching, and "volunteering" that little constructive planning was possible.

Women were extremely visible in the press, receiving promotion awards or certificates following short refresher courses in traditionally accepted women's fields such as education and health. Glowing reports of KOAW successes in carrying out its directive to revitalize and organize new women's groups in all parts of the country were frequently published. The announced goal was to absorb 12,000 women, and the KOAW was reported to "now have complete influence among toiling women" (*Kabul Times*, 3/8/79).

After the PDPA had been created, each of its factions, Khalq and Parcham, organized small clandestine cells in government departments, educational institutions, and youth groups and directed members to spread discontent by constantly harping on discriminatory practices and the disregard evidenced by the power elite toward women. The women who joined these cells came from various backgrounds. Ages ranged between 18 and 30; many were schoolgirls, particularly from Kabul University. The majority were unmarried, but wives of officials and housewives also participated. The Khalq faction tended to draw members into its cells from the middle class and minority groups, predominately in urban provincial centers. They were educated and employed, but not often in high-level positions. Parcham members were from more liberal, elitist families and mainly from Kabul, although some landed gentry from the provinces were also represented. Most were more highly educated, and numbers had travelled abroad because they were affluent. Many held important positions in government because their higher social status provided them with better contacts inside the establishment.

The members' reasons for joining either PDPA faction were as varied as their backgrounds. In pre-DRA days, when legislation permitting political parties was held in abeyance there was only the establishment and the left. Moderate liberals were not organized. The frustrated and the activist opposed to the establishment had only the left to turn to, and there individuals were more important than ideology. Women gathered around charismatic personalities, like Dr. Anahita. Male party members were influential in recruiting female members. One of Taraki's most often quoted statements regarding women was that men and women are like "the two wings of a bird" (*Kabul Times*, 3/8/79); in order to fly both wings must move, and no great movement can achieve victory without the participation of women because they form half of the society (8/23/79). It was incumbent upon male party members, therefore, to enlist the cooperation of the women in their families.

Some women were persuaded to join by their friends. Others joined because of general dissatisfaction, usually concerning male-female relationships at home. The young were particularly attracted by promises of loosening parental control. Most had no ideological reasons for joining. They joined for the sheer excitement of doing something different, of defying their elders. At first it was daring to associate clandestinely with PDPA members. Moreover, party meetings provided an alternative to cloistered, family-chaperoned outings. Party gatherings were mixed, and it was considered perfectly acceptable for boys to invite girls—and even for girls to invite boys—to them. In addition, Parcham meetings presided over by Dr. Anahita and Babrak Karmal were famous for ending in lively disco parties.

Disco parties were particularly attractive in the late 1960s and early 1970s, when a plethora of night clubs and discotheques flourished in Kabul. These public clubs were expensive and patronized mainly by the social elite. The middle class youth could not afford them, nor did their families consider them suitable places for their children.* The PDPA meetings provided these youth with an alternative and the psychological satisfaction of being "mod" and "with it."

*The number of night spots in Kabul in 1972 comes as a surprise to many. Being off limits to most middle class youth, they became symbols of elitist alienation, pushing the middle class toward the left. For a descriptive list, see N. Dupree 1972:159-61.

In both PDPA factions much attention was paid to organization. Each institution, including the DOAW/KOAW had committees responsible for the indoctrination of specific sections inside government ministries and city wards. Close links were maintained with the PDPA central hierarchy, which issued the directives. The members were instructed to establish control over their sections and play up latent female frustrations in order to increase membership.

After the PDPA gained power, it became fashionable to join it—and for less palatable reasons. Prospective members were lured by promises of good positions in the government and promotion. Conversely, those who hesitated were threatened with demotion or dismissal, or even denouncement and arrest.* Daughters whose parents objected to their going out unchaperoned threatened to turn in their elders for hindering the revolution by keeping them from party meetings. Small girls were told that if they joined the youth groups, they would be cleansed of the stigma of having parents who had associated with past regimes. As members of the party, they could grow up with pride as true daughters of the revolution dedicated to the service of the motherland.

None of these reasons, coercive or otherwise, had much to do with ideology or the practical furtherance of the emancipation movement. There was little perception that women should be given the opportunity to develop into a distinct group capable of defining problems specifically related to women, and that they should possess socioeconomic and political power to solve these problems. The ideology was still being provided by men, and the women's movement was obligated to share common political goals.

KHALQ STEPS TOWARD EMANCIPATION

A principal task assigned to the KOAW by the Khalq leadership was the eradication of illiteracy in Kabul and provincial centers. "The roots of rotten customs and traditions are nurtured in ignorance," the Khalq preached (*Kabul Times*, 10/18/78). Khalq spokesmen adapted Lenin's dogma that "An illiterate person stands outside

---

*All such incidents discussed in the text are from personal communications with Afghan refugees and mujahidin. Names have been purposely omitted to protect the interviewees.

politics; he must first learn his ABC's. Without that there can be no politics";* they "Afghanized" it by claiming that "An illiterate woman cannot carry on the struggle, cannot handle properly the family affairs, and cannot rear properly sound and healthy children." A *jihad* (holy war) against illiteracy was called (3/8/79). By September the remarkable—and improbable—figure of 926,141 men and women enrolled in literacy courses was announced (9/8/79).

In sum the KOAW was primarily enlisted to continue women's traditional, sex-oriented occupations as teachers "to extend civic and political education to women, to enable women to understand their rights and responsibilities, to equip them with epoch-making ideology of the working class" (*Kabul Times*, 3/10/79). While these were worthy objectives, in practice the literacy classes were merely political meetings in disguise. Instead of beginning with A, B, or C, Lesson No. 1 began with *jim, dal, kha,* and *alif* for Jamhuriyat-i Demokratik-i Khalqi Afghanistan—the Dari (Afghan Persian) equivalent of PDPA. Marxist ideology dominated the curriculum. Practical, non-formal, functional teaching materials which had been developed a few years previously were shelved.†

The KOAW cadres used heavy-handed tactics to harass illiterate women—a politically vulnerable group—and the tactics stiffened the opposition. Taraki told a group of journalists that "[We] have in no case enrolled women [in the literacy courses] by force. Not even a single one" (*Kabul Times*, 5/3/79), but countless refugees pouring into Pakistan during the summer of 1979 listed the forceful implementation of the literacy program among women as a major reason for their departure. In the recalcitrant city of Kandahar three KOAW workers were killed as symbols of the unwanted revolution.

As dissension continued to mount, the PDPA initiated steps to create an aura of solidarity. Girls continued to be exploited in a very public manner in street demonstrations and volunteer projects—activities which would have been considered unacceptable for girls in the past. Now they were not only acceptable, but patriotic as well. One immediate result of such deviations from traditional behavior

---

*Quoted by Dr. Anahita 1980.

†Daoud's republic had placed great stress on the initiation of "functional" literacy courses, in which the "main objective was to improve vocational skills . . . on the basis of the *choice* of the participants" (*Kabul Times*, 3/28/76).

patterns was an increase in aggressiveness, a basic personality trait among Afghan women. In the past, however, women displayed assertiveness with quiet propriety. Shouting slogans in the streets now gave decorum a new dimension, and the girls exploited this first opportunity to express themselves in public by flaunting their sexuality. This was most noticeable at Kabul University, where the Khalq girls were notorious for their un-Afghan forward, unladylike behavior.

Even the most liberal male proponents of emancipation were embarrassed by the Khalq women's brashness. The traditionalists watched with horror and became even more convinced of their contention that if women were educated and allowed to move freely in the society, sexual anarchy would be the result. By their unorthodox behavior the Khalq girls strengthened the traditionalists and dealt a blow to centrist-conservatives and modernists alike.

The DRA abrogated the 1977 constitution when it came to power and periodically issued decrees to address specific situations. On 17 October 1978 Decree No. 7 was issued. Entitled "Dowry (Mahr) and Marriage Expenses," its stated purpose was to ensure "equal rights of women with men and in the field of civil law and for removing the unjust patriarchal feudalistic relations between husband and wife for consolidation of further sincere family ties." Considering the lofty goals, Decree No. 7 was a very sketchy document of only six articles — the shortest decree issued by the DRA. It was inadequate and simplistic, leading observers to suspect it had been hastily compiled with little reflection. Moreover, as the following discussion details, the six articles benefited the male rather than the female, in contradiction to the rhetoric.

Article 1. "No one shall engage a girl or give her in marriage in exchange for cash or commodities." It was well to decree that an unscrupulous father should no longer be allowed to give his daughter to the highest bidder or for payment of debts without considering her emotional preferences. But in most normal circumstances the exchange is not a "sale" or "wife buying." It compensates for the loss of an economically functioning member of a household and defrays wedding expenses as well as the cost of the goods a bride is expected to bring with her. In most instances the payment equals, or covers barely more than, the expenses. To be equitable the article should have mentioned some limitation on the expectations of the groom's family; these can be exorbitant.

Until attitudes and attendant practices such as arranged marriages change, the issue of prestige cannot be discounted when considering the well-being of brides. A bride's status and treatment in her new home often depend, rightly or wrongly, on the price she has commanded and the goods she brings with her. Honor too is involved. If a father accepts too small an amount, it may appear that he does not value his daughter. If she arrives in her husband's home without the clothes and necessities that allow her to move in with pride, her position suffers further.

Article 1 was of dubious value for girls. However, since the necessity of marriage payments had often delayed marriage for less affluent men until unfairly late in life, the total elimination of the payments was highly advantageous for men.

Article 2. "No one shall compel the bridegroom or his guardians to give holiday presents to the girl or her family." Avaricious mothers of brides-to-be inflict unjust hardships on less than affluent prospective bridegrooms by taking advantage of a custom according to which a fiancée is considered part of the groom's family and therefore entitled to receive gifts on four major religious holidays during each year of the engagement. Like Article 1, Article 2 makes a shortsighted attempt to right this wrong while ignoring the frequent situations in which a bride is less than wealthy and dependent upon holiday gifts—usually sets of clothing—to complete a suitably prestigious trousseau. Therefore, like Article 1, Article 2 caters to men.

Article 3. "The girl or her guardian shall not take cash or commodities in the name of dowry [mahr] in excess of ten *dirham* [Arabic coinage] according to Shari'at [Islamic law], which is not more than 300 afs. [about U.S. $10] on the basis of the bank rate of silver." According to Islamic law, the mahr is the exclusive property of the woman, but in practice fathers demand exorbitant sums and appropriate much of them, and husbands frequently neglect to pay them on demand. A predominate number of court cases involving women concern the mahr. While the writers of Decree No. 7 attempted to protect men from grasping, demanding women, they considered only half the problem and once again discriminated against women. Without accompanying protective legislation, Article 3 deprives women of the principal buffer in cases of separation, divorce, or abandonment, for there is no alimony in Islam.

Article 4. "Engagements and marriages shall take place with the full consent of the parties involved: (a) No one shall force marriage; (b) No one shall prevent the free marriage of a widow or force her into marriage because of family relationships [the leverite] or patriarchal ties; (c) No one shall prevent legal marriages on the pretext of engagement, forced engagement expenses, or by using force." Article 4 is a catchall listing age-old unjust practices without presenting guarantees for enforcement. The problems are identified, but such simplified legislation cannot eliminate the practices. Only evolving attitudinal changes can do so.

Article 5. "Engagement and marriages for women under sixteen and men under eighteen are not permissible."

Article 6. "(1) Violators shall be liable to imprisonment from six months to three years; (2) Cash or commodities accepted in violation of the provisions of this decree shall be confiscated."

Principles crucial to true emancipation, such as the equal right of women to demand divorce, work opportunities, and inheritance — all guaranteed by Daoud's Civil Law — were not considered. Hopes that the DRA would affect a meaningful direction for the women's rights program were dimmed by the lack of guarantees in Decree No. 7. Like earlier pronouncements against child marriages, forced marriages, the leverite, and exorbitant brideprices made since the days of 'Abdur Rahman, Decree No. 7 by itself was doomed to be ineffective. A government such as the DRA, which professed to have "sprung from the toiling masses," "practiced dialogue with the masses," and "learned from the masses," should have realized that trifling half-heartedly with deep-seated socio-religious customs was courting disaster. The unjust discriminatory practices toward women which had persisted for centuries were too deeply rooted in the culture to be uprooted by mere pronouncements. They had proved to be immune to mere legislative reforms, and they would remain so without attendant attitudinal changes and legal guarantees.

The DRA "welcomed" Decree No. 7 with great fanfare, however. A special stamp was issued to commemorate the decree. For months government ministries and organizations, schools and factories, workers and peasants in the capital and in the provinces staged grand functions, sometimes lasting from 9 a.m. to 4 p.m.

(*Kabul Times*, 10/28/78), ending in marches with "hundreds of thousands" carrying "thousands of photos of our Great Leader" (5/8/79). The speakers, predominately male, most often touted Decree No. 7 as a harbinger of cataclysmic change and a "deadly blow to feudalism" which had with a single stroke "delivered women from the tyrannical patriarchal relations of the past" and "gained for women and mothers . . . full independence and released them from the shameful customs of the medieval ages." It "ensured rights of men and women in a real sense" and "for the first time in history ended the practice of selling girls." It was a "chain-breaking" decree which "eliminated feudalistic patriarchal relations" and "delivered millions from outmoded mores and customs." As Professor Mrs. R.S. Siddiqi phrased it, "No more will a girl be plucked from the garden of innocence . . . and thrown into the clutches of a blood-thirsty beast and never have the opportunity to develop" (11/16/78). There were few such sparks of originality in the rhetoric. The same phrases appeared over and over in speeches delivered at myriad grand functions in Kabul and in the provinces. The PDPA propaganda machine in Kabul was in full swing, and the catechized KOAW cadres dutifully mouthed their lessons.

Tragically, the promoters of the campaign to sell Decree No. 7 neglected to even infer that all the principles contained in the decree conformed to Islamic injunctions. The omission was one more example of how the DRA totally disregarded any attempt to identify its reform programs with Afghan culture—i.e., with the people of Afghanistan. The rhetoric served instead to inflame conservative listeners.

Despite the rhetoric, little positive transpired because Decree No. 7 set ablaze the already smoldering dissent. Revolts in the countryside escalated and fractious disputes among the Khalq leadership paved the way for the rise of Amin (Prime Minister after March 1979), who eliminated Taraki in September 1979. Less and less was said about Decree No. 7, and the women's movement was kept in low profile, for it became a sensitive point of contention between the DRA and its tradition-bound opponents. The Marriage Registration Office in Kabul, which normally took in thousands of afs. a month, reported an average take of 160 afs. a month as the end of 1979 approached. Marriages were taking place in local mosques, but without civil registration and without benefit of Decree No. 7 (personal communication).

On 1 October 1979 a fifty-eight-member Constitution Drafting Committee was appointed. It contained a token four women: Fawjiyah Shahsawari (Vice President of KOAW) on the Subcommittee for Regulating the Political System of the Society; Dr. Aziza (DRA Director of Nursing; she replaced Dilara Mahak as president of KOAW after Taraki was eliminated) and Shirin Afzal (President of the Reformatory Schools), both on the Subcommittee for Regulations between the State and Individuals; and Alamat Tolqun (President of Kindergartens) on the Subcommittee for Regulating Foreign Policy and International Affairs. The Working Subcommittee, the Subcommittee for Regulating Administrative Affairs, and the Subcommittee for Ensuring Judicial Justice had no female representatives—a deplorable situation since the need to effectively guarantee women's legal rights by eradicating legal injustices and implementing Decree No. 7 should have been a primary goal of the DRA's legislation.

In any case the efforts toward emancipation proved purely cosmetic. The government overresponded to increasing successes of the resistance movement with severe repression, which brought about a breakdown of many fine Afghan traditions (L. Dupree 1980f). One of the traditions to suffer most was respect for women. Women seeking the whereabouts of their menfolk from the Ministry of Interior were screamed at in abusive language and curtly turned away with such insults as "Go! Find yourself another man." Women and children were imprisoned.* There were no trials and no proofs of guilt.

The country slid rapidly into chaos. In a desperate attempt to establish solidarity, Amin opened the Plenary Session of the National Organization for the Defense of the Revolution (NODR) on 5 December 1979. The delegates—a total of 580, including members of KOAW—had been selected for their "profound loyalty to the aspirations of the Saur Revolution; their irreconcilability to domestic and foreign enemies; political and social piety [sic], and popularity." It was at this time that reportedly "20,000 crusading compatriots were armed" (*Kabul Times*, 12/11/79).

---

*Including Suraya (former president of the DOAW and a cousin of Babrak's) and Jamilah Nahid, daughter of Dr. Anahita (see *New World Review*, July-August 1980:6).

THE WOMEN'S MOVEMENT AFTER THE SOVIET INVASION:
27 DECEMBER 1979-?

Less than a month after the NODR was established, the Soviets invaded. On the night of 24 December 1979, they airlifted many thousands of troops into Afghanistan. On 27 December Amin was killed; the airlifts recommenced, accompanied by a massive land invasion from Soviet Central Asia. Babrak Karmal was brought back as puppet Prime Minister, General Secretary of the PDPA, and President of the Revolutionary Council. Dr. Anahita was appointed a Basic Member of the Politburo of the PDPA Central Committee (PDPA/CC), a member of the Revolutionary Council of the DRA (RC/DRA), and Minister of Education. Two other women were appointed to the RC/DRA with Dr. Anahita: Suraya, reappointed President of the DOAW, which regained its pre-Khalq name; and Jamilah Palwashah from the Ministry of Education, a prominent leader in the DOAW who was also an alternate member of the PDPA/CC. The leading women under the Taraki-Amin Khalq regimes disappeared from public view.

Once again women were soon called upon to support the nation and the "Glorious 27 December Uprising," as the second wave of the Soviet invasion was billed. On 1 January 1980 a "Message to Oppressed Women and Mothers of the Homeland" alluded to heroic women of the past and concluded as follows: "It is the duty of the revolutionary government of Afghanistan to guarantee the rights and freedom of women in all social, political, cultural, and other spheres of life. Women of Afghanistan!, defend the dignity and honor of your homelands!" The PDPA Revolutionary Council's "Greetings to the Heroes of Freedom" spoke even more forcefully to women:

We believe that the vanguards and standardbearers of the people of Afghanistan derive their strength from serving . . . the mothers of the country who have given birth to and fed them. So long as they belong to their mothers . . . no enemy or devil can defeat them (*Kabul New Times*, 1/1/80).

Verbal attacks on Amin's excessive repressions were even more venomous than those previously directed against the defunct "feudals." All the attacks were vehement, but the most vitriolic denouncements came from Dr. Anahita, who upheld the tradition that Afghan women are implacable when crossed. She characterized Amin as a "cruel and criminal murderer with a fraudulent devil's soul," "a savage despot with ruthless fascistic manners," "a beastly lunatic [guilty of] savage acts of looting, killing, and outraging the honor of the suffering and noble people of Afghanistan in order to keep his throne"—and much, much more (*Kabul New Times*, 1/2/80). Her phrases were less elegant than those of past poet-heroines, but they were certainly rousing.

The party newspaper *Haqiqat-i Inqilabi Saur* (Truth of the April Revolution) published a long diatribe on the tyranny of Amin's "sanguinary" followers, "those dolls who had no will of their own ... stupid, empty-headed, brainless yes-men ... who massacred patriots and plundered their properties"; it characterized Amin as "a version of Hitlerites, Mussolinis, and Genghis Khans ... more murderous and cruel than all the hangmen and murderers of history. His reign of terror will form the most bloody pages in our history.... He was not a cultured man. He repeatedly insulted and humiliated women who sought their husbands from him" (*Kabul New Times*, 1/5/80). Released prisoners likened Amin to Zuhak, a legendary despot possessed by the devil who feasted on human brains (*Kabul New Times*, 1/10/80).

The daily newspapers carried pictures and accounts of the countless women who had been jailed and subjected to attacks "violating human dignity." An eighteen-year-old boy reported witnessing scenes of sexual molestation while he was being interrogated at the Ministry of Interior. Worse yet, he had been threatened with being forced to witness the sexual molestation of his fiancée and other female members of his family unless he confessed to anti-Khalq activities (*Kabul New Times*, 1/3/80). A "Message to Mothers," published on 15 January 1980, appealed to raw emotions. It called on women

> who know that those who have been martyred in the glorious struggle against the bloody, beast-like, fascist, and dark-hearted murderer have spiritual links with the sisters and mothers of this land. Come!, and take part in the mourning ceremonies of this day, the day of martyrs and the day of renewal of pact and oath for revolutionary struggles and lament over the martyred heroes!"

The DRA had declared Mothers' Day, previously celebrated on 14 June, as "null and void" in June 1978. It held that in the past the Women's Association had observed Mothers' Day "in a deceitful manner, unmindful of the conditions of millions of toiling women." Instead, International Women's Solidarity Day (IWSD), initiated by the International Conference of Women Socialists in 1910 in Copenhagen, would be observed on 8 March each year because it marked "the solidarity of women in their struggle against tyranny and imperialism, discrimination and racism, and highlighted freedom and equality" (*Kabul Times*, 6/17/78).*

Gala functions were held to celebrate the seventieth anniversary of IWSD on 8 March 1980. Using the motto "Awaken the political consciousness of Afghan women!," the celebrations mirrored those held to welcome Decree No. 7, now conspicuously unmentioned. The grandest function, held at the Polytechnic Gymnasium and graced by one of Mrs. Babrak Karmal's rare ceremonial appearances, passed a resolution condemning the "adventurous and irresponsible policy of the American reactionaries, China, Pakistan, Egypt, and Israel . . . against the Afghan revolution and disinterested assistance of the Soviet Union to Afghanistan" (*Kabul New Times*, 3/9/80). The use of the DOAW for disseminating political propaganda continued to be prominent, but the DRA stressed the following:

> One important criterion of a progressive regime is the efforts it makes to ensure equality between males and females. . . . It was not religion that stood against women's progress . . . for Islam made learning incumbent upon both men and women . . . but men used women as second-rate citizens and did not allow them to acquire knowledge and therefore women are not aware of their rights (Editorial, *Kabul New Times*, 3/16/80).†

*From its inception the DRA attempted to identify the Afghan women's movement with the world-wide women's socialist movement. Afghan delegations attended numbers of international conferences, beginning with the International Democratic Federation of Women meetings (which opened in Moscow on 15 May 1978), at which Afghanistan became a member. Delegations of women from Communist countries periodically visited Afghanistan.

†An American leftist correspondent reporting on an October 1980 interview with Suraya makes no reference to Decree No. 7, however, listing only the familiar youth-indoctrination programs, promotion of nurseries and kindergartens, and literacy as the "special practical measures" being taken to provide equality for women (Bechtel 1981).

A new directive outlining the "Fundamental Principles of the Democratic Republic of Afghanistan" was issued by the Babrak government on 20 April 1980. Unlike Article 12 of the "Basic Lines" issued under Taraki, the new set of guidelines made no reference to women. Presumably this followed the logic advanced by the framers of the 1964 constitution, who held that specific mention of women would in itself be a type of discrimination.

Chapter 2 of the new "Fundamental Principles," entitled "Fundamental Rights and Obligations of Citizens," states that "Citizenship of the DRA is shared equally by all the peoples of Afghanistan." In its eight articles all citizens are ensured of the following rights (among others): "equality before the law irrespective of their racial, national, tribal and linguistic affiliations or sex, domicile, religion, education, parentage, assets and social status . . . in all economic, political, social and cultural fields"; security; full freedom of practice of Islam or other faiths; work; health protection; education; expression; individual or collective complaint before state organs; and to be considered innocent until proven guilty. At the same time, citizens are "obligated to respect and observe the laws and standards of social conduct, human manners and morals." This requirement will remain amorphous until legislation suggests an alignment of the contradictory "laws and standards" inherent in custom, religion, and reform. Finally, "Defense of the motherland and the gains of the Saur Revolution, loyalty to its objectives and aspirations and service to the people comprise the lofty sacred obligation of each citizen" (Asia Society 1980:51-52).

Literacy continued to be hailed as imperative for the socialization of the populace. On 28 May 1980 the DRA announced its goal to eliminate illiteracy completely in the cities in seven years and in the provinces in ten years. The DOAW and KOAY—renamed the Democratic Organization of Afghan Youth (DOAY)—were assigned decisive roles in the project. In an interview with *Soviet Woman* in February, Dr. Anahita had deplored

> some errors, in particular the compulsory education of women. The reactionary elements immediately made use of these mistakes to spread discontent among the population. In this connection the former leadership of the Ministry of Education slowed down to some extent the solution of the problem of eliminating illiteracy (1980:3).

330

However, in May 1980 Dr. Anahita quoted some remarkable statistics: "At present, 500,000 have completed literacy training in 27,000 courses throughout the country. Further, 12,500 literacy courses have been set up in the army where about 200,000 soldiers have achieved literacy" (*Kabul New Times*, 5/29/80). As we have indicated, Afghan statistics are dubious. At its strongest, the Afghan army never consisted of more than 100,000 men, and by May 1980 desertions had considerably depleted its ranks. In contrast to her detailed quotation of such achievements, it is significant to note that when Dr. Anahita mentioned that the government's goal was to educate all males in Afghanistan between the ages of ten and fifty, she omitted any reference to women. Literacy for women remained a politically volatile subject.

The media contributed some constructive and practical education for women on radio and television, such as programs on the activities and services of the Family Guidance Association (established in 1968). Magazines and newspapers in Dari and Pashto carried feature articles especially for women. The *Kabul New Times* published a weekly page for women. Many of the feature articles were inane, but interviews with Afghan women—from housewives to factory workers—discussing successes in employment situations as well as frustrations and maltreatment, arranged and forced marriages, problems with mothers-in-law and nagging, and extravagant husbands were full of substance. Articles on women's achievements in other countries continued Mahmud Beg Tarzi's vision seven decades earlier concerning a more equitable role for women in Afghan society.

Most heartening to women was that a special reporter from the *Kabul New Times* was assigned to the Special Court for Family Affairs. The court, an inspiration of the late Justice Ghulam Ali Karimi in 1975 and one of the more positive accomplishments of the Afghan women's movement, continued to function after the Saur Revolution. The court is customarily headed by a male religious judge and includes a male and female judge trained in secular law as well as Islamic jurisprudence. The newspapers carried case histories and interviews of women seeking divorce or redress from maltreatment by husbands and in-laws and the court's attempts to affect reconciliation. (Significantly, it is generally the women who are asked to return to their husbands.) These articles were both positive and educational. No amount of rhetoric could accomplish what these straightforward interviews achieved.

In June 1980 a staff reporter for the women's page of the *Kabul New Times* made some refreshingly honest and pertinent remarks:

There is nothing more ridiculous than granting privileges on paper without pushing them through practically. . . . There must be an effective law-enforcing apparatus to put into effect each right granted . . . so that every man who does not believe in women's attitudes may be convinced that he is wrong. . . . If women are too passive, . . . no amount of legislation can help them. . . . In order to raise the status of women we must first raise the standards of their men (6/16/80).

Unfortunately, beginning in July 1980 the women's page was gradually preempted by a variety of topical features, such as the Moscow Oympics.

Despite the government's attempts to appear to be functioning normally and implementing progressive programs, the presence of foreign invaders occupying Afghan soil was anathema. The mujahidin extended their effective control over the countryside and disaffection mounted in the cities, rapidly eroding Parcham's political base — particularly among university and college students, who were originally its staunchest supporters. The very girls who had been most revolutionary and politically militant became decidedly unrevolutionary, reticent, and obstructive. They felt disillusioned by the empty rhetoric, shocked and betrayed by the Soviet invasion. Any euphoria that was left from April 1978 faded as Khalq and non-PDPA members were arrested in increasing numbers.

On 27 April 1980 the citizens of Kabul were called out to applaud a parade of Afghan, Soviet, and Soviet-bloc dignitaries celebrating the second anniversary of the Saur Revolution. As the cavalcade passed a large girls' school, a girl named Nahidah began calling out anti-government, anti-Soviet slogans. Others joined her spontaneously and the clamor increased. Bricks and stones flew toward the cavalcade; shots followed from die-hard party members and militiamen. When the riot was finally brought under control, some seventy people lay dead, Nahidah among them. She has now joined the ranks of Afghanistan's heroines as the new Malalay.

Having sparked the resistance movement in Kabul, girls capitalized on their recent experiences in the streets and almost daily organized demonstrations and processions. Jeering at the police and soldiers sent to break up the demonstrations, the girls snatched off the caps of the men and threw them their *chadars* (head scarves), calling: "Here! Wear these. Go! Shut yourselves up in your houses. We girls will defend the motherland!" (personal communication; see also an article from New Delhi in *Pakistan Times*, 6/13/80:1). The girls had taken the lead, expressing their indignation over the Soviet occupation and their distaste at being forced to parrot pro-Soviet propaganda. The Parcham authorities put down the demonstrations (mainly of students) with brutality, swelling the ranks of the dissidents.

The demonstrations continued through May and June in defiance of government prohibitions, and hundreds of girls were carted off to jail. The unmanly, disrespectful treatment of girls, in addition to increasing incidents of abuse by Russian soldiers, fanned the emotions of Afghan men. The Afghans sent to subdue the girls were beset with conflicting emotions between duty and traditional respect for women. A taxi driver cried in shame as he watched girls fighting "like cats" as they were manhandled into a police van (personal communication). A policeman taking six girls in for questioning refused to hand them over to four Russian soldiers who demanded them; he shot the Russians and himself rather than allow the girls to be subjected to insult (personal communication).

The girls remained defiant in spite of the arrests and violence. In Mazar-i Sharif, the capital of Balkh province, women demonstrated in protest after Russian soldiers stomped through the women's section of the sacred shrine of Hazrat-i Ali without removing their shoes. Assaults on female honor caused the Russians to be regarded with revulsion and fear. Women sent requests to the mujahidin for small pistols with silencers which they could carry under their veils. Bodies of Russians were found in the streets with increasing frequency. Some fathers with young daughters opted for exile, saying: "We have nothing left . . . but still we Afghans know how to save the honor of our women" (*Pakistan Times*, 6/13/80:1).

In the very conservative city of Kandahar the protection of honor took more drastic forms. When rumors circulated that Soviet troops had entered the city, two men killed all the women in their families to prevent them from dishonor. These acts infected the entire city, prompting one girl to send a desperate call for protection to her brother in Kabul. When he arrived, he found his two brothers stationed on the roof, armed with knives, watching for the first sign of a Russian, at which, they vowed, they would kill their women. The Kabul brother, known for his liberal views, was powerless. He sent for two of the most conservative members in the family, who argued successfully with the brothers on the roof, that although men were bound by Islam to protect their women to the death, it was incumbent upon the women to protect themselves should their male protectors die. To kill women in anticipation of dishonor, they said, was un-Islamic (personal communication).

Dissidence also appeared in less violent and public forms. Women in government offices began slowdowns, particularly in the Ministry of Education's literacy program. Books and papers were purposely delayed, misdirected, lost, and damaged. More than the usual time was spent in the office gossiping, knitting, and thumbing through magazines. False attendance reports were submitted (personal communication). These actions were as courageous as the public demonstrations, for informers were everywhere who were anxious to enhance their positions with the authorities by turning people in.

The mujahidin encouraged noncooperation by girls in the areas they controlled. On taking over the Nangarhar University in Jalalabad, the mujahidin asked girls to return to their homes in order to protest the Soviet occupation. They promised to reinstate education for girls when they succeeded in expelling the foreigners and chivalrously paid each girl transportation costs plus 200 afs. spending money (personal communication).

Conflicting views on the role of women—particularly their education—constitute one of the more devisive ideological controversies among the resistance groups. Among the refugees who have fled rule by "infidels and godless invaders," fundamentalist attitudes prevail, and those professing liberal views on women risk being branded as traitors and collaborators. By bringing the most fanatic attitudes toward women to the surface, the revolution has seriously jeopardized women. It has so widely polarized conservatives and modernists that fundamentalist reaction threatens to destroy previous accomplishments of the women's movement. This has given rise to the belief that the mujahidin leaders totally reject education for women. The most conservative groups call for women to return behind the veil, but also hold that women have "the right" to education and work opportunities—in separate institutions (Hizb-i Islami N.D.a).* The more liberal manifestos pledge basic freedoms for individuals; free and universal suffrage; compulsory education of all Afghan school-age children; social and economic justice and political freedoms and opportunity for "all Afghans, men and women, to participate individually or collectively in the affairs related to the welfare of Afghanistan"; and "that every individual is entitled to a fair and impartial trial . . . with an opportunity to defend himself or herself and demand the process of law" (National Islamic Front of Afghanistan N.D.).

Legend and fact combine in the accounts of women in the resistance movement. For instance, Nuristani women were credited with destroying the first Afghan army patrol to be annihilated (end of 1978). The government blamed the Nuristani mujahidin, but in Kabul many believed the story that Nuristani women hidden in trees pretending to pick walnuts did the deed. The patrol was taken unawares (the story goes) because it would have been disrespectfully un-Afghan of the soldiers to glance up at the women. Fact or fiction, the story enhances the reputation of Afghan women for being fierce, indomitable foes.[†] In the 1 January 1980 "Message to Oppressed Women," Babrak called upon this acknowledged quality in Afghan women to defend the honor and dignity of the nation. The women have responded, but not entirely as he intended.

The innate courage of Afghan women has been exemplified in many ways. Widows lament they have been denied the honor of becoming *shahid* (martyrs) and plead for guns to fill the empty hands of their infant sons to revenge the deaths of their fathers (personal communication). Many wives and mothers have encouraged their men

---

[*]One young member of Hizb-i Islami, a fundamentalist group, explained that the group's insistence on separate institutions, especially in work situations, was largely economic: "You have seen it yourself, *khanum* [lady]. When there are girls in the office, the men do not pay attention to their work. Much time is lost. And time is money. We have so much to do. How can we develop when so much time is lost?" (personal communication).

[†]Rudyard Kipling expressed British dread of Afghan women on the warpath:

When you're wounded and left on Afghanistan's plains
And the women come out to cut up what remains,
Jest roll to your rifle and blow out your brains
    An' go to your Gawd like a soldier

("The Young British Soldier," in Kipling 1945: 416).

335

to flee arrest while they remain behind to sell property and wind up other affairs. Then alone they face the hazards of crossing the border illegally. In the Kandahar area a band of female smugglers actively assists such women.

The revolution has split many families in permanent ways. Women unable to countenance life under Soviet domination have left husbands who elected to cooperate with the puppet regime. They have gone into exile alone, where they necessarily function as individuals making their own decisions. One wife sent the wedding ring she had worn for fourteen years back to her husband with the following message: "Come with this ring—or forget me." Meanwhile she struggles to make a new life for herself and her two young sons while she assists her fellow refugees. When congratulated on her courage, her eyes flashed as she said: "But I must be strong. For my sons and for my country. But I can make it! And so can Afghanistan!" (personal communication). Her resolve best sums up the spirit of the revolutionary Afghan woman.

While the women in the resistance movement consolidate their positions, the Babrak regime offers women only token representation. Although a hard core remains active in Kabul, women as a group are still largely excluded from positions of real power—with the exception, of course, of Dr. Anahita, member of the PDPA Central Committee Politburo, only female member of the Presidium of the Revolutionary Council, Minister of Education, President of the DRA Peace, Solidarity, and Friendship Organization, and President of the DOAW. She greets all foreign dignitaries, addresses major meetings, and makes frequent trips abroad.

The Babrak regime has made increasingly frantic attempts to enlist women in its desperate fight for survival, however. The Fourth Seminar of the DOAW, held in Kabul on 2 September 1980, was directed "to search for scientific ways to mobilize the enlightened women of Afghanistan." The DOAW, the prime institution promoting women, was defined as "the voice calling upon women to struggle against the counterrevolution," and women were admonished as follows:

As a mother, as a sister, and as a woman you should not leave your sons alone on the long path of struggle for safeguarding the gains of the revolution that for the first time in history . . . has declared in the laws the equality of the rights of women with men ("DOAW's Call on Heroic Women"; *Kabul New Times*, 8/30/80).

On 20 November 1980, the First Conference of the City Council of Representatives of the Women of Kabul City was organized by the DOAW specifically "to organize the women of Afghanistan in defending the revolution." A major objective of this conference was "to further expand the closed ranks of militant women in the country." In addition, it elected representatives to a nationwide conference on Afghanistan's women.*

The nationwide conference, the first international seminar on women to be held in Afghanistan, was entitled "Unity and Solidarity of the Ranks of International Democratic Women and Their Role in Mobilizing the Progressive Forces of the World." It was opened with great fanfare by Babrak on 28 November 1980 in the Salam Khanah, 'Abdur Rahman's Durbar Hall now used as the headquarters of the DRA Revolutionary Council (*Kabul New Times*, 11/29/80). Dr. Anahita was the chair. Delegations from a number of foreign countries and international organizations attended, including Angola, Britain, Bulgaria, Chile, Congo, Cuba, Czechoslovakia, Democratic Republic of Germany, Ethiopia, Hungary, India, Kampuchea, Lebanon, Mexico, Mongolia, Palestinian Liberation Organization, Poland, Soviet Union, Vietnam, All-African Women's Organization, and International Democratic Women's Federation. Twelve Afghan women "represented various strata of Kabul" (11/30/80; 12/1/80).

In its message to the conference, the PDPA/CC pointed out that the conference was being held "under sensitive ... conditions ... when, with the victory of the glorious and liberating uprising of December 27, the new evolutionary phase of the Saur Revolution

*The nationwide women's conference was the first of a veritable bombardment of conferences called as the first anniversary of the Soviet invasion approached. Tribal groups and special interest groups were gathered in Kabul so that Babrak could make impassioned, personal appeals for support of his National Fatherland Front, launched at a "great historic conference" called on 27 December 1980. Among the conferences were the following: 5 December—*buzkashi* teams composed of Uzbek and Turkmen horsemen from the north—to whom Dr. Anahita was chosen to present winning trophies! (the sport of buzkashi is described on p. 198n. above); 6 December—Nuristanis; 8 December—Safi Pashtun; 11 December—First Congress of Agricultural Cooperatives; 15 December—Afridi and Shinwari Pashtun; 21 December—the people of Bamyan; 29 December—Jaghatu (Hazarah).

emerged." After reiterating the party's duty to implement the DRA's Fundamental Principles, it continued: "Under the present circumstances the training of sacrificing and firm adherents to . . . the Saur Revolution . . . is the great duty . . . and prideful responsibility of every mother. The Party and State will never spare any help to mothers in this noble task." The PDPA further pledged that along with developing the national economy, industry, and agriculture, it would set up "kindergartens, nurseries, schools, hospitals, and clubs" and attempt to attract women to take an active part in "social life and productive affairs" to build a new society.

The message digressed to praise Babrak's visit to the USSR (October 1980), the PDPA's link with world revolutionary processes and consolidation of world peace, and Afghan support of "the untiring efforts of the Soviet Union . . . in [its] struggle for peace, detente, and complete and general disarmament." Finally, it expressed the party's appreciation for "the activities of the DOAW toward organizing the women of the country, consolidating solidarity with the women of the world, and their struggle for the prosperity and tranquility of peoples, limitation of the arms race, prevention of the threat of war, and ensuring freedom, democracy, and progress" (*Kabul New Times*, 11/30/80). Quite some tasks for the beleaguered women's movement in Afghanistan! The first day ended with a concert and a fashion show of local costumes and modern dress.

The concluding session on 30 November was again attended by Babrak, but Dr. Anahita was the main speaker. Her long, long speech included fulsome thanks to Karmal and the PDPA/CC for their support of the women's movement, gratitude for "the aid of the brotherly people of the Soviet Union," and quotes from Brezhnev on the "victories gained" by Babrak's visit to the USSR.* Emphasizing the role women had played in the historic struggle for national liberation, she exhorted "enlightened women" to go out "to raise the level of political and social consciousness and disclose the real nature of the reactionary, plundering circles of thieves, rebels and collaborators" (*Kabul New Times*, 12/1/80), described in the speeches by foreign delegates as "U.S. imperialists, Chinese chauvinists, and reactionary circles of the region and of the world" (11/30/80). With warmth and

---

*The speech was so long that it was reprinted in four parts in *Kabul New Times*: Part 1 (12/1/80); Part 2 (12/2/80); Part 3 (12/3/80); Part 4 (12/4/80).

fervor Dr. Anahita concluded: "Let the enemy die because we are undefeatable" (12/4/80).

The organizers of the conference issued a message to "the noble women, gallant mothers, and tortured sisters of the country" (*Kabul New Times*, 12/2/80) and presented the resolutions it had passed unanimously.* Dr. Anahita was unanimously elected president of the DOAW (12/1/80), with a forty-six-member Central Council, also elected unanimously. Representatives of DOAW central councils "in the provinces will be elected later," it was announced (12/1/80).

The revolutionary rhetoric continues unabated, but the feminist movement in Afghanistan has become inextricably enmeshed with the political fortunes of individual leaders—and with foreign invaders well versed in directional indoctrination. The promised cataclysmic changes have not materialized. The psychological relationships between men and women have not been altered. By allowing themselves to be manipulated as tools of party politics, the militant activists subordinate the women's movement to male domination, adding a sinister dimension to the traditional "patriarchal" attitudes their rhetoric condemns. Thus after a century of liberalizing effort, Afghan women still struggle to be recognized as individuals rather than stereotypes and symbols.

APPENDIX

RESOLUTIONS OF THE CONFERENCE ON UNITY AND SOLIDARITY

We have decided to:

1. Promote the role of Afghanistan's women in defense of the gains of the Saur Revolution. . . .

2. Be always decisive against the enemies of revolution. . . .

3. Take part in actions for the gradual, stage-by-stage attraction of women to the process of social production, ensuring the right of women to work . . . for economic independence of women, and their equality in family and society. . . .

*The conference's resolutions were reprinted in *Kabul New Times*, 12/1/80: 4. We reproduce them in summary in the appendix at the end of this chapter.

4. Actively take part in the campaign against illiteracy. . . .

5. Pay attention to the promotion of the cultural level of women and see that they have access to education and acquire vocational know-how in factories and special centers, including villages and rural areas.

6. Take the initiative in advancing specific proposals to the state . . . for the . . . promotion of laws on women's work, payment of wages, work security, and child and mother care.

7. Take care of the health and education of children and help in the promotion of the material level of the life of families, take active and great part in state . . . systems devised for child and mother care. . . .

8. Strengthen our solidarity with the world women in the struggle for peace, relaxation of tension, and prevention of the horrible arms race and atomic conflict. . . .

9. Expand our mutual friendship and cooperation with the women of the Soviet Union and other socialist countries. . . .

GLOSSARY

AFGHAN TERMS

Afandi (afandî) Honorific used in reference to some ruhani families; religious dignitary

Agha (âghâ) Honorific used in reference to the descendants of the Prophet Muḥammad

Akhund (âkhund) Learned Islamic religious leader or scholar

Akhundzadah (âkhundzâdah) Descendants of akhund

Al-amr bi-l-ma'ruf wa-l-nahy 'an al-munkar (al-amr bi-l-ma'rûf wa-l-nahy 'an al-munkar) Commanding what is good and forbidding what is abominable

Alaqadar (alâqadâr) Subdistrict commissioner/administrator (Dari term)

Alaqadari (alâqadârî) Subdistrict headquarters (Dari term)

Alif (alîf) Letter of Dari alphabet; = A

'Alim ('âlim) Learned religious leader (singular of 'ulamâ)

Amir (amîr) Prince, lord, or nobleman; former title of the ruler of Afghanistan

Aqrab ('Aqrab) Eighth month of Islamic solar calendar covering 23 October–21 November; scorpion

Aqsaqal (âqsaqâl) Village elders (Uzbek term)

Arabi ('arabî) Breed of sheep presumably from Arabia

Arbab (arbâb) Official village headman

Arbabha-i rishwat khur (arbâbhâ-i rishwat khûr) Bribe-eating arbabs

Ariza ('ariża) Petition

Ariza nawis ('ariża nawîs) Petition writer

Ashkhasi namdar (ashkhâsi nâmdâr) Local magnates; famous people

Ashkhasi sarshinas (ashkhâsi sarshinâs) Local magnates; people of repute

341

Ashrar (ashrâr)	Riffraff; reactionaries
Avghan (avghân)	Afghan; local term for Pashto-speaking population of southern Afghanistan and western Pakistan
Awghan (Awghân)	Afghan; local pronunciation of the term
Awliya (awliyâ)	"Saints" (plural of walî)
Azan (âzân)	Call for prayers from the minaret
Badi (badî)/Badal	Factional vendettas among Pashtun
Bay (bây)	Title used for indigenous local leader or wealthy person in northern Afghanistan
Bismillah (bismillâh)	Dedication; invocation (In the name of Allah)
Buzkashi (buzkashî)	Game on horseback to gain possession of animal carcass
Chadar (châdar)	Head scarf
Chadari (châdarî)	Veil
Dal (dâl)	Letter of Dari alphabet; = D
Dar al-Islam (dâr al-Islâm)	Land of Peace; Muslim territory
Dawa (da'wâ)	Dispute; court claim
Da wulus zur da Khuday zur (da wulus zûr da Khudây zûr)	The people's power is God's power
Dihqan (dihqân)	Farmworker; farmer
Din (dîn)	Religion
Diniy khaluk (dîniy khaluk)	Men of religion
Dukandar (dukândâr)	Shopkeeper
Dunya (dunyâ)	World
Faqir (faqîr)	Religious intermediary who has relinquished worldly goods for spiritual gains
Fi sabil Allah (fî sabîl Allâh)	In the way of Allah
Fitwa (fitwâ)	Islamic legal pronouncement
Gharibkar (gharibkâr)	Laborer, usually casual
Ghulam bacha (ghulâm bacha)	Page boy; slave boy in Afghan court
Hakim (hâkim)	District commissioner/administrator (Dari term)
Hanafi (Hanafî)	Sunni school of Islamic law named after its founder, Abu Hanifah

Hukumat (ḥukûmat)	Goverment or district office (Dari term)
Hukumat-i a'la (ḥukûmat-i a'lâ)	Subprovince
Ibtidaiya (ibtidâ'ya)	School with grades 1-6; elementary school
Ilbegi (ilbêgî)	Representative between Arabs and central government; community elder (Turkic word)
Inqilab (inqilâb)	Revolution
Iqamat (iqâmat)	Call for prayers inside the mosque
Ishan (îshân)	Religious dignitary with Sufi affiliation; descendant of the Prophet (Tajik and Turkic term)
Istismar (istismâr)	Exploitation
Jama'a (jamâ'a)	Society; association
Jawza (Jawzâ)	Third month of Islamic solar calendar covering 22 May-21 June
Jihad (jihâd)	Islamic war of liberation; holy war for the cause of Islam
Jihad al-'aql (jihâd al-'aql)	Effort to spread Islam by means of reason
Jihad al-da'wah (jihâd al-da'wah)	Effort to spread Islam among unbelievers by peaceful means
Jihad al-lisan (jihâd al-lisân)	Educational jihad; jihad of the tongue
Jihad al-nafs (jihâd al-nafs)	Struggle against oneself
Jihad al-qalam (jihâd al-qalam)	Educational jihad; jihad of the pen
Jihad al-tarbiyah (jihâd al-tarbiyah)	Realization and spread of Islamic values and institutions within Muslim society
Jim (jîm)	Letter of Dari alphabet; = J
Jirib (jirîb)	Land measure equal to 0.2 hectare
Kafir (kâfir)	Infidel
Kamisar (kamisâr)	High-ranking military officer serving as commissioner of a frontier post
Kar (kâr)	Work
Karamat (karâmat)	Spiritual or moral essence
Khalifah (khalîfah)	Representative of a shah among Ismaʿilis of Badakhshan
Khan (khân)	Local leader or chief (Turkic term)
Khanum (khânum)	Lady; wife
Khayrat (khayrât)	Charitable deeds; charities

Khel (khêl)	Lineage
Khujah (khûjah)	Title for those who claim descent from one of the first three caliphs of Islam
Khush bashen (khush bâshên)	Be happy
Lalmi (lalmî)	Dry farming
Loy wuluswali (lôy wuluswâlî)	Subprovince (Pashto term)
Maldar (mâldâr)	Pastoralist
Maliki (mâlikî)	Sunni school of Islamic law named after its founder, Malik
Mawlawi (mawlawî)	Religious scholar
Mazar (mazâr)	Holy shrine
Milmastya (milmastyâ)	Hospitality (Pashto term)
Ming bashi (ming bâshî)	Representative of an Arab clan; "head of a thousand men" (Turkic term)
Mir (mîr)	Local chief
Mirab (mirâb)	Water watchman
Miyan (miyân)	"Saint" (Pashto term)
Mizan (Mîzân)	Seventh month of Islamic solar calendar covering 23 September-22 October
Muhajirin (muhâjirîn)	Refugees
Mujahid (mujâhid)	Muslim resistance fighter; Muslim freedom fighter (plural: mujahidin [mujâhidîn])
Mulkdar (mulkdâr)	Landowner
Mullah (mullâh)	One who has some Islamic religious education; learned man
Mullaha-i Farangi (Mullâhâ-i Farangî)	"Foreign Mullahs" who allegedly served British interests in late nineteenth and twentieth centuries
Mullah imam (mullâh imâm)	Prayer leader of a mosque
Murid (murîd)	Disciple of a wali or Sufi leader
Nangiy pakhtanah (nangiy pakhtânah)	Tribal code of conduct
Napokha (nâpôkha)	Ignorant; raw; uncooked; unripe (Pashto term)
Naqib (naqîb)	Honorific used for some prominent ruhanis among Pashtun

Orustan atang bolsa janingda paltang bolsun (Ŏrŭstan ătang bŏlsa janingda paltang bŏlsun)	If your father was a Russian, carry an axe with you (Kirghiz proverb)
Padawan (pădawăn)	Cattle herder
Padshah gardushi (pădshah gardushĭ)	Time of succession of one monarch by another
Pahlawan (pahlawăn)	Hero; champion; wrestler
Pakhtanah (pakhtănah)	Pashtun tribal code of conduct
Pakhto kawul (pakhtŏ kawul)	To "do Pakhto"
Pakhto wayul (pakhtŏ wayul)	To speak Pakhto
Pakhtunwali (pakhtŭnwălĭ)	Pashtun tribal code of conduct
Pashtunwali (pashtŭnwălĭ)	Pashtun tribal code of conduct
Pir (pĭr)	"Saint"
Pirzadah (pĭrzădah)	Descendants of pirs
Qala (qală)	Fortress; fortified household compound (Pashto term)
Qaryadar (qaryadăr)	Official village headman
Qawmwali (qawmwălĭ)	Tribalism
Qazi (qăzĭ)	Judge
Qisas (qisăṣ)	Eye-for-eye doctrine of punishment or execution
Rasmi (rasmĭ)	Official
Rasti (răstĭ)	Genuine; correct; truthful
Rayat (ra'yat)	Citizen; economic and political dependent of khans and bays
Rish safed (rĭsh safĕd)	Village elders; white beards (Tajik term)
Ruhani (rŭhănĭ)	Religious dignitaries; spiritual leaders; Sufi
Rushanfikran (rŭshanfikrăn)	Intelligentsia; progressive ones
Sahibzadah (săhibzădah)	Honorific used for some prominent ruhanis among Pashtun
Sanduq (sandŭq)	Box; chest
Saratan (Saratăn)	Fourth month of Islamic solar calendar covering 22 June-22 July
Sarhadar (sarhadăr)	Junior military officer serving as chief of frontier guards detachment
Sayyid	Ruhani who claims descent from the Prophet

345

Ser (sêr)	Measure of weight equal to about 7.1 kilos
Shah (shâh)	King; religious dignitary among Isma'ili of Badakhshan
Shahid (shahîd)	Martyr (plural: shuhadâ)
Shari'a (Shari'a)/Shari'at (Shari'at)	Canon law of Islam
Sharwal (shârwâl)	Mayor (Pashto term)
Shaytan (shaytân)	"Devil"; Satan
Shaytani (shaytânî)	Mischievous
Siyasi (siyâsî)	Political
Taliban (tâlibân)	Pupils training to be mullahs; seekers of knowledge (plural of talib)
Tarawih (tarâwih)	Special prayers performed nightly during the month of Ramazan (fasting)
Tariqa (tariqa)/Tariqat (tariqat)	Sufi order; mystic path
Ta'wiz (ta'wîz)	Amulets
Tufangi filtai (tufangi filtaî)	Matchlocks
'Ulama ('ulamâ)	Learned religious leaders or scholars (plural of 'alim)
Umma ('umma)	Community and brotherhood of all Muslims
Wakil (wakîl)	Deputy to provincial council or parliament
Wali (walî)	An accomplished Sufi; a "saint"
Watan az shumast (watan az shumâst)	The country is yours
Watanfurushha raftand (watanfurûshhâ raftand)	The sellers of the country have gone
Wilayat (wilâyat)	Spiritual accomplishment through Sufi practices; God's friendship to "saints"; province
Wuluswal (wuluswâl)	District commissioner/administrator (Pashto term)
Wuluswali (wuluswâlî)	District headquarters (Pashto term)
Zakat (zakât)	Almsgiving; one of the five pillars of Islam
Ziyarat (ziyârat)	Holy shrine

NAMES AND PLACES

Habiburrahman, Shahid (Shahīd Ḥabi-
burraḥmān)

Haqiqat-i Inqilabi Saur (Ḥaqīqat-i Inqi-
lābi Saur)

Harakat-i Inqilab-i Islami (Ḥarakat-i
Inqilāb-i Islāmī)

Hari River (Hari)

Hashimi, Mansur (Mansūr Hāshimī)

Hazaragi Hazāragi)

Hazarah (Hazārah)

Hazarajat (Hazārajāt)

Hazrat-i Ali (Haẓrat-i 'Alī)

Herat (Hirāt)

Herawi, Spina (Spīna Hirawī)

Hikmatyar, Gulbudin (Gulbudīn Ḥik-
matyār)

Hindu Kush (Hindū Kush)

Hizb-i Islami (Ḥizb-i Islāmī)

Hotak, Mir Ways (Mīr Ways Hōtak)

Hotaki (Hōtakī)

Ibrahim, Muhammad Isma'il (Muḥammad Ismā'īl Ibrāhīm)

Ibrahim Beg (Ibrāhīm Bēg)

Id-i Qurban ('Id-i Qurbān)

Ikhwan (Ikhwān)

Ikhwan al-Muslimin (Ikhwān al-Muslim-
īn)

Imam (Imām)

Imami (Imāmī)

Imam Sahib (Imām Ṣāhib)

Ishaqzai (Isḥāqzai)

Ishaqzai, Taju Khan (Tājū Khān Isḥāqzai)

Ishkashim (Ishkāshim)

Ishkashimi (Ishkāshimī)

Isma'ili (Ismā'īlī)

Itihadi Islami Baray Azadyi Afghanistan
(Itiḥādi Islāmī Barāy Āzādyi Afghanistan)

Itihadi Islami Mujahidini Afghanistan
(Itiḥādi Islāmī Mujāhidīni Afghanistan)

Jabal ul-Siraj (Jabal ul-Sirāj)

Jabha-i Milli Nijat (Jabha-i Millī Nijāt)

Jabha-i Najat-i Milli (Jabha-i Najāt-i
Millī)

Jabha-i Nuristan (Jabha-i Nūristān)

Jadran (Jadrān)

Jalalabad (Jalālābād)

Jamal (Jamāl)

Jamhuriyat-i Demokratik-i Khalqi Afghanistan (Jamhūriyat-i Demōkrat-
ik-i Khalqi Afghanistan)

Jamiat-i Islami (Jam'iat-i Islāmī)

Jamiat-i 'ulama (Jam'iat-i 'ulamā)

Jamshidi (Jamshīdī)

Jan, Muhammad (Muḥammad Jān)

Jawanan-i Musulman (Jawānān-i Musul-
mān)

Jawzjan (Jawzjān)

Juggi (Juggī)

Kabir, Muhammad (Muḥammad Kabīr)

Kafiristan (Kāfiristān)

Kakar (Kākar)

Kalat (Kalāt)

Kamdesh (Kāmdēsh)

Kamyar, Ruhafza (Rūḥafzā Kāmyār)

Kandahar (Kandahār)

Kandaharis (Kandahāris)

Kapisa (Kāpīsā)

Karimi, Ghulam Ali (Ghulām 'Alī Kari-
mī)

Karmal, Babrak (Babrak Kārmal)

Kashan (Kāshān)

Kashghar (Kāshghar)

Kashmund Qala (Kishmand Qal'a)

Kayan (Kayān)

Khalili (Khalīlī)

Khalis, M. Yunus (M. Yūnus Khālis)

Khalqi (Khalqī)

Karim Khan, Prince (Karim Khān)

Khanabad (Khānābād)

Khash Valley (Khāsh)

Khawhan (Khāwhān)

Khaybar, Mir Akbar (Mīr Akbar Khaybar)

Khayr Muhammad Khan, Haji (Ḥajī
Khayr Muḥammad Khān)

Khost (Khōst)

Rabbani, Burhanuddin (Burhânuddîn Rabbânî)

Rafi, Muhammad (Muḥammad Rafi')

Ragh (Râgh)

Rahman, 'Abdur ('Abdur Rahmân)

Rahman Qul, Haji (Hâji Rahmân Qul)

Ramazan (Ramazân)

Rashid, 'Abdur ('Abdur Rashîd)

Rashid, Qays 'Abdur (Qays 'Abdur Rashîd)

Rasul Khan, Ghulam (Ghulâm Rasûl Khân)

Ratib, Ahmad (Ahmad Ratîb)

Ratibzad, Anahita (Anâhitâ Ratibzâd)

Rustaq (Rustâq)

Sada-i Nuristan (Sadâ-î Nuristân)

Safi (Sâfî)

Salam Khanah (Salâm Khânah)

Samangan (Samangân)

Sangcharak (Sangchârak)

Sayf Akhundzadah (Sayf Akhundzâdah)

Sayyaf, 'Abdur Rabbur Rasul ('Abdur Rabbur Rasûl Sayyâf)

Sazman (Sâzmân)

Sazmani Azadibakhsh-i Mardum-i Afghanistan (Sâzmâni Âzâdibakhsh-i Mardum-i Afghanistân)

Shab-Namah (Shab-Nâmah)

Shah, Yosuf Ali (Yôsuf 'Alî Shâh)

Shah Mahmud (Shâh Mahmûd)

Shahran-i Khash (Shahrân-i Khâsh)

Shahsawari, Fawziyah (Fawziyah Shahsawârî)

Shara'iyat (Shara'iyât)

Shar'i, 'Abdul Hakim ('Abdul Hakîm Shar'î)

Sharif Jan (Sharîf Jân)

Sher Agha (Shêr Âghâ)

Shi'a (Shî'a)

Shi'a Hazarah (Shî'a Hazârah)

Shiburghan (Shiburghân)

Shinwar (Shinwâr)

Shinwari (Shinwârî)

Shirin Tagaw (Shirin Tagâw)

Shor Bazar (Shôr Bâzâr)

Shor Darya (Shôr Daryâ)

Shughnan (Shughnân)

Shu'la-i Jawid (Shu'la-i Jâwîd)

Siddiqi, R. S. (R. S. Siddîqî)

Siraj al-Akhbar (Sirâj al-Akhbâr)

Siraj ul-Banat (Sirâj ul-Banât)

Sistan (Sistân)

Sitami Milli (Sitami Millî)

Sufi (Sûfî)

Sulayman Khel (Sulaymân Khêl)

Suraya (Surayâ)

Tahiri (Tâhirî)

Tajik (Tâjîk)

Takhar (Takhâr)

Taliqan (Tâliqân)

Taraki

Taraki, Nur M. (Nûr M. Tarakî)

Tarzi, Mahmud Beg (Mahmûd Bêg Tarzi)

Tashkand (Tâshkand)

Tashqurghan (Tâshqurghân)

Taymani (Tâymanî)

Terin Kut (Têrîn Kût)

Tokhi (Tôkhî)

Tolqun, Alamat ('Alâmat Tôlqûn)

Turkistan (Turkistân)

Turkistani (Turkistânî)

Ubaidullah ('Ubaidullâh)

Umar ('Umar)

Umayd ('Umayd)

Usman ('Usmân)

Waigal (Wâigal/Vâygal)

Wakhan (Wâkhân)

Wakhi (Wâkhî)

Wakil, 'Abdul ('Abdul Wakîl)

Wali of Swat (Wâlî of Swât)

Wardak, Amin (Amîn Wardak)

Warduj (Wardûj)

Wilayat-i Kunarhar (Wilâyat-i Kunarhâr)

Wulusi Jirgah (Wulusî Jirgah)

Yarkand (Yârkand)

Yusuf, Muhammad (Muhammad Yûsuf)

Zabihullah (Zabihullâh)

Zabul (Zâbul)

Zahir Shah (Zâhir Shâh)

Zarghunah (Zarghûnah)

Zibak (Zîbâk)

Zibaki (Zîbâki)

Zuhak (Zuhâk)

.

BIBLIOGRAPHY

'Abduh, Muhammad, and Rida, Muhammad Rashid. 1948-53. *Tafsir al-Manar*. 12 vols. Cairo: Dar al-Manar. (An interpretation and commentary on the Quran.)

Adamec, Ludwig W. 1979. *First Supplement to the Who's Who of Afghanistan: Democratic Republic of Afghanistan*. Graz, Austria: Akademische Druck.

_____, ed. 1972. *Historical and Political Gazetteer of Afghanistan: Badakhshan Province and Northeast Afghanistan*, vol. 1. Graz, Austria: Akademische Druck.

Afghan Demographic Studies. 1975. *A Provisional Gazetteer of Afghanistan*, vol. 2. Kabul: Central Statistics Office, Prime Ministry. Report Series no. 1.

Afghanistan, Ministry of Information and Culture—MIC (Kabul). *Democratic Republic of Afghanistan Annual*. Various issues.

_____, _____. 1977. *Women in Afghanistan: A Progress Report*.

_____, Ministry of Planning. 1972. *Statistical Pocketbook of Afghanistan*. August.

Afghanistan: The Target of Imperialism. 1983. Kabul: Party Printing Press.

Afghanistan Forum Newsletter. 1983. 11, 4 (22 May): 2 ("Resolution of the Islamic Unity of Afghan Mujahideen") and 21-23 ("Notes on the Resistance").

Afghanistan National Fatherland Front. 1981. *Documents of the Founding Congress*. Kabul, 15-16 June. New Delhi: Communist Party of India Publication.

Afghanistan Times (Los Angeles). Various issues. (Published by the Afghanistan Freedom Organization.)

Ahmad, Eqbal. 1971. "Revolutionary Warfare and Counter-Insurgency." In Miller and Aya, eds.

Ahmed, Akbar S. 1976. *Millennium and Charisma among Pathans*. London: Routledge and Kegan Paul.

_____. 1980. *Pakhtun Economy and Society*. London: Routledge and Kegan Paul.

Alavi, Hamza. 1965. "Peasants and Revolution." In Miliband and Saville, eds. pp. 241-77.

_____. 1973. "Peasant Classes and Primordial Loyalties." *Journal of Peasant Studies* 1, 1: 23-62.

'Alibek, Mirza Afzal. 1907. *Tarikh-i Badakhshan* (Badakhshan history). Osh: Present Tajik USSR. Handwritten manuscript in Persian reproduced in facsimile in the USSR. According to 'Alibek, the manuscript is a corrected and updated version of earlier works by Mirza Sang Muhammad and Mirza Fazilbik.

Allworth, E., ed. 1967. *Central Asia: A Century of Russian Rule*. New York: Columbia University Press.

Amin, Abdul Rasul. 1973 (1351 A.H.). *Social Status of Women in Ningarhar, Laghman and Kunar Provinces*. Research Center of Kabul University. In Persian.

Amin, Tahir. 1982. *Afghanistan Crisis*. Islamabad: Institute for Policy Studies.

Anahita, Dr. *See* Ratibzad, Anahita.

Anderson, Jon W. 1975. "Tribe and Community among Ghilzai Pashtun." *Anthropos* 70: 575-601.

_____. 1978a. "There Are No Khans Anymore: Economic Development and Social Change in Afghanistan." *Middle East Journal* 32, 2: 167-86.

_____. 1978b. "Introduction and Overview." In Anderson and Strand, eds., pp. 1-8.

_____. 1983a. "Khan and Khel: Dialectics of Pakhtun Tribalism." In R. Tapper, ed.

_____. 1983b. "Cousin Marriage in Context: Constructing Social Relations in Afghanistan." *Folk* 24: 7-28.

_____, and Strand, Richard F., eds. 1978. *Ethnic Processes and Intergroup Relations in Contemporary Afghanistan*. New York: Asia Society, Afghanistan Council. Occasional Paper no. 15.

Anis (Kabul). After 1981 the official organ of the National Fatherland Front. In Dari and Pashto.

Ansari, Javed. 1981. "Islam Finds Marxism Wanting." *Arabia: The Islamic World View* 1, 1: 64-65.

Arnold, Anthony. 1981. *Afghanistan: The Soviet Invasion in Perspective*. Stanford: Hoover Institution.

_____. 1983. *Afghanistan's Two Party Communism*. Stanford: Hoover Institution.

Arunova, Mariam. 1981. "Glimpses from the History of the Liberation Struggle of the Afghan People in the 18th Century." In Editors of *Social Sciences Today*, pp. 60-75.

Asia Society, Afghanistan Council. *Newsletter*. 7, 1 (January 1979); 8, 3 (June 1980); June 1982.

Aslanov, Martiros. 1981. "The Popular Movement 'Roshani' and Its Reflections in the Afghan Literature of the 16th-17th Centuries." In Editors of *Social Sciences Today*, pp. 28-44.

AUFS [American Universities Field Staff] Reports. 1959-1980. Various issues.

Avery, P. 1967. *Modern Iran*. London: Ernest Benn.

Aya, Roderick. 1979. "Theories of Revolution Reconsidered." *Theory and Society* 8, 1: 39-99.

Azoy, G. Whitney. 1982. *Buzkashi: Game and Power in Afghanistan.* Philadelphia: University of Pennsylvania Press.

Bain, R. B. 1982. *Afghanistan Will Not Die.* Calcutta: Satyam Shivam.

Balland, M. D. 1974. "Vieux sédentaires tadjik et immigrants pachtoun dans le sillon de Ghazni (Afghanistan oriental)." *Bulletin de l'Association des Géographes* 417-18: 171-80.

Barfield, Thomas J. 1978. "The Impact of Pashtun Immigration on Nomadic Pastoralism in Northeastern Afghanistan." In Anderson and Strand, eds.

_____. 1981. *The Central Asian Arabs of Afghanistan.* Austin: University of Texas Press.

Barth, Fredrik. 1959. *Political Leadership among Swat Pathans.* London: Athlone Press. London School of Economics Monographs on Social Anthropology no. 19.

_____. 1964. *Nomads of South Persia.* Oslo: Universitetsforlaget.

_____. 1966. *Models of Social Organization.* Royal Anthropological Institute of Great Britain and Ireland. Occasional Paper no. 23.

_____. 1969a. "Pathan Identity and Its Maintenance." In Barth, ed., 1969b.

_____, ed. 1969b. *Ethnic Groups and Boundaries.* Oslo: Universitetsforlaget.

_____, ed. 1973. *Scale and Social Organization.* New York: Werner-Gren.

Bates, Daniel. 1971. "The Role of the State in Peasant-Nomad Mutualism." *Anthropological Quarterly* 44, 3: 109-31.

BBC Summary of World Broadcasts. BBC Monitoring Service, Caversham, Reading. Various issues.

Beattie, Hugh. 1982. "Kinship and Ethnicity in the Nahrin Area of Northern Afghanistan." *Afghan Studies* 3/4: 39-51.

Bechtel, M. 1981. "Afghanistan: The Proud Revolution." *New World Review* 49, 1.

Beck, Sam, and McArthur, Marilyn. Forthcoming. "Class and Ethnicity in Romanian Development." In Lockwood, ed.

Ben David, Joseph, and Clark, T. N., eds. 1977. *Culture and Its Creators: Essays in Honor of Edward Shils.* Chicago: University of Chicago Press.

Bennigsen, Alexandre. 1975. "Islam in the Soviet Union." In Bociurkiw and Strong, eds.

_____. 1980-81. "Religious Belief in Soviet Islam: The Current Status." *Journal Institute of Muslim Minority Affairs* 2, 2 and 3, 1: 37-41.

_____, and Lemercier-Quelquejay, Chantal. 1967. *Islam in the Soviet Union.* London: Praeger.

_____, and _____. 1979. "'Official' Islam in the Soviet Union." *Religion in Communist Lands* 7, 3: 148-59.

Berry, Willard. 1966. *Aspects of the Frontier Crimes Regulation in Pakistan*. Durham, N. C.: Duke University Press.

Bhargava, G. S. 1983. *South Asian Security after Afghanistan*. Lexington, Mass.: D. C. Heath and Co.

Biographical Accounts of Chiefs, Sardars and Others of Afghanistan. 1888. Calcutta: Foreign Office, India.

"B. M." 1982. "The Present Situation in the Hazarajat." *Central Asian Survey* 1, 1: 79-91.

Bociurkiw, Bohdan R. 1980-81. "Changing Soviet Image of Islam: Domestic Scene." *Journal Institute of Muslim Minority Affairs* 2, 2 and 3, 1: 9-25.

_____, and Strong, J. W., eds. 1975. *Religion and Atheism in the USSR and Eastern Europe*. London: Macmillan.

Bohannan, P. 1967. "The Impact of Money on an African Subsistence Economy." In Dalton, ed.

Bowers, Stephen R. 1980-81. "Islam and Soviet Policy: The International Dimension." *Journal Institute of Muslim Minority Affairs* 2, 2 and 3, 1: 26-36. Jeddah: King Abdulaziz University.

Bradsher, Henry. 1983. *Afghanistan and the Soviet Union*. Durham, N. C.: Duke University Press, Policy Studies.

Canfield, Robert L. 1973a. "The Ecology of Rural Ethnic Groups and the Spatial Dimensions of Power." *American Anthropologist* 75, 5: 1151-68.

_____. 1973b. *Faction and Conversion: Religious Alignments in the Hindu Kush*. Ann Arbor: University of Michigan, Museum of Anthropology. Anthropological Papers, no. 50.

_____. 1978. "Religious Myth as Ethnic Boundary." In Anderson and Strand, eds.

_____. 1981. "Soviet Gambit in Central Asia." *Journal of South Asian and Middle Eastern Studies* 5, 1: 10-30.

Caroe, O. 1965. *The Pathans; 550 BC-AD 1957*. London: Macmillan.

Centlivres, Pierre. 1972. *Un Bazar d'Asie Centrale: forme et organisation du bazar de Tashqurghan [Afghanistan]*. Weisbaden: Dr. Ludwig Reichert Verlag.

_____. 1976a. "Problèmes d'identité ethnique dans le Nord de l'Afghanistan." *Actes du XXIXe Congrès International des Orientalistes. Iran Moderne*, vol. 1. Paris.

_____. 1976b. "L'Histoire récente de l'Afghanistan et la configuration ethnique des provinces du Nord-Est." *Studia Iranica* 5, 2: 255-67.

_____. 1976c. "Structure et évolution des bazars du Nord Afghan." In Grötzbach, ed.

_____. 1979. "Groupes ethniques: de l'hétérogénéité d'un conept aux ambiguités de la représentation. L'exemple afghan." In Ehlers, ed., pp. 25-37.

_____. 1980. "Identité et image de l'autre dans l'anthropologie populaire en Afghanistan." *Revue Européene des Sciences Sociales et Cahiers Vilfredo Pareto* 13, 53: 29-41.

Centlivres-Demont, M. 1976. "Types d'occupations et relations interethniques dans le Nord-Est de l'Afghanistan." *Studia Iranica* 5, 2: 269-77.

Chaffetz, David. 1979. "Afghanistan, Russia's Vietnam." New York: Asia Society, Afghanistan Council. Special Paper no. 4.

_____. 1980. "Afghanistan in Turmoil." *International Affairs* 56, 1: 15-36.

Chaliand, Gerard. 1981. "Bargain War." *New York Review of Books* 28, 5 (2 April).

_____. 1982. *Report from Afghanistan.* Trans. Tamar Jacoby. New York: Penguin Books.

Charpentier, C.J. 1972. "Bazaar-e-Tashqurghan: Ethnological Studies in an Afghan Traditional Bazaar." *Studia Ethnographica Upsalensia*, no. 37. Uppsala: Uppsala University, Institionen for Allman och Jamforande Ethnografi.

_____. 1979. "One Year After the Saur Revolution." *Afghanistan Journal* 6, 4: 117-20.

Chu, Solomon, Hill, Robert, and Graham, Saxon. 1975. *National Demographic and Family Guidance Survey of the Settled Population of Afghanistan*, vol. 1: *Demography*. Kabul: Government of Afghanistan and USAID.

Cohen, Abner. 1979. "Political Symbolism." *Annual Review of Anthropology* 8: 87-113.

Cole, Donald. 1975. *Nomads of the Nomads.* Chicago: Aldine.

Comaroff, J.L., ed. 1980. *The Meaning of Marriage Payments.* London: Academic Press.

Crapanzano, V. 1973. *The Hamadsha: A Study in Moroccan Ethnopsychiatry.* Berkeley: University of California Press.

Croll, E. 1981. *The Politics of Marriage in Contemporary China.* London: Cambridge University Press.

Daily Telegraph (London). Various issues.

Dalton, G., ed. 1967. *Tribal and Peasant Economies.* Garden City, N.Y.: Natural History Press.

Dastarac, Alexandre, and Levant, M. 1980. "What Went Wrong in Afghanistan?" *MERIP Reports* 10, 6 (July-August): 3-12.

Davies, C. Collin. 1932. *The Problem of the North-West Frontier 1890-1908.* Cambridge: Cambridge University Press.

Dekmejian, R. Hrair. 1980. "The Anatomy of Islamic Revival: Legitimacy Crisis, Ethnic Conflict, and the Search for Islamic Alternatives." *Middle East Journal* 34, 1: 1-12.

Despres, Leo A., ed. 1975. *Ethnicity and Resource Competition in Plural Societies*. The Hague: Mouton.

Dupree, Louis. 1959. "The Burqa Comes Off." *AUFS Reports* 3, 2.

_____. 1966. "Islam in Politics: Afghanistan." *Muslim World* 16, 4: 269-76.

_____. 1967. "The Political Uses of Religion: Afghanistan." In Silvert, ed.

_____. 1971. "A Note on Afghanistan." *AUFS Reports*, South Asia Series, 15, 2.

_____. 1973. *Afghanistan*. Princeton: Princeton University Press.

_____. 1976a. "Anthropology in Afghanistan." *AUFS Reports*, South Asia Series, 20, 5.

_____. 1976b. "The First Anglo-Afghan War and the British Retreat of 1842: The Functions of History and Folklore." *East and West* (Rome) (new series) 26, 3-4: 503-29.

_____. 1977a. "Afghan and British Military Tactics in the First Anglo-Afghan War (1838-1842)." *Army Quarterly and Defence Journal* (UK) 107, 2: 214-21.

_____. 1977b. "USAID and Social Scientists Discuss Afghanistan's Development Prospects." *AUFS Reports*, South Asia Series, 21, 2.

_____. 1978a. "Toward Representative Government in Afghanistan, Part I." *AUFS Reports*, Asia, no. 1.

_____. 1978b. "Toward Representative Government in Afghanistan, Part II." *AUFS Reports*, Asia, no. 14.

_____. 1979a. "Afghanistan under the Khalq." *Problems of Communism* 28 (July-August): 34-50.

_____. 1979b. "The Democratic Republic of Afghanistan: 1979." *AUFS Reports*, Asia, no. 32.

_____. 1979c. "Red Flag over the Hindu Kush, Part I: Leftist Movements in Afghanistan." *AUFS Reports*, Asia, no. 44.

_____. 1979d. "Red Flag over the Hindu Kush, Part II: The Accidental Coup, or Taraki in Blunderland." *AUFS Reports*, Asia, no. 45.

_____. 1980a. *Afghanistan*. First paperback ed.

_____. 1980b. "Militant Islam and Traditional Warfare in Islamic South Asia." *AUFS Reports*, Asia, no. 21.

_____. 1980c. "Red Flag over the Hindu Kush, Part III: Rhetoric and Reforms, or Promises! Promises!" *AUFS Reports*, Asia, no. 23.

_____. 1980d. "Red Flag over the Hindu Kush, Part IV: Foreign Policy and Economy." *AUFS Reports*, Asia, no. 27.

_____. 1980e. "Red Flag over the Hindu Kush, Part V: Repression, or Security Through Terror, Purges I-IV." *AUFS Reports*, Asia, no. 28.

_____. 1980f. "Red Flag over the Hindu Kush, Part VI: Repressions, or Security Through Terror, Purges IV-VI." *AUFS Reports*, Asia, no. 29.

_____. 1980g. "Afghanistan: 1980, The World Turned Upside Down." *AUFS Reports*, Asia, no. 37.

_____. 1980h. "Islam: Design for Political Stability." *Christian Science Monitor*, 25 February, p. 15.

_____. Forthcoming. *The First Russo-Afghan War: 1979-???*. Bloomington: Indiana University Press.

_____, and Albert, Linette, eds. 1974. *Afghanistan in the 1970s*. New York: Praeger.

Dupree, Nancy Hatch. 1972. *An Historical Guide to Kabul*, 2nd ed. Kabul: Afghan Tourist Organization.

_____. 1978. "Behind the Veil in Afghanistan." *Asia* 1, 2 (July/August): 10-15.

_____. 1979. "A Few Comments on Afghan Women." Unpublished manuscript.

_____. 1980. "The Rights of Afghan Women." *Christian Science Monitor*, 25 June, p. 22.

_____. 1981. *Revolutionary Rhetoric and Afghan Women*. New York: Asia Society, Afghanistan Council. Occasional Paper no. 23.

Editors of *Mirror of Jehad* (Peshawar). 1982a. "Aim and Goals of Jamiat-i-Islami Afghanistan." *Mirror of Jehad* 1, 1: 8-13.

_____. 1982b. "A Brief Biography of Professor Burhanuddin Rabbani, the Revolutionary Leader of Jamiat-i Islami Afghanistan." *Mirror of Jehad* 1, 1: 14-18.

_____. 1982c. "Interview with Professor Burhanuddin Rabbani." *Mirror of Jehad* 1, 2 (22 February): 8-13.

_____. 1982d. "Editorial: What Is Jehad and Who Is a Mujahid?" *Mirror of Jehad* 1, 3: 3-9.

Editors of *Pakistan Progressive* (Journal of the Organization of Progressive Pakistanis, New York). 1980. "Interview with an Afghan Marxist." *Pakistan Progressive* 3, 2: 22-47.

Editors of *Social Sciences Today*. 1981. *Afghanistan: Past and Present*. Moscow: USSR Academy of Sciences, Oriental Studies in the USSR.

Ehlers, Eckert, ed. 1979. *Beiträge zur Kulturgeographie des Islamischen Orients*. Marburg/Lahn: Geographisches Institut der Universität Marburg.

Eickelman, D. F. 1976. *Moroccan Islam: Tradition and Society in a Pilgrimage Center*. Austin: University of Texas Press.

_____. 1981. *The Middle East: An Anthropological Approach*. Englewood Cliffs, N.J.: Prentice-Hall.

Einzmann, Harald. 1977. *Religiöses Volksbrauchtum in Afghanistan: Islamische Heiligenverehrung und Wallfahrtswesen im Raum Kabul*. Wiesbaden: Franz Steiner Verlag.

Elphinstone, M. 1972. *An Account of the Kingdom of Caubul: and Its Dependencies in Persia, Tartary and India . . .* , 2 vols. London: John Murray.

d'Encausse, Hélène C. 1967. "Civil War and New Governments." In Allworth, ed.

_____. 1978. *L'Empire éclate*. Paris: Flammarion.

Engert, C. van H. 1924. *A Report on Afghanistan*. Washington, D.C.: Government Printing Office.

Etienne, G. 1972. *L'Afghanistan, ou les aléas de la coopération*. Paris: Presses Universitaires de France.

Evans-Pritchard, E. E. 1949. *The Sanusi of Cyrenaica*. Oxford: Clarendon.

Farhadi, A. G. Ravan, comp. 1977. *Maqalati Mahmud Tarzi dar Seraj-al-Akhbar, 1290-97* (Mahmud Tarzi, 1865-1933). Pamphlets, editorials, and major articles from *Seraj-al-Akhbar*, 1911-18. Kabul: Baihaqi Publishers. In Persian.

Ferdinand, K. 1962. "Nomad Expansion and Commerce in Central Afghanistan." *Folk* 4: 123-59.

Firth, R. 1950. *Primitive Polynesian Economy*. New York: Humanities Press.

Fischer, Michael J. 1980. *Iran: From Religious Dispute to Revolution*. Cambridge, Mass.: Harvard University Press.

_____. 1982. "Islam and the Revolt of the Petit Bourgeoisie." *Daedalus* (Winter): 101-25.

Fry, Maxwell J. 1974. *The Afghan Economy: Money, Finance and Critical Constraints to Economic Development*. Leiden: E.J. Brill.

Gage, Nicholas. 1980. "Islamic Zeal and Talent for War Help Rebels to Hold Out." *New York Times*, 20 July, pp. 1ff.

Gall, Sandy. 1983. *Behind Russian Lines: An Afghan Journal*. London: Sidgwick and Jackson.

Geertz, Clifford. 1959. "Ritual and Social Change: A Javanese Example." *American Anthropologist* 61: 991-1012. Reprinted in Geertz 1973.

_____. 1973. *The Interpretation of Cultures*. New York: Basic Books.

_____. 1977. "Centers, Kings and Charisma: Reflections on the Symbolics of Power." In Ben David and Clark, eds.

Gellner, E. 1969. *Saints of the Atlas*. Chicago: University of Chicago Press.

Ghani, Abdul. 1921. *Review of the Political Situation in Afghanistan*. Lahore: Khosla Brothers.

Ghani, Ashraf. 1978. "Islam and State-Building in a Tribal Society: Afghanistan 1880-1901." *Modern Asian Studies* 12, 2: 269-84.

_____. 1983. "Disputes in a Court of Sharia, Kunar Valley, Afghanistan, 1885-1890." *International Journal of Middle East Studies* 15, 3: 353-67.

Ghobar, Mir Ghulam Muhammad. 1967. *Afghanistan Dar Masir-i Tarikh* (Afghanistan's path through history). Kabul: Government Press. In Persian.

Gilsenan, Michael. 1973. *Saint and Sufi in Modern Egypt*. Oxford: Oxford University Press.

_____. 1982. *Recognizing Islam*. London: Croom Helm.

Girardet, Edward. 1982. "With the Resistance in Afghanistan." *Christian Science Monitor*, 22 and 28 June; 2, 7, 9, 19, and 26 July.

Glatzer, B. 1977. *Nomaden von Gharjistan: Aspekte der Wirtschaftlichen, Sozialen und Politischen Organisation Nomadischer Durrani-Paschtunen in Nordwestafghanistan*. Wiesbaden: Franz Steiner Verlag.

Glukhoded, Vladimir. 1981. "Economy of Independent Afghanistan." In Editors of *Social Sciences Today*, pp. 222-45.

Grachev, A. S., ed. and comp. 1980. *The Undeclared War: Imperialism vs. Afghanistan*. Moscow: Progress Publishers.

Gregorian, Vartan. 1969 and 1974. *The Emergence of Modern Afghanistan: Politics of Reform and Modernization, 1880-1946*. Stanford: Stanford University Press.

Griffiths, John C. 1981. *Afghanistan: Key to a Continent*. Boulder, Colo.: Westview Press.

Gronhaug, R. 1973. "Scale as a Variable in Analysis: Fields in Social Organization in Herat, Northwest Afghanistan." In Barth, ed., 1973.

Grötzbach, E. 1972. *Kulturgeographischer Wandel in Nordost-Afghanistan seit dem 19. Jahrhundert*. Meisenheim am Glan: Verlag Anton Hain.

_____, ed. 1976. *Aktuelle Probleme der Regionalentwicklung und Stadtgeographie Afghanistans*. Meisenheim am Glan: Verlag Anton Hain.

The Guardian (London). Various issues.

Gurevich, Naum. "Problems of Agricultural Production in Afghanistan." In Editors of *Social Sciences Today*, pp. 157-77.

Habiburrahman, Shahid. 1977 (1356 A.H.). *Jihan Binyi Islami* (Islamic world view). Peshawar: Hizb-i Islami. In Persian.

Hallet, S. I., and Samizay, R. 1980. *Traditional Architecture of Afghanistan*. New York: Garland STMP.

Halliday, Fred. 1978. "Revolution in Afghanistan." *New Left Review* 112 (November-December): 3-44.

_____. 1979. *Iran: Dictatorship and Development*. New York: Penguin.

_____. 1980a. "War and Revolution in Afghanistan." *New Left Review* 119 (January-February): 20-41.

_____. 1980b. "Wrong Moves in Afghanistan." *The Nation* 230, 3 (26 January): 70-72.

_____. 1980c. "The Limits of Russian Imperialism." *New Statesman* (London), 5 December.

Hammond, Thomas T. 1984. *Red Flag over Afghanistan*. Boulder, Colo.: Westview Press.

Harrison, Selig S. 1978. "After the Afghan Coup: Nightmare in Baluchistan." *Foreign Policy* 32.

_____. 1981. *In Afghanistan's Shadow: Baluch Nationalism and Soviet Temptations*. New York: Carnegie Endowment for International Peace.

_____. 1983. "A Breakthrough in Afghanistan?" *Foreign Policy* 51 (Summer): 3-26.

Hikmatyar, Gulbudin. 1980. *Khuday Wayi: Islami Ummat Jul Kulay* (God says: Establish an Islamic community). Speeches to community leaders. Peshawar: Hizb-i Islami. In Pashto.

_____. 1983. Interview in *Afghan Realities* (Paris) 9 (January/February); published by Afghan Information and Documentation Center. Reprinted in *Afghanistan Forum Newsletter* 11, 3: 12-13.

Hizb-i Islami. 1981. *Rah-i Haq*, 1 September (Tehran).

_____. N.D.a. *Aims of Hizb-i Islami Afghanistan*. Peshawar: Hizb-i Islami Afghanistan.

_____. N.D.b. *Nadiry Kuranay aw de Afghanistan Sarparasty* (The Nadir family and their leadership in Afghanistan). Peshawar: Hizb-i Islami Afghanistan. In Pashto.

Hodgson, M.G.S. 1974. *The Venture of Islam: Conscience and History in a World Civilization*, 3 vols. Chicago: University of Chicago Press.

Honigmann, J.J., ed. 1973. *Handbook of Social and Cultural Anthropology*. Chicago: Rand McNally.

Howe, Marrine. 1980. "United Front Still Eludes Afghan Guerrillas." *New York Times*, 28 May.

Hujwiri, A. 1910 (orig. c. 1050). *The Kashf al-Mahjub: The Oldest Persian Treatise on Sufism*. Trans. R. A. Nicholson. Leiden: Brill; London: Luzac.

Huntington, Samuel P. 1968. *Political Order in Changing Societies*. New Haven: Yale University Press.

Hyman, Anthony. 1982. *Afghanistan under Soviet Domination*. London: Macmillan.

Ilyinsky, Mikhail. 1982. *Afghanistan: Onward March of the Revolution*. New Delhi: Sterling Publishers.

Irons, William. 1974. "Nomadism as a Political Adaptation: The Case of the Yomut Turkmen." *American Ethnologist* 1, 4: 635-58.

Jamiat-i Islami Afghanistan (JIA). 1981. *Inqilabi Islami Afghanistan* 5, 10 (8 September). Tehran: JIA Central Office.

_____. N.D.a. *Fishurada-i ahdaf wa Marami Jamiat-i Islami Afghanistan* (Summary of aims and goals of JIA). Peshawar: JIA. In Persian.

_____. N.D.b. *Munasibat-i Afghanistan wa Rusiya wa Jinayati Rus dar Afghanistan* (Relations between Afghanistan and Russia and the Russian atrocities in Afghanistan). Peshawar: JIA. In Persian.

_____. N.D.c. *De Marxism pu Bara Kushy Dersh Poshtany* (Thirty questions about Marxism). Peshawar: JIA. In Pashto.

_____. N.D.d. *Chi Naw' Mubariza* (What kind of a campaign). Peshawar: JIA. In Persian and Pashto.

_____. N.D.e. *Az Haqiqat ta Iftira* (From truth to slander). Peshawar: JIA. In Persian.

_____. N.D.f. *A Brief Biography of Professor Burhanuddin Rabbani, the Revolutionary Leader of Jamiat-i Islami Afghanistan.* Peshawar: Political Committee of JIA.

_____. 1359-60 A.H. "Remembrance of Prof. Ghulam Muhammad Niyazi, Founder of the Islamic Movement in Afghanistan." *Mithaqi Khun* 1-5.

Jarring, G. 1939. "On the Distribution of Turk Tribes in Afghanistan." *Lunds Universitets Arsskrift* N.V., Avd. I, BD35, no. 4.

Jettmar, Karl. 1961. "Ethnological Research in Dardistan 1958." *Proceedings of the American Philosophical Society* 105, 1: 79-97.

_____, ed., in collaboration with Lennart Edelberg. 1974. *Cultures of the Hindukush: Selected Papers from the Hindu-Kush Cultural Conference Held at Moesgård 1970.* Beiträge zur Südasienforschung, Südasien-Institut, Universität Heidelberg. Wiesbaden: Franz Steiner Verlag.

JIA. *See* Jamiat-i Islami Afghanistan (JIA).

Jones, Schuyler. 1974. *Men of Influence in Nuristan: A Study of Social Control and Dispute Settlement in Waigal Valley, Afghanistan.* New York: Academic Press.

_____. 1980. "Nuristan: Factors Influencing Attitudes toward the Kabul Government." Paper presented to the American Anthropological Association, Washington, D.C., 3-7 December.

Kabul Times and (after 1 January 1980) *Kabul New Times.* Various issues.

Kakar, M. Hasan Kawun. 1971. *Afghanistan: A Study in Internal Political Development, 1880-1901.* Lahore: Panjab University Press.

_____. 1979. *Government and Society in Afghanistan: The Reign of Amir 'Abd al-Rahman Khan.* Austin: University of Texas Press.

Kamrany, Nake M. 1969. *Peaceful Competition in Afghanistan: American and Soviet Models for Economic Aid*. Washington, D.C.: Communication Service Corporation.

Karmal, Babrak. 1982. In *Kabul New Times*, 25 February.

Kasatkin, Dmitri. 1980. "Protecting the Gains of the April Revolution." *Asia and Africa Today* 3: 15-18.

Kazemi, Farhad, and Abrahamian, Ervand. 1978. "The Nonrevolutionary Peasantry of Modern Iran." *Iranian Studies* 9: 259-304.

Keddie, Nikki, ed. 1962. *Scholars, Saints, and Sufis: Muslim Religious Institutions since 1500*. Berkeley: University of California Press.

Keiser, R. Lincoln. 1971. "Social Structure and Social Control in Two Afghan Mountain Societies." Unpublished Ph.D. dissertation, University of Rochester.

_____. 1981. "The Relevancy of Structural Principles in the Study of Political Organization: A Case Against Optimization Theory." *Anthropos* 76.

Kemali, M. H. 1976. "Matrimonial Problems of Islamic Law in Contemporary Afghanistan." Unpublished Ph.D. dissertation, University of London.

Khalfin, Naftula. 1981. "The Struggle of the Peoples of Afghanistan for Independence and against the British Colonialists." In Editors of *Social Sciences Today*, pp. 99-129.

Khalid, D. 1980. "Afghanistan's Struggle for National Liberation." *Internationales Asienforum* 11, 3-4: 197-228.

Khalili, Khalilullah. 1980. *'Ayari az Khurasan: Amir Habibullah, Khadim-i Din-i Rasul Allah*. Peshawar: Jamiat-i Islami Afghanistan.

Khalilzad, Zalmay. 1980. *The Return of the Great Game*. Santa Monica, Ca.: California Seminar on International Security and Foreign Policy (September).

Khan, Sultan Muhammad. 1900. *The Constitution and Laws of Afghanistan*. London: Murray.

Kipling, Rudyard. 1945. *Rudyard Kipling's Verse*. Garden City, N.Y.: Doubleday, Doran, and Co.

Knabe, Erika. 1977a. *Frauenemanzipation in Afghanistan*. Afghanische Studien 16. Meisenheim am Glan: Verlag Anton Hain.

_____. 1977b. "Women in the Social Stratification of Afghanistan." In von Nieuwenhuijze, ed.

Kolarz, Walter. 1966. *Religion in the Soviet Union*. London: Macmillan.

Korgun, Victor. 1981. "The First Stage of Afghanistan's Independent Development." In Editors of *Social Sciences Today*, pp. 130-56.

Kraus, W., ed. 1972. *Afghanistan: Natur, Geschichte und Kultur, Staat, Gesellschaft und Wirtschaft*. Tubingen and Basel: Horst Erdmann Verlag.

Kushkaki, B. 1923. *Rahnuma-i Qataghan Wa Badakhshan* (Guide to Qataghan and Badakhshan). Kabul: Ministry of Defense. In Persian.

Lambton, A. 1969. *The Persian Land Reform 1962-1966*. Oxford: Oxford University Press.

Levy, Bernard Henry. 1982. From *Le Matin*, 14 September 1981. In Bain, ed., pp. 92-99.

Lewis, John W. 1974. *Peasant Rebellions and Communist Revolutions in Asia*. Stanford: Stanford University Press.

Lockwood, William G., ed. Forthcoming. *Ethnicity and Economic Development: East and West*.

Mair, L. 1971. *Marriage*. New York: Pica.

Male, Beverly. 1982. *Revolutionary Afghanistan*. New York: St. Martin's Press.

Manzar, A.M. 1980. *Red Clouds over Afghanistan*. Islamabad: Institute for Policy Studies.

Mayer, A. C. 1967. "Pir and Murshid: An Aspect of Religious Leadership in West Pakistan." *Middle Eastern Studies* 3, 2: 160-69.

McCagg, William O., Jr., and Silver, Brian, eds. 1979. *Soviet Asian Ethnic Frontiers*. New York: Pergamon Press.

McClelland, David C. 1970. "The Two Faces of Power." *Journal of International Affairs* 23, 1: 29-47.

Medvedev, Roy. 1980. "The Afghan Crisis." *New Left Review* 121: 91-96.

MERIP. Middle East Research and Information Project.

MIC. *See* Afghanistan, Ministry of Information and Culture.

Middle Eastern Economic Digest (London). Various issues.

Miliband, R., and Saville, J., eds. 1965. *The Socialist Register*. London: Merlin.

Military Reports on Afghanistan (Pt. 1—History). 1941. Simla: General Staff of India.

Miller, Norman, and Aya, Roderick, eds. 1971. *National Liberation: Revolution in the Third World*. New York: Free Press.

Miner, H. 1965. *The Primitive City of Timbuctoo*. Garden City, N.Y.: Doubleday.

Ministry of Information and Culture. *See* Afghanistan, Ministry of Information and Culture.

Misra, K. P., ed. 1981. *Afghanistan Crisis*. New Delhi: Vikas Publishing.

Le Monde (Paris). Various issues.

Monks, Alfred L. 1981. *The Soviet Intervention in Afghanistan*. Washington and London: American Enterprise Institute for Public Policy Research.

Moore, Barrington, Jr. 1966. *Social Origins of Dictatorship and Democracy: Lord and Peasant in the Making of the Modern World.* Boston: Beacon Press.

Mukherjee, Sadhan. 1981. *What Is Happening in Afghanistan.* New Delhi: Communist Party of India. Publication no. 9, July (C353).

Muradov, Ghulam. 1981. "The Democratic Republic of Afghanistan: Second Stage of the April Revolution." In Editors of *Social Sciences Today*, pp. 178-99.

Naby, Eden. 1980. "The Ethnic Factor in Soviet-Afghan Relations." *Asian Survey* 20, 3: 237-56.

National Islamic Front of Afghanistan. N.D. (ca. 1980). *Manifesto.* Peshawar.

Nayar, Kuldip. 1981. *Report on Afghanistan.* New Delhi: Allied Publishing.

Newell, Nancy P., and Newell, Richard S. 1981. *The Struggle for Afghanistan.* Ithaca, N.Y.: Cornell University Press.

Newell, Richard S. 1972. *The Politics of Afghanistan.* Ithaca, N.Y.: Cornell University Press.

_____. 1979. "Revolution and Revolt in Afghanistan." *World Today* (November): 432-42.

_____. 1980. "Islam and the Struggle for Afghan National Liberation." In Pullapilly, ed.

New World Review. Various issues.

Olesen, Asta. 1982. "Marriage Norms and Practices in a Rural Community in Northern Afghanistan." *Folk* 24: 111-41.

Ovesen, Jan. 1981. "The Continuity of Pashai Society." *Folk* 23.

_____. 1982. "The Construction of Ethnic Identities: The Nuristani and the Pashai, Eastern Afghanistan." Paper presented at the Symposium on Identity—Personal and Socio-Cultural, Uppsala, August 1982.

Pakistan Times (Rawalpindi/Lahore). Various issues.

Paul, Jim. 1980. "The Khalq Failed to Comprehend the Contradictions of the Rural Sector: Interview with Feroz Ahmad." *MERIP Reports* 10, 6 (July-August): 13-20.

Peters, Rudolph. 1977. *Jihad in Mediaeval and Modern Islam.* Leiden: E. J. Brill.

_____. 1979. *Islam and Colonialism: The Doctrine of Jihad in Modern History.* The Hague and New York: Mouton.

Petkov, Boris. 1983. *Afghanistan Today: Impressions of a Journalist.* New Delhi: Sterling Publishers.

Poullada, Leon B. 1973. *Reform and Rebellion in Afghanistan, 1919-1929: King Amanullah's Failure to Modernize a Tribal Society.* Ithaca, N.Y.: Cornell University Press.

Poulton, R. et al. 1973. "Services for Children within Regional Development." Report submitted to government of Afghanistan and UNICEF by Compagnie d'Etude Industrielle et d'Amenagement du Territoire (CINAM), Kabul.

Pullapilly, Cyriak K., ed. 1980. *Islam in the Contemporary World*. Notre Dame, Ind.: Cross Roads Books.

Rabbani, Burhanuddin. 1976 (1366 A.H.). *Faji 'a-i 26 Saratan wa Sima-i Za'amati Daoud Khan* (The atrocious event of 26 Saratan [17 July 1973] and the appearance of Daoud's leadership). Originally published by Independence Movement of Iran Outside the Country and recently by Jamiat-i Islami Afghanistan. In Persian.

_____. N.D.a. *Daoud Khan dar Guzashta-i Nangin, Haziri Jinayatbar Wa Mustaqbali Hawulnak* (Daoud Khan's shameful past, criminal present, and dreadful future). Peshawar: Jamiat-i Islami. In Persian.

_____. N.D.b. *Islam wa Kamunizm* (Islam and communism). Peshawar: Jamiat-i Islami. In Persian.

Rahman, Fath-ur, and Qureshi, A. 1981. *Afghans Meet Soviet Challenge*. Peshawar: Institute of Regional Studies, no. 1.

Rahman, Fazlur. 1966. *Islam*. New York: Holt, Rinehart and Winston.

Rasul, Sayyid. 1980 (1359 A.H.). *Isti'mar-i Balshawik wa Asiya-i Markazi* (Bolshevik colonialism and Central Asia). Peshawar: Jamiat-i Islami Afghanistan.

Ratibzad, Anahita. 1980. Interview in *Soviet Woman*, no. 5 (February): 2-3.

Ratnam, Perala. 1981. *Afghanistan's Uncertain Future*. New Delhi: Tulsi Publishing.

Reshtia, Seyed Qassem. 1984. "The National United Front." *Afghanistan Forum Newsletter* 12, 1: 2. Summary of paper presented at International Conference on Afghan Alternatives, Monterey Institute of International Studies, 15-18 November 1983.

Robertson, George Scott. 1896. *The Kafirs of the Hindu-Kush*. London: Lawrence and Bullen.

Rodinson, Maxime. 1979. "Islam Resurgent?" *Gazelle Review* 6: 1-17.

Roy, Olivier. 1981. "What Is Afghanistan Really Like?" *Dissent* (Winter): 47-54.

_____. 1983. "Neither Bled to Death nor Deserted." *Manchester Guardian Weekly* 129, 25: 12, 14.

Rubinstein, Alvin Z. 1982. *Soviet Policy toward Turkey, Iran and Afghanistan*. New York: Praeger.

Sabiq, Sayyid. N.D. *Jihad dar Rahi Khuda* (Jihad in the way of God). Trans. Abu Idris Fazl al-Rahim Fazl al-Karim, from Arabic *Fiqh al-Sunna*. Peshawar: Jamiat-i Islami Afghanistan. In Persian.

Salzman, Philip. 1971. "National Integration of the Tribes in Modern Iran." *Middle East Journal* 25: 325-36.

_____. 1975. "Islam and Authority in Tribal Iran: A Comparative Comment." *Muslim World* 65, 3: 186-95.

_____. 1978. "Ideology and Change in Tribal Society." *Man* 13: 618-37.

Sarwari, M. Sidiq. 1353-54 A.H. *De Afghanistan Kalanay* [Afghanistan annual], vol. 41. Kabul: Ministry of Information and Culture. In Persian and Pashto.

Sattar Khan, A. 1353 A.H. *Ouza-'ye Geographi-ye Woleswali-ye Nahrin*. Kabul: Kabul University Library. Photocopy.

Sayigh, R. 1981. "Roles and Functions of Arab Women: A Reappraisal." *Arab Studies Quarterly* 3, 3: 258-74.

Sayyaf, Abdur-Rabbur Rasul. 1983. "Jihad Is a School." Interview in *Afghan Mujahid* 2, 8: 10-11.

Schinasi, May. 1979. *Afghanistan at the Beginning of the Twentieth Century*. Naples: Istituto Universitario Orientale.

Schurmann, H. F. 1962. *The Mongols of Afghanistan: An Ethnography of the Mongols and Related People in Afghanistan*. The Hague: Mouton.

Shah, Iqbal Ali. 1928. *Afghanistan of the Afghans*. London: Diamond.

_____. 1939. *Modern Afghanistan*. London: Low, Marston.

Shahrani, M. Nazif. 1979a. *The Kirghiz and Wakhi of Afghanistan: Adaptation to Closed Frontiers*. Seattle: University of Washington Press.

_____. 1979b. "Ethnic Relations under Closed Frontier Conditions: Northeast Badakhshan." In McCagg and Silver, eds., pp. 174-92.

_____. 1981a. "The Kirghiz Odyssey." In *Odyssey: The Human Adventure*, ed. Jane E. Aaron. Boston: Public Broadcasting Associates, pp. 16-19.

_____. 1981b. "Islamic Resistance to Russian Communism: The *Basmachi* and the Afghan Mujahideen." Paper presented to Middle East Studies Association, Seattle, Washington, 7 November.

_____. 1983. "Traditional Local Leadership and Modern Political Conflict." Paper presented to American Anthropological Association, Chicago, 16-20 November.

Shalinsky, Audrey C. 1979a. "Central Asian Emigres in Afghanistan: Social Dynamics of Identity Creation." Ph.D. dissertation, Harvard University.

_____. 1979b. "Central Asian Emigres in Afghanistan: Problems of Religious and Ethnic Identity." New York: Asia Society, Afghanistan Council. Occasional Paper no. 19.

_____. 1980. "Homeland Lost and Regained?: The Conflicted Allegiances of Central Asian Emigrants in Afghanistan." Paper presented to the American Anthropological Association, Washington, D.C., 5 December.

Shorish, Mobin. 1983. "Educating the Afghan Refugee Youth." Paper presented to a panel on "The Status and Significance of the Crisis in Afghanistan," Middle East Studies Association, Chicago, 3-6 November.

_____. 1984. "The Impact of the Kemalists' 'Revolution' on Afghanistan." *Journal of South Asian and Middle Eastern Studies* 7, 3.

Siegel, J. T. 1969. *The Rope of God*. Berkeley: University of California Press.

Silber, Irwin. 1980. *Afghanistan—The Battle Line Is Drawn*. San Francisco: Line of March Publications.

Silvert, K. H., ed. 1967. *Churches and States*. New York: American Universities Field Staff.

Skocpol, Theda. 1979. *States and Social Revolutions*. Cambridge: Cambridge University Press.

Smith, Harvey H., et al. 1973. *Area Handbook for Afghanistan*, 4th ed. Washington, D.C.: Government Printing Office.

Smith, W. C. 1963. *The Meaning and End of Religion*. New York: Harper and Row.

Snoy, P. 1972. "Die Ethnischen Gruppen." In Kraus, ed.

Sorokin, P. 1937. *Social and Cultural Dynamics*, 3 vols. Boston: Sargent.

Spain, David W. 1963. *The Pathan Borderland*. The Hague: Mouton.

Stauffer, Thomas. 1965. "The Economics of Nomadism in Iran." *Middle East Journal* 19: 284-302.

Steul, Willi. 1981. *Paschtunwali: Ein Ehrenkodex und seine rechtliche Relevanz*. Wiesbaden: Franz Steiner Verlag.

Stewart, Rhea Talley. 1973. *Fire in Afghanistan, 1914-1929: Faith, Hope and the British Empire*. New York: Doubleday.

Stork, Joe. 1980. "U.S. Involvement in Afghanistan." *MERIP Reports* 89.

Strand, Richard F. 1973. "Notes on the Nuristani and Dardic Languages." *Journal of the American Oriental Society* 93, 3: 297-305.

_____. 1974a. "Principles of Kinship Organization among the Kom Nuristani." In Jettmar, ed., pp. 51-56.

_____. 1974b. "A Note on the Rank, Political Leadership, and Government among the Pre-Islamic Kom." In Jettmar, ed., pp. 57-63.

_____. 1975. "The Changing Herding Economy of the Kom Nuristani." *Afghanistan Journal* 2, 4: 123-34. Graz: Akademische Druck-u. Verlagsanstalt.

_____. 1976a. "Review of Schuyler Jones, *Men of Influence in Nuristan*." *Journal of Asian Studies* 35, 4: 712-13.

_____. 1976b. "Tribal versus National Government in Nuristan." Paper presented at the Conference on Rural Life in Afghanistan: The Prospects for Development. Center for Afghanistan Studies, University of Nebraska at Omaha, 23-25 September.

_____. 1978. "Ethnic Competition and Tribal Schism in East Nuristan." In Anderson and Strand, eds., pp. 9-14.

_____. 1980. "A People Facing Extinction." *Pacific News Service* (San Francisco).

Tapper, Nancy. 1973. "The Advent of Pashtun Maldars in Northwestern Afghanistan." *Bulletin of the School of Oriental and African Studies* 36, 1: 55-79.

_____. 1977. "Pashtun Nomad Women in Afghanistan." *Asian Affairs* 7, 2: 163-70.

_____. 1979. "Marriage and Social Organization among Durrani Pashtuns in Northern Afghanistan." Ph.D. dissertation, University of London.

_____. 1980. "Matrons and Mistresses: Women and Boundaries in Two Middle Eastern Tribal Societies." *European Journal of Sociology* 21: 58-78.

_____. 1981. "Direct Exchange and Brideprice: Alternative Forms in a Complex Marriage System." *Man* 16, 3: 387-407.

_____. 1983. "Abd al-Rahman's North-West Frontier: The Pashtun Colonisation of Afghan Turkistan." In R. Tapper, ed.

Tapper, Richard. 1974. "Nomadism in Modern Afghanistan: Asset or Anachronism?" In L. Dupree and L. Albert, eds.

_____. 1979. *Pasture and Politics: Economics, Conflict and Ritual among Shahsevan Nomads of Northwestern Iran.* New York: Academic Press.

_____, and Tapper, Nancy. 1972. "The Role of Nomads in a Region of Northern Afghanistan." Final Report to Social Science Research Council (UK) on Project HR 1141/1.

_____, ed. 1983. *The Conflict of Tribe and State in Iran and Afghanistan.* London: Croom Helm.

Teplinsky, Leonid. 1981. "Soviet-Afghan Cooperation: Lenin's Behest Implemented." In Editors of *Social Sciences Today*, pp. 200-21.

Tilly, Charles. 1973. "Does Modernization Breed Revolution?" *Comparative Politics* 5, 3: 425-47.

Toepfer, H. 1972. *Wirtschafts- und sozialgeographische Fallstudien in ländlichen Gebieten Afghanistans.* Bonn: Ferd. Dummlers Verlag.

_____. 1976. *Untersuchungen zur wirtschafts- und sozialstruktur der Dorfbevölkerung der Provinz Baghlan.* Meisenheim am Glan: Verlag Anton Hain.

Uberoi, J.P. Singh. 1968. "District Administration in the Northern Highlands of Afghanistan." *Sociological Bulletin* 17 (March): 65-90.

United Nations. 1978. *Yearbook of National Accounts Statistics*, vol. 2. New York.

Urff, W., et al. 1974. *Der wirtschafliche Situation Pakistans nach der Sezession Bangladeshs.* Wiesbaden: Franz Steiner Verlag.

USAID. 1975. *National Demographic and Family Guidance Survey of the Settled Population of Afghanistan*, vol. 1. Sponsored by the Government of Afghanistan and USAID; Contract to State University of New York (Buffalo).

Valenta, Jiri. 1980. "The Soviet Invasion of Afghanistan: The Difficulty in Knowing Where to Stop." *Orbis* 24, 2: 201-18.

van den Berghe, Pierre L. 1975. "Ethnicity and Class in Highland Peru." In Despres, ed.

Verduin, Leonard. 1964. *The Reformers and Their Step Children*. Grand Rapids, Mich.: Baker.

_____. 1976. *The Anatomy of a Hybrid: A Study of Church/State Relationships*. Grand Rapids, Mich.: Eerdmans.

Victor, Jean-Christophe. 1983. *La Cité des murmures*. Paris: Editions Jean-Claude Lattes.

Vogel, Heinrich, ed. 1980. *Die Sowjetische Intervention in Afghanistan*. Baden-Baden: Nomos Verlagsgesellschaft.

Volkov, Y., Gevorkyan, K., Mikhailenko, M., Polonsky, A., and Svetozarov, A., comps. 1980. *The Truth about Afghanistan: Documents, Facts and Eyewitness Reports*. Moscow: Novosti Press.

von Nieuwenhuijze, C. A. O., ed. 1977. *Commoners, Climbers and Notables*. Leiden: E. J. Brill.

Wallerstein, I. 1974. *The Modern World-System: Capitalist Agriculture and the Origins of European World-Economy in the Sixteenth Century*. New York: Academic Press.

Watt, W. Montgomery. 1968. *Islamic Political Thought: The Basic Concepts*. Edinburgh: Edinburgh University Press.

Weinbaum, M. 1980. "Legal Elites in Afghan Society." *International Journal of Middle Eastern Studies* 12: 39-57.

Whitten, N. E., and Wolfe, A. W. 1973. "Network Analysis." In Honigmann, ed.

Wiegandt, Winfried F. 1980. *Afghanistan: Nicht aus Heiterem Himmel*. Zurich: Orell Fussli Verlag.

Wilber, D. 1962. *Afghanistan: Its People, Its Society, Its Culture*. New Haven: Human Relations Area Files (HRAF) Press.

Wilbur, D. N. 1955. "The Structure and Position of Islam in Afghanistan." *Afghanistan* 10: 7-14.

Wolf, Eric. 1969. *Peasant Wars of the Twentieth Century*. New York: Harper Torch Books.

Woodsmall, Helen. 1960. *Women and the New East*. Washington, D.C.: Middle East Institute.

Yapp, Malcolm E. 1962. "Disturbances in Afghanistan, 1839-42." *Bulletin of the School of Oriental and African Studies* 25: 499-523.

_____. 1963. "Disturbances in Western Afghanistan, 1839-41." *Bulletin of the School of Oriental and African Studies* 26: 288-313.

_____. 1964. "The Revolutions of 1841-2 in Afghanistan." *Bulletin of the School of Oriental and African Studies* 27: 333-81.

el-Zein, A. H. M. 1974. *The Sacred Meadows: A Structural Analysis of Religious Symbolism in an East African Town*. Evanston, Ill.: Northwestern University Press.

Zekrya, Mir-Ahmad B. 1976. "Planning and Development in Afghanistan: A Case of Maximum Foreign Aid and Minimum Growth." Ph.D. dissertation, Johns Hopkins University.

ADDENDUM: MUJAHIDIN PUBLICATIONS

Al Jamiat. Weekly newspaper published in Peshawar by Jamiat-i Islami Afghanistan (JIA). In Urdu.

Al Mawqif. Journal published in Peshawar by Hizb-i Islami. In Arabic.

Al Sobh. Weekly newspaper published in Wiesbaden, Germany, by Hizb-i Islami. In Persian and Pashto.

Al Sobh. Journal published in Wiesbaden, Germany, by Hizb-i Islami. In Persian and Pashto.

Bisharat. Weekly newspaper published in Baghlan province by JIA.

De Islam Zhagh. Daily newspaper published in Quetta, Baluchistan, by JIA beginning 30 November 1980. Primarily in Pashto for southwestern Afghanistan.

De Shahid Ziyray. Monthly journal published in Peshawar by JIA since 1981. In Persian and Pashto.

Inqilab-i Islami Afghanistan. Weekly newspaper published in Tehran by JIA since 1979. In Persian.

Itihadi Islami. Newspaper published in Peshawar by Professor Sayyaf, who headed a coalition which dissolved a few months after its formation in 1980. In Persian and Pashto.

Jabha-i Milli Nijat Afghanistan. Newspaper published in Peshawar by a group of the same name led by Sibghatullah Mujadidi.

Khahar-i Musulman. Journal published in Peshawar by Hizb-i Islami. In Persian and Pashto.

Khahar-i Shahid. Newspaper published in Kabul by Hizb-i Islami. In Persian and Pashto.

Mirror of Jehad. Bimonthly journal published in Peshawar by JIA since January 1982. In English.

Mithaqi Khun. Monthly journal published in Peshawar by JIA since 1980. In Persian and Pashto.

Mujahid. Weekly and daily newspaper published in Peshawar by JIA since 1978. In Persian and Pashto.

Payami Mujahid. Newspaper published in Panjsher by JIA. In Persian.

Rah-i Haq. Weekly newspaper published in Tehran by Hizb-i Islami. In Persian.

Sada-i Nuristan. Newspaper published by Nuristani mujahidin. In Persian and Pashto.

Sangar and *Nida-i Jihad.* Weekly newspapers published in Parwan province by JIA. In Persian and Pashto.

Saut al-Jihad. Monthly/bimonthly journal published in Peshawar by JIA since 1981. In Arabic.

Shafaq and *Sima-i Shahid.* Journals published by Hizb-i Islami. In Persian and Pashto.

Shahadat. Daily and weekly newspaper published in Peshawar by Hizb-i Islami. In Persian and Pashto.

Wahdat. Journal published in Wiesbaden, Germany, by Hizb-i Islami. In Turkish.

NOTE: Since early 1982, in accordance with the charter of the Islamic Unity of Afghan Mujahidin (IUAM), a coalition of seven Islamic revolutionary groups formed during the summer of 1981, all publications of its member organizations in Peshawar have been discontinued. In 1981 the IUAM launched a new series of publications expressing the collective views of the coalition. Thus far the following have come to the editors' attention:

Afghan Mujahid. Journal and weekly newspaper published in London. In English.

Al-Nafirul 'am. Monthly/bimonthly journal published in Peshawar. In Arabic.

Hijrat. Journal published in Peshawar. In Urdu.

The Jihad Rays. Monthly/bimonthly journal published in Peshawar since 1982. In English.

Qiyami Haq. Bimonthly journal published in Peshawar. In Persian and Pashto.

Shahid Paygham. Bimonthly journal published in Peshawar. In Pashto and some Persian.

Wahdati Islami. Daily newspaper published in Peshawar. In Persian and Pashto.

The alliance of the three traditionalist resistance groups also has its own publications. Thus far the editors are aware of the following:

Itihadi Islami. Newspaper published in Peshawar. In Persian and Pashto.

Ariza nawis, 199

Army: and conquest of Kafiristan (Nuristan), 98; Khalq-Parcham combat in Badakhshan, 160-63; Khalq-Parcham combat in Darra-i Nur, 120-22; Khalq-Parcham combat in Nahrin, 204-5; Khalq-Parcham combat in Nuristan, 89-91, 335; Khalq-Parcham conscription policies, 125; literacy training for, 331; military skills in Darra-i Nur, 133; Musahiban modernization of, 34-35, 176-77, 178-79; prospects for advancement in 1960s, 37; responses to Khalq, 170, 182, 333

Asadabad. *See* Chagha Saray

Ashkhasi namdar, 34

Ashkhasi sarshinas, 34

Ashrar, 160

Ataturk, 176

Atsakzai (Pashtun tribe), 236

Avghan. See Pashtun

Awakened Youth, 35-36

Awghan. See Pashtun

Aymaq. *See* Chahar Aymaq

Azan, 147

Aziza, Dr., 326

Babrak. *See* Karmal, Babrak

Baburi (non-Pashtun tribe), 236

Bacha-i Saqaw, 8, 164, 196, 204, 242, 308

Badakhshan, 13n, 22, 53, 68, 139-69, 251, 304

Badakhshan, 158

Badakhshi, Tahir, 154, 156-57, 160, 165

Badghis, 68, 250, 253

Badi, 244, 300

Badzgil, 90

Baghlan, 9, 157, 185-86, 189, 190, 199-200, 204

Baharak (Badakhshan), 145, 153, 157, 160, 166

Bajaur, 87

Bakhtyari (non-Pashtun tribe), 236

Balkh, 68, 242

Balkhi, Rabia, 313

Baluch, 6, 236, 237, 243, 246

Baluchistan, 273

Bamyan, 13n, 211-29, 232, 337n

Baqi, 'Abdul, 91

Barakat, 151

Barakzai (Pashtun tribe), 236

Barikot, 90

Baruti (non-Pashtun tribe), 236

Baryalay, Mahmud, 64

"Basic Lines . . . of the DRA," 12, 312, 330

Basir, 'Abdul, 162

Basmachi, 26n, 143, 204, 226n

Bay, 173-75, 244

Bhutto, Zulfikar Ali, 157n

Bilchiragh, 232

Bismillah, 267

Bolshevik, 143

Bragimatal, 77, 106

Bribery. *See* Corruption and bribery

Brideprice. *See Mahr*

Bukhara, 143, 232

Bureaucracy, 34-36, 59, 148, 153-54, 160. *See also* Government; Government officials; Teachers

Burqa Valley, 185

Buzkashi, 198, 201, 243, 337

Central Asia, 50, 65, 70-71, 143, 204, 226n, 327. *See also Basmachi*; Turkistan

Central Committee (PDPA), 315

Chagha Saray, 87, 88, 98, 103

Chahar Aymaq, 186, 233, 234, 238-43 passim, 253, 261, 303

Chandak. *See* Tsunuk

Chapu, 89

Charikar, 202

China. *See* People's Republic of China

Chindawul, 222

Chiqin, 148

Chitral (Pakistan), 89, 143

Christianity, 227n, 294

Class, 230-46; and "class interests," 11, 165, 180-81; and inequality, 38, 40; and marriage reforms, 305; and

Kakar, 236

Kalasha (of the Vaygal Valley), 49, 81, 94-118

Kamdesh. *See* Kombřon

Kamdesh district, 77, 87

Kamisar, 150

Kamu, 90

Kamyar, Ruhafza, 314

Kandahar, 206n, 214n, 313, 321, 333, 336

Kandahar province, 13n

Kandahar riots (1959), 164, 178

Kapisa, 68

Karamat, 216, 217, 218, 219

Karimi, Ghulam Ali, 331

Karim Khan, Prince. *See* Aga Khan

Karmal, Babrak: deposition of, 64, 316-17; under DRA, 62; as head of government, 327, 337n; and negotiations for Khalq-Parcham coalition, 61; and reform policies, 10, 21, 205n, 330, 335, 336. *See also* Khalq-Parcham coalition; Parcham

Kashghar, 143

Kashmund Qala, 120, 125

Kati, 77, 82, 89

Kayan, 222

Khalifah, 150, 219

Khalili, 302

Khalis, M. Yunus, 46, 47

Khalq: anti-Islamic stance of, 80, 88; evolution of, 39, 60; and factional struggles with Parcham, 44, 64, 160, 184, 316-17; increased repressions of, 160, 161; opposition to Musahibans of, 40, 41; organization and membership composition of, 318-20; Pashtun dominance of, 112, 156; propaganda campaigns of, 89-90, 200-201, 318; reform policies of 186-99, 202, 207-8, 320-26; during Republic of Afghanistan, 41, 61; resistance to, 162, 168; responses to reform policies of, 203-5; and Saur Revolution, 77, 159, 170, 184; similarities to Amanullah of, 186,

205-6; and Soviet invasion, 183, 332

Khalq Organization of Afghan Women (KOAW), 317, 318, 320, 321, 325, 326, 330. *See also* Democratic Organization of Afghan Women

Khalq Organization of Afghan Youth (KOAY), 318

Khalq-Parcham coalition: anti-Islamic stance of, 97-98, 111, 116; and differential privileges, 9, 54; dissolution of, 64, 332; factional struggles within, 44, 316; jihad against, 27, 42, 44, 52; organization and membership composition of, 41, 184, 318-20; Pashtun dominance of, 122; reforms of, 10-25, 179-83, 337-38; repressions of, 43-44; resistance to, 4-5, 49, 135, 139-40, 159, 164-67, 169; similarities to Amanullah of, 183; Soviet domination of, 50; support for, 43

Khan(s): and class structure, 238, 244; as feudal landlords, 10, 18, 87, 127, 133, 148, 236, 237; government repression of, 196-97; local opposition to, 50-51, 241-44; opposition to Amanullah of, 33, 34; and religious authority, 278, 281; in resistance movement, 5, 42, 122, 164. *See also Mir*

Khan, Gengis, 233

Khanabad, 195

Khash Valley, 162, 163

Khawhan (Badakhshan), 145

Khaybar, Mir Akbar, 62

Khayrat, 258

Khayr Muhammad Khan, Haji, 236

Khel, 273

Khomeini, Ayatolla, 216, 221n, 225

Khost, 206, 269, 275n

Khost Rebellion, 176, 308

Khujah, 150, 234

Khutan, 143

Kinship: and class structures, 230; and group feuds, 67-68; and marriage,

FOR INDIANA UNIVERSITY PRESS

Lesley Bolton   PROJECT MANAGER/EDITOR
Tony Brewer   COMPOSITION COORDINATOR
Sophia Hebert   ASSISTANT ACQUISITIONS EDITOR
Brenna Hosman   PRODUCTION COORDINATOR
Katie Huggins   PRODUCTION MANAGER
Bethany Mowry   ACQUISITIONS EDITOR
Rachel Rosolina   MARKETING AND PUBLICITY MANAGER
Leyla Salamova   BOOK DESIGNER